THE LIBRARY OF EMMANUEL COLLEGE, CAMBRIDGE, 1584–1637

This book provides a detailed record of the early history of the library at Emmanuel College, Cambridge, from the foundation of the College in 1584 to the completion of the seventh major inventory of the library's contents in 1637. This half-century formed a dynamic period in the religious and political as well as the educational life of the nation. The influence of Emmanuel, a notoriously Puritan college from its founding, was felt especially in the striking prominence of its alumni among New World settlers (among them John Harvard) and, during the English Civil War, in the placement of Emmanuel men in many key positions, including the Masterships of numerous Cambridge colleges. While these men were being educated Emmanuel's library expanded dramatically, and the seven increasingly large inventories of library books recorded there during the period give an indication of their concerns and their scholarship. Now, for the first time, the intellectual resources – by no means narrowly 'Puritan' – of this major institutional library are available for the study of all who are interested in the history of the period.

Professor Bush and Dr Rasmussen here present the largest inventory, that of 1637, using the earlier inventories and other documentary evidence to supply full bibliographical information as well as the acquisition history of each item in the library during these years. The catalogue also provides full information on donations, arrangement of the collection, and present class marks of the many surviving volumes from the early library. By supplementing these details with tables, illustrations, and an historical introduction, the editors give a full picture of the growth and contents of what was in its time a large and modern library at a college of unique historical importance.

This will be a valuable reference work not only for historical bibliographers but for anyone engaged in study of the intellectual, religious, and educational history of the late sixteenth and early seventeenth centuries.

THE LIBRARY OF EMMANUEL COLLEGE, CAMBRIDGE, 1584–1637

Sargent Bush, Jr
and
Carl J. Rasmussen

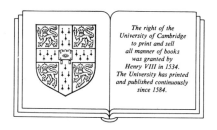

The right of the
University of Cambridge
to print and sell
all manner of books
was granted by
Henry VIII in 1534.
The University has printed
and published continuously
since 1584.

CAMBRIDGE UNIVERSITY PRESS

Cambridge
London   New York   New Rochelle
Melbourne   Sydney

Published by the Press Syndicate of the University of Cambridge
The Pitt Building, Trumpington Street, Cambridge CB2 1RP
32 East 57th Street, New York, NY 10022, USA
10 Stamford Road, Oakleigh, Melbourne 3166, Australia

First published 1986

Photoset and printed in Malta by Interprint Limited

British Library cataloguing in publication data

Bush, Sargent, Jr
 The Library of Emmanuel College, Cambridge,
 1584–1637
 1. Emmanuel College. *Library* — History
 I. Title   II Rasmussen, Carl J.
 027.7426'59   Z792.E4

Library of Congress cataloguing in publication data
Bush, Sargent, Jr.
 The Library of Emmanuel College, Cambridge; 1584–1637.
 Includes index.
 1. Emmanuel College (University of Cambridge).
Library—History. 2. Libraries, University and college
—England—Cambridge (Cambridgeshire)—History—1400–
1600. 3. Libraries, University and college—England—
Cambridge (Cambridgeshire)—History—17th–18th
centuries. I. Rasmussen, Carl J. II. Title.
Z792.E45B87   1986   027.7426'59   85–31443

ISBN 0 521 30846 1

IP

CONTENTS

ILLUSTRATIONS

All photographs were taken by Frank Stubbings, to whom we are grateful.

Figures

Tables

ACKNOWLEDGEMENTS

This work would never have been undertaken and could not have been completed without the generous encouragement, cooperation, and active assistance of Dr Frank H. Stubbings, Fellow and lately Librarian of Emmanuel College. He made all of the library's resources available to us, adding, for good measure, his abiding patience and good humor. His unusual generosity and hospitality were always seconded by the sublibrarians and assistants in the College Library, Martin Everett, Mrs Margaret Bevan, and Mrs Norma Searby. Emmanuel's Master, Derek Brewer, also extended the hospitality of the college to us and we are grateful for his interest in the project.

The generous financial support which has permitted both of the authors to spend extended periods on the project has been a crucial factor in its completion. We wish to thank the University of Wisconsin Graduate School's Research Committee for funds which supported Carl Rasmussen as a graduate assistant for two academic years at the outset of our work, and for salary support to Sargent Bush for the summers of 1978 and 1979. His travel to Cambridge in the summer of 1978 was funded by the same source and in the summer of 1979 by a grant from the American Philosophical Society. S.B. also benefited greatly from a semester as Fellow of the Institute for Research in the Humanities. Finally, a subsidy to the Cambridge University Press from the Governing Body of Emmanuel College has helped see this work into print. For all of this practical support, we are extremely grateful.

Other aid came in a variety of ways. The assistance and counsel of fellow scholars and colleagues has been particularly gratifying; we want to thank especially G. Thomas Tanselle, Merton M. Sealts, Jr, William M. Gibson, and Everett H. Emerson. Norman Roth gave invaluable help in dealing with the Hebrew titles in the collection. George Goebel provided expert advice on the Greek and the more opaque Latin that we encountered. Philip Gaskell, Librarian of Trinity College, Cambridge, generously permitted S.B. to read the manuscript of his book on the early history of the Trinity College Library before it was published. David McKitterick of the Cambridge University Library and the Cambridge Bibliographical Society has also given generously of his time, knowledge, and encouragement. Cynthia Bush assisted in numerous ways at all stages of the project but particularly in Cambridge where she helped substantially with the research done in the Emmanuel College Library. Catherine Rasmussen read page proofs. Others in Wisconsin who have given valuable practical assistance include Lynda Reigstad, Cindy Townsend, Jane Renneberg, Maggie Brandenburg, Elizabeth Reinwald, Bielha Mirkan, and Jean McGruer. And for over four years as we progressed through various stages of the work, most of our difficult typing was done by Deanna Briley. To all of these helpers, we owe much thanks.

Having had such exceptional support and assistance, we wish it were reasonable to promise a flawless product. But for those errors which may be inevitable in such a work, the authors accept full responsibility.

Madison, Wisconsin
January, 1985

INTRODUCTION

In recent years catalogues from sixteenth- and seventeenth-century libraries have begun to receive the careful scholarly attention which they deserve. Bibliographers have long recognized the intrinsic interest of such inventories; of late, scholars in the humanities and social sciences have begun to turn to these catalogues more frequently to gain fuller understanding of the cultural and intellectual history of both England and America. Sears Jayne, whose publication in 1956 of an extensive list of largely unknown *Library Catalogues of the English Renaissance* did much to inspire interest in the field, has made the claim that "a large and careful English library catalogue is ... the shortest and most accurate route to a knowledge of what was known in renaissance England about any subject."[1] Even though it is true that not all books on library shelves – then as well as now – were read, Jayne's assessment of the value of such inventories is quite correct. Early library catalogues, with their abundance of detail, provide a valuable body of data to support or correct the sometimes easy and sweeping generalizations that have been used to characterize a richly interesting, complex, and influential historical period. The kind of information such inventories provide is particularly useful when it illuminates the thought and illustrates the mission of historically important personages and institutions.

Emmanuel College, Cambridge, in its first half-century, was just such an institution, and its library holdings represent a heretofore untapped resource of knowledge about that college and the era to which it so substantially contributed. The work which follows is, therefore, an attempt to make available a full knowledge of the particularly ample resources of a college of unique historical significance in the period of its great initial influence, 1584–1637.[2]

For the past 350 years the Emmanuel College archives have safeguarded seven inventories of the books in the early college library. The first six are in a narrow folio account book and the last is in a somewhat larger notebook. The first of these lists, which is undated, was apparently compiled in or about 1597, some thirteen years after the founding of the college in 1584. The second was not made until 1621. Five successive inventories were compiled in the next sixteen years, doubtless reflecting an increasing concern for the careful management of the college's library. In all, these seven lists, compiled in c. 1597, 1621, 1622, 1626, 1628, 1632, and 1637, represent a full and accurate record of the growth of one of the larger college library collections of the period. Sears Jayne calls this series of inventories the "most remarkable" of Cambridge college library inventories from the seventeenth century.[3] They surely comprise an unusually detailed record, not only of exactly what books the college owned but also of the nature of the library's growth during a half-century in which college libraries were increasingly valued after a period of decline. Emmanuel College offers an unusually interesting case because of the special nature of the college's history, its particular mission in the period, and the unique contributions by its alumni in both England and America during these years and the subsequent decades.

The character of the early Emmanuel College

In 1583 the land and buildings of a defunct Dominican monastery were acquired by Laurence Chaderton, a fellow of Christ's College, Cambridge, and his kinsman, Richard Culverwell of London, who promptly conveyed the property to Sir Walter Mildmay, Queen Elizabeth's Chancellor of the Exchequer and a member of her Privy Council. Sir Walter had formed plans for a new college, and the Queen granted a charter for its founding in January 1584. Chaderton became the first master of the college, a post he held for thirty-six years. Three fellows were appointed, one coming from Christ's College and two from Clare Hall. Later in the same year they were joined by four new fellows, two from Christ's and two from Clare. By July of 1585 there were eighteen scholars. The financial footing of the college was gradually strengthened, and major building projects began almost immediately, most notably the construction of the Founder's Range (now the Westmorland Building).[4]

The diplomatic and financial skill of Sir Walter Mildmay was surely an important factor in the rise to prominence of this new college which by the early seventeenth century enrolled more students than any other college in Cambridge except Trinity. Sir Walter's intentions, however, were not simply to establish another college; he had a particular goal in mind. Mildmay, from his seat in Parliament and the Privy Council, was a forceful defender of the great need to protect the godly Puritan preachers from too severe treatment at the hands of the government. Chaderton voiced similar views in one of his very few published sermons.[5] Tradition holds that after she had granted the charter, Queen Elizabeth said to Sir Walter with considerable displeasure, "I hear, Sir Walter, you have erected a Puritan foundation," to which the accomplished diplomat responded with a carefully chosen metaphor: "No, Madam, far be it from me to countenance anything contrary to your established laws, but I have set an acorn, which when it becomes an oak, God alone knows what will be the fruit thereof."[6] In the early statutes of the college and in his comments on those statutes, Mildmay returned to his planting and harvesting metaphor, saying that he had established Emmanuel College as a "seed-plot of learned men for the supply of the Church" so that "from this seed-ground the English Church might have those that she can summon to instruct the people and undertake the office of pastors, which is a thing necessary above all others." "We have founded the college," he said, "with the design that it should be, by the grace of God, a seminary of learned men for the supply of the Church."[7] In order to insure that the fellows at Emmanuel did not become so comfortable as to forget their duty to the world, Mildmay wrote into the original statutes the stipulation that no fellow could remain more than ten years after receiving his M.A. or more than one year past his D.D. Such a regulation did indeed assure that the college would be a continuous source

2

of ministers for the kingdom and also that the college's body of fellows would, perforce, receive a steady flow of new blood. This regulation remained in effect until 1627 when, in the mastership of John Preston, a royal dispensation was granted suspending the rule.[8]

Regardless of Mildmay's denial of subversive intent, Emmanuel College was, from the start, a Puritan institution. It became notorious for its departures from prescribed form in the observation of the sacrament of communion and in the refusal by its clerics to wear the surplice in the church service. Even the first chapel was out of line, facing north rather than east as was customary. These were only the most conspicuous signs of the college's ecclesiastical nonconformity, a characteristic which encouraged numerous Puritan families in the country to send their sons there for their education. A prominent procession of church leaders, scholars, colonists, and, to a lesser extent, political figures issued from Emmanuel during its first half-century. Though Sir Walter died only five years after his college was born, his vision of its fruitfulness was not long in being realized.

Emmanuel's early graduates and fellows were very often, as Mildmay intended they should be, important presences and voices in the church. William Bedell was among the very first to enroll at Emmanuel, being admitted on November 1, 1584. He would become chaplain to the Ambassador to Venice, Sir Henry Wotton, and later Provost of Trinity College, Dublin, and Bishop of Kilmore and Armagh. Joseph Hall, a minister and man of letters who became chaplain to James I and later Bishop of Exeter and then of Norwich, was another early Emmanuel graduate and fellow to achieve special prominence in the church. More typically, Emmanuel graduates became a part of the large force of prophesying Puritan preachers active in the English countryside. Such names as John Rogers, Ezekiel Culverwell, John Cotton, Thomas Shepard, Timothy and Nehemiah Rogers, and Thomas Hooker became all too familiar to the Anglican Church hierarchy, many of them being silenced during the late 1620s and 1630s. Many of the delegates to the Westminster Assembly in the 1640s were Emmanuel men, including Stephen Marshall, William Bradshaw, John Yates, the Independents Jeremiah Burroughs and Sidrach Simpson, and even Francis Cornwall, whose nonconformity ultimately became the more radical Baptism. Other men found preferment at other colleges as fellows and masters. Among the most prominent of these were two of the original seven fellows, John Richardson and William Branthwaite. Richardson became Master of Peterhouse (1609–15), then Master of Trinity College (1615–25) and Regius Professor of Divinity, while Branthwaite, an accomplished Greek scholar, became Master of Gonville and Caius College (1607–19). Both were among the translators of the Authorized Version of the Bible, as was Samuel Ward, another Emmanuel fellow, who became Master of Sidney Sussex (1610–43). During the interregnum, an Emmanuel College background was sufficient recommendation for preferment. Under the Protectorate, when new masters were imposed on many of the colleges by the political authorities, as many as twelve of the masters of Cambridge colleges were Emmanuel graduates. It was in this period that Thomas Fuller, the early historian of the University of Cambridge, after quoting Mildmay's prophetic oak tree metaphor, declared that "at this day it hath over shadowed all the University, more than a moiety of the present masters of colleges being bred therein."[9] In the years 1644–

53 Emmanuel itself was led by one of her own, Anthony Tuckney, also a Westminster Assembly delegate and previous Master of St John's College. The sole Emmanuel graduate before Tuckney to become the Master of his alma mater was William Sandcroft (1628–37), uncle of the more famous Archbishop of Canterbury William Sancroft, also an Emmanuel graduate.

Earlier in the seventeenth century, many of the strongest and most outspoken Puritans among the Emmanuel alumni had committed themselves to the Great Migration to New England. Most of these men left England in the 1630s, having been exiled, in effect, by being denied the right to practice their preaching or teaching gifts in England. Indeed, it is well known that no college in the land contributed nearly so many leaders of the early New England colonial enterprise as did Emmanuel. In the first generation of settlement, 1620–45, some 130 college-educated settlers went to New England. About 100 of these· were from Cambridge colleges, thirty-five being Emmanuel men. The college contributing the next highest number of college-graduate colonists was Trinity College, Cambridge, with thirteen.[10] The Emmanuel men in New England included governors and magistrates such as Thomas Dudley, Simon Bradstreet, and Richard Saltonstall; powerful preachers and town founders such as Thomas Hooker, Thomas Shepard, and Samuel Stone; ministers who also wrote the first body of laws, Nathaniel Ward and John Cotton; and a book-collecting minister who gave his library and his name to the first college in America, John Harvard. Moreover, it was Emmanuel which served as the chief model for Harvard College's curriculum, its educational philosophy, and even the floor plan of its residential buildings. As Samuel Eliot Morison has suggested in his histories of Harvard College, Emmanuel was, in many ways, the mother of Harvard.[11] The fruits from Sir Walter's seed-plot were even more abundant and far-flung than he had hoped or imagined a half-century earlier.

All of the men mentioned in this brief and highly selective list were at Emmanuel College during the period in which the seven early library inventories were compiled. It might be argued, indeed – without diminishing subsequent contributions – that it was this period in which Emmanuel College achieved its greatest prominence and made its profoundest impact on the history of England and of the western world. At any rate, as a Puritan institution, Emmanuel was born at a most opportune moment: the seventy-five years after its birth saw the triumph of Puritanism. Emmanuel men, as we have suggested, had an important role as teachers and practical leaders of this movement on both sides of the Atlantic.

College libraries in the period

1584 was also an excellent time for the creation of a college library. From the Henrican Reformation until the accession of Elizabeth, the English Universities had been in turmoil, and this turmoil adversely affected the college libraries, which were severely diminished. A major purge of libraries occurred in 1535 when Roman Catholic works of canon law along with books by scholastic Biblical commentators were largely cast out. Around mid-century under the brief reign of Edward VI some of the libraries suffered the effects of Puritan censors, and in 1557 in his visitation of Cambridge, Cardinal Pole rooted out Protestant works. Public book-burnings in the market place were among the consequences of the Pole visitation, made all the more dramatic in February 1557 by inclusion in the fire of the remains of Martin Bucer and Paul Fagius, exhumed from Great St Mary's Church. On Elizabeth's accession, fortunately, a more enlightened attitude towards books and learning came to prevail.[12]

Political and ecclesiastical vicissitudes were not, however, the only causes of the weakening of college libraries in the sixteenth century. Fully as many books – perhaps more – were lost by the mismanagement of the collections. The case of King's College has been particularly well documented in this respect. Even though the Visitation of 1557 represents the nadir for most Cambridge libraries, in the thirteen years after 1557, "what was left of King's Library almost entirely disappeared."[13] In both Cambridge and Oxford people were simply walking off with books and manuscripts. Although all college libraries through much of the sixteenth century continued the medieval practice of chaining their books, most such libraries also kept a portion of their collections for loan. This was the "electio sociorum," which allowed fellows of the college to take books and manuscripts to their rooms for extended periods. All libraries had difficulty enforcing the rules of this system, and a great many books were simply never returned. Merton College, Oxford, discontinued the system as early as 1519, though most libraries stayed with it much longer, to their loss. Several scholars have documented the decline in the holdings of college library collections in the first three-quarters of the sixteenth century; it was not unusual for collections of four or five hundred volumes to have been reduced to between one and two hundred in this period.[14]

By the time Emmanuel College was founded, however, the climate had changed. It is now generally agreed that the period of about 1585 to 1640 represents what Neil Ker calls "a new era" in the history of college libraries.[15] The date of Emmanuel's founding thus could not have been more fortunate for building a library collection. Indeed, from the outset the Emmanuel library took on a rather modern approach in its shelving methods and its rules. Though some extant college libraries remained chained well into the seventeenth century,[16] Emmanuel's books were never chained. This innovation probably reinforced the tendency already present in other colleges to do away with their chains. As Philip Gaskell has explained in his history of Trinity College Library, removal of the chains and the heavy binding boards required by the chains made possible new, more efficient shelving methods.[17] Offsetting this apparent new openness, however, were rules limiting access to most libraries to fellows of the colleges. In this regard as well Emmanuel's practice appears to have been more liberal than the norm.

Emmanuel's earliest library: physical details

Not a great deal is known about the physical characteristics of the first library at Emmanuel. Robert Willis and John Willis Clark conclude that it must have been located in "the small range which extended from the north end of the Kitchen-range to the street and formed the north side of the small court called 'Bungay Court'."[18] Their reasoning is based mainly on the details in David Loggan's engraving of the college

Table 1. *Reconstruction of classis 4, inferior, from the 1621 and 1622 Emmanuel College Library catalogues*

The 1621 and 1622 catalogues show identical data on this classis. Note, however, that the fore-edge numbering reflects the presence of more volumes in the classis than does the numbering of the items on the inventories of 1621 and 1622. This suggests that books were added shortly before the application of the fore-edge numbering sometime in the period 1622–6, and before the major rearrangement of the collection in 1626. **RBR** stands for Register of Books Removed.

1621–22 location	Running number on fore-edge	1637 location	Author, short title, date of publication	Present class mark
4.I.1		22.I(2).14	Altensteig, Lexicon Theologicum	MISSING
4.I.2	"2"	23.S(2).4	Nausea, Homiliarum Centuria Tres (1532)	308.3.51
4.I.3		—	Aretius in Psalmos. Last recorded 1628. 3.1.5	MISSING since 1628
4.I.4		22.S(3).9	Fricius [Modrevius], De Republica....	MISSING, (RBR, p. 29, 1. 14)
4.I.5	"5"	22.S(1).6	Sedulius, In Epistolas Pauli (1528)	310.5.1
4.I.6	"6"	23.I(1).4	Sadoletus, In Pauli Epistolas ad Romanos (1536)	306.2.32
4.I.7		22.I(3).4	Hosius, Opera Omnia	MISSING
4.I.8		22.S(3).10	Vives, De Veritate Fidei Christianae	MISSING, (RBR, p. 38, 1.3)
4.I.9	"9"	22.I(3).9	Pighius, Hierarchiae Ecclesiasticae Assertio (1538)	307.3.4
4.I.10	"10"	22.I(3).11	Vadianus, Aphorismorum ... De Consideratione Eucharistiae (1536)	307.3.10
4.I.11	"11"	22.I(3).2	Stapleton, Principorum Fidei Doctrinalium.... (1581)	305.1.7
4.I.12	"12"	22.I(3).3	Canisius, Opus Catechismus (1579)	308.3.36
4.I.13	"13"	22.I(3).10	Lindanus [van der Lindt], Panoplia Evangelica (1575)	307.3.8
4.I.14	"14"	22.I(3).17	Lindanus, Apologeticum ad Germanos pro Relig. Cath. (1568[−70])	301.5.68
4.I.15		23.I(1).26	Lindanus, Paraphrases in Psalmos	MISSING
4.I.16	"16"	7.1.19	Molinaeus, Tractatus Commerciorum (1555)	FB9
4.I.17	"17"	22.I(3).16	Constantio [pseud. Gardiner]. Confut. Cavil.... Eucharistiae (1552)	301.5.69
4.I.18	"18"	22.I(3).23	Billick, Judicii Universitatis et Cleri Coloniensis adversus.... (1545)	301.5.92

4.1.19	[22]1.I(3).22	"19"	Fisher (Roffensis), De Veritate Corporis et Sanguinis Christi in Eucharistia (1527)	334.3.68
4.1.20	[23]S(2).14		Pepin, Expositio in Genesim, 2 Vols.	MISSING?
4.1.21	[23]1.I(1).27		Titelmann, In Omnes Epistolas Apostolicas	MISSING?
4.1.22	[23]1.I(1).29		Guilliandus, In Canonicas Apostolorum	MISSING
4.1.23	[22]1.I(3).35	"24"	Peresius, De . . . Apostolicis, atque Ecclesiasticis Traditionibus (1549)	321.4.107
4.1.24	2.I.29	"26"	Lossius, Annotationes Scholasticae in Evangelia Dominicalia (1560)	321.6.11
4.1.25	[21]1.I.46	"27"	Bodius, Unio Dissidentium (1531)	321.6.39
4.1.26	[22]1.I(3).34	"28"	Cologne, Cathedral, Antididagma . . . . (1544)	338.5.30
4.1.27	[22]1.I(3).36		Gerlacher, Erasmus, & Luther, De Libero Arbitrio, etc.	MISSING?
4.1.28	[23]S(2).16	"30", "31"	Culmann, Concionum . . . .2 Vols. (1550)	326.4.98,99
4.1.29	2.I.15	"32", "33", "34"	Sarcerius in Matthew, Mark, & John, 3 Vols. (1538 39,40)	321.6.15–17
4.1.29	2.I.16	"35","36"	Sarcerius in 1 & 2 Cor., 2 Vols. (1544)	323.5.113 and 321.7.75
4.1.29	2.I.17	"37"	Sarcerius, Postilla (1538)	321.6.14
4.1.29	2.I.18	"38", "41"	Sarcerius, Loci Communes, 2 Vols. (1539, 40)	338.5.41 and 326.4.90
4.1.29	2.I.19	"39"	Sarcerius, De Consensu Verae Ecclesiae & Sanctorum Patrum . . . super praecipuis Christianae . . . .(1540)	338.5.43
4.1.29	2.I.20	"40"	Sarcerius, Catechismus, & Spalatinus & Castalione (1542, 44, 45)	321.7.76

(c. 1688) which shows seven windows on the south side of that range's second story. These windows would have been ideal for a library, they argue. Other evidence, again supportable by a detail in the Loggan print, suggests another location for the library, however. An entry in the college's accounts book for 1657 refers to a payment for installing "doggs and SS of iron for the Library." Two of the three outside walls on the Bungay Court building thought by Willis and Clark to be the library are clearly shown in the Loggan picture, but neither has an "S" bracket. Two such brackets are visible, however, one clearly depicted on the west end (in the immediate foreground) and one barely discernible in the shadows on the north wall of the extension of the Founder's Wing which runs out perpendicular to St Andrew's Street (originally Preachers' Street).[19] This building is south of but parallel to the Bungay Court building and thus also on an east–west axis, a requirement for the Emmanuel Library, Willis and Clark note, because of the 1637 inventory's division of the collection into a "pars occidentalis" and a "pars orientalis."

As to the furnishings of the library, we may note that three of the seven inventories include supplementary lists of property other than books in the library. All the lists take note of certain objects such as "The founders picture with a curtayne of blew saye & an Iron rodd" and the "Terrestriall globe with a waynscot frame." Another recurrent entry is "Nyne glass windows & 3. Casements." Loggan's view shows only a window with two lights on both the first and second floors of the west end of the extension. It does seem likely, though, that the room nominated by Willis and Clark must have had more than nine windows, while the wing with the "S" brackets must have had a smaller number because a large chimney occupies part of the south wall.

Included on the inventories of physical property in the first list (c. 1597) are "Nyne fayre desks of oake each one having three degrees." These were supplemented shortly after 1622 by "2 other desks of oake having each of them 6. degrees, the upp[er] bord of one wanting" and by "1 other desk of deale having 6 degrees." This last item does not appear on the 1637 list but the other eleven "desks" do. As Willis and Clark point out, the word "desk" was sometimes used synonymously with "classis," each term referring to a book case or press, usually having two shelves and a lectern desk at the top where the large folios could be laid comfortably close to eye level for the standing reader. It is not certain that the lectern-style cases were used in Emmanuel's first library but it seems highly likely. At any rate, it is clear that, though most of the desks had three "degrees" or shelves, only two were used for storing books, leaving the top of the case unoccupied.[20]

It is not clear exactly how these cases were arranged around the room, though most of them probably projected from the wall at right angles, with windows between, in the manner common to medieval and early Renaissance libraries. The nine desks with three shelves may not have been of uniform size judging from the variation from list to list of the number of books stored in each. Still, they seem to have conformed in style and function to those in most Cambridge libraries of the period. The two extra-tall classes first appear in the property list appended to the 1621 book inventory and were first integrated into the functional library furnishings between 1622 and 1626. They were surely acquired to help accommodate the large influx of new books in 1622–6, of which more will be said shortly.[21]

The books were shelved standing on their bottom edges with the fore-edges facing outwards. Lists of the books in a given case were probably posted on the end of the case, according to standard college library procedure for the period. At first this was probably all the help one had in finding a given work in the Emmanuel Library, though there was a rough subject division of the books. At some point it was decided, as the collection grew larger, that the books themselves should bear designations indicating the author and/or title or subject. Consequently short author and/or title designations were written on the fore-edges; as one looked at a shelf one saw, usually at the tops of the fore-edges, such short titles as "Prosper" and "Naz. graec" to designate volumes of the Opera of St Prosper of Aquitaine and a Greek version of the works of St Gregory of Nazianzus.

At a slightly later date it seems to have occurred to those in charge of Emmanuel's library that running shelf numbers assigned to each volume would help keep the shelving system in order. These numbers were probably written on the list of books posted at the end of the lectern desks, but they were also written directly on the books' fore-edges, above or, more commonly, below the author/title designation. The shelving order was substantially changed at least three times during the period with which we are concerned, and it can be shown that this fore-edge numbering system appeared shortly after the 1622 inventory and before the major rearrangement of 1626 (see Table 1). Once it appeared, however, the system was of limited usefulness. New books had to be added to the old subject classes, so that the fore-edge numbers quickly went out of date. Some of these numbers were altered, but the futility of this process must soon have become apparent. Probably there was a period when the new running numbers were not written on or in the books at all. Sometime after 1637 the Emmanuel Librarian began writing tripartite class marks, along with the library's ownership designation, on the title pages or flyleaves of the volumes. Consequently many of the early volumes contain an inscription such as: "Coll: Eman: Cant:/ G.3.35," though in many cases only the class mark was written in. The final number, the running shelf location number, also appeared on a small paper tab glued around the edge of the front cover near the top of the fore-edge.[22] Such tabs were common in Cambridge libraries and since tabs are replaceable, they proved more practical than fore-edge writing. During the period in which the inventories were made, however, fore-edge writing was the only method used at Emmanuel for indicating a book's shelf location, and it was not applied to all books. The fore-edge writing on some books was trimmed away when these books were rebound in the seventeenth and eighteenth centuries, but where it remains, it has been especially valuable evidence for our reconstruction of the early library.

The founder's books

In 1584 immediately after receiving the charter, Sir Walter Mildmay already had a hand-picked Master, at least three fellows, and sufficient financial resources to begin operation of the college. It seems likely, therefore, that he had given some careful thought to and made preliminary plans for the acquisition of a suitable library for the college. Yet, relatively little is known about the Emmanuel Library during its first fifteen years. It is not mentioned in Mildmay's Statutes for the college. By the time the first surviving inventory of the library was made in about 1597, however, the collection already contained at least 443 volumes, and perhaps as many as 481.[23] This was a very respectable number since, as Philip Gaskell and others have said, 500 volumes was about the most that any college library contained at this date, the main restriction on growth being lack of space.[24] Trinity College, which was founded in 1546 through a merger of two earlier institutions and their libraries, and whose collection eventually grew to be the gem of the Cambridge college libraries, had only about 325 volumes of printed books in 1600.[25] It seems clear that Emmanuel had made a determined effort to build a good book collection from the very start.

Mildmay, for all of his other talents, was not known as a book collector, though he was a friend and occasional patron of authors. He did give to Emmanuel a small collection of a dozen books, doubtless intended to serve as the core of the new library. They are books which came from his own private library, and most of them bear his signature, sometimes with the date on which he acquired the volume.[26] Most also contain his marginal notes. This cluster of books displays Mildmay's own varied interests, but it may also suggest something of his sense of what a college library should contain and even what a college should be. Three of the works have to do with divinity: a Latin vulgate Bible (Lyons, 1557), a French language Bible (Geneva, 1588), and the second volume of Theodore Beza's *Tractationum Theologicarum* (Geneva, 1573). Each of these is interesting for unique reasons. The Latin vulgate Bible was lost sometime in the first decade of the seventeenth century (it was one of some thirty books recorded as missing on October 4, 1610). The French Bible bears a hand-written inscription on its title page: "Ex dono Ministrorum totius Ecclesiae Geneuensis Octavo Calendas Junij 1588. W. A.: Mildmaye". After he received this book from the Geneva divines, Mildmay must have presented it very promptly to the college library since he lived just under a year after the gift was inscribed. It thus probably came to the library slightly later than the rest of his gift books. The Beza volume was dedicated to Sir Walter and the copy at Emmanuel is the dedication copy.

His desires for this "seed-plot" were that it should produce "learned men for the supply of the church" but the Mildmay nucleus for the library was by no means narrowly theological. His donation of books also included a volume on logic (Rodolphus Agricola), two of rhetoric (the *Orationes* of Isocrates in Greek and Latin and The Latin *Orationes* of the sixteenth-century English author Walter Haddon), and two on ancient history (Appian in Greek and Livy in Latin, both important for their style as well as content). Much farther afield from the broad subject area of divinity were the remaining books in Mildmay's donation: three on mathematics (Dürer, Finé, and Tunstall), and one reflecting the founder's immediate practical interests in the law (Charles Du Moulin on contracts).

One of the most striking things about this rather diverse list is its reflection of trends in Cambridge education in the period. The copy of Agricola's *De Inventione Dialectica* (Cologne, 1527) is a case in point. This book has been singled out by Lisa Jardine as one of the four or five most important dialectic texts in Cambridge by the second half of the seventeenth century.[27] It follows Valla and precedes Ramus and Melanchthon in giving the study of dialectic a new humanistic emphasis. Agricola's is, says Jardine, a "reformed dialectic.... Agricola is first and foremost a *humanist* in his emphasis on Cicero and Quintilian at the expense of Aristotle, and in his insistence on elegant Latin as the model for discourse."[28] She has observed that in the private book collections of members of the university in this period "Agricola's ... occurs twice as often as Melanchthon's textbook, and three times as often as any other [dialectics] textbook."[29]

But there are other signs that Mildmay was in tune with the trends in Cambridge education. The two history books given by Mildmay are Appian's *Romanae Historiae* (Paris, 1551) in Greek and the Basel, 1535 edition of Livy. Although Greek was taught at Cambridge, it was not a part of the undergraduate curriculum until well into the seventeenth century.[30] But the presence of the Greek version of Appian's history of Rome, an important resource for the study of literature as well as of Roman history, suggests that Mildmay's "learned man" was expected to know Greek. It clearly had a place in a body of resources which were providing the basis for the strengthening of the humanities at Cambridge. This is all the more true of the volume of Livy, who was "the favorite Roman historian of the early humanists" until after the turn of the century when he was replaced by Tacitus.[31]

Also striking in these few books given by Mildmay is the presence of contemporary works in both law and literature. The study of law had been in disarray at the universities since the abolition of canon law by Henry VIII. William T. Costello goes so far as to say "there was no study of law worth a doit at Cambridge between 1600 and 1670."[32] Mildmay had himself studied at Gray's Inn after leaving Christ's College, however, and had a strong practical bent in his thinking. His gift of the French jurist Charles Du Moulin's *Tractatus Commerciorum, et Vsurarum* (Paris, 1555), suggests that for Mildmay the well-rounded "learned man" would do well to mingle the law with his study of the other disciplines.

Likewise, Mildmay's decision to bestow a copy of Walter Haddon's Latin poetry and orations on his college's library is noteworthy. While Haddon is no Sidney or Spenser, the presence of *any* contemporary poet in a college collection in the 1580s was more than a little unusual.[33] The ancient poets were there, but modern poets, even in Latin versions, were only just beginning to appear. A volume of Petrarch was present at the time of Emmanuel's first inventory; Chaucer did not appear in the collection until sometime between 1628 and 1632, and nothing whatever of Spenser was in the library by 1637 nor were the modern English poets, George Herbert and Francis Quarles, who were so popular with the Puritans. Mildmay's choice of Haddon can probably be explained by the fact that he was a personal friend, being, like Mildmay, a Cambridge graduate, a sometime member of Gray's Inn, a Member of Parliament, and a counsellor to the Queen. One of his Latin poems, in fact, was written about Mildmay.[34] Still, while Haddon's *Orationes* makes a somewhat peculiar companion to the Greek *Orationes* of Isocrates, Mildmay may have reasoned that both the modern and the ancient offered instruction to the student of eloquence.

The only branch of learning as fully represented as divinity in Mildmay's gift books is mathematics, a field which, like law, was not much taught at sixteenth- and early seventeenth-century Cambridge. Costello, again adopting a hyperbolic style, says simply that "early seventeenth-century Cambridge is almost a mathematical desert."[35] A letter by the eminent Emmanuel graduate, John Wallis (B.A. 1637), on the state of learning in the field which particularly attracted him, has often been quoted. Having long since established his eminence as a professor of astronomy at Oxford, as an old man he complained that:

> I had none to direct me, what books to read, or what to seek, or in what method
> to proceed. For mathematics, (at that time, with us) were scarce looked upon as
> academical studies, but rather mechanical; as the business of traders, merchants,
> seamen, carpenters, surveyors of lands, and the like; and perhaps some almanac-
> makers in London. And amongst more than two hundred students (at that time) in
> our college, I do not know of any two (perhaps not any) who had more of
> mathematics than I . . . which was then but little.[36]

Curiously, another man who achieved eminence in the same field in a much shorter life than Wallis's, Jeremiah Horrocks, had also matriculated at Emmanuel in 1632, the year Wallis enrolled. Both had been preceded there by Samuel Foster, the mathematician and astronomer, who had taken his B.A. and M.A. in 1619 and 1623 respectively. Somehow, despite the scarcity of knowledgeable instructors, these three members of the same college received sufficient nurture in their undergraduate (and, in Foster's case, graduate) training to sustain an interest in and establish a fundamental body of knowledge about mathematics on which to build in later years. It would be foolish to claim too much for Sir Walter Mildmay's foresight in his gift of Albrecht Dürer's *Institutiones Geometricae* (Paris, 1535), Oronce Finé's *In sex priores libros Geometricorum elementorum Euclidis Megarensis demonstrationes* (Paris, 1544), and Cuthbert Tunstall's *De Arte Supputandi* (Paris, 1529). But the fact remains that these books were in the library from its beginnings and did provide a core of books to which a few others were added in the next four decades, so that the likes of Wallis, Horrocks, and Foster were hardly stranded in an intellectual desert. Also present in the Emmanuel library by 1632 were Ptolemaeus's *Almagestum* (Venice, 1515), acquired in the period 1598–1621, Euclid's *Geometrica Elementa*, with Grynaeus's commentary (Basel, 1533) and the important *Opera Mathematica* of Christoph Clavius (Mainz, 1612), both of which were acquired in the period 1628–32. These works, together with books on cosmography by Apianus and Münster, helped make up a small but respectable collection for its day. Since, after all, mathematics was taught and mathematics textbooks were available in Cambridge, it is proper to suppose with Mark H. Curtis that to some degree extreme statements like that of the aged John Wallis demonstrate that "the memories of impatient genius, even when recalled in the tranquility of old age, may be less than fair to bygone times."[37]

Mildmay's gift of books, then, established a small core collection which signaled that Emmanuel's ministers would have a humanist background and at least some oppor-tunity for acquaintance with the practical disciplines of law and mathematics. It would be a mistake to make too much of the possible motivations for Mildmay's gift of these few books since in fact we know nothing definite about it. He may simply have been disposing of his duplicate copies! But, considering his seriousness in establishing his college, it seems fair to assume that his selection of a few books for the new library was a matter of more than passing interest to him. Mildmay, being himself something of an Elizabethan man of *virtu*, by his example – and his donation of books – encouraged the members of his college to aspire to as broad a range of command as had the founder.

The first inventory

The first of Emmanuel's seven early catalogues is the only one which was not dated by its compiler. Until very recently it had been assumed that the list was drawn up in 1610.[38] Careful examination of the evidence, however, points to another date. The 1610 misdating probably stems from the fact that this first catalogue, recorded on nine pages of an early college accounts book (BUR. 8.1), is followed, on the verso of the final page (f. 192), by a list of books missing from the library on October 4, 1610. On that date, we are told, "there were found in the Library...503 bookes," but there is also a "Memorandum that at our accounts Octob. 4, 1610. there were wanting in the Library thirty books in number." These missing books are then carefully listed by author, short title, and location (classis, shelf, and running number). This list of missing books itself provides ample evidence that the preceding nine-page catalogue was made before 1610. The catalogue and the 1610 notes are written in decidedly different hands, and a count of the volumes in the earliest list yields, at most, 481 and, for reasons which will be explained shortly, probably fewer. Finally, all thirty of the items listed as missing on October 4, 1610, were present for the earlier inventory. Moreover, we can tell from evidence of two other kinds that the earliest catalogue was compiled at least as early as 1598.

In the year 1600 Thomas James, the Oxford librarian and bibliophile, published his catalogue of manuscripts in Oxford and Cambridge libraries, *Ecloga Oxonio-Cantabrigiensis*. His list of Emmanuel's manuscripts includes nine volumes, of which only six were present when the first catalogue was compiled. The remaining three volumes of manuscripts seen by James, probably sometime in 1599 or very early 1600, include two which we know were gifts to the library in 1598. One of these, a collection of writings by St Chrysostom, carries the inscription: "Given by George Barcroft, Ecclesiae Cathedralis Eliensis Αρχέχορος, A.D. 1597. Mart, 5°."[39] This old-style date translates to March 5, 1598; it is the earliest recorded date of a gift to the library of an item which had not appeared on the first catalogue. Consequently, the first catalogue must be dated no later than very early March of 1598. Other inscribed gift books support this dating: Samuel Wright's 1598 gift of a partial Greek New Testament in manuscript (4.4), three books given by Richard Lister in 1599 (1.1.5, 9.S.1, [2]3.I(3).4), and Ralph Cudworth's gifts of at least three and probably four manuscripts in 1600 (4.6, 4.8, 4.14, 4.18) do not appear on the earliest catalogue.[40]

Unfortunately, these items are the first gifts to the library to bear such clear and precise information, such inscriptions becoming common only at about this time. Though there are several items in the earliest catalogue which we can safely assume were given to the library by their owners at some date before 1598, almost none of them – including even the founder's books – unambiguously specifies the date of the gift.[41] Three volumes, however, do bear the boldly written inscription, "Ex dono W. Fletewoode Recordatoris London 1586."[42] Fleetwood was the Recorder of London and, during the 1580s, Member of Parliament for London. A man of considerable influence in official circles and a well-known antiquary and owner of several valuable manuscripts,[43] Fleetwood was a Parliamentary and court acquaintance of Sir Walter Mildmay, who was some fifteen years his senior. In the very year of his gifts to the Emmanuel library he was promised the office of Baron of the Exchequer. It seems likely that Mildmay, then Chancellor of the Exchequer, prevailed on Fleetwood to give these few books to the new college, though it is of course equally possible that Fleetwood was of a sufficiently charitable nature that the thought occurred to him voluntarily. At any rate, political intrigue aside, these three volumes – Ptolemy's *Geography* in Latin (Strassburg, 1520) (7.2.6), Antoninus's *Opus…hystoriarum seu cronicarum* [Lyons, c. 1512] (6.4.12), and a Strassburg incunable folio edition of Joannes Balbus's *Summa que vocatur catholicon* (^{2}3.I(3).1) – are all listed in the first catalogue, which must therefore date from no earlier than 1586. Thus, we know that that catalogue was compiled sometime in the period 1586–98. The best estimate of the date, however, is probably c. 1597 since it seems likely that a collection of over four hundred volumes would have taken a good deal more than the first two years of the college's existence to accumulate and since we know that in 1610 the collection included only about fifty more volumes than were recorded at the time of the first inventory.

Another important group of books which appears to have come to Emmanuel's library in time to be included in the first inventory deserves special attention. This is a group of some twenty-five volumes from the library of John, Lord Lumley. In every instance but one, these books had been part of the library of Archbishop Thomas Cranmer before he was martyred.[44] They thus bear on their title pages the distinctive small and very regular signature of "Thomas Cantuarien*sis*" as well as the larger, rounded signature "Lumley." Since the listing of Emmanuel's books from the Lumley collection which appears at the back of the published catalogue of the entire Lumley Library is both inaccurate and incomplete in certain details, we have provided a correct list of Emmanuel's Lumley books (see Table 2), including the same information as that in the Lumley Catalogue but adding the location of the books in three of Emmanuel's early catalogues and the fore-edge markings on the Emmanuel copies. What makes the library's acquisition of these works particularly interesting is that it appears to have occurred at such an early date. The modern editors of the Lumley Catalogue, Sears Jayne and Francis R. Johnson, state that immediately after a 1596 catalogue was made, Lumley set about disposing of the many duplicates in the collection, showing "characteristic generosity and interest in institutions of learning," being particularly partial to Cambridge.[45] Considering the fact that the first inventory of the Emmanuel library could not have been compiled later than early March of 1598 and was probably done slightly earlier than that, it would appear that these books were distributed by the Lumley Library at least as early as the eighty-nine folios which went to the Cambridge University Library in 1598 and perhaps earlier. (The Bodleian Library did not acquire its thirty-four volumes from the Lumley collection until still later, in 1599.) The claim by the editors of the Lumley Library Catalogue that no books went from the Lumley collection to college libraries, as distinct from the university libraries, until after Lumley's death in 1609 may very well be incorrect. The only reason for any doubt about this is that the date of acquisition is nowhere indicated in the books or the college's records. If we assume that the Cranmer/Lumley copies are the same copies as those seen by Emmanuel's first cataloguer and not replacements of books with identical contents, then we have to conclude that they arrived at Emmanuel before early March of 1598. It surely seems more than merely coincidental that items 86, 87, and 88 on the catalogue of c. 1597 mention a total of twenty-one volumes of which the twenty that are still present all bear the Lumley and Cranmer signatures. It is impossible to say how or why Emmanuel was able to obtain books from that collection so early in the period of its first distribution. But whatever the means of their acquisition, the Lumley books appear to have been among Emmanuel's earliest additions to the collection and remain today among the most prized items.

There are other uncertainties in the earliest catalogue. The most important of these is the duplication of eleven entries. These items appear near the beginning of the catalogue and turn up again near the end. Perhaps the library simply had duplicate copies of these works and shelved them in different cases, but since two of the duplicated items are manuscripts, this is unlikely. One of these manuscripts is described only in rather general terms: "Commentarius manuscript super Epist." Since this title appears apparently as the very last item on one shelf and then as the sixth item on the next shelf, it is possible that there were two manuscript commentaries on Paul's Epistles. In this 1600 catalogue, however, Thomas James lists only one, the beautifully illustrated and very large folio of Gorranus (4.9), a rare prize to this day. Repetition of a single item by the scribe seems much more likely here. The other twice-mentioned manuscript appears as the sixty-first entry on the list, "liber perantiquus de anima & corpore gr," and then as the 382nd entry: "Liber perantiquus gr. de anima corp: manuscript." This readily identifiable item is the eighth of the nine manuscript volumes listed by Thomas James in 1600 (4.25). Apparently these two manuscript volumes, and some nine printed books, of which eight are Hebrew works, were shifted within the collection while the first catalogue was being made. This would suggest that this first list was compiled over a period of time, as opportunity or inclination dictated.

The catalogue of c. 1597 contains a total of 396 unnumbered entries plus "6 bookes of monumts of Martyrs," which are listed with the physical property (founder's picture, nine glass windows, etc.) rather than with the books but which are a set of manuscripts by and about sixteenth-century Protestant martyrs. This collection is still present in the library, now rebound in three volumes. If we consider the martyrs' "monuments" as one entry, and adjust for the eleven duplicated items, the total number of items is 386. These items include 449 volumes, some of which, of course, contained two or more discrete books bound together. At the end of the catalogue, also with the physical property, the scribe mentions "Thyrty eight boks to be sold or changed for others." This was later crossed out and the word "gone" added. If these thirty-eight books were not enumerated in the catalogue, as the entry seems to suggest, the total number of volumes would come to 487.

This early collection was arranged according to rough subject divisions, getting

Table 2. *Lumley books in the Emmanuel College Library*

Location on c. 1597 catalogue	Numbers on fore-edge*	Location on 1621 catalogue	Location on 1637 catalogue	Author, short title, place & date of publication	Signed by†	Present Emmanuel classmark	Lumley catalogue number
86	1–6	3.I.1	²²2.I(4).2	Bible [Latin] with Postilla of St Hugh of Cher. [6 vols.] Basel, 1498–1502	TC, L	MSS1.13–18	—
87	7,8	3.I.2	²²2.I(2).10	Dionysius Carthusianus. In Sententiae. [2 vols.] Cologne, 1535.	TC, L	309.3.2,3	261,262
87	9	3.I.3	Missing. (See note on ²²2.I(4).12)	Dionysius Carthusianus. In Boethius, Cassianus, Scala Paradisi. Cologne, 1540.	TC, L	301.3.1	(270)
87	[10]	3.I.5	²²2.I(4).4	Dionysius Carthusianus. In Pentateuchum.	?	Missing	—
87	11	3.I.6	²²2.I(4).7	Dionysius Carthusianus. In Sapientiales. Cologne, 1539.	TC, L	302.2.45	—
87	12	3.I.7	²²2.I(4).6	Dionysius Carthusianus. In Psalmos. Paris, 1542.	TC, L	302.2.43	—
87	13	3.I.8	²²2.I(4).8	Dionysius Carthusianus. In Prophetes. Cologne, 1543.	TC, L	302.2.46	—
87	14	3.I.9	²²2.I(4).9	Dionysius Carthusianus. In Evangelistas. Cologne, 1538.	TC, L	302.2.47	(270)
87	15	3.I.10	²²2.I(4).10	Dionysius Carthusianus. In Pauli Epistolas, Acta Apostolorum, & Apocalypsum. Cologne, 1536–38.	TC, L	302.2.47A	—
88	19–24	3.I.14	²²2.I.(4).1	Bible [Latin] with glosses of Nicholas of Lyra. [6 vols.] Basel, 1508.	TC, L	303.2.61,62 302.2.1–4	—
51	11	2.I.9	²¹1.I.14	St Basil the Great. Opera [Greek]. Basel, 1532.	TC, L	304.4.29	135

65	— (rebound and trimmed, 18th c.)	2.I.25	[2]1.I.28	St Gregory of Nyssa & St Hilary. Opera. Basel, 1550.	TC, L	304.4.32	362
60?	—	1.I.4	[2]1.S.12	Eusebius, Ecclesiasticae Historiae, Lib. X. Paris, 1544.	A, L	309.1.47,46	1097
37	— [acquired in Sancroft donation, 1693]	1.I.8	6.4.6	Josephus, *Flavius*. Opera. Basel, 1524. Erasmus. De Libero Arbitrio.	TC, L / TC, L	310.1.7 / S5.4.56	1232 / 324a

*The fore-edge numbering was apparently written on the books sometime between 1622 and 1626 since the numbering follows the same order as the shelf order of the inferior sectio of the third classis in 1621 and 1622, though a few non-Lumley books had by 1621 been shelved among the Lumley volumes there. In the sequence of fore-edge numbers, 1–24, indicated above, the missing numbers, if we can judge from the 1621 and 1622 inventories, were the following books, which were not a part of the Lumley donation.

—	[16]	3.I.11	[2]2.I(4).3	Dionysius Carthusianus. Operum Minorum, Tomus Secundus. Cologne, 1532.		Missing, but replaced by 302.2.57,59 sometime between 1622 and 1626.	NA
—	[17, 18]	3.I.12,13	[2]2.I(14).12	Dionysius Carthusianus. In Epistolas & Evangelistas; De Sanctis. 2 vols.		302.2.60	NA

†TC = Thomas Cantuariensis (Thomas Cranmer, Archbishop of Canterbury)
L = Lumley (John, first Baron Lumley)
A = Arundel (Henry Fitzalan, eleventh Earl of Arundel)

17

rougher as one progresses through the list. Although classis divisions are indicated by means of a horizontal line at periodic points on the list, the cataloguer abandoned these markers after recording only a little more than half the collection. The first eighteen items are Bibles and Testaments in various languages, proceeding from the first item, the eight-volume Antwerp polyglott Bible of Arias Montanus to item eighteen, a Latin concordance. Then follows a section of some two dozen books in or about the Hebrew language or people, including five by Josephus and Philo on Jewish history, with a few other miscellaneous books mingled in amongst them. Then follows a considerable collection of the Church Fathers – Augustine in eight volumes, Jerome in four, Ambrose in three, Origen in two, Chrysostom in five, and numerous others, often in both Greek and Latin versions. Then the mix becomes a bit more eclectic, though the dominance of divinity books continues as theology and Biblical commentary by medieval scholastics – Hugo of St Cher in six volumes, Nicholas of Lyra in six, Thomas Aquinas in six, Gorranus in two – are mixed with occasional sixteenth-century Reformers and Counter-Reformers. On the third page of the catalogue a large section of Reformation theology and particularly Biblical commentary begins, followed by a section of Latin and Greek classics and a variety of contemporary secular writings including most of the science and mathematics, ethics, rhetoric, history, and grammar books in the collection. The last half of the list consists largely of Reformation authors, interspersed with occasional recent Roman Catholic Biblical commentary, and a smattering of books of history, law, and rhetoric. This rough arrangement of the books was gradually refined over the years, and successive catalogues show both increasing numbers of books and increasing control over the subject divisions.

A systematic breakdown of the subjects represented in the collection of c. 1597 shows, predictably, a preponderance of divinity books. Indeed, Bibles, Biblical commentaries, theological disputation, church polity, and related matters comprise two-thirds of the collection, or about 66%. History accounts for another 10%, lexicography and philology, 6%, the Greek and Latin orators, poets, and works of aesthetics, 5%. An interesting nucleus of books on preaching and collections of sermons makes up another 4% of the total, while the remaining books are in science and mathematics, 4%, law, 2%, and logic, 1%. Mildmay's example of distribution among several fields was thus followed in principle but not in proportion. A heavy concentration on divinity books was, in fact, the norm for college libraries. This was true in our period for both the King's and Trinity College libraries, though neither college had as precisely defined a religious mission as Emmanuel. In 1600 52% of Trinity's library was divinity books, while in 1612 64% of King's College's Library was made up of divinity books. Both of these libraries had a good many more law books than did Emmanuel, with the consequence that the remainder of their collections were somewhat narrower than Emmanuel's.[46]

Surely one of the striking things about the Emmanuel library of c. 1597 is its rather large collection of Hebrew books. The great majority of the books of lexicography and philology are devoted to the Hebrew language – some thirteen volumes in all. In addition, some eight of the Bibles are in Hebrew, giving Emmanuel's earliest scholars a solid core of books to assist them in mastering Hebrew, certainly a requisite for any truly learned minister of the day. It seems likely that Laurence Chaderton, the first

Master, was in part responsible for this collection. He was learned in Latin, Greek, and Hebrew, and on occasion, as the early accounts books show, he made journeys to London to buy books for the library. Books in other languages were also present, particularly Greek which, apart from the dominant Latin, was the most common, with at least twenty-seven items wholly or partly in Greek. There are also three items in Aramaic, five in the Chaldaic dialect of Hebrew, two French books, one in Italian, and a smattering of English works. Among the college's early distinguished scholars were Samuel Ward, William Branthwaite, Laurence Chaderton, and John Richardson, all among the translators of the King James Bible and distinguished for their command of the Biblical languages. Certainly Emmanuel's library both reflected and encouraged such interests.

One other body of books in the earliest collection merits special mention. Books of Reformation theology and polity account for just about one hundred of the divinity items in the list. This is a substantial number for a late sixteenth-century English college library. What is perhaps even more surprising, however, is that at least two-thirds of these works are by Lutherans as opposed to some 30% by those of the Reformed branch of the new Protestantism. By 1598 the library had acquired sixteen separate published works of Luther, some of which were probably quite rare in England, as well as several by Philipp Melanchthon, his chief follower. But the collection goes well beyond the chief Lutheran theologians and Bible commentators. Johann Brenz, the Württemberg reformer, is represented in seven volumes of his Bible commentary and homilies, and Erasmus Sarcerius, the German Lutheran who ultimately opposed Melanchthon, in ten volumes. Lucas Lossius, though known chiefly as a Protestant musician, is represented by one book, and Christoph Hoffman, a largely forgotten Lutheran follower, was known to the Emmanuel scholars in three volumes. By contrast, the Swiss Reformers, whose Zwinglian/Calvinist bias might seem likely to have been the dominant theological influence in Puritan Emmanuel's library, were much less prominent in the collection. Until sometime in 1598 Calvin was represented only by a single volume, his *Institutes*, though in that year, after the first catalogue had been completed, a twelve-volume collection of his writings came to the library and was noted at the end of the catalogue of c. 1597 in a hand different from that in which the list had been written.[47] There were four volumes of Zwingli, eight of Bullinger, and two of Peter Martyr, with single volumes by Beza, Zanchius, and Marot. Among those who can best be considered mediators between the German and Swiss/French branches of Reformation thought, Oecolampadius and Bucer were represented by five and four volumes respectively. While the major names of both branches of continental Reformation thought are present, the Lutheran position is decidedly better represented.

The received view is that Luther ceased to have any influence in England after Henry VIII stamped out a fledgling Lutheran movement and that by the late sixteenth and early seventeenth centuries Luther's thought was accessible in England mainly at second hand, through English translations of a small number of works.[48] Emmanuel's collection, particularly of Luther's own works, suggests that at least some influential Englishmen, either within Emmanuel or benefactors of the college, had a deep interest in Luther. Still more, it points up dramatically the importance to English scholars of the original Latin continental editions of Luther and his followers. English translations were only a small part of the picture.

In the forty years after 1598 the number of Reformed works grew more noticeably than the number of Lutheran works.[49] The collection of Reformation literature in general, however, did not grow as rapidly after the earliest years as did other sections of the library.

Shortly after the first catalogue was compiled, some tightening of the administration of the library occurred. On April 8, 1600, for instance, the master and fellows issued the order that "no fellow or scholler shall at anie time hence forwards take anie booke out of the Library into his owne chamber or study or into his owne private custody for his private benefitt unless he shall first obtayne leave of the master and the greater part of the fellows, and shall leave under his hand a note of remembrance that it may appear from time to time what booke be lent and to whom." Besides indicating that books had been circulating rather freely, this order also implies that undergraduates ("scholler[s]") as well as fellows and postgraduate students probably had access to the library's books; if so, Emmanuel departed from the usual practice of excluding undergraduates. Then in 1608 a new lock was installed on the library door, and in 1609 the practice of taking books out of the library at all was prohibited, with a stiff fine of 40 shillings for offenders.[50] These measures were well justified and seem to have done some good. Between 1597 and October of 1621, numerous books were, it seems, taken from the library and never returned. The list of "bookes wanting" on October 4, 1610, totalled thirty. These books may have been checked out of the library before the 1609 regulation went into effect. Subsequent catalogues indicate that only two of them were eventually returned.

More than ninety items dropped out of the collection in the two decades intervening between the first and second catalogues. Many of these losses can be attributed to an orderly acquisitions procedure by which newer, more comprehensive editions of various authors' collected works were purchased to replace the more fragmentary collections of occasional volumes often present in the first library. No better example of this procedure can be cited than in the case of Luther's books. By 1621 the sixteen Luther volumes cited on the first list had been reduced to eight, mainly because of the acquisition in that period of the seven-volume *Omnia Opera* (Wittenberg, 1554–83). The sixteen original volumes, it can be assumed, were sold off or traded for other books, as had been done with thirty-eight volumes mentioned at the end of the first catalogue. This acquisition and replacement procedure went on consistently throughout the seventeenth and into the eighteenth century. At some time towards the end of the seventeenth century – probably on receipt of the Sancroft collection in 1693 – the Library Keeper began making a record of duplicates. A college order passed on March 20, 1712, authorized the sale of these duplicates.[51] This record, which we have called the Register of Books Removed, still survives (LIB.1.3) and we have used it extensively in determining some of the library's early contents. It lists both the place and date of publication for most of the books removed from the collection as well as the donor of the books so discarded, where one was known. This register has made it possible for us to identify precisely just over one hundred books present in the library in 1637 but no longer in the collection.

20

But, however careful and effective this replacement system became, books from the early collection were, perforce, sometimes simply lost. Among the early holdings lost and never replaced were the founder's gift of a Latin Vulgate Bible (Lyons, 1557), a Chaldaic *Thargum*, a Greek and Latin edition of Plato's *Phaedo*, Erasmus's catechism as well as his *De Matrimonio Christiano* and his *Enchiridion*, Aesop's Fables in Greek, and a volume of Ovid, to name only a few.

The growth of the library

Inventories appear to have been taken in Emmanuel's library on two sorts of occasions. One was after a major shifting of books due to new acquisitions, as in 1621, 1626 and 1632. The other was upon changes of the mastership of the college, as in 1622 when John Preston rather abruptly succeeded the octogenarian but still vigorous Laurence Chaderton, in 1628 when William Sandcroft succeeded Preston after the latter's death, and in 1637 on Richard Holdsworth's assumption of the office. The reason for the creation of the first catalogue cannot so easily be surmised, though it was clearly at a point when the collection had become quite large; its compilation was probably an initial step in the exercise of stricter management of the collection. Since one of these presumed motives for the cataloguing, the change in mastership, had nothing to do with the library itself, the inventories taken on those occasions show little change from the immediately preceding ones. It is only the 1621, 1626 and 1632 inventories which show significant change in the size and arrangement of the collection, though of course books were being added all the time.

The remarkable growth of the library in the first fifteen years to at least 449 volumes leveled off in the next two decades. By 1610 there were 503 volumes and by 1621 just 533, giving a net gain in number of volumes between 1597 and 1621 of only eighty-four. This is partly due to loss of books but still more to the kind of consolidation we noticed in the Luther collection, which was reduced from sixteen to eight volumes without weakening the collection. Consequently, while the number of catalogue entries is two fewer in 1621 than in c. 1597, the number of volumes has increased by 19%.

The collection remained virtually unchanged between the 1621 and 1622 catalogues, but the 1626 catalogue reveals a significant increase in the number of volumes and works in the library. This particular growth is due to many gifts but especially to the bequest of John Richardson, one of the first fellows and sometime Master of Trinity College, who in 1625 willed £120 to the Emmanuel College Library. Richardson's bequest alone was responsible for the addition of more than 170 volumes to the collection. The growth of the library in just four years, therefore, was impressive: from 381 entries and 543 volumes in 1622 to 735 entries and 990 volumes in 1626.

Changes in the next catalogue (1628), in either additions or location of the books, were negligible. The 1632 inventory reveals another influx of new works, many of which had been listed at some time between 1626 and 1632 as being temporarily shelved "In the window, new bought" and "on the other side" of the room. By 1632 they had been distributed by subject into their proper places.[52] By that time the inventory included 795 entries while the number of volumes had grown to 1103. By 1637 another twenty volumes had been added, so that in its fifty-third year the college library owned 1123 volumes.

Book donations

In the sixteenth and early seventeenth centuries the strength of college libraries depended in large measure on the generosity of the members, friends, and benefactors of the college. Few libraries had either permanent curators or specially designated funds for the acquisition of new books. They were heavily dependent on gifts. At Emmanuel it appears that some money was available for both the upkeep of the library and the purchase of books, but donors were still of crucial importance to the college's hopes for a library of high quality. A brief survey of some of the most important donations will bear this out.

Books from the earliest collection have survived which contain signatures suggesting that Mildmay may have prevailed on certain of his friends and political acquaintances to contribute books, as he certainly prevailed on them to contribute both cash and real estate in the five years he lived after founding the college. Gifts to the college of cash and property declined in number after his death in 1589, and it is perhaps fair to assume that new sources of books also had to be sought. We have already noted the gift by William Fleetwood of three books in 1586. A more important benefactor was Edward Leeds, who had been Master of Clare College from 1560 to 1571. Leeds gave a substantial cash contribution and a small annuity as well as some property to the college. He also appears to have donated to the library at least six volumes containing eight works, probably at the time of his death in February of 1589.[53] Laurence Chaderton is known to have donated the two-volume Bomberg Bible in the same period. And the coat of arms of Cambridge University, together with the initials R. C. for Richard Culverwell, is blind stamped on seven volumes, five of which were recorded in the first inventory. They were apparently donated by Culverwell himself, who was related to Chaderton and was a college benefactor. Only one of the five contains specific information about the donation. A folio Paris, 1574 edition of St Cyprian's collected writings (^{2}2.S(1).2) bears an inscription on the title page: "Richardus Culverwell Colleg: Eman. D.D. L.M.Q. 1584. Res tuas age. 1584." The five books are uniformly bound and were probably presented to the library at the same time, making them the earliest known gift of books to the library. The two remaining Culverwell books came to Emmanuel as part of the bequest of William Branthwaite in 1619, which is discussed below.

The London printer, George Bishop, who having been Master of the Stationers' Company may have been known to Mildmay, once owned five volumes which were recorded on the earliest inventory and which remain at present in the Emmanuel collection. In four of these, controversial works by William Fulke which Bishop himself

22

published,[54] he wrote on the title pages, "ex dono George Bysshop," neglecting to name the recipient. That it was Emmanuel College seems a safe but not a certain surmise. But despite these contributions to the early college library, the origin of the great majority of the books on the first inventory is simply not known. A certain Mr Shipton at one point gave enough books to the library to create the need for new "desks" to hold them. Payment for these desks is recorded in the college's accounts book for 1607.[55] Given the relatively high survival rate of the books in the early collection through the centuries, it seems highly unlikely that all of the books in such a major benefaction would have disappeared by now. But since no books now in the collection bear any mention of Shipton, it seems that, even as late as 1607, no one was routinely recording the donor's name in gift books. The same is true of the gift of Richard Ashton, whom the college's book of benefactors says gave £13. 6s 8d "ad Bibliothecam ornandam" but whose name is nowhere mentioned in any surviving books.

An important donation came to the library sometime between the first inventory and 1621. This was a group of some forty-five volumes, comprised almost entirely of the collected works of major reformers – seven volumes of Luther, six of Melanchthon, five of Peter Martyr, eight of Musculus, and others, including Hemming, Zanchy, Sadeel, and Gesner. The books from this group which remain in the collection are identifiable by a bookplate with a coat of arms and the inscription: "Ex dono T.S." The identity of this benefactor remained a mystery until Frank Stubbings recently determined that the coat of arms was that of the London Grocers' Company and that one Thomas Southaicke was elected second warden of the company in 1621. This man, who seems to have had no immediate connection with Emmanuel College, was in all likelihood the donor of these important books. A separate page (205) in the college's accounts book gives a list of all the books in the "T.S." donation. The publication dates of the surviving books in this important collection enable us to place the donation after 1604 and before 1621, when they first appear on an inventory.

Though most of the donors of books mentioned so far had no formal affiliation with the college, after 1600 most of the donors were Emmanuel men. For some of these, who chose to give a single volume to the college library on the occasion of receiving a degree or on leaving the college, the act seems to have been a gesture of good will or gratitude. John Cotton, later famous for his preaching and writing in Lincolnshire and New England, in 1612 gave a copy of Martin Chemnitz's *Examen Concilii Tridentini* (Frankfurt, 1609), and the year before, Joseph Alliston, just vacating his fellowship, gave a crisp folio copy of Philippe de Mornay's Latin history of the papacy, *Mysterium Iniquitatis* (Saumur, 1611). Other fellows who thus contributed included Richard Lister (three volumes in 1599), Ralph Cudworth, father of the Platonist (four important manuscript volumes in 1600), Thomas Pickering (a two-volume German Bible in 1600), Robert Booth (four volumes in 1616), and William Sandcroft (two volumes of Capreolus in 1618).

Four of Emmanuel's earliest and most distinguished fellows, William Bedell, Samuel Ward, William Branthwaite, and John Richardson, all bestowed books on their alma mater, though in widely varying numbers. The only known gift of Ward, who for thirty-three years was the Master of Sidney Sussex College, was, interestingly, the just-published *Apology for the Oath of Allegiance* by King James I in both Latin and

English, donated in September of 1609 just before Ward left Emmanuel for Sidney Sussex. Ward's friend and correspondent, William Bedell, later Provost of Trinity College, Dublin, gave a copy of Erasmus's New Testament in Greek and Latin in the Basel, 1570 edition. In 1621 Bedell also gave the college a collection of pamphlets in Latin and Italian having to do with the dispute between Pope Paul V and the civil government of Venice during Bedell's residence in that city (1607–10) as chaplain to Sir Henry Wotton, England's ambassador. The thirty pamphlets are bound as three volumes and comprise a unique documentary record of that controversy over the Pope's excommunication of the Venetian Senate.[56]

William Branthwaite's gift was a bequest on his death early in 1619. He had been Master of Gonville and Caius and gave most of his books to that college but specified some seventeen volumes which were to go to Emmanuel, most of which were works of the Church Fathers.[57] Just six years later Thomas Hanscombe, a much younger and less distinguished fellow, surpassed all three of these former fellows in generosity to the library by leaving Emmanuel at least seventeen separate works, totalling twenty-eight volumes, on his premature death in October of 1625. Numerous other fellows and graduates gave books or money for the purchase of books in the 1620s and 1630s, including Thomas Ball, John Preston's special friend and a well-known tutor under Preston's mastership, and Anthony Tuckney, the cousin of John Cotton who would later follow Holdsworth as Emmanuel's fifth master (1645–53).

All of these donations together, however, fail to equal the gift of one man, Dr John Richardson, whose 1625 bequest was more responsible than any other identifiable cause for the significant growth of the library between the 1622 and 1626 inventories – indeed, during the entire first half-century of its existence. Richardson, one of the founder's hand-picked group of four original fellows, had amply fulfilled his early scholarly promise. Near the end of his Emmanuel fellowship he took the D.D. degree and later became Master of Peterhouse for six years and Regius Professor of Divinity for ten (1607–1617). His final ten years were spent as Master of Trinity College (1615–25). But he was best known as an eminent scholar. It was in Richardson's personal library at Peterhouse that Isaac Casaubon, whom Scaliger called "the most learned man in Europe," had pursued his studies while in Cambridgeshire in 1611.[58] Richardson's magnificent bequest of £120 for the purchase of books is all the more interesting considering his reputation for friendliness to Arminianism, a doctrine strenuously opposed by many of Emmanuel's preaching alumni.

It seems likely that Richardson's generosity to Emmanuel may have been encouraged by his observing the great impact on the Trinity College Library in the decades just before and during his mastership there of numerous large gifts of money, books, and manuscripts. He would have been aware of the tremendous effect such donations had on the quality of a college library.[59] In any case, the impact of his contribution is still evident in the college's rare books collection, where volume after volume bears the label which was printed and affixed to most of the volumes purchased from the Richardson bequest. Still others, which were sold when subsequent gifts of books duplicated Richardson gifts, can be traced through the Register of Books Removed where "Dr Rich" at the end of an entry indicates the removal of one of the Richardson gift volumes.[60] Doubtless a few of his gifts still present in the library can no longer be identified because of the occasional loss of a gift label, but at least 136 entries involving at least 172 volumes on the inventories from 1626 on are known to have been purchased with the Richardson bequest. This one donor, in other words, was responsible for the presence of at least 17% of the books in the collection in 1626. Such a fact makes dramatically evident the crucial importance to seventeenth-century college libraries of the individual benefactor.

Though Richardson was primarily responsible for the library's growth between the inventories of 1622 and 1626, many new books appeared on the 1626 list which cannot be traced to Richardson, Hanscombe, or any other known donor. It is clear that pains were now being taken about the contents of the library. Subject areas that had been poorly represented now became substantially strengthened, while very few works were being added in the subject categories which had been strong from the start. While few Bibles and little Reformation literature were purchased at this stage, many books of history were being added. Now for the first time, too, large numbers of recently published books of Roman Catholic and anti-Catholic controversial writing were added, especially commentaries on Aquinas and Peter Lombard and Catholic books in the field of moral theology. The dramatic increase in the number of history books during the early twenties is especially noteworthy since it suggests again Emmanuel's participation in the general strengthening of the post-scholastic humanities curriculum at Cambridge in the late sixteenth and early seventeenth centuries.[61] The new books included the works of important contemporary historians like the Frenchman, Jacques-Auguste de Thou (two volumes), and the Englishman, William Camden. Janus Gruter's eight-volume *Chronicon Chronicorum* (Frankfurt, 1614) was one of the major additions in the Hanscombe donation, but the types of histories added at this time ranged from ecclesiastical to secular, from oriental to Russian, Polish, Sicilian, Florentine, and British, while also including some of the traditional chronicles tracing all of history from the birth of Adam down to Tudor times. These works were shelved in the eighth classis in 1626 and 1628 but before 1632 were shifted to the sixth classis and remain there in the 1637 catalogue, which follows hereafter. Among the ancient historians included in these acquisitions is Tacitus, whom F. J. Levy cites as the chief exemplar of "politic history," a school of historiography followed by authors such as Camden, Samuel Daniel (whose poetic history of the Wars of the Roses was added for the first time at Emmanuel in 1626), and others including Machiavelli (whose work was not present in the Emmanuel library), his follower Guicciardini (whose Italian history was added in 1626), and Henry Savile (whose *Rerum Anglicarum Scriptores* [London, 1596] had been acquired almost as soon as it was published). The additions to the history collection thus reflect the dual principles which are still sound policies for acquisitions: filling in lacunae while keeping abreast of current directions in scholarship.

Another trend may be detected in these pre-1626 purchases in the strengthening of the collection of books on moral theology and casuistry. By 1626 there was still not very much generally available in the way of Protestant casuistry, but there was clearly an interest in the subject at Puritan Emmanuel. The works of the great Cambridge Puritan, William Perkins, which were by no means chiefly in the field of casuistry but did include his *Cases of Conscience*, had been in the Emmanuel library from early in the century; William Ames's *De Conscientia* (1603), however, had not found its way into the collection even by 1637. Other Protestant writers on morality such as Joseph Hall and John Dod were also among the missing, even though both of these authors had Emmanuel connections (a factor, incidentally, which seems to have had little or no importance in the college's decisions about which authors to collect). The library turned to continental works, in 1622–6 adding the works of the Portuguese Enrique Henriquez and Spaniards Thomas Sanchez, Domingo de Soto, Raymond of Penafort, and Juan Azor. Azor's three-volume *Institutiones Morales* (1613–17) is a particularly significant acquisition since it presented departures in the analysis of moral theology and was a model for later writings on the subject.[62] It is clear, at least, that the library of this intensely Protestant college was aggressively acquiring the very latest works of continental Roman Catholic thinking on moral theology.[63] A case in point is a group of five works on the subject which were the gift of Elias Pettit shortly after he received his M.A. in 1626. The authors, an international lot, all wrote from the Catholic perspective. They include the Austrian Paulus Laymann, the Italians Vincenzo Filliucci and Paulus de Blanchis, the Spanish Franciscan Antonio de Cordoba, and an Englishman, Robert Sayre, who had attended Caius College in the 1580s. The works by Laymann, Filliucci, and de Blanchis were all published in the 1620s and thus were acquired almost as soon as they became available. This trend was reinforced by other significant purchases such as the two-volume collected works of both the Italian Neoplatonist, Pico della Mirandola, and the German Nicholas of Cusa, whose work reflects the influence of Neoplatonism. The presence of these authors doubtless helped make the environment congenial for the gradual shift in theological bias around mid-century when Ralph Cudworth and his younger followers among the Cambridge Platonists, several of whom were educated at Emmanuel, rose to prominence.

The collection as it stood in April of 1637, when the last of these early inventories was made, was a mature one. The college's mission to educate its members in divinity above all was strongly supported by the library's collection. But divinity had become more broadly understood. While popular anti-Catholic sentiment was if anything perhaps more prominent in England during the 1620s when the troubling news of the wars in the Palatinate was a frequent subject of discourse in pulpits as well as government and private circles, Cambridge scholars wished to know about the positions of both Catholics and anti-Catholics. In addition to the books on moral theology, a great many Roman Catholic Biblical commentaries were added for the first time in the period 1622–6 as were numerous controversial writings dealing with Counter-Reformation issues. The writings of Andrewes, Cartwright, Morton, Sandys, Donne, Collins, Barlow, Cowell, and others who opposed Catholic positions are balanced by the works of Catholic polemicists such as Sanders, Netter, Gretser, Hosius, Bellarmine, and others.

By comparison with these acquisitions, the additions in the areas of law, science, and medicine were small, though significant. There was certainly not growth in the number of science books comparable to that which Philip Gaskell has documented at the Trinity College Library between 1600 and 1640, for instance.[64] But the large numbers of acquisitions in a variety of fields between 1622 and 1632 clearly indicate a high level of intellectual activity at the college generally during that period.

Later growth

Though this study concentrates on the period up to 1637, gifts continued to come into the library after the 1637 inventory. Indeed, some books were added to that list shortly after its compilation, though soon, separate entries were made in the inventory book on the pages following the 1637 inventory, where one can note the thirty-one volumes given by Francis Ash in 1651 and 1653, the fourteen volumes in Hebrew and Arabic given by Dr Robert Johnson in the 1640s, and many others. Since there is no extant thoroughgoing inventory of the collection between 1637 and approximately 1680, by which time the collection had increased substantially, we have made no attempt to include here any acquisitions after 1637 except where they may appear as additions to the list proper. Where we have been able to identify such cases, we have noted them.[65]

It remains simply to observe that the library continued to profit from the beneficence of a variety of contributors throughout the rest of the century. The second John Richardson was a major benefactor in the latter half of the century as was the Master of Emmanuel, John Breton. The greatest of all the gifts, however, was that of William Sancroft, who was briefly Master in 1662–5 and later Archbishop of Canterbury. Sancroft's gift, given in 1693 shortly before his death, consisted of over five thousand volumes, now displayed in cases of seventeenth-century style in the shelf order recorded on the inventory which was made when they were first arranged in the library.[66] When this gift was received – somewhat assuaging the college's sense of deprivation at having lost the still larger library of Richard Holdsworth in the legal dispute with the University Library at mid-century – many duplicates of books already in Emmanuel's library were discovered. The college followed the frugal practice of removing the older duplicates from the shelves. These were recorded in the Register of Books Removed and then presumably were sold, with the proceeds probably going to further book purchases. The donation which seems to have been most severely depleted by this practice was that of the second John Richardson. It is possible that in some cases a late seventeenth-century gift – by Breton or Richardson, for instance – replaced an earlier copy and was then in turn replaced by an identical or similar volume from the Sancroft donation. Such cases cannot be identified, and where they may exist any bibliographical information about the original book has been lost for good.

Having cited Sears Jayne's claim for the immense importance of early library inventories, we must be careful about the degree to which we infer intellectual influences from contents or lacunae. What does it mean, for instance, that the notoriously Puritan college, Emmanuel, did *not* own during the first fifty-three years of its existence – its most pronouncedly Puritan years – a single copy of the work of Peter Ramus, whose logic and rhetoric books were among the most important tools of the Puritans' education as preachers, reasoners, writers, and interpreters of the human condition? It certainly does not mean that Ramus was not important at Emmanuel College. We know he was because the earliest regulations of the college about the curriculum stipulate the works of Ramus as required reading.[67] Instead, it simply means that certain books – textbooks in octavo, in particular – were not high on the library's list of purchasing priorities. Certainly the reason for this in the case of Ramus's works was that scholars and fellows were expected to own private copies. Thomas Thomas's 1584 Cambridge University Press edition of the *Dialecticae libri duo* assured an ample supply of copies. It is useful to notice the example of a fellow of Emmanuel College, named Alexander Clugh, whose sizeable collection of books was recorded for legal purposes at the time of his death in 1621. This catalogue of his library is preserved in the Cambridge University Library.[68] Of the sixty volumes which he owned, five were works by Ramus and two others were the Temple and Piscator commentaries on Ramus. Even though these works were not a part of the college library collection which was catalogued in the same year, Ramus was thus very much a part of the life of the Emmanuel College scholar.

Still, the case of the Ramus lacunae, though not unique, is the exception. The Puritans were, of course, committed to encouraging education at all levels. Taken as a whole, the record of the first fifty-three years of the Emmanuel College library's development illuminates the intellectual resources of a rapidly growing, extremely influential college of the period. It is especially important to note that Sir Walter Mildmay's purpose in founding a college to supply the Church with "learned men" was interpreted liberally when it came to accumulating a core collection of books. The collection as it stood at the end of this period was by no means narrowly Calvinistic, as one might have suspected. Nor was it even narrowly Protestant. The library included an impressive cross-section of theological literature, offering the standard early sixteenth-century editions of the church fathers, numerous examples of medieval literature, especially the works of Aquinas and Lombard and their many commentators, as well as the more recent polemical religious literature of various kinds, though this was added later and far from comprehensively. From beginning to end of the period the library reflects an emphasis on Biblical scholarship, with commentaries by leading scholars representing a variety of perspectives. The new tendency toward humanistic emphases is clearly reflected here. Emmanuel's collection of books of history would itself surely reward the concentrated attention of the modern historiographer.

These several areas, indeed, remained the greatest strengths of the Emmanuel collection in the period during which the lists were made. Although other libraries grew more significantly than did Emmanuel's in certain subject areas – Trinity College in science, King's College in law, for instance – the few books present in Emmanuel's collection in 1637 in such areas as geography, law, mathematics, and even surgery comprise a core collection of books of fundamental importance in these fields. The "learned man" on leaving Emmanuel College could be expected to have been exposed to books other than Calvin's *Institutes*, and to subject areas other than those in the regular curriculum. Any man who made use of the Emmanuel library as a place to gain exposure to the broad range of knowledge in his day had an opportunity to study several subjects in great depth and to study the essentials of many others. No college library of the period could be said to have been comprehensive; all were subject to the restrictions of limited resources and the usually haphazard generosity of their alumni and friends. But those in charge of the Emmanuel library were apparently well aware of the opportunity and responsibility which they had, and in the period when college libraries generally were showing new strength Emmanuel's collection became an outstanding repository of "the best that is known and thought" during a period of great intellectual growth and ferment. The catalogue which follows, detailing the collection as it stood at the end of the first fifty-three years of growth and documenting as precisely as possible the dates of acquisition of all items, provides a unique opportunity for understanding not only this important college in the days of special Puritan strength in England and America but also the state of learning generally. We offer it in the hope that it will prove a valuable resource for scholars in a variety of fields, having special interests which we are unable in many cases to predict. In such a detailed catalogue as this, we believe, one can truly feel the intellectual pulse of a crucial era in our collective past.

Notes

1 Sears Jayne and Francis R. Johnson, eds., *The Lumley Library: The Catalogue of 1609* (London: Trustees of the British Museum, 1956), pp. 28, 29. After Jayne's *Library Catalogues of the English Renaissance* (Berkeley and Los Angeles: University of California Press, 1956; reissued with new Preface and Notes, Godalming, Surrey: St Paul's Bibliographies, 1983), the most important work in the field includes N. R. Ker, "Oxford College Libraries in the Sixteenth Century," *Bodleian Library Record*, 6 (1959), 459–515; Mark H. Curtis, "Library Catalogues and Tudor Oxford and Cambridge," *Studies in the Renaissance*, 5 (1958), 111–20; J. R. Liddell, "The Library of Corpus Christi College, Oxford, in the Sixteenth Century," *The Library*, 4th Series, 18 (1937–8), 383–416; John M. Fletcher and James K. McConica, "A Sixteenth-Century Inventory of the Library of Corpus Christi College, Cambridge," *Transactions* of the Cambridge Bibliographical Society, 3 (1961), 187–99; Ker, *Records of All Souls College Library, 1437–1600* (Oxford, 1971); Lisa Jardine, "The Place of Dialectic Teaching in Sixteenth-Century Cambridge," *Studies in the Renaissance*, 21 (1974), 31–62; David McKitterick, "Two Sixteenth-Century Catalogues of St John's College Library," *Transactions* of the Cambridge Bibliographical Society, 7 (1978), 135–55; and Philip Gaskell, *Trinity College Library: The First 150 Years* (Cambridge: Cambridge University Press, 1980).

2 Although the terminal date of 1637 is entirely determined by the date of the last of the series of library inventories made during the college's first fifty-three years, it approximates a significant point of historical demarcation as well. 1640 was of course a great watershed in British history, marking the point at which the royalist and parliamentary factions had their critical falling out, followed by civil war, the Protectorate, and finally the Restoration. Against this historical backdrop, changes were also beginning at Emmanuel College which, by the time of the Restoration, would see a shift in the college's theological/ecclesiastical bias. By 1637 the men who would become known as the Cambridge Platonists had already begun to appear at Emmanuel, though the shift away from the college's pronounced Puritan bias would be gradual and progressive. The years from 1584 to 1637 thus mark a coherent era in English and, even more, in Emmanuel College's history.

3 Jayne, *Library Catalogues of the English Renaissance*, p. 42. Jayne claims there are nine catalogues in this series. In fact, there are seven. The two extras in his list are the "1610" and "1640" catalogues. The former is only a list of thirty books missing from the library in 1610 which is discussed below. The "1640" list is an undated and as yet unidentified library catalogue in Emmanuel's archives (Emm. Coll. MSS 188) but which clearly describes some other library which was many times larger than was Emmanuel's in 1637 and which used

different classis designations than those in the Emmanuel library around 1640. The early twentieth-century historian of the college, E. S. Shuckburgh, who is reliable in many respects, erroneously claimed that "in a volume of inventories lists are copied out in 1603, 1606, 1609, 1610, and 1620," *Emmanuel College* (London, 1904), pp. 188–9. In fact, there is no inventory for any of these years, though one of the dates (1610) was apparently meant to refer to the first (undated) inventory whose dating is discussed below. Finally, we should mention a catalogue which was made of the Emmanuel collection some time much later in the century, probably after the important John Breton bequest (1676) and before that of Archbishop William Sancroft. We have not attempted to date this catalogue but assume it is c. 1680. The essential facts in the library's history are succinctly stated in Frank Stubbings's pamphlet, *A Brief History of Emmanuel College Library* (Cambridge, 1981).

[4] James Bass Mullinger, *The University of Cambridge*, II (Cambridge: Cambridge University Press, 1884), 310–11, and Shuckburgh, pp. 3–5.

[5] Mullinger, II, 311; Shuckburgh, pp. 19, 24–5.

[6] Mullinger, II, 312. See also Thomas Fuller, *The History of the University of Cambridge from the Conquest to the Year 1634*, ed. Marmaduke Prickett and Thomas Wright (Cambridge, 1840), p. 278. Fuller's book was first published in 1655.

[7] Shuckburgh, pp. 24, 23; Mullinger, II, 314.

[8] *The Statutes of Sir Walter Mildmay for Emmanuel College*, trans. and ed. Frank Stubbings (Cambridge: Cambridge University Press, 1983), pp. 19, 95–8. See also Mullinger, II, 315–18.

[9] Fuller, p. 278.

[10] Samuel Eliot Morison, *The Founding of Harvard College* (Cambridge, Mass.: Harvard University Press, 1935), Appendix B, pp. 359–410.

[11] Morison, *The Founding of Harvard College*, pp. 92–107.

[12] H. C. Porter, *Reformation and Reaction in Tudor Cambridge* (Cambridge: Cambridge University Press, 1958), pp. 56–7.

[13] W. D. J. Cargill Thompson, "Notes on King's College Library, 1500–1570, in Particular for the Period of the Reformation," *Transactions* of the Cambridge Bibliographical Society, 2 (1954), 38–54. The University Library, according to J. C. T. Oates and H. L. Pink, declined from some 500–600 volumes in 1528 to no more than 175 in 1556, "Three Sixteenth-Century Catalogues of the University Library," *Transactions* of the Cambridge Bibliographical Society, 1 (1952), p. 311. Most Cambridge colleges, excepting Gonville and Caius, Peterhouse, and Pembroke, experienced similar declines. See J. C. T. Oates, "The Libraries of Cambridge, 1570–1700," in Francis Wormald and C. E. Wright, *The English Library before 1700: Studies in its History* (London: University of London, 1958), p. 215. See also C. E. Wright, "The Dispersal of the Libraries in the Sixteenth Century" in Wormald and Wright, pp. 169–71.

[14] H. W. Garrod, "The Library Regulations of a Medieval College," *The Library*, 8 (1927), 312–35 and Ker, "Oxford College Libraries in the Sixteenth Century," *passim.*

[15] Ker, "Oxford College Libraries in the Sixteenth Century," p. 498. See also Sir Edmund Craster, *The History of All Souls College Library*, ed. E. F. Jacob (London: Faber and Faber, 1971), p. 49 and ff.

[16] J. C. T. Oates suggests that "the first general unchaining of books at Cambridge" was in 1627 when Clare College occupied a new library; Oates, "The Libraries of Cambridge, 1570–1700," p. 217. At Oxford – and at King's College, Cambridge – the chaining continued into the eighteenth century; see J. N. L. Myres, "Oxford Libraries in the Seventeenth and Eighteenth Centuries" in Wormald and Wright, pp. 246–47. The standard book on the subject is B. H. Streeter, *The Chained Library* (London, 1931).

[17] Gaskell, pp. 97, 93.

[18] Robert Willis and John Willis Clark, *The Architectural History of the University of Cambridge and of the Colleges of Cambridge and Eton* (Cambridge, 1886), II, 702.

[19] These details are noted by J. B. P[eace] in "Chapters in College History. The College Buildings in the Eighteenth Century" in *Emmanuel College Magazine*, 9 (1898), pp. 84, 94. See Plate 1. Stubbings provides a detail from David Loggan's view of the college in his *Brief History of Emmanuel College Library*, plate 1, where he also cites the importance of these details, observing that Loggan's "accuracy is usually impeccable" (p. 1).

[20] This cannot be proven for the first inventory but the other six all refer to "Superior" and "Inferior" sections in most of the classes. For discussion of the evolution of book cases, see Willis and Clark, III, 438–71.

[21] These taller "desks" are classes 7 and 8 in the 1626 and 1628 inventories and classes 6 and 7 in 1632 and 1637.

[22] Gaskell discusses this practice, pp. 97, 102–3. Many of these tabs no longer survive in the Emmanuel books.

[23] See discussion on p. 15.

[24] David McKitterick informs us, however, that Elisabeth Leedham-Green's research on private libraries has shown that Peterhouse had acquired about 1,000 books from Andrew Perne by 1590.

[25] Gaskell, p. 38.

[26] The library now has fifteen volumes which belonged to the founder. From his gift of twelve, two have been lost: a Latin Bible and a volume of Walter Haddon's *Orationes*. Five of Mildmay's volumes apparently came to the library after 1637 since they do not appear on the inventories up to that date. These are: Homer, *Ilias et Vlyssea* (Basel, 1535) (present class mark FB8); Francis I, King of France, *Exemplaria Literarum quibus Rex Franciscus, ab Aduersariorum maledictis defenditur* (Paris, 1537) (FB10); Thomas Smith, *De Recta & Emendata Linguae Angliae ... & ... Linguae Graecae* (Paris, 1567) (FB11); *Nouum Testamentum* [2 vols., Greek] (Paris, 1549) (FB14, 15).

Well before the founding of Emmanuel, Sir Walter had made a similar gift of books to his alma mater, Christ's College. On this donation, see Stanford E. Lehmberg, *Sir Walter Mildmay and Tudor Government* (Austin: University of Texas Press, 1964), p. 222.

[27] Jardine, "The Place of Dialectic Teaching in Sixteenth-Century Cambridge," pp. 50–1. Also important, especially for its discussion of Agricola's predecessors and the appearance of their books in the private collections of sixteenth-century Cambridge men, is Jardine's "Humanism and the Sixteenth-Century Cambridge Arts Course," *History of Education*, 4 (Spring 1975), 16–31.

[28] Jardine, "The Place of Dialectic Teaching in Sixteenth-Century Cambridge," p. 53.

[29] Ibid., p. 46, n38.

[30] Mark H. Curtis, *Oxford and Cambridge in Transition, 1558–1642* (Oxford: Clarendon Press, 1959), pp. 88, 92, 94.

[31] F. J. Levy, *Tudor Historical Thought* (San Marino, Calif.: The Huntington Library, 1967), p. 249. See also Denys Hay, *Annalists and Historians: Western Historiography from the Eighth to the Eighteenth Centuries* (London: Methuen & Co., 1977), pp. 122–58.

[32] William T. Costello, *The Scholastic Curriculum at Early Seventeenth-Century Cambridge* (Cambridge, Mass.: Harvard University Press, 1958), p. 137. Mark Curtis remarks that by 1621 "Oxford and Cambridge produced only nine or ten bachelors and doctors in [civil law] each year," p. 151.

[33] Philip Gaskell notes that in 1600 Trinity College Library's non-divinity books were "a very scrappy lot," including "virtually no Latin literature, mathematics, medicine, or law. There was of course no English literature," p. 40.

[34] The six-line poem is printed in *The Poetry of Walter Haddon*, ed. Charles J. Lees (The Hague: Mouton, 1967), p. 211.

[35] Costello, p. 103.

[36] Quoted in Curtis, p. 244.

[37] Ibid., p. 246.

[38] This date was suggested by H. S. B[ennett], "The College Library, 1584–1694," *Emmanuel College Magazine*, 38 (1955–6), p. 38. Correct dating is established in Bush and Rasmussen, "Emmanuel College Library's First Inventory," *Transactions* of the Cambridge Bibliographical Society, 8 (1985), 514–15, which includes a catalogue of the library's holdings in c. 1597, with cross-references when appropriate to entries in the present volume.

[39] This volume appears as the twenty-fourth item in the fourth classis of the 1637 collection, which is printed below. Hereafter, when referring to particular books in the collection, we shall cite their locations in the 1637 list in parentheses, as: (4.24).

George Barcroft was a Trinity man who became a priest and musician and at the time of his gift was organist and Minor Canon of Ely. See John and J. A. Venn, *Alumni Cantabrigiensis*, I. 83, and *Dictionary of National Biography (DNB)*, I, 1095.

⁴⁰ Two other dated gifts are worth mentioning. On October 2, 1598, "Thomas Crocus" (probably the Thomas Crooke who *fl.* 1582, *DNB*) gave the library a volume containing four commentaries on various prophets and Job by Oecolampadius (Geneva, 1558, 1567) (5.I.15). This is the last entry on the earliest inventory and was added, with three entries just above it, in a hand different from that of the compiler of the main part of the list. In 1601 John Newcourt of Devonshire gave a huge folio fifteenth-century Latin manuscript Bible (4.1).

⁴¹ The single exception is a group of five books given by Richard Culverwell in 1584. See discussion on p. 22.

⁴² This is the exact wording in ²3.I(3).1. The wording varies slightly in 6.4.12 and 7.2.6.

⁴³ C. E. Wright mentions this in "The Elizabethan Society of Antiquaries and the Formation of the Cottonian Library" in Wormald and Wright, p. 183. For his role in efforts to stem the influx of Roman Catholic books to England in the 1580s, Fleetwood has been described as a "zealous persecutor of papists," Leona Rostenberg, *The Minority Press & the English Crown: A Study in Repression, 1558–1625* (Nieuwkoop: B. DeGraaf, 1971), p. 39.

⁴⁴ Cranmer's library was confiscated by Queen Mary, who assigned it to the keeping of her Lord High Steward, the Earl of Arundel. Arundel's daughter, Jane, married John, Lord Lumley, who ultimately assumed ownership of the library.

⁴⁵ Jayne and Johnson, eds., *The Lumley Library*, p. 12.

⁴⁶ Gaskell, pp. 44–5.

⁴⁷ This is in the group of entries mentioned in n. 40. The four items, in the order in which they have been added to the list of c. 1597 are: (1) a two-volume Bomberg Bible (1.S.4); (2) the twelve volumes of Calvin (5.S.1); (3) "Rerum Anglicarum Scriptorum post Bedam," doubtless the Henry Savile collection (6.5.24); and (4) the Oecolampadius commentaries mentioned in n. 40 (5.I.15).

⁴⁸ This issue is discussed in William H. Clebsch, "The Elizabethans on Luther" in *Interpreters of Luther: Essays in Honor of Wilhelm Pauck*, ed. Jaroslav Pelikan (Philadelphia: Fortress Press, 1968), pp. 97–120. Perhaps Clebsch and others who have discussed the subject have tended too readily to equate knowledge of Luther's writings with the availability of Luther in English translations. Other important studies containing informed discussions on the matter of Luther's direct and indirect influence in England include: Gordon Rupp, *The Righteousness of God: Luther Studies* (New York: Philosophical Library, 1953), pp. 37–43, A. G. Dickens, *The English Reformation* (London: B. T. Batsford, 1964), Rupp, *Studies in the Making of the English Protestant Tradition* (Cambridge: Cambridge University Press, 1947), and Philip Hughes, *The Reformation in England* (London: Burns and Oates, 1950), esp. Vol. I.

⁴⁹ The second classis in 1637 held the Lutheran Reformers' books. Of the fifty-one entries there, twenty-eight had been present since the first inventory. The books of Calvinist/Zwinglian Reformers were in the fifth classis, where only eleven of the thirty entries had been present from the time of the first list.

⁵⁰ Bennett, "The College Library, 1584–1694," pp. 39–40.

⁵¹ Frank Stubbings, *A Brief History of Emmanuel College Library* (Cambridge, 1981), p. 5.

⁵² Five other books were added to the 1632 inventory in a different hand from that of the scribe at the end of the third classis under the heading "Ex dono Edovard: Thornton." Thornton was an Emmanuel graduate (B.A., 1628–9, and M.A., 1632) who died in late 1635. Since one of the books in his donation was published in 1636 it is probably safe to assume that he left a small amount of cash to the library and that the books were acquired in 1636 or early 1637 and duly added to the most recent catalogue. They remain in the same location in the 1637 inventory, where they are catalogue items 3.14–18.

⁵³ These books appear on the first inventory and all carry Leeds's signature. On the 1637 catalogue they are: 2.I.11, 7.2.3 (first 4 vols.), and ²1.I.15.

⁵⁴ On Bishop's interest in and support of Fulke, see H. S. Bennett, *English Books and Readers, 1558–1603* (Cambridge: Cambridge University Press, 1965), p. 284.

[55] Emmanuel MS BUR.8.1. The exact date of Shipton's gift is not known but the book of benefactors (COL. 20.1) records its acceptance: "Mr Shipton Civis Londinensis librorum quorundam pretio bibliothecae huius ornatui consuluit." John Shipton was admitted in 1604 and received the B.A. degree in 1607/8 but it is not certain that he was the donor.

[56] When he died, Bedell also gave a handsome three-volume manuscript Hebrew Bible, dating from 1284. It was received by the library in or after 1641 and therefore does not appear in the 1637 catalogue. We owe special thanks to F. H. Stubbings for clarifying the details of this donation.

[57] Branthwaite's bequest to Emmanuel is recorded in an itemized manuscript list, which is Gonville and Caius MSS 734/782. We are grateful to Miss B. A. Parnell, Assistant Librarian at Gonville and Caius, for providing us with a copy of this document. An identical list is in the Emmanuel Library. The late Professor Edward Wilson of Emmanuel College first called Branthwaite's gift to our attention while he was the visiting Johnson Professor at the Institute for Research in the Humanities at the University of Wisconsin.

[58] This relationship is mentioned by Mullinger, II, 493, and in *DNB*, III, 1166–70.

[59] There are relatively few such references to Dr Richardson in this Register but a great many to books originally donated by another John Richardson later in the century. The later Richardson is designated "Mr Rich" in the Register of Books Removed. See fig. 3.

[60] On Trinity's acquisitions of books and manuscripts in this period see Gaskell, chapters 11 and 12.

[61] We refer here to the liberalizing tendency to broader instruction in "humanities" courses which has been discussed by recent historians such as Jardine, Curtis, Levy, and others.

[62] The *Institutiones Morales* was "a new type of moral treatise in which the basic division followed that of the Commandments, not the virtues. This ... is rightly considered the forerunner of the modern manuals of moral theology," R. A. Couture, *New Catholic Encyclopedia*, I (New York: McGraw-Hill, 1967), p. 1144.

[63] N. R. Ker makes passing reference to "the new interest in the medieval schoolmen and in Catholic theology which can be discerned in these years [1585–1640]" in "Oxford College Libraries in the Sixteenth Century," p. 498.

[64] Gaskell, pp. 241–58.

[65] In two places in the catalogue books were added after the inventory was taken, though how much after is not known. This is apparently the case with items 4.29–31, 9.I.16–18, and perhaps 4.28.

[66] See F. H. Stubbings, "The Sancroft Library," *Emmanuel College Magazine*, 58 (1975–6), 15–17.

[67] F. H. Stubbings's transcription of the College Orders of 1588 (Emmanuel College Archives, COL. 14.1) includes the following sentences: "Item that the books thought necessarie to have redd through [be] Ramus Logick Aristotles Organon Ethicks Politicks and Physiques: and if they can or will they may read Phrigius his naturall Philosophie," in *The Statutes of Sir Walter Mildmay*, p. 101.

[68] Cambridge University Archives, Wills. VC's court inventories, bundle 9.

A NOTE ON THE CATALOGUE
DESCRIPTIONS

Despite many excellent specialized bibliographies and catalogues of the major library collections, we still lack a comprehensive record of what was published in Europe between 1500 and 1700.[1] This lack presents something of a dilemma: in the absence of complete information on all editions published on the continent, we have no way of knowing the exact editions – indeed in some instances the works – to which particular entries on the Emmanuel inventories refer. Other kinds of evidence thus become crucial.

We must emphasize that many of the books cited on the hand-written inventories can, through physical evidence, be located among the present Emmanuel holdings. Besides donor inscriptions and bookplates – which conclusively identify many original copies – we have relied heavily on fore-edge writing and numbering to identify books which were in the early collection. When we have been able to identify a specific book, we describe that book – down to the present Emmanuel Library class mark (call number, in American terminology) – in our annotation. When a book has not been susceptible to conclusive identification but appears to be a likely candidate nonetheless, we describe that particular book in the annotations, but we also place the bibliographical information in brackets and preface it with a cautionary "possibly" (or rarely a more assertive "probably"). In some cases we can be sure that the edition is correct, but we may be unsure that we have located the original copy. In these cases we place only the class mark in brackets. With this judicious use of brackets, we are able to use the present Emmanuel holdings as part of our evidence for what might have been there in 1637 without expansive claims for doubtful information.

In some cases a work is missing entirely from the present Emmanuel collection – or such works as the Emmanuel library might hold clearly cannot be the ones to which the early inventories refer. In such cases, lacking other information, we include in the annotation only the author and title and designate the book "Missing." About such cases we have chosen silence as to possible editions rather than cluttering up the descriptions with tortuous inferences. However, even in the case of "Missing" books we are not without resources. Indeed, the present Emmanuel holdings prove useful in this regard. Many of the books to which the inventories refer were displaced – probably sold – to make way for the editions in donations from later benefactors, including especially Archbishop Sancroft whose library came to Emmanuel College in 1693.[2] Consequently the Sancroft books often stand between us and the original library. In the case of "Missing" books, therefore, we have included information about any Sancroft editions, thus suggesting the possibility that the original copy was replaced by the later acquisition. A second source of information that has enabled us to identify the editions of "Missing" books with certainty is the seventeenth-century manuscript record of books discarded from Emmanuel that we have called the Register of Books Removed (Emm. Coll. Archives LIB. 1.3). This record provides information not only about the specific editions but about the donors as well. A final category of missing books includes the many volumes which appear on the earlier inventories but which drop out of the library before 1637. These disappeared before the Register of Books Removed was created. Thus, our catalogue of these books, which follows the 1637 catalogue, includes only authors and titles.

The initial line of each of our catalogue descriptions cites, from left to right, the classis and shelf numbers, the inventory entry, exactly as it appears on the 1637 catalogue, and the date or limits of possible dates when the book entered the library. The original hand-written inventories do not employ this full numbering of each item: the c. 1597 inventory does not number individual entries at all, and the more orderly later inventories contain only the final digits designating shelf position. We have chosen, nonetheless, for convenience to cite the full location description for each item in the 1637 catalogue. We have reproduced the entries as accurately as possible, expanding scribal abbreviations and contractions, indicating such practice with italics. Our main source of information for dates of entry has been the lists themselves. Thus the limiting dates of acquisition are usually coincident with inventory dates, e.g. "1597–1621" for a work not present on the c. 1597 inventory but recorded on that of 1621.

A brief key to the entries is as follows:

classis and shelf number	inventory entry [supplemented with earlier inventory entries where helpful]	entry date
	description and identity of donor, where applicable	**present Emmanuel class mark**

As we have indicated, an important element in the dynamics of the library's growth from the very beginning was the purposeful removal, and the occasional outright loss, of books from the collection. Because seven full catalogues and one list of "books wanting" have survived for the period from 1584 to 1637, we have been able to chart the flow of books out of as well as into the library. Immediately following the catalogue of the holdings as of 1637, we have appended a list of books lost or replaced up to that year.

Throughout, our primary concern has been the recreation of a library from fragmentary evidence. Our ability to identify and describe discrete books has been shaped considerably by our sources. We have sought in the annotations to contain uncertain information in brackets where it can suggest contours without making definite claims, rather in the way that one will use new clay to fill in the missing pieces of a reconstructed vase.

Notes

1 See Denys Hay, "1500–1700: The Bibliographical Problem: A Continental S.T.C.?" in R. R. Bolgar, ed., *Classical Influences on European Culture A.D. 1500–1700* (Cambridge: Cambridge University Press, 1976), pp. 33–9.

2 See F. H. Stubbings, "The Sancroft Library," *Emmanuel College Magazine*, 58 (1975–6), 15–17.

REFERENCE BOOKS CITED

Adams
H. M. Adams, *Catalogue of Books Printed on the Continent of Europe, 1501–1600, in Cambridge Libraries*, 2 vols. Cambridge, 1967.

CMA
"Librorum Manuscriptorum Collegii S. Emanuelis in Universitate Cantabrigiensi Catalogus," *Catalogi Librorum Manuscriptorum Angliae et Hiberniae.* Oxford, 1697, I, 89–92.

Darlow & Moule
T. H. Darlow & H. F. Moule, *Historical Catalogue of the Printed Editions of Holy Scripture In the Library of the British and Foreign Bible Society*, 4 vols. London, 1903–11.

Hain
L. F. T. Hain, *Repertorium Bibliographicum.* Stuttgart, 1826–38; repr. Milano, 1948.

M. R. James
Montague Rhodes James, *The Western Manuscripts in the Library of Emmanuel College.* Cambridge, 1904.

T. James
Thomas James, "Catalogus Librorum Manuscriptorum in Bibliotheca Coll. Emmanuelis Cantabrigiae," *Ecloga Oxonio-Cantabrigiensis.* London, 1600, pp. 136–7.

Proctor
R. G. C. Proctor, *An Index to the Early Printed Books in the British Museum: From the Invention of Printing to the Year 1500, With Notes on Those in the Bodleian Library.* London, 1898–1906; repr. 1960.

STC
A. W. Pollard & G. R. Redgrave, *A Short Title Catalogue of Books Printed in England, Scotland, & Ireland and of English Books Printed Abroad, 1475–1640.* London, 1926.

Steinschneider
M. Steinschneider, *Catalogus Librorum Hebraeorum in Bibliotheca Bodleiana.* Berolini, 1852–60; repr. Hildesheim, 1964.

Venn
John Venn & J. A. Venn, *Alumni Cantabrigienses*, Pt. I: *From the Earliest Times to 1751*, 4 vols. Cambridge, 1922–7.

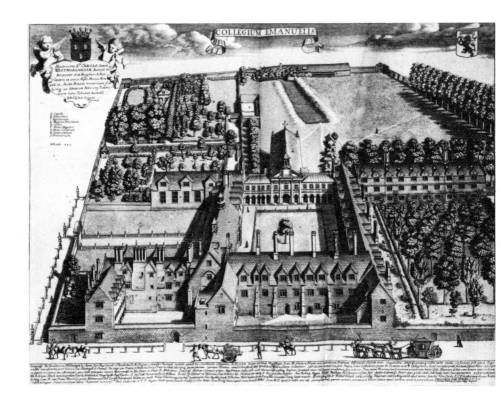

1 David Loggan's view of Emmanuel College (c. 1688). Some of the buildings shown, including the chapel, post-date the period covered by the early library catalogues, but the illustration shows the library in the right foreground with one of the two "S" brackets on the wall facing the viewer.

2 The upper half of an opening of the inventory book (CHA.1.4B) showing, on the left, an inventory of furnishings in the library and, on the right, the beginning of the inventory of books dated April 27, 1637.

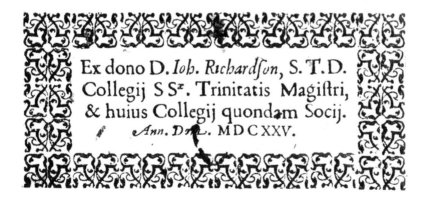

Ex dono D. *Ioh.* Richardſon, S. T. D.
Collegij S Sᵡ. Trinitatis Magiſtri,
& huius Collegij quondam Socij.
Ann. Dñī. MDCXXV.

3 The bookplate identifying volumes purchased with
the 1625 bequest of Dr John Richardson.

39

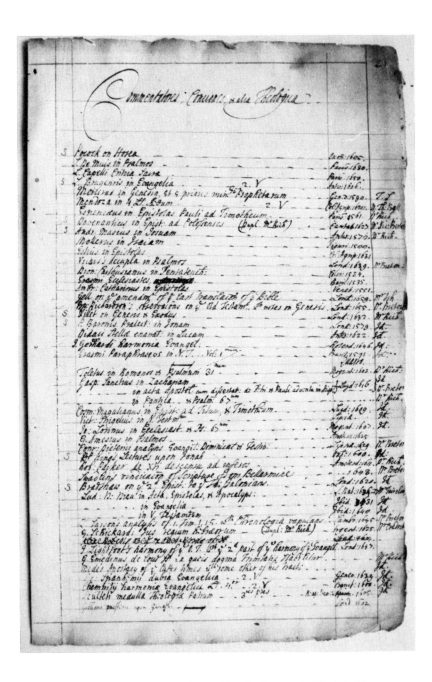

4   Folio 21 from the Register of Books Removed (LIB.1.3). The column on the far right lists donors. The list is a valuable source of information regarding books long since replaced. Fifteen of the items listed on this page, for instance, were copies acquired in the period before 1637.

40

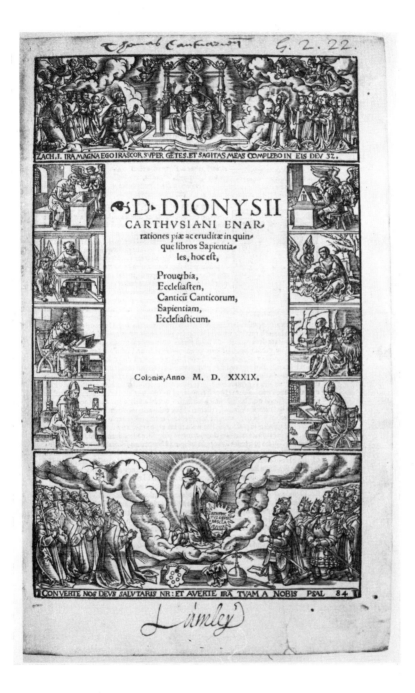

5 One of the Lumley Library books containing the signatures of John, first Baron Lumley, and Thomas Cranmer when Archbishop of Canterbury ("Thomas Cantuarien*sis*"). See [2]2.I(4).7 and Table 2.

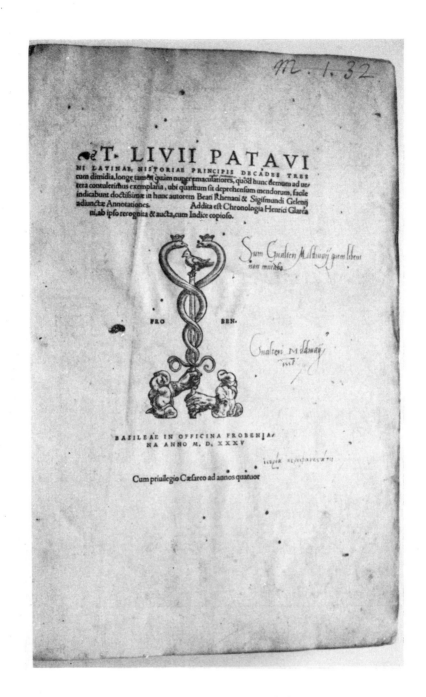

6 Sir Walter Mildmay's donation copy of Livy. See 7.3.14.

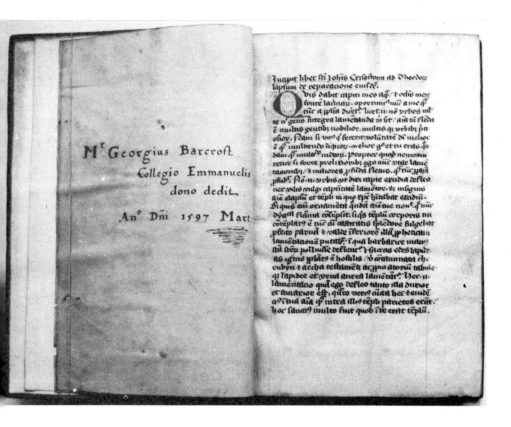

7 The beginning of a manuscript of the writings of St Chrysostom, showing the donation inscription on the flyleaf opposite. This is the earliest identifiable addition to the library after the completion of the first inventory. See 4.24.

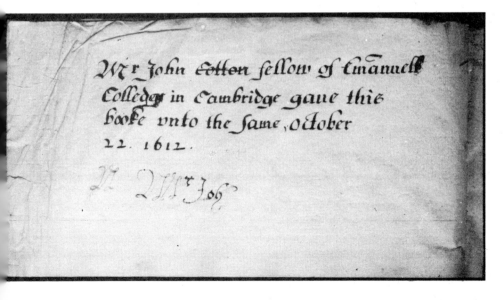

8 The inscription on the flyleaf of the copy of *Examinis Concilii Tridentini* (1609) by the German Lutheran, Martin Chemnitz, given by John Cotton when he received his B.D. degree and left the college in 1612 (2.S.6).

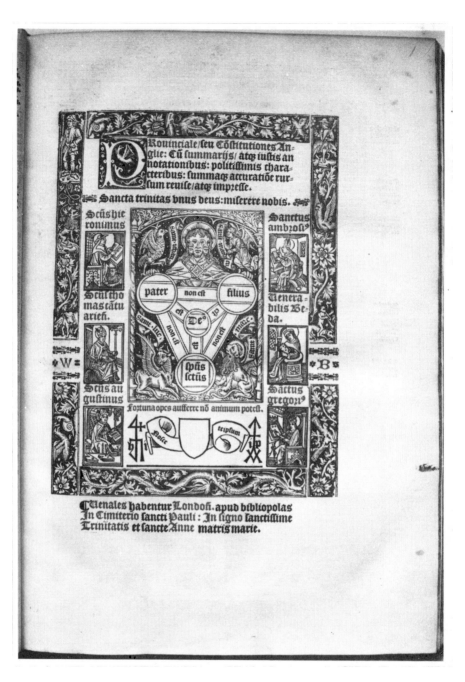

9 The elaborate woodcut title page in Bishop William Lyndwood's *Provinciale,*
   seu Constitutiones Anglie (London, 1505). See 7.1.4.

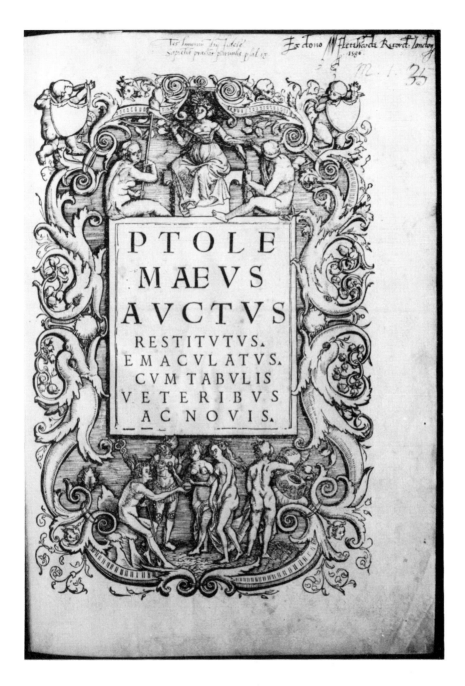

PTOLE
MAEVS
AVCTVS
RESTITVTVS.
EMACVLATVS.
CVM TABVLIS
VETERIBVS
AC NOVIS.

10 The title page of the volume of Ptolemy's *Geographia* donated by William
Fleetwood, Recorder of London and friend of Sir Walter Mildmay (7.2.6).

45

Memorandum Anno dñi.
1610, there were found
in the library Octob:
4th 503 bookes.

Memorandu that at our
accounts Octob: 4. 1610. there
were wanting in the Library
thirty books in number vz.

I

Class. sup:
  11 Biblia Latina
  35 Liber psalm. cum annot. Steph.

Class. mser.
  25. Jo:dy. bitæ. 12. Dic. com: Med. pr
  29. Jo: Sleid de statu reip: & relig

III
Class. sup.
  + 9 Dionys. de Jc. Hierarch.
  24 Burchardi decreta
  26. Rab: Mau. de cler. mstit:

IV
Class. sup.
  34. Fulk against Staplet. Lat.
  36. Calb. English:
  39. Riby. lib. de erroribj. pontif:
  41. Melancth: loc. com.
Class. mser.
  57. Lutheri. Apol. a Thed. mbis dam:

11 Part of the list of books missing in 1610. (BUR.8.1).

12 A reconstruction of part of the second classis, inferior, as listed in the inventories of 1621 and 1622, showing numbering and author and title designations on the fore-edges. See Table 1.

47

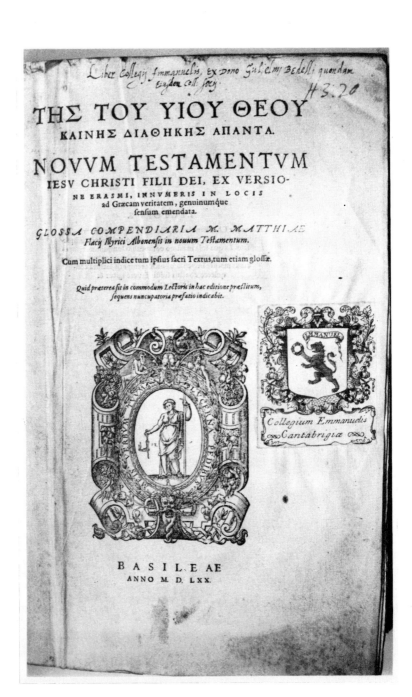

13. The title page of the copy of Erasmus's *Novum Testamentum* in Greek with the "Glossa Compendiaria" of Matthias Flacius (2.S.9) donated by William Bedell.

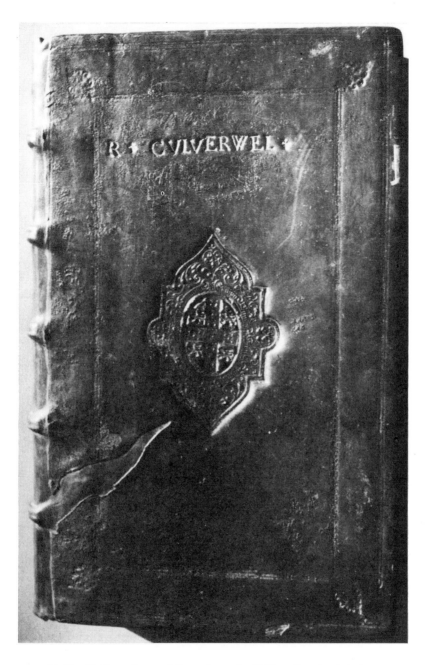

14. The binding of one of the volumes in William Branthwaite's bequest of 1620, displaying the Cambridge University arms. The book
had obviously been owned by Richard Culverwell, another Emmanuel benefactor, some of whose gifts to the library bear similar
bindings, though usually the initials "R" and "C" appear on either
side of the University arms. This volume was thus owned successively by two of the friends of Emmanuel before its acquisition by
the Library ([2]1.S.24).

CATALOGUE OF THE LIBRARY,
APRIL 27, 1637

ANNO DOMINI 1637: APRILL: 27th
A CATALOGUE OF ALL THE LIBRARY
BOOKES:

Pars Orientalis

Classis primae superior sectio

1.S.1   Biblia Regia Hispanica 8 vol: 1584–97
        [1621 inventory (1.S.1): "Ariae Montani Biblia in 8 Vol: in fol:"]
        Bible [The Antwerp Polyglot]. Biblia sacra Hebraice, Chaldaice, Graece,
        & Latine. Philippi II reg. Cathol. pietate, et studio. *Ed.* B. Arias Mon-
        tanus. Antuerpiae, excud. Christophorus Plantinus, 1569–72. 8 vols. F°,
        pp. 743; 720 [731], 213; 83, 73–679, 130; 919, 141; 499 [501], 566; 147,
        186, 114, 166; 191; 24, 118, 26, 23 [19], 14, 10, 18, 6, 11, 22, 33, 31. Adams
        B970. Darlow & Moule 1422. Missing. Register of Books Removed,
        p. 1, 1. 1: "Arie Montani Biblia—8V—Antw."

1.S.2   Biblia Gallica   1588(?)
        Bible [French]. La Bible, qui est Toute la Saincte Escriture du Vieil &
        du Nouveau Testament: Autrement L'Anciene & la Nouvelle Alliance.
        Geneue: 1588. F°, ff. 548, 94, 167. Adams B1150. Darlow & Moule 3736.
        Inscription on title page: "Ex dono Ministrorum totius Ecclesiae
        Geneuensis Octavo Calendas Junij 1588. W A: Mildmaye." Fore-edge:
        "Biblia Franc./9". Donor: Sir Walter Mildmay.   **FB.1**

1.S.3   Novum Testamentum Syriacum Tremel   1584–97
        Bible, New Testament [Polyglot; Gk, Lat., Syriac]. [Possibly:
        Testamentum Novum ... Est autem interpretatio Syriaca Novi Testamenti,
        Hebraeis typis descripta, plerisque etiam locis emendata.... Autore
        Immanuele Tremellio. (Also contains his) Grammatica Chaldaea et Syra.
        (Geneva.) excud. Henr. Stephanus, 1569. F°, ff. 709, coll. 98 + preface.
        Adams B1701. Darlow & Moule 8949.   **308.1.27**]

1.S.4   Biblia Bombergi 2 vol   c. 1598
        Bible, Old Testament [Hebrew] Biblia Rabbinica. Venice: Daniel Bomberg
        [year unknown]. Missing. Donor: Laurence Chaderton. Register of Books
        Removed, p. 1, 1. 4: "Biblia Bombergica—2.V—Venet. Dr Chader[ton]".
        The Bomberg Bible was first published in 1517 and in revised editions in
        1524–5 and 1546–8, each time in 4 volumes. Later editions were by other

printers. See Darlow & Moule 2403, 2404, 5083, 5084, 5085, and 5093. The work first appears in the Emmanuel collection at the end of the c. 1597 inventory, the first of four items added in a hand different from that of the list proper. One of these four new items is known to have been donated on October 2, 1598 (see 5.I.15). The Bomberg Bible was probably acquired at about the same time. It is Chaderton's only known gift to the library.

1.S.5   Biblia Hebr Hutteri   1587–97
Bible, Old Testament [Hebrew]. דרך הקדש ... hoc est via sancta... sive Biblia sacra... Authore Elia Huttero. Hamburgi, typis Elianis per Iohannem Saxonem, 1587. F°, pp. 1572. Adams B1235. Darlow & Moule 5108. Steinschneider 276. Fore-edge: "Bibl. Hutter/12".   **308.1.32**

1.S.6   Biblia Graec: Septuag: 1622–6
Bible, Old Testament [Greek]. [Possibly: Vetus Testamentum iuxta Septuaginta ex auctoritate Sixti v. Pont. Max. editum. (By Cardinal Carafa and many others.) Romae, 1586. F°. Darlow & Moule 4647.] Missing.

1.S.7   Concord: Lat Stephani   1584–97
Stephanus. [Possibly: Robertus, *the elder*. Concordantiae Bibliorum utriusque Testamenti, Veteris & Novi. (Paris,) Oliva Rob. Stephani, 1555. F°, pp. 548. Adams S1798.   **304.2.9**]

1.S.8   Concord No: Testam: Graec: Steph   1622–6
Stephanus, Henricus. Concordantiae Testamenti Novi Graecolatinae. [By Robert and Henri Estienne, Theodore Beza, and others.] [Geneva?] Ex typographeio Henr. Stephani, 1594. F°, pp. 535. Adams (S1756) omits Emmanuel's copy. Fore-edge: "Concor/Graec".   **304.2.25**

1.S.9   Testam: Graec: 1: Baezae cum eiusdem annotationib*us* majorib: 1622–6
Bible, New Testament [Polyglot]. Iesu Christi D. N. Novum testamentum, sive Novum foedus... Eiusdem Th. Bezae Annotationes... tertia editione. *Tr.* Theodore Beza. [Gk & Lat.] [Geneva, H. Stephanus,] 1582, F°, pp. 525, 488 + indices. Adams B1708. Darlow & Moule 4643. Fore-edge: "Test: Beza".   **304.2.3**

1.S.10   Biblia Anglica MS vers: Antiq   1584–97
A vellum manuscript of John Wycliffe's translation. "Cent. xiv late, finely written," M. R. James 21, T. James 2. Fore-edge: "Biblia [?]/13".   **MSS1.1.21**

1.S.11   Biblia Lat vers vulgaris   1584–97
[1621 inventory (1.S.10): "Biblia vulgata Hyeron:"]
Bible [Latin]. Biblia Sacrosancta Veteris & Novi Testamenti, iuxta Divi Hieronymi vulgatam aeditionem. [With woodcuts from drawings by

H. Holbein.] Lugduni, apud Ioannem Frellonium, 1551. F°, ff. 284, coll. 283 + index. Adams B1044. Not in Darlow & Moule. Fore-edge: "Biblia/Lat:/20". Inscription on title page: "i563./Joh*ann*es Dister ex dono R G:". **304.2.18**

1.S.12   Biblia Haebr Munsteri 2 vol   1584–97
Bible. Old Testament [Polyglot]. מקדש'' ... Hebraica Biblia Latina planeque nova Sebast. Munsteri tralatione. [2 vols.] Basileae, ex off. Bebeliana, impendiis Michaelis Isingrinii et Henrici Petri, 1534–5. F°, ff. 795, consecutive pagination through 2 vols. Adams B1240. Darlow & Moule 5087. Fore-edges: I: "Biblia hebra/ica münster/14/pars pri*mus*"; II: "Biblia hebr:/munster/15".   **304.2.21, 22**

1.S.13   Testamentum novum Erasmi   1584–97
Bible, New Testament [Polyglot]. Novum Testamentum Omne, tertio iam ac Erasmo Roterodamo recognitum. [Gk & Lat.] [Possibly: (Basileae,) 1522. F°, pp. 562 + prefaces, indices. (Vol. I only.) Adams B1681. Darlow & Moule 4599.   **305.4.68**]

1.S.14   Ejusdem annotationes in Testam: 1584–97
Erasmus, Desiderius. Annotationes in Novum Testamentum. Missing. Emmanuel's present copy (Basel, 1542: Adams E895) was a Sancroft gift: S7.2.11.

1.S.15   Psalt Nebiense Hebr: Gr: Chald: Arab: cum interpret Lat   1584–97
Bible: Psalms [Polyglot]. Psalterium, Hebr*ae*um, Gr*ae*cum, Arabic*um*, & Chald*ae*um, cu*m* tribus latinis i*n*terp*r*etatio*n*ibus & glossis. [*Ed.* Augustinus Justinianus, Bp of Nebbio.] Genuae, impressit Petrus Paulus Porrus in aed. Nicolai Iustiniani Pauli, 1516. 4°. Isaac 13835. Adams B1370. Steinschneider 25. Darlow & Moule 1411. Fore-edge: "Psal: [?]:/[?] Neb:".
304.2.23

1.S.16   Biblia Tremel: 2 vol   1593–7
[1622 inventory (1.S.7): "Biblia Latina Tremellij & Iunij: 2 Vol.ˢ fol."]
Bible [Latin]. [Possibly: Testamenti Veteris Biblia sacra ... Latini recens ex Hebraeo facti ... ab Immanuele Tremellio & Francisco Junio quibus etiam adjunximus Novi Testamenti libros ... Secunda cura F. Junii. Londini, Excudebant G. B(ishop), R. N(ewbury), & R. B(arker), 1593, 1592. F°, pp. 177, 104, 75, 129, 74, 198. STC 2061. Darlow & Moule 6185.] Missing? Emmanuel's copy is now bound as one vol.:   **305.4.77**

1.S.17   Testament: Hibernicum   1602–21
Bible, New Testament [Irish]. Tiomma Nuadh ar d'Tighearna agus ar Slanaightheora Iosa Criosd. *Tr.* Huilliam O'Domhnuill. [Dublin,] Seon Francke [i.e. J. Franckton], 1602. F°, ff. 214. STC 2958. Darlow & Moule 5532. Writing on the gilt and gauffered fore-edge is illegible. **MSS. 4.2.2**

1.S.18 Concord: Kircheri Septua: 2 vol   1622–6
Bible, Old Testament Concordance [Hebrew]. Conrad Kircher.
Concordantiae Veteris Testamenti Graecae, Ebraeis Vocibus
Respondentes. Francofurti, apud Claudium Marnium, & heredes Iohannis
Aubrii. 1607. [3 pts.] 4°. Missing. Register of Books Removed, p. 1, 1. 19:
"Kircheri (Conrad) Concordantia V. Testam^{ti}:... 2. V——Franf^{ti} 1607."
Emmanuel's present copy was a Sancroft gift: S1.3.18.

1.S.19 Biblia Germanica 2 Vol   1604
Bible [German]. Bibel Teutsch das ist alle bücher Alts und Nüws
Testaments. [2 vols.] [Zurich, C. Froschauer,] 1549. 8°, pp. 344, 324.
Donor: Thomas Pickering. Inscription on title page of vol. I: "Collegio
Emmanuelis Cantabrigiae, in perpetuum d amoris ac pietatis monimentum
dicavit Thomas Pickering S. Theologiae Baccalaureus, ejusdemque Collegij
Socius. Anno Domini. 1604. Martij. 15°." This inscription, with slightly
different wording, also appears in vol. II. Fore-edges: "Biblia Ger./38";
"Biblia Ger. II/39".   **326.3.43.44**

Classis I^{ae} Infer: Sect

1.I.1 Hutteri Cubus   1584–97
[1621 inventory (1.S.23): "Cubus Hutteri in Psal: 119."]
Hutter, Elias. [Possibly: Cubus alphabeticus sanctae Ebraeae linguae.
Ed. D. Wolder. Hamburgi, excud. Iacobus Wolfius, 1588. F°.] Missing.

1.I.2 Talmud: 7 vol   1584–97
Talmud [Babylonian]. Berakhot [-Niddah]. [With commentaries of
Solomon ben Isaac Rashi, "Tosefot," and Asher ben Yehiel. (Second
edition)] Venice, Daniel Bomberg, [1520]. F°. Steinschneider 1568.
Uncatalogued; not in Adams.   **308.1.37**

1.I.3 Pagnini Thesaurus   1597–1621
Pagninus, Sanctes. Thesaurus Linguae Sanctae, sive Lexicon Hebraicum.
[Ed. Ioannes Mercer, Ant. Cevallarius, & B. Cornelius Bertramus]
Lugduni, apud Bartholomaeum Vincentium, 1575. F°. Fore-edge: "Pagnin:
Thesaur:/25". Binding is stamped "CE/1592". Adams P39.   **312.1.5**

1.I.4 Concord: Hebr: 1622–6
Bible, Old Testament. Concordance [Heb.] [Possibly: Concordantiae
Sacrorum Bibliorum Hebraicorum, in quibus chaldaicae etiam librorum
Esdrae & Danielis suo loco inseruntur.... Auctore... Mario de Calasio.]
Missing.

1.I.5   Pagnini Isagog: in Script   1599
[1621 inventory (2.I.29): "Pagnini Isagoge ad sacras Script, & ad. mysticos
Scripturae sensus."]
Pagninus, Sanctes. Isagogae ad Sacras Literas Liber unicus.... Isagoge
ad mysticos sacrae scripturae sensus, Libri XVIII. Coloniae [*pr.* Euch.
Cervicornus] impens. Iohannis Soteris, 1540. F°, pp. 902 + index. Donor:
Richard Lister. Inscription on title page: "RICHAR: LISTERVS/EMAN:
COLLEGIO/DEDIT. ANN: DOM: 1599."   **306.4.58**

1.I.6   Arca Noae Lexic: Hebr Brixiani   1625
Marinus, Marcus, *of Brescia.* Arca Noe. Thesaurus Linguae Sanctae
Novus. [2 pts.] [And:] Collectio Messis. Dictionarium Latino-Hebraeum
Ex Thesauro Decerptum. Venetiis, apud Iohannem Degaram, 1593. F°, ff.
492, 288, [37]. Adams M597. Donor: Dr John Richardson. Inscription on
title page: "Ex dono Johan. Richardson S.T.D./Coll. S.S.ᵈ Trinitatis Mʳⁱ/&
hujus Collegij quonda*m* Socij/An. Dⁿⁱ 1625/Coll. Eman." Fore-edge:
"Arca. Noe".   **312.1.8**

1.I.7   Eliae Levitae Methurgeman   1622–6
Elias, *Levita.* מיתורגמן. Lexicon Chaldaicum Authore Eliia Levita,
Quo nullum hactenus a quoquam absolutius aeditum est, omnibus
Hebraeae linguae studiosis, imprimis & utile & necessarium. Isnae, 1541. F°.
Adams E121. Steinschneider 4960.26. Fore-edge: "Lexic Chald. Eliae
Levitae".   **302.3.31**

1.I.8   Avenarij Lexic Hebr   1622–6
Avenarius, Johannes. סֵפֶר הַשָּׁרָשׁים Liber Radicum seu Lexicon Ebrai-
cum. Witebergae per Haeredes Iohannis Cratonis. 1589. F°, pp. 860.
Missing. Register of Books Removed, p. 1, 1. 13: "Avenarij lexicon hebr....
Witteb: 1589". Emmanuel's present copy (Adams A2306) was a Sancroft
gift: S1.2.20.

1.I.9   Evang Matthaei Hebr Munsterj   1584–97
Bible: Matthew [Polyglot]. [Possibly: Evangelium secundum Mat-
thaeum ... una cum epistola ... ad Hebraeos. (Lat. & Heb.) *Ed.* S. Munster.

Steinschneider 6591.27.   **330.6.118**]
Basileae, apud Henricum Petri, 1557. 8°, pp. 396. Adams B1886.
1.I.10 Placi Lexic Bibl   1584–97
Placus, Andreas. Lexicon biblicum. Coloniae, ex off. Melchioris Novesiani,
1536. F°, ff. 208. Adams P1388. Fore-edge: "Lexicon/biblicum/28".
                                                                   318.2.18

1.I.11 Galatinus et Reuchlinus de *verbo* mirifico   1625
Two works, paged consecutively, with one title page:
(1) Columna, Petrus, *Galatinus.* Opus de Arcanis Catholicae Veritatis....

in omnia difficilia loca Veteris Testamenti, ex Talmud, aliis*que* hebraicis libris... commentarius.

(2) Reuchlin, Johann. De Arte Cabalistica, Libri tres. Item, libri tres de Verbo mirifico. Basileae, per Ioannem Hervagium, 1561. F°, pp. 651. Adams C2420. Donor: Dr John Richardson. Fore-edge: "Galatin*us*/Reuchlin/de verbo mi/rifica". **308.4.67**

1.I.12   Joseph Ben = Gorion Heb: Lat Munst   1622–6
Joseph, ben Gorion, *pseud.* Josephus Hebraicus... ex Constantinopolitano exemplari iuxta Hebraismum opera Sebastiani Munsteri versus, & annotationibus atque collationibus illustratus. [Lat. & Heb.] Basileae, apud Henricum Petrum, 1541. F°. Steinschneider 6033.2. Missing. Register of Books Removed, p. 25, I. 23: "Josephus hebr: versione Munsteri.... Basil: 1541." Emmanuel's present copy (Basileae, 1559: Adams J346) was a Sancroft gift: S8.3.15.

1.I.13   Kimchij lib radicum   1597–1621
Kimchi, David. [Possibly: Compe*n*dium Michlol, Hoc est absolutiss. Grammatices Davidis Chimhi. *Ed.* R. Baynes. Parisiis, apud Carolum Stephanum Typographum Regium, 1554. 4°, pp. 141. Adams K54. Steinschneider 4524. **333.2.71**]
"Kimhi's first work was his philological treatise, the *Mikhlol*, written in two sections: the grammatical portion... which itself came to be known as the *Mikhlol*..., and the lexicon... known independently as the *Sefer ha-Shorashim*," or the book of roots. *Encyclopedia Judaica* (Jerusalem, 1971), X, 1002.

1.I.14   Barbenel   1626–32
Abravanel, Isaac. [Possibly: (with Moses Alschech) Comment. in Esaiae Prophetiam 30. cum additamento eorum quae R. Simeon e veterum dictis collegit. Lugduni Batavorum, ex officina Bonaventurae & Abrahami Elzevir. Academ. Typograph. 1631. 8°, pp. 291. Steinschneider 5302.18.
       323.6.70]

1.I.15   Menorah Hamaor   1626–32
[Probably: Aboab, Isaac. ספר מנורת המאור. (System of moral laws as explained in the Talmud.) Venetia, Appresso gli Illustris. Sig. Pietro e Lorenzo Brag(adini) 1623. F°. Uncatalogued; not in Adams. Steinschneider 5294.8.   **305.4.80**]

1.I.16   Ricij coelest agric^ra   1584–97
[1621 inventory (2.S.23): "Ricius de coelesti agriculturâ, de Mosaicae Legis mandatis, & farrago ex Thalmud."]
Ricius, Paulus. [Opera] De Coelesti Agricultura. [ff. 122; other works of Ricius. ff. 123 210.] Augustae Vindelicorum, per Henricum Stayner,

1541. F°. Adams R 520. Fore-edge: "Pau/lus/Ric*ius*/de coelest/agricult."

307.4.17

1.I.17 Postellus de Orbis conc^a 1622–6

Postel, Guillaume. De Orbis Terrae concordia Libri Quatuor. Missing. Emmanuel's present copy (Basle, 1544; Adams P2020) was a Sancroft gift: S2.2.29.

1.I.18 Reuchl: Rudiment: Hebr 1625

Reuchlin, Johann. Principium Libri. [De rudimentis Hebraicis liber primus (-tertius).] Phorce, in aedib. Tho. Anshelmi, 1506. F°, pp. 621. Adams R383. Proctor 1174. Donor: Dr John Richardson. **305.4.55**

1.I.19 Jarchi Ab Ez Kimchi in 4 prophet minores 1622–6

Bible, Minor Prophets [Hebrew and Aramaic]. [Possibly: הושע (יואל ובו עם תרגום) יונה עובדיה עמום עמום, Hosee (-Jonah) cu*m* Thargum, id est Chaldaica paraphrasi Ionathan, & co*m*mentariis R. Selomo Iarhi, R. Abraham Aben Ezra, & R. D. Kimhi. (Paris, R. Estienne, 1556. 4°. pp. 243. Adams B1289. Steinschneider 146. **328.2.64**]

This work contains commentaries on five minor prophets rather than the four indicated in the catalogue description. The volume has no fore-edge markings and may be a later acquisition. The Register of Books Removed, p. 1, 1. 20, may describe the original copy, though it too is somewhat ambiguous in mentioning just three prophets and Ruth: "Jonathan Targum in Hoseam, Joelem, Amosum, cum anonym: in Ruth: &c. Cat: p*er* Quinquasbor: Paris: 1556."

1.I.20 Eliae Levitae Thisbites 1584–97

[1621 inventory (2.S.34): "Thibites Elia Levitae & Apotheg: Patru*m*"]
Two books bound together:
(1) Mishnah *Nezikin*, Aboth. Sententiae Vere Elegantes... quas פרקי אבות id est Capitula, aut si mavis Apophtegmata Patrum nominant. *Tr.* Paulus Fagius. [Heb. & Lat.] Isnae in Algavia, 1541. 4°, pp. 151. Adams (M1484) omits Emmanuel's copy. Steinschneider 1435.
(2) Elias, *Levita.* Opusculum recens Hebraicum...תשבי id est Thisbites. Isnae in Algavia, 1541. 4°, pp. 371 + prefaces, errata. Adams E124. Steinschneider 4960.46. **[Possibly: 332.2.47]**

1.I.21 Ricij Opusc: Erasmi: Paraph in E*pisto*las ad Cor. et Opusc: Zasius in Ecciu*m* 1597–1621

Three books bound together:
(1) Ricius, Paulus. 4 works: [I] De Sexcentum et tredecim Mosaice sanctionis edictis, [II] Caballistarum seu allegorizantium Eruditionem Isagogae, [III] Philosophica Prophetica ac Talmudistica pro Christiana veritate tuenda... disputatio, [IV] De Novem Doctrinarum

Ordinibus. Pt. I, Augustae Vindelicorum, officina Millerana, 1515; pt II, Augustae impressum Anno 1515; pt III, aedibus Milleranis, 1514; pt IV, officina Ioann. Miller, 1515. 4°, ff. 41, 26, 40, 24. Proctor 10825, Adams R522.

(2) Erasmus, Desiderius. 2 works: [I] Paraphrasis in Duas Epistolas Pauli ad Corinthios. In Basilea, apud Ioannem Frobenium, 1519. 4°, pp. 222. Adams E789. [II] Enchiridion Militis Christiani, Saluberrimis praeceptis refertum... Cui accessit... Praefatio. Et Basilius in Esaiam commentariolus ... Cum alijs. Argentorati, apud Schurerium, 1519. 4°, pp. 303, [16]. Adams E363.

(3) Zasius, Udalricus. Apologetica defensio contra Ioannem Eckium... Defensa Magni Erasmi assertio, quam in elegantiss. scholijs sup. septimo Matthei capite docuit. Basileae, apud Ioannem Frobenium, 1519. 4°, pp. 71. Adams Z85.   [Possibly: 330,2.58]

1.I.22   Element: prim linguae Syr: 1622–6
[Possibly: Severus, *Patriarch of Alexandria.* Syriacae linguae prima elementa.] Missing. Emmanuel's present copy (Adams S1023) was a Sancroft gift: S3.4.21.

1.I.23   Cheshek Shelomoh. Comment in Proverb   1626–32
Bible, Proverbs [Hebrew]. חשק שלמה ... Solomon ben Duran. [Commentary on Proverbs, with text.] Venice, Pietro and Lorenzo Bragadini, 1623. 4°. Uncatalogued. Steinschneider 6911.2. Inscription on flyleaf: "Cheshek Shelomoh/Comment: in Proverb:".   **328.2.73**

1.I.24   Sepher Hacozri   1626–32
Judah ben Samuel, *the Levite.* ספר הכוזרי [*Tr.* Judah ibn Tibbon]. Venice, Juan di Gara, 1594. 4°. Uncatalogued. Steinschneider 5738.3. Adams (J401) omits Emmanuel's copy. Inscription on flyleaf: "Sepher Hacozri".   **328.2.72**

1.I.25   Sepher Jedi Moshe   1628–32
Moses ben Baruch, *Almosnino* ספר ירי משה והוא פירוש המש מגלות [Commentary on the Five Scrolls: Ruth, Esther, Ecclesiastes, Song of Solomon, and Lamentations.] Venice, Daniel Zannetti, 1597, 4°. Uncatalogued. Steinschneider 6430.3. Adams (M1864) omits Emmanuel's copy. Inscription on flyleaf: "Sepher Jede Mosche: h.c./ Manus Moses Commentarius/in Megilloth Quinque,/Cantica Canticorum/Ruth/Lamentati./Ecclesiastes/Esther". Fore-edge: "in Hag[io]/ grapha".   **328.2.78**

1.I.26   Lechem dingnah   1626–32
Bible, Lamentations [Hebrew]. ספר להם דמעה [With commentary by Samuel ben Isaac of Uceda.] Venice, Daniel Zannetti. 1605 [1600]. 4° [ff.

120]. Uncatalogued. Adams (B1591) omits Emmanuel's copy. Steinschneider 336.   328.2.75

1.I.27   Mincah Belulah   1626–32
Abraham Menahem Rabe Rapaport. מנחה בלולה [Commentary on the Pentateuch.] Verona, in casa di M. Francesco dalle Donne, 1594. 4°. Uncatalogued. Steinschneider 4289.1. Adams (A27) omits Emmanuel's copies. Fore-edge: "Mincah/Belulah." Emmanuel has a duplicate copy (328.2.89) which lacks fore-edge marking and appears to be a later acquistion.   **328.2.96**

1.I.28   Gnabod Hacodesh   1626–32
Solomon Adret. עבודת הקודש [Laws of the Sabbath and Festivals.] [Pt I] בית נתיבות [Domus semitarum] [Pt II] Missing: בית מועד [Domus conventus]. Steinschneider 6891.22. [Also includes:] כעלי הנפש [Viri animi anxii]. Steinschneider 4213.1. Venice, Daniel Zannetti, 1601–2. 4°. Uncatalogued. Fore-edge: "Gnabod hakedesh".

                                                                    328.2.77

1.I.29   Mishnaioth 2 vol   1626–32
Talmud [Babylonian]. Mishnah. [Possibly: פש נ י ו ת (Commentary by Obadiah Bertinoro and Yom Tov Lipmann Heller.) (2 vols.) Prague, Joseph Bezalel Katz, 1614–17. 4°. Uncatalogued. Steinschneider 1991.

                                                                328.2.79, 80]

1.I.30   Alphunsi dial: R Sam de Mess et Colloq X^ti cum Judaeo   1584–97
Two books bound together:
(1) Alfunzi, Petrus. Dialogi... in quibus impiae Iudaeorum opiniones... confutantur.... Accessit libellus... Rabbi Samuelis, veri Messiae parastasim continens. Coloniae, apud Ioan. Gymnicum, 1536. 8°, pp. 395 + indices. Adams A741. Steinschneider 4409.1.
(2) Munster, Sebastian. Messias Christianorum et Iudaeorum Hebraice & Latine. [2 pts in 1 vol.] Basileae, apud Henricum Petrum, 1539. 8°. Adams M1935. Steinschneider 6591.29.   **[Possibly: 321.6.20]**

1.I.31   Munsterj diction Heb: 1584–97
Munster, Sebastian. Dictionarium Hebraicum, Iam Tertio ab autore Sebastiano Munstero ex Rabinis, praesertim ex radicibus David Kimhi, auctum & locupletatum. Basileae, per Hieronymum Frobenium & Nicolaum Episcopium, 1535. 8°. Adams M1923. Fore-edge: "Dict./Munsteri/Heb./32".   **329.7.5**

1.I.32   Aurogalli Gram^ca Heb: Munst anomal: Heb: 1584–97
Two books bound together:
(1) Elias, *Levita*. Vocabula Hebraica Irregularia. [*Tr.* Sebastian Munster]

Basileae excudebat Henricus Petrus, 1536. 8°, pp. 196. Adams E128. Steinschneider 4960.15.

(2) Aurogallus, Matthaeus. Grammatica Hebraeae Chaldeaeque linguae. Vitebergae in aed. Iosephi Clugi, 1531. 8°. Adams A2272. Fore-edge: "Ano/mala/heb/Muns/teri/Aurogal/Gram H. C./38". **329.7.95**

1.I.33   Psalm: Heb: Reuchl. in Ps: poenitent Eliae Levitae Elect   1584–97
Four books bound together:

(1) Psalterium Hebraicum cum radicibus in margine. Lipsiae in aedib. Melchioris Lottheri, per Antonium Margaritam genere Israelitam, 1533. 8°. Adams B1350. Steinschneider 73.

(2) [Reuchlin, Johann.] Septem Psalmi Poenitentiales Hebraici cum grammatica tralacione Latina. [Wittemberg, Joseph Klug, 1529?] 8°, pp. 18.

(3) Reuchlin, Johann. In septem psalmos poenitentiales hebraicos interpretatio de verbo ad verbum, & super eisdem commentarioli sui. Wittembergae apud Iosephum Clugum, 1529. 8°. [Heb. & Lat.] Adams B1499. Steinschneider 62.

(4) Elias, *Levita* רוחבה רפס Liber Grammaticae. Mantuae, 1556. 8°. Uncatalogued. Adams (E120) omits Emmanuel's copy. Steinschneider 4960.11. Fore-edge: "Psal. Poe/nit. hebr/12".   **329.8.48**

1.I.34   Bibliae Hebr: pars   1584–97
[1621 inventory (2.S.10): "Bibliorum Hebraic. pars prior."]
Bible, Pentateuch [Hebrew] [Possibly:
either: Venice, Daniel Bomberg, 1525. 4°. Pt I only. Uncatalogued. Steinschneider 59. Darlow & Moule 5086. Fore-edge: two faded and illegible lines of writing. On bottom edge: "G. Fuliambe (?) in/(?)(?)". Signature on title page: "gnod Fulia*m*be".   **328.2.68**
or: Antwerp, Christopher Plantin, 1580–2. 4°. Uncatalogued. Steinschneider 257. Darlow & Moule 5104. Adams (B1234) omits Emmanuel's copy.   **327.2.5]**

1.I.35   Kimchi in Joel, et Amos   1584–97
David Kimchi produced Hebrew versions of the twelve minor prophets: Duodecim prophetae cum comentariis R. David Kimhi. [*Ed.* F. Vatablus] Parisiis, ex off. Roberti Stephani, 1539–40. 4°. Emmanuel's book was probably a collection of two, or perhaps three, of these commentaries in Hebrew. Missing. There is some disagreement among the several inventories as to what this volume contained: c. 1597 inventory (368): "Kimhi in Joel Mallach & Amos"; 1621 and 1622 inventories (2.S.6): "David Kimki in Joelem Hebraic."

1.I.36   Eliae Levitae Gram: 1584–97
[1622 inventory (2.S.12): "Grammat: Eliae Levitae: Et Munster de accentib*us* Hebrae."]

Elias, *Levita*. Grammatica Hebraica absolutissima ... nuper per Sebastianum Munsterum iuxta Hebraismu*m* Latinitate donata ... Institutio
elementaria in Hebraica*m* Linguam eodem Sebast. Munstero autore.
[2 pts.] A Preface is entitled: Accentum Hebraicorum compendium, per
Sebastian Munsterum. Basileae, apud Io. Frobenium, 1525. 8°. Adams
E114, Steinschneider 4960.7.   **329.7.75**

1.I.37   Ejusdem Massorah Ham*m*ass: 1584–97
Three books bound together:
(1) [Elias, *Levita*] ספר מסורת המסורת. Basileae, per Henricum
Petrum, 1539. 8°. Adams E131. Steinschneider 4960.22.
(2) Munster, Sebastian. הַוִּיכוּחַ Christiani Hominis Cum Iudaeo pertinaciter prodigiosis suis opinionibus & scripturae violentis interpretationibus addicto, colloquiu*m*: per Sebastianu*m* Munsterum. Basileae, per
Henricum Petrum, 1539. 8°. Adams (M1905) omits Emmanuel's copy.
Steinschneider 6591.29.
(3) Elias, *Levita*. ספר הטעמים ... Accentuum Hebraicorum Liber unus.
Basileae, apud Henricum Petrum, 1539. 8°, pp. 109. Adams E109.
Steinschneider 4960.22. Fore-edge: "Massoreth/[Two faded lines of
illegible Hebrew]/24".   **329.8.24**

1.I.38   Munst: Gram: Heb: 1584–97
[1621 and 1622 inventories (2.S.19): "Institutio in Haebr. Linguam"]
Munster, Sebastian. [Possibly: Institutiones grammaticae in Hebraeam
linguam. (Basel), in off. Frobeniana, 1524. 8°. Adams M1931. Title page
bears the signature "Martino Bucero". This book is now bound with
another work: Munster's Proverbia Salomonis iam recens iuxta
Hebraica*m*. [n.p., n.d.] This joint binding probably post-dates 1637.

                                                              329.7.66]

1.I.39   Ejusdem Gram Hebr Compend   1584–97
[1621 inventory (2.S.14): "Gram*matica* Hebraea Rabbi Mosche Kimki &
Munsteri"].
Three books bound together:
(1) Kimchi, ˙Moses. Grammatica ... iuxta Hebraismum per Sebastianum
Munsterum versa. Accessit ... Eliae Levitae commentarium. [Heb. &
Lat.] [2 pts.] Basileae, apud Andream Catandrum, 1531. 8°, pp. 51.
Adams K58. Steinschneider 6498.7.
(2) Munster, Sebastian. קיצור של הדקדוק Compendium Hebraicae
grammaticae, ex Eliae Iudaei ... libris per Sebastianum Munsterum
concinnatum. Basileae [Froben], 1529. 8°. Adams M1906.
(3) Munster, Sebastian. Christiani Hominis cum Iudaeo pertinaciter prodigiosis suis opinionibus, & scripturae violentis interpretationibus
addicto, Colloquiu*m*. [Heb.] Basileae, Froben, 1529. 8°. Adams M1904.
Fore-edge writing is badly faded: "[?]/[?]/compe*n*/[?]/[?]/17". **329.6.4**

1.I.40   Josippi Hist Heb: Lat   1584–97
Joseph ben Gorion, *pseud.* [Possibly: De Bello Iudaico. Deinde decem
Iudaeorum captivitates & Decalogus. (*Comm.* R. Aben Esra. *Tr.* S.
Munster.) (Heb. & Lat.)] Missing. Emmanuel's present copy (Basileae,
1559: Adams J347) was a Sancroft gift: S12.5.5.

1.I.41   Praecepta Mosaica. 613   1584–97
Moses ben Jacob, *of Coucy*. Praecepta Mosaica sexeenta at*que* tredecim.
[*Ed.* Sebastian Munster] [Heb. & Lat.] [Possibly: Basileae, excud.
Henricus Petrus, 1533. 8°. Adams M1871. Steinschneider 6453.6.
                                                                        329.8.44]
This book and the following one (1.I.42) are now bound together with
other works on Hebrew grammar. The binding appears to post-date 1637.
The edges were trimmed at the time of rebinding, removing any fore-edge
writing.

1.I.42   Agath Gram: Heb: 1622–6
Guidacerius, Agathius. [Possibly: In hoc libello continetur, De Literis
Hebraicis. Parisiis, in off. Christiani Wecheli, 1537. 8°. Adams G1547.
                                                                        329.8.44]
See note to 1.I.41.

1.I.43   Bibliandri Gram Heb: 1584–97
[1621 inventory (2.S.15): "Grammat. Hebr. Bibliandri cum Alphabet: Hebr."]
Bibliander, Theodorus. Institutionum grammaticarum de lingua Hebraea
liber unus. Tiguri, in off. Froschoviana, 1535. 8°, ff. 105. Adams B1981.
Bound with De Usu Tabulae Coniugationum Bibliandri, pp. 6, *and*
Alphabetum Hebraicum. Parisiis, excudebat Christianus Wechelus, 1534,
pp. 11.   **329.7.85**
These works are now bound with a volume of Cicero; the binding appears
to post-date 1637.

1.I.44   Clenardi Gram: Heb   1584–97
Clenardus, Nicolaus. Tabula in Grammaticen Hebraeam. [Possibly:
Salingiaci, Ioannes Soter excud., 1540. 8°, pp. 155. Adams C2163.
                                                                        329.6.19]
This work is now bound with three other books. The binding appears to
post-date 1637. The edges were trimmed at the time of rebinding, thus
removing any fore-edge markings.

1.I.45   Rabbi Symeonis Log[a]   1584–97
Simeon, *Rabbi* [*Pseud.*: Maimonides]. הזהיור Logica Sapientis Rabbi
Simeonis, per [*Tr.*] Sebastianum Munsterum. [Heb. & Lat.] Basileae,
apud Io. Frob., 1527. 8°. Adams (M163) omits Emmanuel's copy. Steinschneider 6591.9.   **324.7.35**

2.S.1   Lutheri Op*era* 7. vol   1604–21
Luther, Martin. Tomus Primus [-Septimus] Omnium Operum. [7 vols.]
Witebergae, Vols. 1, 3 typ. Zachariae Lehmani (1582, 1583), Vol. 2 excud.
Laurentius Schwenck (1562), Vols. 4, 5 excud. Iohannes Lufft (1574, 1554),
Vol. 6 excud. Matthaeus Welack (1580), Vol. 7 per Thomam Klug (1557).
F°, ff. 495, 510, 599, 529, 653, 678, 614. Adams L1739, 1742, 1748, 1751,
1752, 1757, 1759. Donor: Thomas Southaicke. All vols. except 5 and 7 have
a gift plate which reads "Ex dono T. S." with the London Grocers' Com-
pany arms. Fore-edges: "Luther/1"; "2"; "3"; "4"; "5"; "6"; "7". **309.3.32–8**

2.S.2   Melancth: Op*era* Theolog: 5 vol   1604–21
Melanchthon, Philipp. Operum...pars Prima – Quinta [5 vols.]
Witebergae. Typis Simonis Gronenbergii, sumptum impendente Zacharia
Schürerio, & eius sociis, 1601. F°, pp. 443, 983, 1084, 843, 746 + indices.
Donor: Thomas Southaicke. Bookplate: "Ex dono T. S." with the London
Grocers' Company arms. Fore-edges: "Melanth/i/8"; "ii/9"; "iii/10";
"iiii/11"; "v/12".   **309.3.26–30**

2.S.3   Lorichij Epitom: in vet Test   1584–97
Lorichius, Gerhardus. Ἐπιτομή hoc est, compendium sive breviarium
textus & glossematon in Omnes Veteris Instrumenti libros (in Omnes Novi
Testamenti libros). Missing.

2.S.4   Chemnitij Harmonᵃ: 2 vol   1625
Chemnitz, Martin. Harmoniae Evangelicae, A ... Chemnitio primum.
Inchoatae & per D. Polycarpum Lyserum Continuatae, Libri Quinque. [2
vols.] Francofurti, apud Iohannem Iacobum Porssium, 1616. F°. Donor:
Thomas Hanscombe. Inscription on second front flyleaf: "1625/Magister
Thomas Hanscombe huius/Collegij Socius, moriens. D.D." Fore-edges:
"Harm/i"; "Harm/ii".   **303.2.59,60**

2.S.5   Ejusdem Loci Theolog: 1625
Chemnitz, Martin. Loci Theologici...quibus et Loci communes D.
Philippi Melanchthonis...explicantur, & ...Christianae typis doctrinae
corpus...proponitur. *Ed.* P. Leyser. Witebergae, typis I. Gormanni, 1623.
[5 pts.] F°. Donor: Dr John Richardson. Missing. Register of Books
Removed, p. 40, 1. 1: "Chemnitii Loci Theologici per Lyserum
fol... Witten: 1623. Dʳ R." This donation replaced an earlier edition of the
same work which had been present at the time of the first inventory (c.
1597). Emmanuel's present copy (Francofurti, 1604) was a Sancroft gift:
S10.3.53–5.

2.S.6   Ejusdem Examen Concilij Tridentini   Oct. 22, 1612
Chemnitz, Martin. Examinis Concilii Tridentini...Opus integrum.

Francofurti, ex officina typographica Iohannis Saurii, impensis Francisci Nicolai Roth, 1609. F°, pp. 816 + index. Donor: John Cotton. Inscription on flyleaf: "Mr John Cotton Fellow of Emmanuell Colledge in Cambridge gaue this booke unto the same, October 22, 1612." Fore-edge: "Chemn/Examen".   **302.3.54**

2.S.7   Idem de 2^{abus} Nat: in X^{to} 1622–6
Chemnitz, Martin. De Duabus Naturis In Christo. *Pref.* N. Selneccer. Lipsiae, Iohannes Rhamba excud., 1580. 4°, pp. 559. Adams C1435. Fore-edge: "CHEMNi:".   **329.1.15**

2.S.8   Illyrici clavis Script   1622–6
Flacius, Matthias, *Illyricus*. Clavis Scripturae S. seu de Sermone Sacrarum literarum. [2 vols. in 1.] Basileae, ex officina Hervagiana, per Eusebium Episcopium, 1580, 1581. F°, coll. 1338, pp. 446 + indices + tables. Adams F557. Fore-edge: "Clauis S. S."   **318.2.7**

2.S.9   Ejusdem Glossa in Nov: Testam: 1597–1621
[1621 inventory (2.S.40): "Testamentum Erasmi"]
Novum Testamentum ... ex versione Erasmi ... Glossa compendiaria M. Matthiae Flacii Illyrici. [Gk & Lat.] Basileae, per Petrum Pernam et Theobaldum Dietrich, 1570. F°, pp. 1394. Adams B1702. Donor: William Bedell. Inscription on title page: "Liber Collegij Immanuelis, ex Dono Gulielmj Bedellj quondam eiusdem Coll: socij." Fore-edge: "Illirici Glossa/[6?]9".   **304.3.20**

2.S.10   Ejusdem Catalogus Testium Veritatis   1622–6
Flacius, Matthias, *Illyricus*. Catalogus Testium Veritatis qui, ante nostram aetatem, Pontificum Romanorum Primatui, variisque Papismi superstitionibus ... reclamarunt. [Possibly: (Geneva), 1608. F°.   **305.1.6**]

2.S.11   Idem de Sectis   1622–6
Flacius, Matthias, *Illyricus*. De Sectis, Dissensionibus, Contradictionibus et Confusionibus doctrinae, religionis, scriptorum & doctorum Pontificiorum Liber. [Possibly: Basileae, per Paulum Queckum, 1565. 4°, pp. 344 + index. Adams F560.   **332.5.91**]

2.S.12   Hemingij Opera 4 vol   1604–21
Hemmingius, Nicolaus. There was no collected *Opera* of Hemmingius. Physical evidence – particularly the fore-edge numbers, which are the correct running shelf numbers for a date shortly after the catalogue of 1622 and before that of 1626 – indicates that the following four volumes are the ones seen by the cataloguer:
(1) Commentariorum in Evangelium secundum Iohannem, Decas Prior [-Pars altera]. [2 vols. in 1.] Basileae, per C. Waldkirch, 1590, 1591.

F°, coll. 651, 422 + indices. Adams H216. Fore-edge: "Hem*m*ing/ in/Iohan°/19".   **308.4.63**

(2) Commentaria In Omnes Epistolas Apostolorum... Et in Eam Quae Ad Hebraeos inscribitur. Argentorati, excud. T. Rihelius, 1586, F°, pp. 981 + index. Adams B1866. Fore-edge: "in/Epist°/20".   **308.4.64**

(3) Enarratio Viginti Et Unius Psalmorum Davidis. [Geneva] apud Petrum Santandreanum, 1592. 8°, pp. 635 + index. Adams B1512. Fore-edge: "21".   **321.7.69**

An undated list of the books in the "T.S." donation in the college's early accounts book (Bur.8.1) calls this volume – apparently incorrectly – "Hemmgius in Psalm. 24 priores".

(4) Opuscula Theologica... additis ... Notis. [Geneva], excud. Eustathius Vignon, 1586. F°, coll. 1680 + index. Adams H209. Fore-edge: "Op*uscu*la/Hemmin/gii/22".   **309.3.21**

Donor of all four volumes: Thomas Southaicke. Vols. 1 & 2 have the bookplate: "Ex dono T.S." with the London Grocers' Company arms.

Classis 2^{ae} Infer: Sect:

2.I.1   Zegedini Loci Com*munes*   1622–6
Kis, Stephanus, *Szegedinus.* Theologiae sincerae Loci Communes de Deo et Homine. Basileae, per Conrad. Waldkirchium, suis & Episcopianorum sumptibus, 1608. F°, pp. 655 + index. Missing. Register of Books Removed, p. 37, 1. 7: "St. Szegedi loci communes... Basil. 1608–10." Emmanuel's present copy was a Sancroft gift: S10.1.32[1].

2.I.2   Pfflatcherj Anal: Typica   1622–6
Pflacher, Moses. Analysis Typica Omnium cum veteris tum novi Testamenti Librorum Historicorum. Basiliae, per Conradum Waldkirch, 1587. F°, pp. 576 + indices. Adams P965. Fore-edge: "PFLACHER".
                                                                304.3.19

2.I.3   Osiandri Harm*.ª* Evang: 1584–97
Two books bound together:
(1) Osiander, Andreas. Harmoniae Evangelicae Libri IIII. [Gk & Lat.], Basileae, apud H. Frobenium & N. Episcopium, 1537. F°, ff. 145 + pp. 67. Adams 0356 (misnumbered 359).
(2) Altercatio Synagogae et Ecclesiae, in qua bona omnium fere utriusque instrumenti librorum pars explicatur: opus pervetustrum ac insigne... interlocutores Gamaliel & Paulus. Coloniae, apud Melchiorem Novesianum, 1537. F°, ff. 118. Adams A814. Fore-edge: "hermonia/euange*ca* osia*n*dri/27".   **303.4.15**

2.I.4 Gastij Parab[ae] 1584–97

Gast, Johannes. Parabolarum, sive Similitudinum ac dissimilitudinum Liber, ex... Ecclesiae Doctorum lucubrationibus... excerptus... Cum Epistola D. Ioannis Brentii. Basileae, per Balthasarem Lasium, 1540. F°, pp. 358. Adams G281. Fore-edge: "GAST:/PARAB/29". **306.4.59**

2.I.5 Hoffman de Penitent 1584–97

Hoffman, Christoph, *of Onoltzpach*. De poenitentia commentariorum Libri tres. Halae Suevorum, ex off. Petri Brubachii, 1540. F°, ff. 232. Adams H650. Fore-edge: "22/hofma*n*/ de peni/tencia". **303.4.64**

2.I.6 Brentius in Lucam 1597–1621

Brenz, Johannes. In Evangelii Quod Inscribitur Secundum Lucam, duodecim posteriora capita, Homiliae octoginta. Halae Suevorum, ex off. Petri Brubachii, 1540. F°, ff. 439–802. Adams B2788, pt 2 only. Fore-edge: "Brentius/in Lucam/8" and, more faintly and running vertically: "brenti*us* in 2[us] pt: Luce". **306.5.73**

2.I.7 Idem in Ioh*ann*em 1584–97

[1621 inventory (7.S.8): "Brentius in Iohann. usq*ue* ad 11. caput".]

Brenz, Johannes. Evangelion quod inscribitur, Secundum Ioannem, usq*ue* ad historiam de Lazaro a mortuis suscitato, octoginta duabus homiliis explicatum. (Undecim posteriora capita.) Missing. Emmanuel's present copy (Halae Suevorum, 1545; Adams B2796) was a Sancroft gift: S10.1.33.

2.I.8 Idem in Ep*isto*las ad Galat: et philip 1584–97

Two books bound together:

(1) Brenz, Johannes. Explicatio Epistolae Pauli ad Galatas. Halae Suevorum, per Petrum Frenitus, [15]46 [colophon: 1548]. 4°, ff. 216. Adams B2808

(2) Brenz, Johannes. Explicatio epistolae ad Philippenses. Halae Suevorum, excud. Petrus Frentius, 1548. 4°, ff. 90. Adams B2812. Fore-edge: "29/Bre. gal./ + philipp." **326.4.72**

2.I.9 Idem in Iob 1584–97

Brenz, Johannes. Hiob cum commentariis. Haganoae, per Iohan. Secerium, 1529. 8°, ff. 291. Adams B2777. Fore-edge: "28". **328.7.87**

2.I.10 Ejusdem Catachism 1584–97

Brenz, Johannes. Catechismus pia et utili explicatione illustratus. Francofurti, ex off. typog. Petri Brubacchii, 1551. 4°, pp. 670 [i.e. 707]. Adams B2751. Fore-edge: "30/Bre*n*tij expla/[?] [?]/chismus". **327.4.79**

2.I.11   Ejusdem Homiliae et Capito in Hos et Bulling de prophet functione.
1584–97
Three books bound together:
(1) Brenz, Johannes. Homiliae XXII sub incursione*m* Turcaru*m* in Germaniam. Haganoae, in off. Seceriana, 1533. 8°. Adams B2758. Signature on title page: "Edouard*us* Leeds".
(2) Capito, Wolfgang. In Hoseam prophetam. Argentorati, apud Ioannem Hervagium, 1528. 8°, ff. 284. Adams B1610.
(3) Bullinger, Heinrich. De Prophetae Officio. Tyguri, apud Christofferum Froschover, 1532. 8°. ff. [37]. Adams B3204. Fore-edge: "31" and (vertically): "homilia Brentii/[?]".   **321.7.70**
Donor: Edward Leeds.

2.I.12   Idem de poenit*entiâ*   1584–97
Brenz, Johannes. De Poenitentia...homili*ae* viginti quinq*ue*. Missing. A "memorandum" at the end of the 1637 catalogue includes "Brentius de penitentiâ" among the eighteen items "missing at the accounts at Easter 1637".

2.I.13   Capitonis Hexaemeron   1584–1621*
Capito, Wolfgang Fabricius. Hexemeron Dei opus explicatum. Argentorati, per Wendelinum Rihelium, 1539. 8°, ff. 299. Adams C597. Fore-edge: "42/Hexemeron/[?]".   **321.7.71**
*The inventory of c. 1597 includes a single volume designated only "Capito." The inventory of 1621 lists both the *Hexemeron* and "Resp: de Missa, de Matrim. &c." (see below). Which of the two entered the collection first is unknown.

2.I.14   Idem de Missa, Matrimonio, et jure Magistratus in Religione*m* 1584–1621*
Capito, Wolfgang Fabricius. Responsio, De Missa, Matrimonio & iure Magistratus in Religionem. Argentorati, per Wen[delinum] Rihelium, 1537. 8°, ff. 207. Adams C598. Fore-edge: "41/Capito de/missa:/matr:/iure".
*See note to 2.I.13.   **339.7.36**

2.I.15   Sarcerius in Mat, Marc, et Joh 3 vol   1584–97
Three separate books:
(1) Sarcerius, Erasmus. In Matthaeum Evangelistam iusta scholia. Francofurti, apud Christianum Egenolphum, 1538. 8°, ff. 367. Adams S404. Fore-edge: "Sarceri*us* in/matheum/32".   **321.6.15**
(2) Sarcerius, Erasmus. In Marcum Evangelistam iusta Scholia. Basileae, ex off. Barptholomaei VVesthemeri, 1539. 8°, pp. 398. Adams S406. Fore-edge: "33".   **321.6.17**
(3) Sarcerius, Erasmus. In Ioannem Evangelistam iusta Scholia. Basileae, apud Bartholomaeum Westhemerum, 1540. 8°, pp. 817 [i.e. 815]. Adams S408. Fore-edge: "Sarcerius/in Joh*annem*/34".   **321.6.16**

2.I.16   Idem in duas Epi*sto*las ad Corinth: 2 vol   1584–97
Two separate books:

(1) Sarcerius, Erasmus. In D. Pauli Epistolas ad Corinthios meditationes. Argentorati, per Wendelinum Rihclium, 1544. 8°, ff. 383. Adams S409. Fore-edge: "35/Sarcerius/super/p^{ia.} epistolam ad/Cor".   **323.5.113**

(2) Sarcerius, Erasmus. Piae et eruditae cogitationes in posteriorem ad Corinthios epistolam. Argentorati, per Wendelinum Rihelium, 1544. 8°, ff. 341 [i.e. 241]. Adams S410. Fore-edge: "36/Sarcerius/sup 2^{dam} epistolam/ad cor".   **321.7.75**

2.I.17   Ejusdem postillae   1584–97
Sarcerius, Erasmus. Postilla in Evangelia Dominicalia. Francofurti, apud Christianum Egenolphum, 1538. 8°, pp. 791. Adams S414. Fore-edge: "37/Postilla/Sarcerij".   **321.6.14**

2.I.18   Ejusdem Loci Comm: 2 vol   1584–97
Two separate books:
(1) Sarcerius, Erasmus. Praecipui sacrae scripturae communes loci. Francofurti, per Christianum Egenolphum, 1539. 8°, ff. 292. Adams S419. Fore-edge: "38/Loc. co./Sarcerij". "TC" stamped on covers.   **338.5.41**

(2) Sarcerius, Erasmus. Tomus Primus [-Secundus] Methodi in Praecipuos Scripturae Divinae locos, ad nuda Didactici generis praecepta, quo certa ratione sanctam Scripturam syncere tractare possint. Franc., apud Chr. Egenolphum, 1540. 8°, ff. 367, 215. Adams S240. Fore-edge: "methodus Sarcerij/41".   **326.4.90**

2.I.19   Idem de Consensu verae Ecclesiae et sanctorum Patrum super praecip: X^{tianae} relig Articulis   1584–97
Sarcerius, Erasmus. De consensu verae Ecclesiae, et SS. Patrum, in primis autem D. Augustini, super praecipuis Christianae religionis articulis, Liber. Francofurti, Christianus Egenolphus excud., 1540. 8°, ff. 263. Adams S399. Fore-edge: "Consensus/vere ecclesie/39".   **338.5.43**

2.I.20   Ejusdem Catechismus et Georgij Spalatini consolatoria exempla et sent^{ae} ex vitis et passionibus sanctorum.   1584–97
Three books bound together:
(1) Sarcerius, Erasmus. Catechismus per Omnes Quaestiones et Circumstantias in usum praedicatorum...absolutus. Francoforti, apud Christ. Egen., 1542. 8°, ff. 90. Adams S396.

(2) Spalatinus, Georgius. Magnifice Consolatoria exempla, & sententiae, ex Vitis & Passionibus Sanctorum & aliorum summorum Virorum. *Pref.* Martin Luther. Vitebergae, ex off. typog. Nicolai Schirlent, 1544. 8°. Adams S1530.

(3) Castellion, Sebastian. Dialogorum sacrorum, ad Linguam simul & mores puerorum formandos, libri quatuor. Basileae, ex officina Roberti Winter, 1545. 8°, pp. 310 [210]. Adams C916. Fore-edge: "40".   **321.7.76**

2.I.21 Gastius adversus Catabapt 1584–97
Gast, Johannes. De Anabaptismi Exordio, Erroribus, Historiis abominandis. Basileae, Robertus Winter excud., 1544. 8°, pp. 509. Adams G279.
Fore-edge: "40/Gast*us errores* [?]/catabap/tismus". **327.3.109**

2.I.22 Cogelij cap^ta Relig Antiqua 1584–97
Cogelius, Charieus. Religionis Antiquae ... Christianae Potissima capita.
Missing. Emmanuel's present copy (Tiguri, 1535: Adams C2313) was a Sancroft gift: S3.5.48.

2.I.23 Meier*us* in Epist*o*las ad Cor: et in Ep*istolam* ad Galat 1584–97
Two books bound together:
(1) Major [also Mayer; Meyer], Sebastian. In utranque...Epistolam ad Corinthios Commentarii. Francoforti, excud. Petrus Brubac, 1546. 8°, ff. 248. Adams M261.
(2) Major, Sebastian. Annotationes Breves et Eruditae...in Epistolam ad Galatas. [With the Latin text.] Apud Aventicorum Bernam, per Mathiam Apiarum, 1546. 8°, ff. 90. Adams B1926.
Fore-edge: "Coment*us*/Meiers/46". **321.6.18**

2.I.24 Hoffman in 2^dam ad Thess et de relig. X^tianâ, et de regno Anti-X^ti 1584–97
Two books bound together:
(1) Hoffman, Christoph, *of Onoltzpach*. Commentarius in Posteriorem D. Pauli ad Thessal. Francofurti, ex off. Petri Brubachii, 1545. 8°, ff. 63. Adams H651.
(2) Hoffman, Christoph, *of Onoltzpach*. De Christiana Religione, Et De Regno Antichristi. Francofurti, ex off. Petri Brubachii, 1545. 8°, ff. 180 + index. Adams H649.
Fore-edge: "HOFMA*N*/43". **321.7.78**

2.I.25 Idem in Epist*o*lam ad Titum 1584–97
Hoffman, Christoph, *of Onoltzpach*. Commentarii in Epistolam Pauli ad Titum. Francofurti, ex off. Petri Brubachii, 1541. 8°, ff. 243. Adams H652.
Fore-edge: "44/hofma*n*/ad titu*m*". **325.7.3**

2.I.26 Ecclesiae Tigurinae Confessio 1584–97
Zurich. Orthodoxa Tigurinae Ecclesiae ministrorum Confessio...una cum...responsione ad vanas...D. Mart. Lutheri calumnias. *Tr.* R. Gualtherus. Tiguri, apud Christ. Frosch., 1545. 8°, ff. 135. Adams Z199.
Fore-edge: "Confess:/Tigurini/40". **321.6.29**

2.I.27 Althameri Sylva nom Biblic 1584–97
Althamer, Andreas. Sylva biblicorum nominum...quorum in sacris Bibliis mentio. Basileae, in aed. Thomae Volfii, 1535. 8°. Adams A823.
Fore-edge: "Althameri*us*/Sylva/20". **321.6.76**

2.I.28 Ejusdem Conciliationes Script^{ae} 1584–97
Althamer, Andreas. Conciliationes Scripturae. Norimbergae, apud Io.
Petreium, 1534. 8°, ff. 236. Adam A816. Fore-edge: "Altha-
meri/Conciliat/6". **321.7.79**

2.I.29 Lossius in Evang dominicalia 1584–97
Lossius, Lucas [ed]. Annotationes Scholasticae in Evangelia Dominicalia,
et ea quae in Festis Iesu Christi, et Sanctorum eius praecipuis, leguntur in
Ecclesia [with the text]. Lipsiae, in officina haeredum V. Papae, 1560. 8°,
pp. 595, 199. Adams B1880. Fore-edge: "L. Lossius/in euangel:/
dominic:/26". **321.6.11**

2.I.30 Chytraeus in Epistolas dominicales 1584–97
Chytraeus, David, the elder. Dispositiones Epistolarum, Quae Diebus
Dominicis et Aliis, in Ecclesia... proponi solent. Vitebergae, excud.
Iohannes Crato, 1566. 8°, pp. 636. Adams C1588. Fore-edge:
"Chytraej/Epist:/45". **321.6.75**

2.I.31 Oecolampadius in Matth: et serm populares et Oratio A° 1526, et de Missa
et de Imaginibus 1584–97
Oecolampadius, Johannes. Enarratio in Evangelium Matthaei... & alia
nonnulla. Basileae, 1536. 8°, ff. 235. Adams O92. Fore-edge: "Oecolampa:/in
Matth./4". **326.4.103**

2.I.32 Idem in Johannem: 1584–97
Oecolampadius, Johannes. Annotationes Piae ac Doctae in Evangelium
Ioannis. Basileae, per And. Cratandrum et Io. Bebelium, 1533. 8°, ff. 381.
Adams O93. Fore-edge: "5/Oecolamped/in Johannem". **321.6.19**

2.I.33 Idem in Epistolam ad Hebr^{os} 1584–97
Oecolampadius, Johannes. In Epistolam Ad Hebraeos. Argentorati, apud
Mathiam Apiarium, 1534. Missing.

2.I.34 Weinrichius in Epistolam ad Rom 1625
Weinrichius, George Silesius. Commentarii Super... Epistolam Romanis
inscriptam & nuncupatam pars prior [and posterior]. Lipsiae, Michael
Lantzenberger exscribebat, sumptibus Thomae Schureri Bibliopolae, 1608.
4°, pp. 507, 404. Donor: Dr John Richardson. Fore-edge: "WENRICH: ad
Roman:". **327.4.73**

2.I.35 Pelargi Bibliotheca Theolog 1622–6
Pelargus, Christophorus. Bibliotheca Theologica. Missing.

2.I.36 Graweri absurda absurdorum &c 1622–6
Grawer [also Grauer], Albert. Absurda, Absurdorum, Absurdissima,

Calvinistica Absurda. Magdeburgi, apud Iohannem Francum, 1606. 4°.
Fore-edge: "Grauerus/Absurd[?]".   **333.4.43**

2.I.37 Idem de Satisfactione X^{ti} 1622–6
Grawer [also Grauer], Albert. Dissertationes de novo ac horrendo errore
circa doctrinam de Satisfactione Christi pro peccatis generis humani,
sophisticationibus C. Ostorodi et F. Socini Neo-Arrianis seu potius
Photinianis oppositae. Missing. A "memorandum" at the end of the 1637
catalogue includes "Grawerus de satisfactione" among the items "missing
at the accounts at Easter 1637".

2.I.38 Wirtenbergenses in lib Concordiae   1625
Würtemberg. Vera et Solida Refutatio Conviciorum...Quas Iesuitae
Duobus Maledicentissimis Libellis...per orbem Christianum sparserunt.
Quorum alter titulum habet: Iudicium Roberti Bellarmini Politiani...de
Libro...Concordiae. Alter vero...inscribitur: Patefactio ingentis
stulticię...Libri Concordiae Lutheranorum. Ad Universos Salutis aeter-
nae amantes commonefaciendos. A Theologis Wirtembergicis Conscripta.
Tubingae, apud Georgium Gruppenbachium, 1587. 4°, pp. 343. Adams
W269. Donor: Dr John Richardson. Fore-edge: "WIRT/emberg/Refut [?]".
                                                                    332.5.114

2.I.39 Lutheri Loci Com*mun*es   **1622–6**
Luther, Martin. Loci Communes...ex scriptis ipsius latinis forma
Gnomologica & Aphoristica collecti...a M. Theodosio Fabricio.
Magdeburgi, typis Andreae Genae, impensis Ambrosii Kirchneri, 1594. 4°,
pp. 125, 153, 206, 88, 152. Adams L2072. Fore-edge: "Lutheri
loci/com*mun*es".   **330.2.42**

Classis 3^a

3.1   Fran: de Mendoza in lib Regum: 2 vol   1628–32
Mendoza, Francisco de. Commentariorum in Quatuor Libros Regum.
Coloniae Agrippinae, sumptibus Petri Henningii, 1628. [2 vols.] F°, pp.
564, 636 + indices. Donor: Thomas Ball. Missing. Register of Books
Removed, p. 21, 1. 6: "Mendoza in 4Ls. Regum.... Cologni: 1628 M. Th:
Ball." Emmanuel's present copy was a Sancroft gift: S7.6.24.

3.2   Nugno in 3^{tiam} Thomae   Aug. 19, 1633
Nugnus, Didacus. Commentaria scholastica in Tertiam partem S. Thomae
Aquinatis...De Sacramentis Ecclesiae. [2 pts in 1 vol.] Coloniae
Agrippinae, ex off. Choliniana, sumpt. P. Cholini, 1630. F°, pp. 456,
485 + indices. Donor: Nicholas Preston. Inscription on flyleaf: "Ex dono
Nicolai Preston in Artibus Magistri/et huiusce collegij alumni Augusti die
19 1633". Fore-edge: "Nugno in 3^{am}/Thom:".   **310.3.39**

3.3 Theophil in Evang Gr: lat May 3, 1632
Theophylactus, *Abp of Ochrida.* Commentarii in Quatuor Evangelia. [Gk & Lat.] *Tr.* Iohannes Oecolampadius, *ed.* Philippus Montanus. Lutetiae Parisiorum, apud C. Morellum, 1631. F°, pp. 848. Donor: John Crossley. Inscription on half-title page: "Ex dono Johannis Crosley in Artibus Magistrij & hujusce Collegij alumni. Maij 3° an° 1632". Fore-edge: "Theophylact/in Evan gr [?]/I". **301.2.47**

3.4 Optatus Milevitanus 1631–3
Optatus, *St, Bp of Mela.* Opera. Parisiis, apud Claudium Sonnium, 1631. F°, pp. 557, 336. Donor: John Poole. Inscription on flyleaf: "Ex dono Johannis Poole in Artibus Magistrij & hujusce Collegij alumni". Fore-edge: "Optatus". **301.2.49**

3.5 Jo: Hussi ~~Historia~~ operu*m* pars 1ᵃ. 1630
Huss, Johann. Ioannis Hus, et Hieronymi Pragensis historia et monumenta. [Prima pars.] Noribergae, in off. Ioannis Montani, & Ulrici Neuberi, 1558. F°, ff. [471]. Adams H1207. Donor: Anthony Tuckney. Inscription on title page: "Ex dono Antonij Tuckney/hujus Collegij Socij/1630."
303.4.61

3.6 Euclides cum Coment 1628–32
Euclid. [Elements, with Proclus's commentary on Bk I.] Στοιχείων βιβλ. ιέ-ἐκ τῶν Θέωνος συνουσιῶν. Εἰς τοῦ αὐτοῦ τὸ πρῶτον ἐξηγημάτων Πρόκλου βιβλ.δ'. [Gk.] *Ed.* Simon Grynaeus. [2 pts in 1 vol.]. Basileae, apud I. Hervagium, 1533. F°, pp. 268, 115. Missing. Register of Books Removed, p. 17, 1. 20: "Euclides cum notis Procli in Ls. 4 priores ... Basil 1533." Emmanuel's present copy was a Sancroft gift: S6.2.8.
   The original copy was a presentation copy from the editor, Grynaeus, to Sir Thomas More. It is now owned by the Bodleian Library (Byw. C.3.3). The book and its provenance are described in J. B. Trapp and Hubertus Schulte Herbrüggen, *"The King's Good Servant": Sir Thomas More, 1477/8–1535* (London, 1978), item 78, p. 52.

3.7 Purchas his Pilgrims 4 vol 1628–32
Purchas, Samuel. Purchas his pilgrimes In Five Bookes, 4 Pts [4 vols.] London, W. Stansby for H. Fetherstone, 1625. F°, pp. 1860 [I and II]; 1973 [III and IV]+indices. STC 20509. Donor: Henry Featherstone. Inscription on flyleaf of each vol.: "Ex dono Mʳ Henrici Fetherstone/Bibliopolae Londinensis." **307.3.21–24**

3.8 Procopius in Esaiam 1628–32
Procopius, *Gaza.* Variarum in Esaiam Prophetam commentationum epitome. [Gk & Lat.] *Tr.* Johannes Curterius. Parisiis, apud Michaelem Sonnium, 1580. F°, pp. 764+index. Missing. Register of Books Removed,

p. 9, 1. 22: "Procopius in Esaiam...Gr: Lat: Cauterij...Paris. 1580".
Emmanuel's present copy (Adams P2157) was a Sancroft gift: S4.2.30.

3.9   Bellarmini Controversias 1 vol   1628–32
       Bellarminus, Robertus. Disputationum...De Controversiis Christianae
       Fidei adversus huius temporis Haereticos. [2 vols. in 1?] Coloniae
       Agrippinae, 1628. Missing. Register of Books Removed, p. 31, 1. 19:
       "Bellarmini Controversia...Col: 1628."

3.10   Philostrati Lemnij opera   1628–32
       Philostratus, Flavius, *the Elder, et al.* Philostrati Lemnii Opera....
       Philostrati Iunioris Imagines, et Callistrati Ecphrases. Item Eusebii
       Caesariensis Episcopi liber contra Hieroclem. [Gk & Lat.] Parisiis, ex
       officina C. Morelli, 1608. F°, pp. 914 + index. Fore-edge: "Philostratus".
                                                              306.3.35

3.11   Pineda in Iob 2 vol.   1628–32
       Pineda, Le P. Juan de. Commentariorum in Iob. 2 vols. Missing. Em-
       manuel's present copy (Paris, 1631 in 1 vol.) was a Sancroft gift: S7.1.16.

3.12   Arriba de grat et lib arbitrio   1628–32
       Arriba, Franciscus de. Operis conciliatorii, gratiae et liberi arbitrii creati
       perfectam concordiam....explicantis...tomus primus. Parisiis, apud
       Laurentium Sonnium, 1622. 4°. Missing. Register of Books Removed, p. 51,
       1. 35: "Fr: de Arriba de Gratiâ, libero arbitrio &c...Par: 1622".
       Emmanuel's present copy was a Sancroft gift: S13.3.20.

3.13   Vrsinus in Isaiam   1628–32
       Ursinus, Zacharias. Commentarium in Prophetiam Isaiae. Missing.

3.14   Theophilact in Epistolas Graecolat   1636–7
       Theophylactus, *Abp of Ochrida.* ἐξήγησις τῶν ἐπιστολῶν τοῦ ἁγίου παύλου.
       Theophylacti...in D. Pauli Epistolas commentarii. [Gk & Lat.] *Ed.* A.
       Lindsell & T. Bayly, *Tr.* P. Montanus. Londini, E. Typographeo Regio,
       1636. F°, pp. 1041. STC 23948. Donor: Edward Thornton. Fore-edge: "II".
          This item and the four following were added to the 1632 inventory in a
       hand different from that of the cataloguer, under the heading: "Ex dono
       Edovardi Thornton." Thornton was an Emmanuel graduate (B.A. 1628–9,
       M.A. 1632) who died Dec. 16, 1635.   **301.2.48**

3.15   Iansenius in Harmoniam Evangelic   1636–7
       Jansenius, Cornelius, *Bp of Ghent.* Commentariorum in suam Concordiam,
       ac totam Historiam Evangelicam Partes IV. Moguntiae, apud
       Balthasarum Lippium, 1612. F°, pp. 615, 312. Donor: Edward Thornton;
       see note to 3.14. Fore-edge: "Ianse/nii Com/Evang".   **306.2.6**

3.16   Becani Opuscula Theolog: vol 2   1636–7
Becanus, Martinus. Opuscula Theologica. Parisiis, apud Ioannem Petit-
Pas, 1633. F°, pp. 111, 177, 107, 116, 328. Donor: Edward Thornton; see
note to 3.14. Missing. Register of Books Removed, p. 51, 1. 15: "Mart:
Becani Opuscula Theologica ... Par: 1633". Emmanuel's present copy was
a Sancroft gift: S13.1.29.

3.17   Estius in Epistolas   1636–7
Estius [also Van Est], Gulielmus. Absolutissima in omnes Beati Pauli et
Septem Catholicas Apostolorum Epistolas Commentaria. Coloniae
Agrippinae, sumptibus Petri Henningii, 1631. F°, pp. 1314. Donor: Edward
Thornton; see note to 3.14. Missing. Register of Books Removed, p. 21, 1.
11: "Estius in Epistolas ... Col: Agrip: 1631". Emmanuel's present copy was
a Sancroft gift: S7.2.1.

3.18   Lessij opuscula   1636–7
Lessius, Leonardus. Opuscula: quibus pleraque sacrae Theologiae mysteria
explicantur. Antuerpiae, ex officina Plantiniana, Apud Balthasarum
Moretum, & Viduam Ioannis Moreti, & Io. Meursium, 1626. F°, pp.
922 + index. Donor: Edward Thornton; see note to 3.14.
                                                          [**Possibly: 308.3.49**]

Classis 4ᵃ

4.1   Biblia Lat fo M:S: 1601
Bible [Latin]. Includes Prologues of Jerome and a genealogy of Christ.
15th-century ornamented ms on vellum. $21\frac{3}{4} \times 15\frac{5}{8}$, ff. 316. Donor: John
Newcourt. Inscription on f.2: "Johannes Newecovrt de Pickwel/in Perochia
Georgeham in/comitatu Deuon. Armiger/dedit istum librum Collegio/
Emanuelis Cantabrigiae: Anno/Domini millessimo sexcentissimo/primo.
Etatis dicti Johanis octoges = /simo/per me Johen Newcovrt". CMA 69; M.
R. James 264.   **Yy.3.17**

4.2   Sundry workes of Martyrs 6 vol M:S: 1584–97
Letters and other writings by many Protestant martyrs. Works by Bishop
Ridley and John Bradford are the most numerous but Cranmer, Hooper,
Careless, Philpot, Tymms, and others are represented. Most are not in the
handwriting of the authors. Now in 3 vols. $13\frac{5}{8} \times 9\frac{3}{4}$; $12\frac{1}{2} \times 8\frac{1}{2}$; $8\frac{1}{2} \times 6\frac{1}{4}$.
According to the three earliest inventories these volumes were not shelved
with the other books but were catalogued with the library's furnishings, an
indication that they were given a place of special prominence and were
perhaps more highly prized by the college than any other books. Not in T.
James; CMA 99–101; M. R. James 260–262. **MSS 4.1.17, 18; MSS 4.2.29**

4.3   Psal: Graec: M: S: 1600–21

Fragment of a 12th-century Greek Psalter on vellum. $10\frac{5}{8} \times 7\frac{1}{4}$, ff. $26 + 1$. Facsimiles of 2 pp. reproduced in *Cambridge Antiquarian Society Proceedings*, 8(1892–3), p. 168 ff. CMA 32; M. R. James 253. **MSS 3.3.22**

4.4   No: Test pars Gr: MS   July 9, 1598

Epistolae Pauli Graece. 10th-11th century. Tiny vellum pages. $3\frac{5}{8} \times 3\frac{1}{8}$, ff. $144 + 1$. Donor: Samuel Wright. Inscription on flyleaf: "Collegio Emmanuelis in Testimonium grati animi D. D. Samuel Wright ejusdem Collegii Alumnus Anno 1598 Pridie nonas Iulias". T. James 3; CMA 3; M. R. James 110. **MSS 1.4.35**

4.5   Gregorius de interna X^ti Locucione MS   1600–21

Kempis, Thomas à. De Imitatione Christi, Books III and IV only. Book III is entitled "De interna Christi locucione ad animam fidelem." $15\frac{9}{16} \times 3\frac{5}{8}$, ff. 108. 15th-century hand on vellum. Probably Flemish. Inscription on f. 2*b*, "Gregorius Man." Fore-edge: "Greg/4 + [?]". CMA 77; M. R. James 94. **MSS 1.4.15**

4.6   Rabanus in Mat M:S: 1600

Rabanus Maurus, *Abp of Mainz.* Commentary on Matthew. 12th-13th-century hand on vellum. $6\frac{1}{4} \times 4\frac{1}{8}$, ff. $203 + 3$. Donor: Ralph Cudworth. Inscription on flyleaf: "Rodolphus Cudworth Collegio/Emmanuelis, dedit/Anno 1600." Fore-edge: "35". CMA 78; M. R. James 91. **MSS 1.4.12**

4.7   A Catalogue of the Lyveings in England and Wales MS   1627-32

Valor Beneficiorum Angliae et Walliae. Written in 1627 on paper. $15\frac{3}{4} \times 10\frac{1}{4}$, ff. $6 + 89$. Not in CMA; M. R. James 119. **MSS 2.1.10**

4.8   Gregorij Moralia MS   1600

Gregory I, *Pope, the Great.* Moralia. $19\frac{1}{2} \times 12$, ff. 223. 14th-century English hand on vellum. Donor: Ralph Cudworth. M. R. James says of the illumination: "The decoration of the volume is of the first class.... The drawing admirable throughout. Altogether a most notable example of English art." Inscription at top of f.1: "Anno 1600 Collegio Emmanuelis Dedit Rodolph: Cudworth. eiusdem Coll: Socius." Fore-edge: "greg". CMA 68; M. R. James 112. **MSS 2.1.1**

4.9   Gorranus in Epistolas, M: S   1584–97

Gorran, Nicolaus de. Super Epistolas Pauli. [And] Super Actus Apostolorum $17\frac{1}{4} \times 12\frac{3}{8}$, ff. $335 + 3$. Two 15th-century hands on vellum. Beautifully painted and illuminated borders. Fore-edge: "Gorran*us*/25". T. James 6; CMA 6; M. R. James 113. **MSS 2.1.3**

4.10   Lyra in Epistolas et Act et Apocal: M:S   1629
Lyra, Nicolas de. Super Epistolas Pauli, Epistolas Canonicas, Actus, Apocalypsin. $15\frac{1}{2} \times 11\frac{1}{2}$, ff. $197 + 2$; paper. Dutch hand, 1460, with decorative initials. Donor: Thomas Ball. Inscription on verso of flyleaf, opposite p. 1: "Ex dono Thome Ball hujus Collegii Socii/Anno D. 1629". Fore-edge, top to bottom: "LYRA IN EPISTOLAS, ACTA, & APOCALYPSIN". CMA 44; M. R. James 118. M. R. James erroneously calls the donor Thomas Bell. Ball was a favorite student of John Preston during his mastership.   **MSS 2.1.9**

4.11   Propositiones et Tractat plurimi de potestate papali et Regali M:S:
                                                                    1584–97
Miscellaneous tracts and other writings copied in a 15th–16th-century hand on vellum. $14\frac{1}{4} \times 10\frac{3}{8}$, ff. $247 + 1$. Fore-edge: "PROPOSITIONES &c:". T. James 1; CMA 1.1–34; M. R. James 9.   **MSS 1.1.9**

4.12   Lethberti flores Psalt MS   1600–21
Lethbertus (*Abbot of St Ruphus.* Selections from the Psalms. 15×11), ff. 117. Late 15th-century non-English hand on paper. Inscriptions at bottom of last page: "Robertus Fowberie" and "Tho: Bywater. 1600". Bywater was probably the donor. CMA 123; M. R. James 120.   **MSS 2.1.11**

4.13   Horologium Sap^ae MS   1600–21
Suso, Henricus. Horologium Sapientiae and other assorted works not by Suso. $8\frac{1}{8} \times 5\frac{1}{2}$, ff. $191 + 3$. 15th-century English hand on vellum. Inscription on flyleaf indicates ownership in 1478 by Robertus Fowberius; inscription on flyleaf recto: "Tho: Bywaters/booke". Bywater was probably the donor. CMA 126; M. R. James 65.   **MSS 1.3.12**

4.14   Aquinas de fide, spe, et charitate MS   1600
Aquinas, Thomas. Tracts on various subjects. $7\frac{3}{8} \times 5\frac{1}{4}$, ff. $163 + 2$. 13th–14th-century hand on vellum. Donor: Ralph Cudworth. Inscription on flyleaf: "Collegii Emmanuelis/Liber: Ex dono/Rodolphi Cudworthi eiusdem/Coll. socii./Anñ domini. 1600." Fore-edge: "34". CMA 41; M. R. James 40.   **MSS 1.2.19**

4.15   Bedae Hist et Gyrald Cambrensis Hist Hibern: M:S   1613–21
Bede, *The Venerable, St,* Ecclesiastical History [Lat.] and Giraldus Cambrensis, geographical and historical writings on Ireland. [Lat.] $14\frac{1}{2} \times 9\frac{3}{4}$, ff. 120. Probably Flemish hand, 1481, on vellum with elaborate ornaments. Donor (?): John White. Inscription on f.1: "Jo: White, 1613." CMA 18; M. R. James 3.   **MSS 1.1.3**

4.16   Orig: Hieron: Lanfranc Anselmus et Beda in omnes pauli epistolas MS
                                                                    1600–21

Robert of Bridlington, *compiler.* Super Epistolas Pauli. $13\frac{7}{8} \times 8\frac{7}{8}$, ff. 232. 12th-century hand on vellum. This manuscript includes the verses of the Epistles in red ink, followed by commentaries in black ink. The commentaries of Origen, Jerome, Lanfranc, Anselm, and Bede are the most prominent. Fore-edge: "14". CMA 17; M. R. James 8.   **MSS 1.1.8**

4.17   Gregorius in Ezech   1600–21
[1626 inventory (10.I.7): "Greg in Ezek M.S."]
Gregory I, *Pope, the Great.* In Ezechielem. $12\frac{1}{2} \times 7\frac{7}{8}$, ff. 130 + 1. Early 12th-century hand on vellum. M. R. James notes: "Written for a monastery dedicated to St. Germanus, probably Selby." Donor: Thomas Bywater. Inscription on flyleaf: "Liber Coll:Emmanuelis/ex dono Tho: Bywatere". Fore-edge: "36". CMA 16; M. R. James 143.   **MSS 2.2.18**

4.18   Tractatus Patriarchae Antiocheni MS   1600–21
Concilium Basileense. Acts of the council, sermons, notes, and miscellanea. $12 \times 8\frac{1}{2}$, ff. 198. 15th-century English hand on paper. Donor: Ralph Cudworth. Inscription at top of f.1: "Ex dono Rodol: Cudworth". CMA 118; M. R. James 142.   **MSS 2.2.17**

4.19   Lactantius: M:S: 1584–97
[1621 inventory (2.I.40): "Augustinus Manuscript:"]
Lactantius Firmianus, Lucius Coelius. A note on p. 1 reads: "NB: This M.S. was written in the year 1424; & contains all the works of Lactantius except 2 or 3 little Poems, which have been disputed by some of the Critics." The manuscript begins with extracts from Augustine and Jerome about Lactantius. This accounts for the 1621 catalogue's description. Flemish. Paper, $11\frac{5}{8} \times 8\frac{1}{2}$, ff. 186. T. James 4; CMA4; M. R. James 238.
                                                                                 MSS 3.3.5

4.20   Cicero de officijs et Parad   1584–97
Cicero, Marcus Tullius. [De Officiis & Paradoxa. Mainz,] Johannes Fust & Petri [Schoeffer] 1465. F°, ff. [88]. [Printed in red and black on vellum. Beautifully illuminated; with the arms of Arthur, Prince of Wales.] Hain 5238. Proctor 80. CMA 47.   **MSS 5.3.11**

4.21   Biblia Lat M:S: 1619–21
Bible [Latin] [Possibly: $9\frac{1}{4} \times 6\frac{3}{8}$, ff. 358. 13th-century ms on vellum with illuminated initials. Donor: John Foxcroft. Inscription on flyleaf: "Magister Foxcroft, hujus olim Collegij alum*nus*, &/scholaris discipulus, Ecclesiae nunc Gothamensis/Rector, huic Bibliothecae D.D.D.Q." John Foxcroft received his B.A. at Emmanuel in 1615, became rector at Gotham, Notts., in 1619, remaining there until his death in 1662. He may have given this ms to Emmanuel on taking that position, though the date of the gift is not specified. CMA 70; M. R. James 23.   **MSS 1.2.2]**

4.22   Isidorus in Pentateuch MS   1597–1600

Isidore, *St, Bishop of Seville.* Super 5 libros. Moysis cum versibus & Epigram. quibusdam. $9 \times 5\frac{5}{8}$, ff. $79 + 3$. 12th-century hand on vellum. Fore-edge: "ISIDORVS". T. James 7; CMA 7; M. R. James 38.   **MSS 1.2.17**

4.23   The Lives of Certayne Philosophers MS   1600–21

Dictes and Sayinges of Philosophers. $8\frac{5}{8} \times 6\frac{1}{2}$, ff. $78 + 1$. 15th-century hand on vellum. Donor: Samuel Starlinge. Inscription at top of flyleaf: "Ex dono Samuelis Starlinge/quondam socii"; "24/The Lyves of certaine/ Phylosophers". CMA 104; M. R. James 31.   **MSS 1.2.10**

4.24   Chrisostomus ad Theodorum Lapsum   Mar. 5, 1598

[1622 inventory (2.I.27); "Chrysost: ad Theodorum Lapsum: Tractatus de Eo quod nemo Laeditur. MS"]

John, *Chrysostom, St* [Includes three tracts:] Ad Theodorum Lapsum de reparacione eiusdem; Libellus quod nemo laeditur nisi a semetipso; De compunctione cordis ad Demetrium $8\frac{1}{2} \times 5\frac{3}{4}$, ff. 88. Donor: George Barcroft. 15th-century hand on vellum. Inscription on recto of flyleaf: "Ex dono M^{ri} Georgij Barcroft Ecclesiae Cathedralis Eliensis Ἀρχεχόρου." and on verso: "Mr Georgius Barcroft Collegio Emmanuelis dono dedit An° Dn̄i 1597 Mart: 5°." Fore-edge: "Chr" CMA 5; M. R. James 37.   **MSS 1.2.16**

4.25   Διοπτρα, dialogus inter Corpus et animam MS   1584–97

Philippus Solitarius. Dioptra [Gk] [and] John, *Chrysostom, St*, Serm. de ramis palmarum. [Gk.] $7\frac{7}{8} \times 5\frac{1}{4}$, ff. 159. 14th-century hand on paper. Donor(?): Hugh Broughton. Signed at top of f.1: "Hugo Broughton D." CMA 8, 80; M. R. James 59.   **MSS 1.3.6**

4.26   Bibl: Hier: Lat: MS   1584–97

Bible [Latin]. [Probably: M. R. James 82. $6\frac{1}{2} \times 4\frac{1}{2}$, ff. 628. 13th-century hand on vellum (uterine). With Jerome's Prologues. Fore-edge: "Bib Hier: vers/33".   **MSS 1.4.3**]

4.27   Coletus in 1^{am} ad Cor: MS   c. 1630

Colet, John. In Epistolam Pauli ad Corinthios 1^a. $9\frac{5}{8} \times 6\frac{1}{4}$, ff. $120 + 2$. Early 16th-century hand (Peter Meghen?) on vellum. Donor: Anthony Tuckney. Inscription on flyleaf: "Coll. Emman. Cantabr./Ex dono M^{ri} Anthonij Tuckney in Sacra/Theologia Baccalaurej, & hujus Collegij Socij." CMA 103; M. R. James 245.   **MSS 3.3.12**

4.28   Libri undecim Allegoriarum MS.   1632–7

Petrus, *Comestor.* Allegoriae. $13\frac{1}{2} \times 9\frac{5}{8}$, ff. 36. 13th-century hand on vellum. CMA 42; M. R. James 126.   **MSS 2.1.20**

4.29   Wicklevi Chronicon Ceremoniarum. M.S. 8vo 1637–49?

English tract on ceremonies ordained by several of the popes. Inscription on end paper: "Wiclevi Caeremoniarum Chronicon cujus initium deest. Balaeus de script. Brit. Cent. 6.I." and, apparently in a different hand, "G. Dill." 7 × 5, ff. 29. 15th-century hand on vellum.

This item and the following two were added to the catalogue after 1637 – perhaps in 1649, when the last item was donated. The handwriting of these three entries is different from that of the rest of the inventory but the same as that used to list at the end of the 1637 catalogue several donations in the years 1649–51. CMA 74; M. R. James 85.   **MSS 1.4.6**

4.30   Biblia latina M.S. 8°   1637–49?

Bible [Latin]. [Possibly: M. R. James 87. $6\frac{1}{4} \times 4\frac{3}{8}$, ff. 387 & 1. 13th-century hand on vellum. With the items preceding and following, this item was added to the catalogue after 1637 – perhaps in 1649, when the next item was donated. See note to 4.29.   **MSS 1.4.8**]

4.31   A book of chirurgerie M.S. 4to 1649

John, *of Ardern*. Begins: "This is a mirrour of bloodletynge in Þe weche Þey Þat wolen beholden it diligently...." etc. Tables and drawings. $8\frac{1}{4} \times 4\frac{3}{8}$, ff. 210. 15th-century hand on paper. Donor: Humphrey Moseley. Inscription: "Collegio Emanuelis sacrum posuit Humfredus Moseley Armiger, & Sociorum Commensalis 1649". CMA 12; M. R. James 69. See note to 4.29.
                                                                  MSS 1.3.17

Classis 5^{ae} Superior Sect

5.S.1   Calvini Opera 12 vol   c. 1598

This entry was one of four which first appeared at the end of the inventory of c. 1597. One of these four new items is known to have been donated in October of 1598 (see 5.I.15). The Calvin volumes were probably added at about the same time.

No true collected *Opera* of Calvin was published until after 1637. This entry therefore describes twelve discrete books. Because of Calvin's popularity in the seventeenth century, his works were amply represented in the libraries of some of Emmanuel's chief late seventeenth-century benefactors, including John Breton, whose bequest came to the library in 1676, and William Sancroft (1693). Their copies apparently supplemented or replaced all of the copies which had arrived in 1598. None of the latter, at any rate, are now present in the Emmanuel collection, while the gifts of Breton and Sancroft are. Oddly, only one of the discarded items appears in the Register of Books Removed. In arriving at the following list of probable works and editions of the earliest Calvin holdings, we have relied on an undated catalogue (Emm. Lib. 1.1) which is supposed to have been made in c. 1680 and which lists thirteen Calvin volumes, one of which appears to describe the Breton gift, a volume containing commentaries on several of Paul's minor epistles (see Adams C331, 332 [omits Emmanuel's copy], 333, 334, 335). We omit this volume from the following list.

Calvin, John [Possibly the following 12 vols.:

[I.   In quinque libros Mosis, commentarii.... Eiusdem in librum Iosue commentarius. (Geneva,) in off. Sanctandreana, 1595. F°, pp. 320, 594, 79. Missing. Catalogue c. 1680, G3.1: "Jo Calvinus in Pentateuchum & Josuam fol: Genev. 1595." Emmanuel's present holdings include only the Joshua Commentary (Geneva, 1564: Adams C280), which was a Sancroft gift: S7.5.12.

[II.   In librum Iobi conciones. *Ed.* Theodore Beza. Genevae, apud haered. Eustathii Vignon, 1593. F°, pp. 764. Missing. Catalogue c. 1680, G3.2: "... in Jobum cum praefatione Theod. Bezae Genev: 1593."

[III. In librum Psalmorum commentarius. (Geneva,) excud. Nicolaus Barbirius & Thomas Courteau, 1564. 8°, pp. 893. Missing. Catalogue c. 1680, G3.3: "... in Psalmos fol: Genev: 1578." Emmanuel's present copy (Geneva, 1564: Adams C287) was a Sancroft gift: S7.4.35.

[IV.   Commentarii in Isaiam Prophetam. *Ed.* N. Gallasius. (Geneva,) Excudebat E. Vignon, 1583. F°, pp. 530. Missing. Catalogue c. 1680, G3.4: "... in Esaiam, fol: 1583." Emmanuel's present copy (London, 1609) was a gift of Samuel Richardson: 313.4.73.

[V.   Praelectiones in librum Ieremiae, et Lamentationes. Tertia ed. Genevae, apud haered. Eustath. Vignon, 1589. F°, ff. 436. Missing. Catalogue c. 1680, G3.5: "... in Jeremiam & Threnos. fol: Genev: 1589."

[VI.   Praelectiones in Ezechielis viginti capita priora. *Ed.* Ioannes Budaeus & Carolus Ionvilaeus (Geneva,) apud Petrum Sanctandreanum, 1583. F°, ff. 128. Missing. Bound with: Praelectiones in librum prophetiarum Danielis, edition unknown. Catalogue c. 1680, G3.6: "... in Ezek: & Danielem: fol: Genev: 1583." Emmanuel's present holdings include only the Ezekiel Commentary (Geneva, 1565: Adams C300), which was a Sancroft gift: S7.4.34.

[VII. Praelectiones in duodecim prophetas minores. Genevae, apud Eustathium Vignon, 1581. F°, pp. 795. Missing. Catalogue c. 1680, G3.7: "... in 12. Prophetas minores fol: Gen: 1581."

[VIII. Harmonia ex Evangelistis tribus composita. Genevae, apud haered. Eustathii Vignon, 1595. F°, pp. 376, 210. Missing. Catalogue c. 1680, G3.8: "... ejus Harmon: in 3 priores Evangelist: cum comment: in eadem fol. Gen: 1595." Emmanuel's present copy (Geneva, 1553: Adams C353 [omits Emmanuel's copy]) was a Sancroft gift: S7.2.26[1].

[IX.   (1) Commentarii in omnes Pauli... epistolas, atque etiam in epistolam ad Hebraeos. (Et) in omnes epistolas canonicas. Genevae, apud Eustathium Vignon, 1580. F°, pp. 624, 116. Apparently bound with: (2) In evangelium secundum Iohannem commentarius. (Paris,) excud. Robertus Stephanus, 1553. F°, ff. 133, and (3) Commentarii in Acta Apostolorum. Genevae, Eustathius Vignon, 1584. F°, pp. 258. Catalogue c. 1680, G3.9: "... in epistolas omnes fol: Genevae 1580. cum commet: in D. Johann: & Acta. fol. ibidem. 1584." Missing. Emmanuel's present copies (Geneva, 1565: Adams C322), (Geneva, 1553: Adams C309), (Geneva, 1573: Adams C316) were all Sancroft gifts: S7.4.33, S7.2.26[2], S7.2.12[1].

[X.   Tractatus theologici omnes. Altera ed., cui accesserunt in libros Senecae de clementia commentarii. (2 pts.) F°, pp. 1003, 75. Genevae, apud Petrum Sanctandreanum, 1597. Missing. Catalogue c. 1680, 13th Classis N. 16: "Jo: Calvini Tractt. Theologici omnes fol. Genev: 1597."

[XI.   Epistolae et responsa. Genevae, apud Petrum Santandreanum, 1575 or 1576. F°. Missing. Register of Books Removed, p. 38, 1.2: "Jo: Calvini Epistola cum responsum... Gen: 1575." Catalogue c. 1680, 13th Classis N. 17: "ejusd: Epistolae & Responsa cum ejus vita per Bezam fol: Genev: 1576." Emmanuel's present copy (Hanoviae, 1597: Adams C391) was a Sancroft gift: S10.4.11.

[XII.   Institutio christianae religionis. Genevae, apud Iohannem le Preux, 1592. F°, ff. 312. Missing. Catalogue c. 1680, 13th Classis N. 18: "ejusd: Institutio Xtianae Religionis. fol: Genev: 1592." (A separate copy of this work had been present for the inventory of c. 1597 but was recorded as "wanting" in 1610.)]]

5.S.2   Bezae Tract Theolog: 3 vol   1584-97
Beza, Theodore. Volumen [primum-tertium] Tractationum Theologicarum, in quibus pleraque Christianae Religionis dogmata adversus haereses nostris temporibus renovatas solide ex Verbo Dei defenduntur. [3 vols.] Genevae, [I:] apud I. Crispinum, 1570; [II:] excud. Eustathius Vignon, 1573; [III.] excud. Eustathius Vignon, 1582. F°, pp. 703; 480, 65; 447. Adams B953, 957, 959. On fore-edges: "Beza I/10"; "Beza II/11"; "Beza III/12".   **309.3.18–20**

5.S.3   Ejusdem opuscula vol: 1[um]   1584?
Beza, Theodore. Volumen Alterum Tractationum Theologicarum. Genevae, excudebat Eustathius Vignon, 1573. F°, pp. 480, 65. Adams B957. Donor: Sir Walter Mildmay. Mildmay's copy; not signed. The book is dedicated to Mildmay and this is the dedication copy, elaborately bound in leather with heavy gilt on cover and edges. Fore-edge: "Beza/13". **FB4**

5.S.4   Sadeelis opera   1605-21
Chandieu, Antoine de la Roche, pseud. Sadeel. Opera Theologica volumine

uno comprehensa ... Editio tertia. [Genevae,] excudebat I. Le Preux, 1598. F°, pp. 926 + index. Donor: Thomas Southaicke. Missing. Register of Books Removed, p. 30, l.1: "Ant: Sadeelis opera Theologica fol:... 1598." Emmanuel's present copy (n.p., 1593: Adams L212) was a Sancroft gift: S9.3.5.

5.S.5   Mornaei Mysterium iniquitatis   1611
Mornay, Philippe de. Mysterium Iniquitatis seu, Historia Papatus.... Asseruntur etiam iura Imperatorum, Regum & Principum Christianorum adversus Bellarminum & Baronium Cardinales. Salmurii, per T. Portaeum, 1611. F°, pp. 644, [1]. Donor: Joseph Alliston. Inscription on front flyleaf verso: "Collegio Emmanuelis Dedit Josephus Alliston/ejusdem Coll: Socius./ Ann° Dnj: 1611 . ". Fore-edge: "62".   **309.1.49**

5.S.6   Idem de Eucharistia   Feb. 14, 1613/14
Mornay, Philippe de. Fowre Bookes, of the Institution, use and doctrine of the Holy Sacrament of the Eucharist in the Old Church. As likewise, how, when, And by what Degrees the Masse is brought in, in place thereof.... The second edition. London, printed by Iohn Windet, for I. B. [,] T. M. and W. P., 1600. F°, pp. 484. STC 18142. Donor: Samuel Bisse. Inscription on second flyleaf: "Ex dono... Samuelis Bisse... Sacra Theol. Doctoris, An° 1613. Feb. 14."   **313.4.74**

5.S.7   Mercerus in Gen: et Proph   1605-21
Mercerus, Johannes. Two books bound together:
(1) In Genesin... Commentarius... Addita Theodori Bezae praefatione. Genevae, ex typographia Matthaei Berjon, 1598. F°, pp. 747 + index.
(2) Commentarii locupletiss. in Prophetas quinque priores inter eos qui minores vocantur. Genevae, excud. H. Stephanus, 1565. F°, pp. 464.
Donor: Thomas Southaicke. Missing. Register of Books Removed, p. 21, l.5: "Mercerus in Genesin, et 5 priores min: Gr Prophetarum... Genev: 1598. T.S." Emmanuel's present copy was a Sancroft gift: S7.1.22.

5.S.8   Idem in Job et Proverb   1605–21
Mercerus, Johannes. Two books bound together:
(1) Commentarii in librum Iob. Adiecta est Theodori Bezae Epistola, in qua de huius viri doctrina, & istorum Commentariorum utilitate differitur. Genevae, excudebat Eustathius Vignon, 1573. F°, ff. 189. Adams M1314.
(2) Commentarii in Salomonis Proverbia, Ecclesiasten, & Canticum canticorum. Genevae, Excudebat Eustathius Vignon, 1573. F°, ff. 168. Adams M1315.
Donor: Thomas Southaicke. Bookplate: "Ex dono T.S." with the London Grocers' Company arms. On fore-edge: "Mercerus/in/Iob & Pr./14".
                                                                304.4.60

5.S.9   Glossa in Evang: Rob Steph   1584–97
Bible, Gospels [Latin]. In Evangelium secundum Matthaeum, Marcum, et
Lucam Commentarii ex Ecclesiasticis Scriptoribus Collecti. [*And*]
Harmonia evangelica. [2 pts in 1 vol.] [Geneva,] Oliva Roberti Stephani,
1553. F°, ff. 312, 38. Missing. Register of Books Removed, p. 20, 1.1: "R.
Stephani Glossa in 4 Evangelia... R.S. 15[55]." Emmanuel's present copy
(Adams B1818) was a Sancroft gift: S7.2.26[1].

5.S.10   Vireti op*era* Gallica   1625
Viret, Pierre. Instruction Chrestienne en la Doctrine de la Loy et
L'Evangile. [3 pts.] Geneva, par Iean Rivery, 1564. F°, pp. 674. Adams
V875. Donor: Dr John Richardson. Fore-edge: "P. Viret/Fra*n*cois".

312.4.31

5.S.11   Aretius in No: Testam[l]:   1605–21
Three books bound together:
(1) Aretius, Benedictus. Commentarii In... Quatuor Sanctos
Evangelistas... Editio Altera. [Geneva,] excud. I. le Preux, 1596. F°,
pp. 572. Adams A1591.
(2) Aretius, Benedictus. Commentarii In Sacram Actuum Apostolicorum
historiam. [Geneva,] excud. I. le Preux, 1600. F°, pp. 168. Adams
A1598.
(3) Aretius, Benedictus. Commentarii In Omnes Epistolas D. Pauli, Et
Canonicas, Itemque In Apocalypsin D. Ioannis... Editio Altera.
[Geneva,] excud. I. le Preux, 1596. F°, pp. 628. Adams A1600.
Fore-edge: "Aretius/in/No. T/15 [corrected to 16]". Donor: Thomas
Southaicke. Bookplate: "Ex dono T.S." with the London Grocers'
Company arms.   **308.4.62**

5.S.12   Ejusdem problemata   1605–21
Aretius, Benedictus. S. S. Theologiae Problemata. Hoc est, Loci
Communes Christianae Religionis Methodice explicati. Bernae
Helvetiorum. Excudebat Ioannes le Preux, 1604. F°, pp. 591. Donor:
Thomas Southaicke. Missing. Register of Books Removed, p. 29, 1. 26:
"Aretii loci communes.... Bern: 1604". Emmanuel's present copy (Bern,
1603) was a Sancroft gift: S9.2.28.

5.S.13   Chamier 4 vol.   1626–28
Chamier, Daniel. Panstratiae Catholicae, sive Controversiarum de
religione adversus Pontificios corpus.... [*Ed.* Adrien Chamier] 4 vols.
Genevae, typis Roverianis, 1626–30. F°. Missing. Register of Books
Removed, p. 29, 1. 11: "Dan: Chamieri Panstratia Catholicae. 4 Vol. (Dupl:
M[r] Rich)... Gen: 1626." Emmanuel's present copy was a Sancroft gift:
S9.1.27–30.

5.I.1 Zwinglius in Evang et Ep*isto*las   1584–97
[1621 inventory (7.S.4): "Zwinglius in Evang: & aliquot Pauli Ep*isto*las &
Jacobi"]
Zwingli, Ulrich. Two books bound together. [Possibly:
(1) In Evangelicam Historiam de domino nostro Iesu Christo, per
    Matthaeum, Marcum, Lucam, et Ioannem conscriptam, epistolasque
    aliquot Pauli, annotationes D. H. Z. per L. Iudae exceptae et aeditae.
    Adiecta est epistola Pauli ad Hebraeos & Ioannis Apostoli Epistola per
    G. Megandrum.
(2) Brevis et luculenta . . . in Epistolam beati Iacobi expositio, per Leonem
    Iudae ex ore eius excepta.]
Missing.

5.I.2 Ejusdem et Oecolampad: Ep*isto*lae   1584–97
Oecolampadius, Johannes and Zwingli, Ulrich. Epistolae Doctorum viro-
ru*m*. Preface by Theodore Bibliander. [Possibly: (Basel, R. Winter,) 1548.
F°, pp. 212, (3). Adams 0108. Fore-edge writing runs vertically, is badly
faded and illegible.   **303.4.66**]

5.I.3 Idem in Isaiam   1584–97
[1621 inventory (7.S.5): "Huldricus Vinglius in Esaia & ejus Apolog."]
Zwingli, Ulrich. Complanationis Isaiae, foetura prima, cum apologia.
Missing.

5.I.4 Ejusdem Op*era* 4 vol: 1626–32
Zwingli, Ulrich. Opera . . . omnia novissime recognita [by R. Gualtherus].
4 vols. [Zurich, C. Froschouer, c. 1545.] F°, ff. 379; 367-646; 388; pp. 599 +
indices. Adams Z216. Fore-edges: "Zuinglii/Opera/.i."; ".ii."; ".3."; ".4."
                                                                                                          303.4.4–7

5.I.5 Idem de vera et falsâ religione   1584–97
Zwingli, Ulrich. De Vera et Falsa Religione, . . . Commentarius. Tiguri.
[Possibly: ex officina Froschoviana (1525?). 8°, pp. 437.] Missing. Register
of Books Removed, p. 33, 1. 28: "Zuinglius de vera & falsa Religione . . .
(Dupl: Mr R.) . . . Tigur." Emmanuel's present copy (Adams Z225) was a
Sancroft gift: S9.4.62.

5.I.6 Idem de providentia dei et ~~Bueeri~~ Brentij Homiliae et Bugenhagius de
Conjugio Episcoporum et diaconor*um*   **1597–1621**
Three books bound together:
(1) Zwingli, Ulrich. Ad illustrissimum Cattorum Principem Philippum,
    sermonis De providentia Dei Anamnema. Tiguri apud Christophorum
    Froschover, 1530. 8°, ff. 80. Adams Z218.

(2) Brenz, Johannes. Homiliae Viginti duae . . . . cum Praefatione Doct. Martini Lutheri. Vitebergae, per Ioannem Weiss, 1533. 8°. Adams B2759.

(3) Bugenhagen, Johannes. De Conjugio Episcoporum & Diaconorum. Argentorati, excudebat Joannes Knoblouchus, 1526. 8°, Adams B3160. Fore-edge: "39 [horizontally]/[vertically: faded and illegible]". The "Buceri" deleted from the entry is a correction of an error first appearing in the 1632 catalogue, when Brenz's work was mistaken for Bucer's.

321.6.27

5.I.7   Musculi op*era* 8 vol   1605–21
        Musculus, Wolfgang.

I.   In Mosis Genesim Commentarii . . . Nunc a multis mendis repurgati. Basileae, per S. Henricpetri, 1600. F°, pp. 815 + index. Adams M2009. Fore-edge: "Muscu/ in/ Genes/5". Donor: Thomas Southaicke.   **302.2.49**

II.   In Davidis Psalterium Sacrosanctum Commentarii. . . Editio postrema. Basileae, per S. Henricpetri [1599]. F°, pp. 1098. Adams M2013. Fore-edge: "Psalm/ 6". Donor: Thomas Southaicke. Book-plate: "Ex dono T.S." with the London Grocers' Company arms. This copy replaced an earlier copy which was present at the time of the earliest inventory. c. 1597 (144: "Musculus sup*er* Psalm").   **302.2.50**

III. In Esaiam Prophetam Commentarii . . . Recens Editi. Basileae, ex off. Hervagiana per E. Episcopium, 1570. F°, pp. 829, [16]. Adams M2015. Fore-edge: "Isaiah/ 7". Donor: Thomas Southaicke.

302.2.51

IV.   In Evangelistam Matthaeum Commentarii Tribus Tomis Digesti. Basileae, ex off. Hervagiana, per E. Episcopium, 1578. F°, pp. 662 + index. Adams M2021. Fore-edge: "Math/8". Donor: Thomas Southaicke. Bookplate: "Ex dono T.S." with the London Grocers' Company arms.   **302.2.53**

V.   In Divi Ioannis Apostoli Evangelium . . . Commentarii In tres Hep-tadas digesti. Basileae, ex off. Hervagiana, per E. Episcopium, 1580. F°, pp. 665 + index. Adams M2028. Fore-edge: "Ioha*n*/9". Donor: Thomas Southaicke. Bookplate: "Ex dono T.S." with the London Grocers' Company arms. This copy replaced an earlier copy which was individually catalogued in the inventories of c. 1597 (153), 1621 (7.S.1), and 1622 (7.S.1): "Musculus in Iohannem".

VI.   Three books bound together:

(1) In Epistolam D. Apostoli Pauli Ad Romanos, Commentarii. Basileae, per S. Henricpetri, 1600. F°, pp. 278, [2]. Adams M2031.

(2) In Ambas Apostoli Pauli ad Corinthios Epistolas Commentarii [2 pts.] Basileae, per Haered. I. Hervagii, 1566. F°, coll. 782, 416. Not in Adams.

(3) In Epistolas Apostoli Pauli ad Galatas & Ephesios, Commentarii. [2 pts.] Basileae, ex off. Hervagiana, per E. Episcopium, 1569. F°, pp. 228, 173. Adams M2038.

Fore-edge: "Epist./10". Donor: Thomas Southaicke. Bookplate: "Ex dono T.S." with the London Grocers' Company arms. **302.2.55**

VII. In D. Pauli Epistolas ad Philippenses, Colossenses, Thessalonicenses ambas, & primam ad Timotheum, Commentarii. Basileae, ex off. Hervagiana, per E. Episcopium, 1578. F°, pp. 377 + index. Adams M2033. Fore-edge: "Phill/&c/11". Donor: Thomas Southaicke.

302.2.52

VIII. Loci Communes Theologiae Sacrae... Editio ultima. Basileae, per S. Henricpetri, 1599. F°, pp. 647. Adams M2044. Fore-edge: "Loci/12". Donor: Thomas Southaicke. Bookplate: "Ex dono T.S." with the London Grocers' Company arms. This copy replaced an earlier edition which was individually catalogued on the earliest inventory, c. 1597 (154): "[Musculus] Loci Communes". **309.3.31**

5.I.8   Mollerus in Isaiam   1622–6

Moller, Henricus. Iesaias in Iesaiam Commentarius. Tiguri, in off. Froschoviana, 1588. F°, ff. 236. Missing. Register of Books Removed, p. 21, 1. 10: "Mollerus in Isaiam... Tiguri. 1588." Emmanuel's present copy (Adams M1578) was a Sancroft gift: S7.1.35.

5.I.9   Pet. Martyr in Gen et Cor   1605–21

Martyr, Peter, *Vermilius*. Two books bound together:

(1) In Primum Librum Mosis, qui vulgo Genesis dicitur commentarii. Tiguri, excud. Christophorus Froschoverus, 1579. F°, ff. 199. Adams M771.

(2) In selectissimam D. Pauli Priorem ad Corinthios Epistolam.... Editio tertia. Tiguri, apud Christophorum Froschoverum, 1579. F°, ff. 242. Adams M790.

Donor: Thomas Southaicke. Fore-edge: "Martir/ in/ Gen & Cor/ 13". Bookplate: "Ex dono T.S." with the London Grocers' Company arms.

303.4.11

5.I.10   Idem in Libros Samuelis   1605–21
Martyr, Peter, *Vermilius*. In Samuelis Prophetae Libros Duos. Tiguri, apud
I. Wolphium, typis Frosch., 1595. F°, ff. 330. Donor: Thomas Southaicke.
Missing. Register of Books Removed, p. 29, 1. 16: "Petri Martyris
Comment: in libros Samuelis... Tiguri, 1595." Emmanuel's present copy
(Adams M779) was a Sancroft gift: S9.1.35.

5.I.11   Idem in Libros Judicum et Regum   1605–21
Martyr, Peter, *Vermilius*. Two books bound together:
(1) In Librum Iudicum... Commentarii. Tiguri, apud Christophorum
     Froschoverum, 1582. F°, ff. 181. Adams M775.
(2) Melachim, id est Regum Libri Duo Posteriores cum commentariis
     Petri Martyris... et Ioannis Wolphii. Heidelbergae, ex off. Andreae
     Cambieri, 1599. F°, ff. 424. Adams M783.
Donor: Thomas Southaicke. Fore-edge: "Regum/0&/Iudic./15". **303.4.12**

5.I.12   Idem de Eucharistiâ: 2 vol: in fol et 4ᵗᵒ   1604–21
[1621 inventory (7.S.10): "Petrus Martyr de Eucharist adv S Gardener";
(7.S.22): "Petrus Mart de Eucher & disput. Ejusd de Eadem in accademiae
Oxon."]
Martyr, Peter, *Vermilius*. Two separate books:
(1) Defensio Doctrinae Veteris et Apostolicae De Sacrosancto Eucharistiae
     Sacramento... adversus Stephani Gardineri... librum. Basileae, ex off.
     P. Pernae, 1581. F°, coll. 1654. Adams M762. Fore-edge: "de/Euch./16".
                                                                 303.4.63
(2) Tractatio de Sacramento Eucharistiae, habita in celeberrima
     Universitate Oxoniensi... Ad hec Disputatio de eodem Eucharistiae
     Sacramento, in eadem Universitate habita. [2 pts.] [Possibly: Londini,
     (R. Wolfe,) 1549. 4°, ff. 67, 96. STC 24673. Fore-edge: "37". **329.1.21**]
The original copies, which were present in c. 1597 were probably replaced
by duplicates in the gift of Thomas Southaicke. The present copies lack his
"ex dono T.S." bookplate.

5.I.13   Ejusdem Loci Communes   1605–21
Martyr, Peter, *Vermilius*. Loci Communes.... Heidelbergae, apud I.
Lancellotum, impensis A. Cambieri, 1603. F°, pp. 1148. Donor: Thomas
Southaicke. Missing. Register of Books Removed, p. 29. 1. 15: "Petri
Martyris Loci communes (Duplic: Lond: 1576 Mʳ Rich)... Heidel. 1603."
Emmanuel's present copy was a Sancroft gift: S9.1.35.

5.I.14 Zanchij Ope*ra* 3 vol   1605–21

Zanchius, Hieronymus. [Possibly *either*: Operum Theologicorum tomi octo. Genevae, ex typographia Samuelis Crispini, 1619. (3 vols.) F°, *or*: Operum Theologicorum. (Heidelbergi,) excudebat Stephanus Gamonetus, 1605. (3 vols.) F°.] Donor: Thomas Southaicke. Missing. Register of Books Removed, p. 29, l. 17: "Hieron. Zanchii opera Theologica 3 Vol:... Gen. 1609." Emmanuel's present copy of the 1605 edition was a Sancroft gift: S9.2.1–3.

We have been unable to locate a 1609 edition of Zanchi's works..

5.I.15 Oecolampad: in proph: et Job   Oct. 2, 1598

Oecolampadius, Johannes. Five books bound together:

(1) In Iesiam Prophetam, Hypomnematon, Hoc Est, Commentariorum... Libri Sex... elucubrationum commonstrat D. Heinrychi Bullingeri... Praefatio. [Geneva,] apud Io. Crispinum et Nicolaum Barbirium, 1558. F°, pp. 320 + index. Adams B1284.

(2) In Ieremiam... Commentariorum... libri tres.... In Threnos & Orationem Ieremiae enarrationes. [Geneva,] e typ. Crispiniana, 1558. F°, pp. 262 + index. Adams B1284.

(3) In Ezechielem... Commentarii... opera Wolphga*n*gi Capitonis in lucem editi. Genevae, e typ. Crispiniana, 1558. F°, pp. 150 [250]. Adams B1284.

(4) In Librum Iob Exegemata.... Eiusdem in Danielem... Libri Duo. [2 vols. in 1.] Genevae, e typ. Crispiniana, 1567. F°, pp. 193, 141 + index. Adams B1307.

(5) In Minores... Prophetas... lucubrationes. Genevae, e typ. Crispiniana, excud. Ioannes Crispinus, 1558. F°, pp. 240 + index. Adams B1284.

Donor: Thomas Crocus. Inscription on the first title page: "Collegio Emmanuelis legavit Thomas Crocus sacrae/Theologiae Londini/in Graiensi hospitio/professor,/2° Octobris *1598* immortalitate/auctus." Fore-edge: "OEcola*m*pad in/Prophetes/56".   **307.4.76**

5.I.16 Simlerus de persona et duabus naturis in X^(to)   1622–6

Simler, Josias. Scripta Veterum Latina, de una persona et duabus naturis Domini et Servatoris nostri Jesu Christi. Tiguri, excud. Christophorus Froschoverus, 1571. F°, ff. 211. Missing. Register of Books Removed, p. 29, l. 36: "Simler's Collectio Script: de unâ personâ & 2^(bus) naturis X/ti... Tiguri 1571." Emmanuel's present copy (Adams S1178) was a Sancroft gift: S9.2.41.

5.I.17 Idem in Exodum   1625

Simler, Josias. Exodus. In Exodum...Commentarii. Tiguri, excud. Christophorus Froschoverus, 1584. F°, ff. 193. Adams S1175. Donor: Dr John Richardson. Fore-edge: "Simler/in/Exod".   **308.4.60**

Classis 6^{ae} sect: 1^a

Classis 6ae sect: 1a

[Empty]

Classis 6^{ae} sect: 2^a

6.2.1 Abbas Vrspergensis   1625
Conradus, *Abbot of Auersperg* [Conradus à Liechtenaw]. Chronicon...
Accesserunt huic editioni... Annales, Rheginonis Abbatis Brumiensis &
Lamberti Schaffnaburgensis Monachi. [3 pts.] Argentorati, sumptibus
Lazari Zetzneri, 1609. F°, pp. 539 + index. Donor: Dr John Richardson.
Fore-edge: "ABBAS/VRSPER:/REGIN:/SCHAF:".   **307.3.60**

6.2.2 Fox: Hist Eccl pars 1^a   1584–97
Foxe, John. Rerum in ecclesia gestarum... Commentarii. Pars prima.
[Possibly: Basileae, per Nicolaum Brylingerum, et Ioannem Oporinum,
1559. Adams F813.   **310.4.74**]

6.2.3 Hospinianus de festis X^{norum}   1622–6
Hospinianus, Rodolphus. Festa Christianorum. [Possibly: Editio secunda.
Tiguri, apud Ioh. Rodolphum Wolphium, 1612. F°, ff. 162.   **310.4.34**]

6.2.4 Ritus Eccles:^{ci} Romanae Ecclesiae   1617–32
[1621 inventory 4.S.4): "Romanae Ecclesiae Ceremoniae Sacrae"]
[Possibly: Piccolomini, Agostino Patrizio. Rituum ecclesiasticorum sive
sacrarum cerimoniarum s.s. Romanae ecclesiae. Libri tres. Venetiis, Gregorii de Gregoriis excusere, 1516. F°, ff. (143). Adams L976. Donor: Thomas
James. Inscription: "Reuerendiss° D. D*omino* Eccl^e Linconien*sis* Antistiti
meritiss°/Iacob*us* Canta Seruulus dono dabat". (Venn records that Thomas
James was matriculated pensioner in 1611, was ordained priest at
Peterborough in March 1617, and "for some years ministered in
Lincolnshire." He emigrated to Massachusetts in 1632.   **336.2.17**]

6.2.5 Theodoricus a Niem de Schismate   1625
Niem, Theodoricus à, *Bp of Verdun*. Historiae... qua res suo tempore...
gestae uberrime exponuntur, Libri IIII....Hisce Iohannis Marii Belgae...
Liber de XXIIII Schismatis in Ecclesia, & Conciliorum Gallicanae
Ecclesiae praestantia & utilitate... adiectus est. Basileae, per Thomam
Guarinum, 1566. F°, pp. 469 + index. Adams N267. Donor: Dr John
Richardson. Fore-edge: "Theodo/de Niem".   **318.3.38**

6.2.6 Platina de vitis Pontific: 1584–97
Platina, Bartolomeo (also Baptista Platina). Historia ... de vitis
Pontificum Romanorum... annotationum Onuphrii Panvinii accessione
nunc illustrior reddita.... Alia quoque cum ipsius Platinae tum Onuphrii
opuscula huic aeditioni nunc recens addita sunt. Coloniae, apud Maternum

Cholinum, 1574. F°, pp. 429, 104, 77 + index. Adams P1425. Fore-edge: "Plantina/de vitis/et onuphrii".   **310.4.27**

6.2.7   Philo Lat, Hegesippus, Krantzi, Saxon   1584–97
            Three books bound together:
            (1) Philo, *Judaeus*. Libri antiquitatum. Quaestionum et solutionum in
                Genesin. Basileae, per Adamum Petrum, 1527. F°, pp. 142. Adams
                P1031.
            (2) Hegesippus. De rebus a Iudaeor*um* principibus in obsidione fortiter
                gestis, deq*ue* excidio Hierosolymorum. *Tr.* St Ambrose. Apud
                Coloniam, per Eucharium Cervicornum, impensa & aere M. Godefridi
                Hittorpii, 1525. F°, ff. 77 + index. Adams H146.
            (3) Crantz, Albert. Saxonia. Coloniae, 1520. F°. Adams C2884.   **310.4.32**
            The first inventory (c. 1597) shows the first two of these books as a single
            item (1597.38) and the Crantz volume as a separate item (1597.106). They
            were either bound together before 1621 or replaced by the copy listed here.

6.2.8   Mariani Scoti Chron: et Martini Poloni Supputati*one*s et Roveri Historia
                                                                                      1625
            Two books bound together:
            (1) Marianus, *Scotus*. Chronica... Adiecimus Martini Poloni... eiusdem
                argumenti Historiam. (2 pts.) Basileae, apud Ioannem Oporinum, 1559.
                F°, coll. 486; pp. 22, coll. 23–251 + indices. Adams M582.
            (2) Pontanus, Roverus. Rerum Memorabilium iam inde ab anno Domini
                M.D. ad annum fere LX in Rep. Christiana gestarum, Libri Quinque.
                Coloniae, apud Iasparem Gennepaeum, 1559. F°, pp. 462. Adams
                P1881.
            Donor: Dr John Richardson.   **306.4.8**

6.2.9   Fasciculus rerum expetendarum et fugiendaru*m*   1622–6
            Gratius, Ortuinus, *ed.* Fasciculus rerum expetendarum ac fugiendarum.
            [Cologne,] 1535. F°, ff. [242]. Adams G1069. Fore-edge: "Fasciul*us*/Reru*m*
            ex".   **307.4.16**

6.2.10   Causabon in Baronium   1614–21
            Casaubon, Isaac. De Rebus Sacris et Ecclesiasticis Exercitationes XVI. Ad
            Cardinalis Baronii Prolegomena in Annales. Londini, ex officina
            Nortoniana, apud Ioan. Billium, 1614. F°, pp. [66,] 775 + index. STC 4745.
            Missing. Register of Books Removed, p. 25, 1. 22: "Is. Casaubonus de rebus
            SS. & Ecclesiasticis... Lond: 1614." Emmanuel's present copy was a
            Sancroft gift: S8.3.14.

6.2.11   Pii 2^di^ Coment: rerum memorabil*ium*   1625
            Pius II, *Pope* (Enea Silvio Piccolomini). Commentarii rerum
            memorabilium, quae temporibus suis contigerunt. *Ed.* Joannes Gobellinus.
            Romae, ex typographia Dominici Basae, 1584. 8°, pp. 749 + index. Adams
            G784. Donor: Dr John Richardson.   **333.2.1**

6.2.12   Anastasius de vitis Pontificum   1625
Two books bound together:
(1) Anastasius, *Bibliothecarius*. Historia, de vitis Romanorum Pontificum.
Moguntiae, in typ. Ioannis Albini, 1602. 4°, pp. 352 + index.
(2) Liutprand, *Bp of Cremona*. Opusculum, de vitis Romanorum
Pontificum. Moguntiae, ex typog. Ioannis Albini, 1602. 4°, pp.
161 + index.
Donor: Dr John Richardson. Fore-edge: "Anast./Vit. Pont".   **334.1.85**

6.2.13   Osiandri Epitome Historiae Eccles:^{cae} p*ars*: ult: sine cent: 16   1625
[The words "p*ars*: ult: sine cent: 16" appear to have been added to the
entry after the completion of the catalogue. None of the earlier catalogues
in which this work appears (1626, 1628, 1632) mention this exclusion of the
sixteenth-century portion of the work. When the copy was discarded or
sold, probably shortly after Sancroft's bequest (1693), only the sixteenth-
century portion of the work was mentioned in the Register of Books
Removed. These details suggest that in the period here in question
(1625–37) the library probably owned the complete work, bound in at least
two volumes, as follows.]
Osiander, Lucas, *the elder*. Epitomes Historiae Ecclesiasticae. [3 vols.]
Tubingae, 1608. Donor: Dr John Richardson. Missing. Register of Books
Removed, p. 25, l. 44: "L. Osiandri Epitome Historiae Ecclesiast:
Centuriae 16th... (Dupl: Mr Rich) Tubingae 1608 Dr Rich". Emmanuel's
present copy (Tubingae, 1604, 1608, 1610) was a Sancroft gift: S8.3.42–44.

6.2.14   Lipomannus de vitis Patrum Tom: 2^{dus} et 3   1625
(1) Lipomanus, Aloysius, *Bp of Bergamo*. Secundus tomus vitarum
sanctorum priscorum patrum. Venetiis, ad signum spei, 1553. 4°, ff. 487.
Adams L739. Donor: Dr John Richardson.
(2) Lipomanus, Aloysius, *Bp of Bergamo*. Vitarum sanctorum priscorum
patrum... tomus tertius. Venetiis, ad signum spei, 1554. 4°, ff. 267.
Adams L740. Donor: Dr John Richardson.   **329.3.5,6**

6.2.15   Zamorensis speculum omnium statuu*m* totius orbis   1625
Sanchez de Arevalo, Roderigo, *successively Bishop of Oviedo, Zamora,
Calahorra, and Valentia*. Speculum omnium statuum totius orbis terrarum.
Hanoviae, apud heredes Ioan. Aubrii, 1613. 4°, pp. 277. Donor: Dr John
Richardson.   **301.5.40**

6.2.16   Thesaurus Politicus   1622–6
[Possibly: Thesaurus politicus... Ex Italico Latinus factus, opera et studio
Gasparis Ens.] Missing. Emmanuel at present has an Italian edition
(Turnoni, 1605), a Sancroft gift: S15.2.67.

6.2.17 Controversia Venª: 3 vol: October 4, 1621
This is a three-volume gathering of miscellaneous works concerning the controversy between Pope Paul V and Venice. Vol. I contains nine works; vol. II, twenty; and vol. III, seven. The books were published in a variety of places but especially Venice and Hanau. Several are anonymous, and many are in Italian. Authors include Bellarmine, Sarpi, Capello and others. Fore-edges: "Venetii/Controv/i"; "ii"; and "iii". A gilt volume number is stamped in the middle of the cover of each. Donor: William Bedell. Each volume carries the following inscription: "Hunc Librum Collegio Emmanuelis DD Guilielmus Beadle ejusdem Colleg: socius/Octob 4 Annº 1621". Bedell, an Emmanuel graduate and fellow, was in Venice as chaplain to Sir Henry Wotton during the years of the dispute. **329.3.10–12**

6.2.18 Historia Regum Daniae et M Adami Historia Eccles. et His: Archiepiscop: Bremens 1622–6
Three books bound together:
(1) Lindenbrog, Erpold, *ed.* Historia... Daniae regum. Lugduni Batavorum, ex off. Plantiniana apud Franciscum Raphelengium, 1595. 4°, pp. 64 + index. Adams D299.
(2) Adam, *of Bremen.* Historia ecclesiastica. *Ed.* Erpold Lindenbrog. Lugduni Batavorum, ex off. Plantiniana, apud Franciscum Raphelengium, 1595. 4°, pp. 156 + indices. Adams A138.
(3) Lindenbrog, Erpold, *ed.* Historia Archiepiscoporum Bremensium. Lugduni Batavorum, ex off. Plantiniana, apud Franciscum Raphelengium, 1595. 4°, pp. 135 + index. Adams B2746. **332.3.20**

6.2.19 Regnorum Mundi Pentaplus 1625
Eytzinger (Aitsinger), Michael. Pentaplus regnorum mundi. Antuerpiae, ex off. Christophori Plantini, 1579. 4°, pp. 110 + folding tables. Adams E1176. Donor: Dr John Richardson. **331.4.45**

6.2.20 Raemundus de Haeresibus huius seculi 1622–6
Raemond, Florimond de. Historia de ortu, progressu, et ruina Haereseon hujus saeculi. (2 pts.) Coloniae, apud Gerhardum Greunbruch, 1614. 4°, pp. 614. Fore-edge: "REMUND/HAER:". **329.3.16**

6.2.21 Godwin de praesulibus Anglic 1622–6
Godwin, Francis. De Praesulibus Angliae Commentarius. (2 pts.) Londini, ex off. Nortoniana, apud Ioannem Billium, 1616. 4°, pp. 664, 180, 16. STC 11941. [Possibly: **329.3.22**]

6.2.22 Chronicon Chronicorum 8 vol 1625
Gruterus, Janus. Chronicon chronicorum ecclesiastico-politicum. [8 vols.] Francofurti, in officina Aubriana, 1614. 8°. Donor: Thomas Hanscombe. Each volume has the following inscription on the front flyleaf: "Magister

Thomas Hanscombe huius Collegij Socius, moriens, D.D." Top-edges: "Ecclesia/stico poli/ticus/Pars 1ᵃ"; "Eccles:/Pars 2ᵃ"; "Cron: BC/Pars 1ᵃ"; "Cron BC/Pars 2ᵃ"; "Cronicon/Polit/Pars 1ᵃ"; "Cron: Pol/Pars 2ᵃ"; "Ecclesias:/tico polit/pars 3ᵃ"; "Ecclesiasti/co poli/pars 4ᵃ". Fore-edges: "1"; "2"; "3"; "4"; "[?]"; "6"; "7"; "8".   **329.3.66–73**

6.2.23   Constantini donatio   1622–6
          Constantine I, *Emperor of Rome, the Great*. Donatio. [Possibly: Adrian IV,
          Pope. Legatio ad Conuentum Nurembergensem Anno M.D.XXII. (*And* De
          donatione Constantini.) Vittembergae, per Ioannem Frischmut, 1538.
          Adams A156. Donor: Elias Travers. Signature on title page: "E. Travers".
                                                                    330.5.42]
          Though this work was commonly called the Donation of Constantine,
          the falsity of this attribution was demonstrated in the fifteenth century by
          Nicholas of Cusa and others.

6.2.24   Major de vitis Patrum   1584–97
          Major, Georg. Vitae patrum, in usum ministrorum verbi. Missing.

6.2.25   Historia Ecclesiastica   1584–97
          [1621 inventory (1.I.19): "Eusebij historia & Psalmi selecti â diversis
          authoribus Lat. carmine redditi"]
          Two books bound together:
          (1) Eusebius, Pamphili, *Bp of Caesarea*. Hystoria ecclesiastica. Ed. G.
              Boussard. Parisiis, a Francisco Regnault [c. 1520]. 8°, ff. [131]. Adams
              E1089.
          (2) Bible, Psalms [Latin]. Psalmi Omnium Selectissimi ... Latino carmine
              redditi per ... Hermannum Novae Aquilae Comiem Philippum
              Melanchtonem. Haganoae, in off. Iohan Secerii, 1532. 8°, pp. 252.
              Adams B1508.
          Fore-edge: "Historia/Ecclesiastica/28".   **322.7.98**

                         Classis 6ᵃᵉ sectio tertia

6.3.1   Speeds History   1611–21
          Speed, John. The History of Great Britaine Under the Conquests of yᵉ
          Romans, Saxons, Danes, and Normans. [Possibly: London, William Hall
          & John Beale for John Sudbury & George Humble, 1611. F°, pp.
          151–898 + index. STC 23045.   **315.1.18]**

6.3.2   Fox Martyrolog 2 vol   1622–6
          Foxe, John. Actes and monuments [the sixth edition]. [2 vols.] London,
          for the Company of the Stationers, 1610. F°. STC 11227. Fore-edges: "I.
          Foxe/Mart/I"; "II".   **309.1.32–3**

6.3.3 Baronius et Bzovius 12 vol   1625
Baronius, Caesar, *Cardinal.* Annales Ecclesiastici [completed by Abraham
Bzovius]. [12 vols.] Coloniae Agrippinae, sumptibus Ioannis Gymnici &
Antonij Hierati, 1609. F°. [12 vols.] Donor: Dr John Richardson. Missing.
Register of Books Removed, p. 25, 1. 6: "Baronij annales cum Bzovij
continuatione... 18 Tomi... 12V... Col. Agrip: 1609. Dʳ Rich". The
twelve volumes were temporarily shelved with a group of "new bought"
books until sometime between 1626 and 1632, at which time they displaced
an incomplete set containing only vols. 1–7, 12, and 13.

6.3.4 Tornellus   1626–32
Tornellio, Augustino. Annales Sacri et Profani ab orbe Condito ad
Eundem Christi passione redemptum. Coloniae Agrippinae, apud
Cornelium ab Egmondt, 1622, 1616. [2 vols.] F°, pp. 484; 420 + index.
Fore-edge: "Tornell*us*".   **309.1.23**

6.3.5 Centuriae Magdeburgens 7 vol   1597–1621
Magdeburg. Magdeburg Centuriators. Ecclesiastica Historia. Ed. Mathias
Flacius. [13 vols. in 7.] Basileae, per Ioannem Oporinum, 1560–74. F°.
Adams M110.la; 110.2b; 110.3b; 110.4; 110.5; 110.6a; 109.7a; 110.8; 110.9;
110.10; 110.11; 110.12; 110.13. Fore-edges: "CENT: Mag/I/II. III/2";
"IV/3"; "V. VI/4"; "VII. VIII/5"; "IX. X. XI/6"; "XII/7"; XIII/8". Binding
stamped: "C.E./1592".   **318.3.10–16**

6.3.6 Iovij Historiae vol: 2^{dum}   1584–97
Giovio, Paolo, *Bp of Nocera.* Historiarum Sui Temporus, Tomus
Secundus. [Possibly: Florentiae, in officina Laurentii Torrentini, 1552. F°,
pp. 506. Adams G649.   **312.1.35**]

Sectio 4ᵃ

6.4.1 Iovij Historiae vol 1um   1584–97
Giovio, Paolo, *Bp of Nocera.* Historiarum Sui Temporis, Tomus Primus,
XXIIII Libros Complectens. Lutetiae Parisiorum, Michaelis Vascosani,
1553. F°, ff. 236 + index. Adams G650. Fore-edge: "P. Ioui*us*/i/23".
                                                                                         309.2.40

6.4.2 Cedreni Annales   1622–6
Cedrenus, Georgius. Annales. Missing.

6.4.3 Nicephori Callistae Histᵃ Eccles et Cassiodori Historia Tripartita   1625
Nicephorus Callistus. Ecclesiasticae Historiae Libri decem et octo...
Adiecimus... Magni Aurelii Cassiodori Tripartitam... Historiam. (2 pts in
1 vol.) Francofurti, impens. Sigismundi Feyerbendii apud Ioannem
Feyrabent, 1588. F°, coll. 1172, pp. 192 + indices. Adams N222. Donor: Dr
John Richardson. Fore-edge: "NICEP. Cal./HIST. Trip."   **309.1.19**

6.4.4   Eusebij, Ruffini, Socratis Theodoreti Sozomeni etc. Eccles: Hist[a] cum Chronogr[a] Bucholceri   1622–6
Eusebius, *Pamphili, Bp of Caesarea.* Eusebii Pamphili, Ruffini, Socratis, Theodoriti, Sozomeni, Theodori, Evagrii, et Dorothei Ecclesiastica Historia. Missing. Emmanuel's present copy (Basileae, 1587: Adams E1099) was a Sancroft gift: S8.3.2.

6.4.5   Iosephus Graec: 1584–97
Josephus, Flavius. Opera. [Gk] Basileae, παρὰ τῶ ἱερονιμω φροβενιω και Νικολαω τω ʽΕπισκοπιω, 1544. F°, pp. 967. Adams J351. The Cambridge University arms and initials of Richard Culverwell are stamped on the covers. He was probably the donor.   **302.3.57**

6.4.6   Iosephus Lat   1584–97
Josephus, Flavius. Opera quaedam Ruffino presbytero interprete. Basileae, apud Io. Frobenium, 1524. F°, pp. 907. Adams (J356) omits Emmanuel's copy. Lumley 1232. Signatures on title page: "Thomas Cantuarien*sis*" (Thomas Cranmer) and "Lumley" (John, First Baron Lumley). Fore-edge (vertically): "Josephus/Josephus".   **310.1.7**

6.4.7   Sabellici Enneades 2 vol   1622–6
Sabellicus, Marcus Antonius. Rapsodiae Historiarum Enneadum. 2 vols. Missing. Apparently replaced by Sabellicus's Opera (Basileae, 1538: Adams S11), which was a Sancroft gift: S5.1.12,13

6.4.8   Funccij Chronologia   1622–6
Funck, Johann. Chronologia. [2 pts.] Witebergae, excud. Matthaeus Welack, typis Iohannis Schwertelii, 1578. F°. Adams F1177. Fore-edge: "Funccius Chrol".   **309.2.14**

6.4.9   Genebrardi Chronologia   1625
Genebrard, Gilbert, *Archbp of Aix.* Chronographiae Libri Quatuor. [2 pts.] Lugduni, sumpt. Ioannis Pillehotte, [1608–]1609. F°, pp. 954, 83+index. Donor: Dr John Richardson. Fore-edge: "GENEB:". **309.1.26**

6.4.10   Petavij doctrina tempor*um* 2 vol   1627–32
Petau, Denis (Petavius, Dionysius). Opus de doctrina temporum. [2 vols.] Lutetiae Parisiorum, sumptibus Sebastiani Cramoisy, 1627. F°, pp. 886, 896+indices. Missing. Register of Books Removed, p. 47, 1. 23: "Dionys: Petavii doctrina temporum 2 vol:... Par: 1627". Emmanuel's present copy was a Sancroft gift: S12.2.32,33.

6.4.11   Scaliger de Emendatione Tempor*um*   1629–32
Scaliger, Joseph Justus. Opus de Emendatione Temporum. Genevae, typis Roverianis, 1629. F°, pp. 52, 784, 59+index. Missing. Register of Books

Removed, p. 13, 1. 5: "Jos: Scaliger de emendatione temporum... Genev: 1629". Emmanuel's present copy was a Sancroft gift: S5.1.14.

6.4.12 Antonini Historia   1586–97
Antoninus, *Abp of Florence*. Opus excellentissimum hystoriarum seu cronicarum. [III *Colophon*: In Lugduno, per Nicolaum Wolff, 1512.] F°, pp. 215+index. [Vol. I only.] Adams A1208. Donor: William Fleetwood. Inscription on title page: "Ex dono W. Fletewoode Seruiensis ad Legem e*st*/Recordat. London 1586".   **305.3.29**

6.4.13 Naucleri Chronolog   1622–6
Nauclerus, Johannes. Chronica. [Possibly: Coloniae, ex off. Petri Quentel, 1544. F°, pp. 1042+index. Adams N72.   **307.3.58]**

6.4.14 Trithemij Opera 2 vol   1626–32
The markings on the fore-edges suggest that these distinct editions were grouped together as a two-volume opera:
(1) Trithemius, Johannes. Opera historica. [2 pts.] Francofurti, typis Wechelianis, apud C. Marnium & heredes I. Aubrii, 1601. F°, pp. 412, 574+indices+preface. Fore-edge: "Trithemius/1".   **309.1.53**

(2) Trithemius, Johannes. Opera pia et spiritualia. Moguntiae, ex typog. I. Albini, 1605, F°, pp. 1226. Fore-edge: "2".   **307.3.9**

6.4.15 Gesneri Bibliotheca   1584–97
Gesner, Conrad. Bibliotheca... collecta primum a C. Gesnero... tertio recognita, per I. Simlerum: iam amplificata per Ioh. Iac. Frisium. Tiguri, excud. Christophorus Froschoverus, 1583. F°, pp. 835+prefaces+index. Missing. Register of Books Removed, p. 13, 1. 20: "Gesneri Bibliotheca... ed: Frisij... Tiguri: 1583". Emmanuel's present copy (Adams G515) was a Sancroft gift: S5.2.17.

6.4.16 Bucholceri Chronolog   1622–6
Bucholtzer, Abraham. Chronologia: Hoc est: Annorum Supputatio. [Possibly: Gorlicii, typis Ambrosii Fritschii, 1584–5. F°, pp. 445. Adams B3064. Fore-edge: "Bucholcer". The arms of William Cecil, Lord Burghley, are stamped on the covers.   **309.1.28]**

6.4.17 Ejusdem Isagoge chronologica   1622–6
Bucholtzer, Abraham. Isagoge Chronologica. [Possibly: Gorlicii, typ. Ambrosii Fritschii, 1580. F°, ff. 54, (6), (121). Adams B3067   **303.1.13]**

6.4.18 Beroaldi Chronologia   1622–6
Beroaldus, Matthaeus. Chronicum, Scripturae Sacrae Autoritate Constitutum. [Geneva,] apud Anton. Chuppinum, 1575. F°, pp.

267 + indices + preface. Adams B757. Fore-edge: "Beroald:". The arms of William Cecil, Lord Burghley, are stamped on the covers. **308.4.18**

Sectio 5[a]

6.5.1   Nicephori Gregorae, gr 1: et Chalcocondylas de Turcis   1622–6
Gregoras, Nicephorus. Romanae, hoc est Byzantinae historiae Libri XI. *Ed. & Trans.* H. Wolf. His adjunximus Laonici Chalcondylae Turcicam historiam. *Trans.* C. Clauser. *Ed.* H. Wolf. [Gk & Lat.] Basileae, per Ioannem Oporinum, 1562. F°, pp. 533 + index + tables. Adams G1082. Fore-edge: "Nic/Greg". The arms of William Cecil, Lord Burghley, are stamped on the covers. **312.1.45**

6.5.2   Florilegium Matthaei Westmonast   1625
Matthew of Westminster. Flores historiarum. Francofurti, typ. Wechelianis apud Claudium Marnium & heredes Ioannis Aubrii, 1601. F°, pp. 696 + index. Donor: Dr John Richardson. Fore-edge: "FLORiLE:/GVS". **309.2.6**

6.5.3   Historia Orientalis 2 vol   1622–6
[?] This item is probably missing and unidentifiable, though Emmanuel's present holdings include a work which could have been one of the two recorded volumes: [Possibly: Ioannes Zonaras, Nicetas Acominatus Choniates, Nicephorus Gregoras, and Laonicus Chalcocondylas. Historia Rerum in Oriente Gestarum. Francofurti ad Maenum. impens. S. Feyrabendius, 1587. F°, ff. 297 + prefaces + indices. Adams H634. Fore-edge: "Zonarae/Annales/Orient:". **310.1.6**]

6.5.4   Thuani Hist[a] 2 Vol: 1622–6
Thou, Jacques-Auguste de. Historiae sui temporis. [2 vols.] Missing.

6.5.5.   Aimonus de rebus gestis Francorum et chron: casinense   1625
Aimonus, *of Fleury*. De Gestis Francorum.... chronicon casinense Leonis Marsicani, Cardinalis. *Ed.* Jacobus de Breul. Parisiis, apud Ambrosium & Hieronymum Drouart, 1603. F°, pp. 618 [918]. Donor: Dr John Richardson. Fore-edge: "Cronica/Aimonij/cassin". **309.2.41**

6.5.6   The Empires of the World, Grimston   1622–6
Avity, Pierre d'. The Estates, Empires, & Principalities of the World.... Translated out of French by Edw: Grimstone. London, A. Islip; for M. Lownes; and Iohn Bill, 1615. F°, pp. 1234. STC988. [Possibly: **310.2.55**]

6.5.7   Onuphrij Coment in fastos   1625
Panvinius, Onuphrius. Fastorum. Libri V a Romulo Rege usque ad Imp.

Caesarem Carolum V Austirium. (3 pts.) [Geneva?] in off. Sanctandreana, 1588. F°, pp. 106, 368, 78[74], 68. Adams P197. Donor: Dr John Richardson. Fore-edge: "Onvph:".   **305.2.41**

6.5.8   Paulus Aemilius de rebus franc   1625
Aemylius, Paulus (Emili, Paolo). De rebus gestis Francorum... Libri X. Arnoldi Ferroni... de rebus gestis Gallorum Libri IX... Chronicon Ioan. Tilii de Regibus Francorum. Basileae, per S. Henricpetri, 1601. F°. Donor: Dr John Richardson.   **307.3.59**

6.5.9   Gaguini Annales de rebus Gallicis   1622–6
Gaguin, Robert. Rerum Gallicarum annales. [Possibly: Francofurti ad Moenum, ex off. typog. And. Wecheli, 1577. F°, pp. 336+index. Adams G25.   **309.2.46**]

6.5.10   Carionis Chronicon   1584–97
Carion, Johannes. Chronicon Carionis. *Ed.* Philipp Melanchthon and Caspar Peucer. Witebergae, excudebant haeredes Iohannis Cratonis, 1580. F°, pp. 746+preface+index. Adams C715. Fore-edge: "Carion". **309.2.39**

6.5.11   Aventini Annales Boio*rum*   1622–6
Aventinus, Johannes. Annalium Boiorum Libri VII. Basileae, excud. Petrus Perna, 1580. F°, pp. 669. Adams A2309. Fore-edge: "Auentin*us*". **309.2.49**

6.5.12   Reusneri Basilicon   1622–6
Reusner, Elias. βασιλικῶν opus Genealogicum Catholicum De Praecipuis Familiis Imperatorum... Orbis Christiani. [Possibly: Francofurti, ex off. typog. Nicolai Bassaei, 1592. F°, pp. 532, 92, 199+index. Adams R396.
                                                              310.2.42]

6.5.13   Rerum Sicularum Historia   1626–32
[Possibly: Fazellus, Thomas, *ed.* Rerum Sicularum Scriptores. Francofurti ad Moenum, apud And. Wechelum, 1579. F°, pp. 705+index. Adams F205.
                                                              306.3.30]

6.5.14   Bizar*us* de rebus Persar*um*   1622–6
Bizzarus, Petrus. Persicarum Rerum Historia. Antuerpiae, ex off. Christophori Plantini, 1583. F°, pp. 451+index. Fore-edge: "Persic/Hist". Adams B2088.   **309.2.48**

6.5.15   Baletij vita Scanderbeg   1584–97
[1621 inventory (1.I.13): "Barletius de vita & rebus gestis Scanderbegi".] Barletius, Marinus. [Possibly: De Vita Moribus ac Rebus Praecipue Adversus Turcas, Gestis, Georgii Castrioti... qui... Scanderbegius... cognominatus fuit, libri Tredecim. Argentorati, apud Cratonem Mylium, 1537. F°, pp. 371+index. Adams B217.   **306.4.11**]

6.5.16   Hist[a] Saracenica Caelij   1584–97
[1621 inventory (1.I.16): "Celij histor. de Sarracenis Turcis & Sultanis Egip.
& Drechlerus de Sarrac. & Turcis."]
Curio, Caelius Augustinus. Sarracenicae Historiae Libri III ... His accessit
Volfgangi Drechsleri ... Chronicon. Basileae, per Ioannem Oporinum,
1567. F°, pp. 163 + index. Adams C3078. Fore-edge: "22". [Bound with two
other books after 1637.]   **318.3.43**

6.5.17   Moscovia Possevini   1622–6
Possevinus, Antonius. Moscovia, et Alia Opera. Coloniae Agrippinae, in
off. Birckmannica, sumpt. Arnoldi Mylii, 1595. F°, pp. 392, 75, engraved
maps. Adams P2006. Fore-edge: "Musco:/via./Possev".   **318.2.34**

6.5.18   Chronic*um* Germanic*um*   1622–6
[Possibly: Germanicarum Rerum Quatuor Celebriores Vetustioresque
Chronographi ... Quorum Nomina Sunt: (1) Iohannes Turpinus De Vita
Caroli Magni et Rolandi. (2) Rhegino Abbas Prumiensis (Annales) ... (3)
Sigebertus Gemblacensis Eiusque Continuator Robertus De Monte. (4)
Lambertus Schaffnaburgensis, Alias Hirsfeldensis Dictus. Francofurti ad
Moenum, apud Georgium Corvinum, Sigismundum Feyrabend, & haered.
Wigandi Galli, 1566. F°, ff. 224 + index. Adams G488. (After 1637 [?],
bound with: Abbatis Urspergensis. Chronicon. Argentorati, 1587. Not in
Adams.)   **309.4.64**]

6.5.19   Historia Florent Aretini   1622–6
[Possibly: Two books bound together:
(1) Aretino, Leonardo Bruni. Historiarum Florentinarum Libri XII.
    Argentorati, sumptibus L. Zetzneri, 1610. F°, pp. 285 + index.
(2) Sleidan, Johann, *tr.* & *ed.* Tres Gallicarum Rerum Scriptores ... Philip-
    pus Cominaeus ... Frossardus in ... epitomen ... Claudius Sesellius.
    Francofurti ad Moenum, ex off. typog. Andreae Wecheli, 1578. F°, pp.
    320, 28. Adams C2463.   **318.3.42**]

6.5.20   Walsingami Hist[a] etc: 1616
Camden, William, *ed.* Anglica, Normannica, Hibernica, Cambrica, a
veteribus Scripta: Ex quibus Asser Menevensis, Anonymus de vita
Gulielmi Conquestoris, Thomas Walsingham, Thomas de la More,
Gulielmus Gemiticensis, Giraldus Cambrensis. Francofurti, impens.
Claudii Marnii, & haeredum Iohannis Aubrii, 1603. F°, pp. 898 + index.
Donor: Robert Booth. Inscription on flyleaf: "Hic liber donatus
bibliothecae huic a Domino Roberto Booth quondam huius Collegij socio
anno dom. 1616". Fore-edge: "Walsing."   **309.2.35**

6.5.21   Polydorus Vergilius   1622–6
Vergilius, Polydorus. Anglicae Historiae Libri Vigintiseptem. Basileae,

apud Thomam Guarinum, 1570. F°, pp. 691 + index. Adams V452. Fore-edge: "Pol. Virg." **309.2.37**

6.5.22 Matthaei Paris: Hist[a] 1622–6
Paris, Matthew. Historia maior. Tiguri, in off. Froschoviana, 1589. F°, pp. 977 + index. Adams P337. Fore-edge: "M. Paris". **309.2.51**

6.5.23 Antiquitas Britannicae Ecclesiae 1622–6
[?]

6.5.24 Anglicae Historiae scriptores post Bedam 1601–21
Savile, Henry, *ed*. Rerum Anglicarum Scriptores Post Bedam Praecipui. Francofurti, typis Wechelianis apud C. Marnium & heredes I. Aubrii, 1601. F°, pp. 916. Missing. Register of Books Removed, p. 47, 1. 28: "H. Savilii Collectio Scriptorum vol: Angl: Historiae post Bedam (Dupl: M[r] Rich) Franc: 1601". Emmanuel's present copy (London, 1596) was a Sancroft gift: S12.2.42. This is one of four works added to the 1597 catalogue in a hand different from that of the rest of the list. It was probably added soon after its publication in 1601.

6.5.25 Walsingami ~~Alfred~~ historiae: una cu*m* Assaris historiae ~~Aelfredi~~ saxonic: charact: 1622–6
Three books bound together:
(1) [Asser, Joannes, *Bp of Sherborne*.] Aelfredi Regis Res Gestae. [London, John Day, 1574.] F°, pp. 48. STC 863.
(2) Walsingham, Thomas. Ypodigma Neustriae vel Normanniae... Ab irruptione Normannorum usq*ue* ad annum 6. regni Henrici quinti. Londini, in aedibus Iohannis Daij, 1574. F°, pp. 199 + index. STC 25005.
(3) Walsingham, Thomas. Historia Brevis... ab Edwardo primo, ad Henricum quintum. Londini, exc. apud Henricum Binneman, 1574. F°, pp. 458. STC 25004.
Fore-edge: "Alfredus/T. Walsing." **309.4.65**

6.5.26 Daniels History 1622–6
Daniel, Samuel. [Possibly: The First Fowre Bookes of the civile wars between the two houses of Lancaster and Yorke. (Also includes the fyft Booke.) London, P. Short, for S. Waterson, 1595. 4°, ff. 108. STC 6244. (Bound with six other books after 1637.) **331.5.28[3]**]

6.5.27 Proceedings ag[t] Traytors: Northampton 1622–6
A True and Perfect Relation of the Whole proceedings against the late most barbarous Traitors, Garnet a Iesuite, and his Confederats: Containing... The Earle of Northamptons Speech. London, Robert Barker, 1606. 4°. STC 11619. **330.4.38**

6.5.28   Antiquitates Oxonij Twinni   1622–6
Twyne, Brian. Antiquitatis Academiae Oxoniensis Apologia. [Possibly:
Oxoniae, excud. Iosephus Barnesius, 1608. 4°, pp. 384, [72]. STC 24405.
326.6.34]

6.5.29   Origines Palat: Freheri   1622–6
Freher, Marquard. Originum Palatinarum Commentarius. [Possibly:
Heidelbergae, ex off. Commeliniana, 1599. 4°, pp. 114, 77. Adams F1001.
Now bound with two other books.   **330.4.21**]

6.5.30   Cambdens remaynes: 1622–6
Camden, William. Remaines of a greater worke concerning Britaine.
Missing. Emmanuel presently has two copies, one (London, 1623; STC
4523) a gift of John Breton in 1676: 330.4.23.

Classis 7ᵃᵉ Sect: 1ᵃ

7.1.1   Corpus juris Civilis Gothofredi 2 vol: 1622–6
Justinian I, *Emperor of the East*. Corpus iuris Civilis in quinque partes
distinctum.... His accesserunt commentarii... Authore Dionysio Gothofredo [i.e. Denys Godefroy].... Secunda editio. [Two volumes:]
(1) Digesta.
(2) Codicis... libri XII; Authenticae seu Novellae Constitutiones; Feu-
dorum consuetudines; Tractatus ad ius varii tomus V... Authore D.
Gothofredo. Lugduni, apud haer. B. Honorati, 1590. F°, coll. xiiii, 100,
2052; 952, 158 [458], 104, 124. Adams C2674. Fore-edges:
"CORP:IVR:CIU:/GOTHOF./I"; "II."   **305.2.43,44**

7.1.2   Lexicon Iuridicum Calvini   1622–6
Calvinus, Johannes, *J.D.* Lexicon iuridicum iuris Romani. Missing.

7.1.3   Hostiensis   1625
Hostiensis, Henricus de Segusio, *Card*. Aurea Summa, Nicolai
Superantii... Adnotationibus &... Fr. Martini Abbatis... illustrata
Coloniae, sumpt. Lazeri Zetzneri, 1612. F°, coll. 1736 + index. Donor: Dr
John Richardson. Fore-edge: "Hosti=/ensius."   **311.4.1**

7.1.4   Lyndewood   1626–32
Lyndwood, William, *Bp of St David's*. PRovinciale, seu Constitutiones
Anglie. London, 1505. F°, ff. 189 + tables. Adams L2116. STC 17109. Fore-
edge: "Linde/woode".   **311.4.8**¹

7.1.5   Ius Gr Rom Leunclavij   1622–6
Leunclavius [Loewenklau], Johannes. Iuris Graeco-Romani Tam Canonici

Quam Civilis Tomi duo. [Gk & Lat.] [2 vols. in 1.] Francofurti, impens. hered. Petri Fischeri; Vol. 2: Hanoviae, excud. Guilielmus Antonius impens. hered. Petri Fischeri, 1596. F°, pp. 563, 278. Adams L598. Fore-edge: "IUS Graec Rom."   **311.4.43**

7.1.6 Imperato*rum* etc statuta Goldasti 2 vol   1625
Goldast, Melchior (Haiminsfeld), *ed*. Imperatorum Caesarum Augustorum, Regum, et Principum Electorum S. Rom. Imperii Statuta et Rescripta imperialia a Carolo Magno... usque ad [Rudolphum II]. [3 vols. in 2.] Tom. I: Francofurdiae ad M., impens. Ioannis Iacobi Porssii & Ioan. Theobaldi Schönwetteri, apud Iohannem Spiessium, 1607; Tom. II: Hanoviae, excud. I. Halbeius, impens. P. Kopfii, 1609; Tom. III: Offenbachi, in off. C. Nobenii., cura P. Kopfius, 1610. F°, pp. 228, 120, 227, 400; 660 + indices. Donor: Dr John Richardson. Fore-edges: I: "Haimens/ [?]/ii"; II: "iii".   **311.4.35,36**

7.1.7 de Jurisdict: Imperato*rum* et Pontific vol 2^{dum} 1622–6
Goldast, Melchior, *ed*. Monarchiae S. Romani Imperii, sive Tractatuum de Iurisdictione Imperiali seu Regia, et Pontificia seu sacerdotali; de*que* potestate Imperatoris ac Papae... Tomus secundus... a Catholicis doctoribus conscripti. [2nd of 2 vols. only.] Francofordiae, typ: N. Hoffmanni, impens. C. Biermanni & Consort., 1614. F°, pp. 1782. Fore-edge: "Go*l*dat/Monar/ii".   **311.4.11**

7.1.8 Occam de Potestate politicâ et Ecclesiast   1622–6
William of Ockham. Opera de ecclesiastica et politica potestate. [Fran-cofordiae,] 1614. [Title page missing.] F°, pp. 313–1360. Fore-edge: "Occam".   **311.4.12**

7.1.9 Bruni op*e*ra tria: Scil: { de legationib*us*   1625
                                      { de ceremonijs
                                      { de Imaginibus

Brunus, Conrad. Opera Tria....De legationibus Libri.... De Caeremoniis.... De Imaginibus. [3 pts.] Moguntiae, apud S. Victorem, ex off. Francisci Behem, 1548. F°, pp. 242, 223, 154 + index. Adams B2959. Donor: Dr John Richardson. Crest and initials E.S. stamped on covers. Fore-edge: "Brun*us*".   **315.4.43**

7.1.10 Budaeus in Pandectas   1622–6
Budaeus, Gulielmus. [Possibly: Annotationes in quatuor & viginti Pandectarum libros. (2 pts.) Parisiis, ex off. Roberti Stephani, 1535. F°, pp. 381, 142. Adams B3086. Inscription on flyleaf: "Masyn".   **311.4.6**]
       Emmanuel's present holdings include two other editions, both Sancroft gifts (Coloniae, 1527; Adams B3079 and Basileae, 1557; Adams B3091): S2.5.75, S2.2.38.

104

7.1.11   Idem de asse   1625

Budaeus, Gulielmus. De Asse. Basileae, apud. Nic. Episcopium, 1556. F°,
pp. 315. Donor: Dr John Richardson. Missing. Register of Books
Removed, p. 13, l. 20: "Budaeus de Asse.... Basil: 1556. Dr Rich".
Emmanuel's present copy (Adams B3111) was a Sancroft gift: S5.2.11[1].

7.1.12   Idem de trans: Hellenismi   1625

Budaeus, Gulielmus. De transitu Hellenismi ad Christianismum. Parisiis,
ex off. Rob. Stephani, 1535. F°, ff. 132. Adams B3127. Donor: Dr John
Richardson.   **303.1.31**

7.1.13   Ejusdem Ep*isto*lae   1622–6

Two books bound together:
(1) Budaeus, Gulielmus. Epistolae. Basileae in aed. Andreae Cartandri,
    1521. 4°, pp. 222. Adams B3130.
(2) Tusanus, Jacobus. Annotata in G. Budaei Epistolas priores. Basileae
    apud Andr. Cratandrum, 1528. 4°, pp. 134. Adams T1206.   **327.2.94**

7.1.14   Statuta ab Hen 3° ad Hen: 8   1625

Statutes... from the time of kyng Henry the thirde, unto the fyrste yere
of... Henry the viii [3 pts.] Londini, in aed. T. Betheleti, 1543. F°, STC
9301. Donor: Dr John Richardson. Inscription on title page: "Ex dono D.
Joh. Richardson &c." Fore-edge: "Statutes/1".   **308.5.51**

7.1.15   Statutes 2 volumes   April 26, 1627

The Statutes at large,...from *Magna Charta*, until the sixteenth yeere of
the Raigne of... Iames. [2 vols.] London, Printed by Bonham, Norton and
Iohn Bill, 1618. F°. Donor: Richard Hunt. Inscription on flyleaf of each
vol.: "Aprilis 26. 1627. Ex dono Richardj Hunt in Sacrâ Theologia
Baccalaurej et hujus Collegii Socii". STC 9326.   **311.4.51,52**

7.1.16   νομοτεχνία Finchij   1622–6

Finch, Sir Henry. Νομοτεχνία; Cestascavoir, un Description del Common
Leys Dangleterre Solonque les Rules del Art. London, for the Societie of
Stationers, 1613. F°, ff. 149. STC 10870. Fore-edge: "Finc^h".   **308.5.53**

7.1.17   Epitome juris Civil Harmenopuli   1625

Harmenopulus, Constantius. Epitome Iuris Civilis Quae Legum Prochiron
Et Hexabiblos inscribitur. *Ed*. Theodoricus Adamaeus. [Gk.] Parisiis,
apud Christianum Wechelum, 1540. 4°, pp. 425. Adams H66. Donor: Dr
John Richardson. Inscription on title page: "Ex dono D. Joh. Richardson
&c". Fore-edge (vertically): "Epitome Iuris, Prochiron".   **333.2.56**

7.1.18   Gratian 2 vol   1584–97; 1622–6

Gratianus, *Bononiensis.* One volume was present from the time of the first inventory. In 1621 and 1622 it was shelved immediately adjacent to the six-volume *Corpus Juris Civilis* (see 7.2.3). As the fore-edge numbering shows, this volume is: Decretum Gratiani. *Ed.* Johannes Thierry. Parisiis, venund. in off. lib. yolande Bonhomme, vidue... Thielmanni Keruer, 1531. 4°, ff. 691. Adams G1050. Fore-edge: "8/Decreta".   **333.2.57**

A "memorandum" at the end of the 1637 catalogue includes "Gratian one vol" among the eighteen items "missing at the accounts at Easter 1637". A note in the left margin, probably assigning responsibility for the book, mentions "Mr Preston". Then follows a statement that "this book shewed/at ye acc: octo: 18/1637". It is unclear, however, whether the reference is to the Gratian volume or the following item, "Puteani Strictura, in Casaubonum" (7.4.4–12).

The second volume is possibly:

either: [Decretorum collectanea. *Ed.* A. de Mouchy. (Paris,) apud Carolam Guillard, vid. Claudii Chevallonii & Gulielmum desboys, 1552. 8°, ff. 285–663 only. Fore-edge: "2". Adams G1052.   **324.8.59**]

or: [Decretum Gratiani: seu verius, Decretorum Canonicorum collectanea. Lutetiae Parisiorum, apud Gulielmum Merlin... & Gulielmum Desboys... ac Sebastianum Nivellium, 1561. F°, coll. 3044 (2144), 220 + index. Adams G1054. Fore-edge: "Gratiani:/Decretvm:".
                                                                        315.4.42]

7.1.19   Molinaeus de Contractibus   c. 1584

Du Moulin, Charles. Tractatus commerciorum, et usurarum, redituumque pecunia constitutorum, et monetarum. Parisiis, apud Audoenum Parvum, 1555. 4°, pp. 816 + index. Adams D1095. Donor: Sir Walter Mildmay. Signature on title page: "Gualteri Mildmay/A° 1560". Fore-edge: "16".

                                                                        FB9

7.1.20   Pithaei Collatio Legum Mosaic et Rom: 1622–6

Pithou, Pierre. Mosaycarum et Romanarum legum collatio. Missing.

7.1.21   Pomeranus de jurisdictione   1622–6

?[Possibly: L. Fenestellae (*pseud.* for Julius Pomponius Laetus). De Magistratibus sacerdotijsque Romanorum libellus, iamprimum nitori restitus. Basileae, 1532.   **322.6.102**]

7.1.22   Goldastus contra Gretserum   1625

Goldast, Melchior. Replicatio pro Sac. Caesarea et Regia Francorum Maiestate illustrissimisque Imperii Ordinibus adversus Iacobi Gretseri Crimina.... Accesserunt insuper... quorundam S. Rom. Imperii Principum Apologiae pro... Henrico IV. Imp.... adversus Gregorii VII

Papae. Hanoviae, apud Thomam Villerianum, impens. Conradi Biermanni, 1611. 4°, pp. 440. Donor: Dr John Richardson. Missing. Register of Books Removed, p. 37, l. 18: "Goldasti replicatio pro Caes: majest: adv: Gretserum, cum Apologia Henr: 4^{ti} adv: Papaeum (Dupl: Apol:) Han: 1611 Dr Rich".

7.1.23 Pleas of the Crowne   1625
Staunford, Sir William. Les Plees del Coron: divisees in plusiours titles & common lieux. London, Richard Tottyll, 1560. 4°, ff. 198 + index. STC 23220. Donor: Dr John Richardson. Inscription at top of title page: "Ex dono D. Joh. Richardson". Fore-edge: "pleas of/ye crown".   **325.3.109**

7.1.24 Swinburne of Testaments   1625
Swinburne, Henry. A Briefe Treatise of Testaments and last Willes. London, for the Companie of Stationers, 1611. 4°, ff. 359 + table. STC 23548. Donor: Dr John Richardson. Inscription on title page: "Ex dono D. Joh. Richardson &c".   **326.5.56**

7.1.25 Smiths Comonwealth of England   1622–6
Smith, Sir Thomas. The commonwealth of England, and the Manner of Government thereof. [Possibly: London (W. Stansby) for J. Smethwicke, 1609. 4°, pp. 134. STC 22862. Fore-edge: "Smith/ & Cowels/Interp:". Present copy bound with 7.1.26, perhaps later than 1637.   **327.5.76¹**]

7.1.26 Cowells Interpreter   1622–6
Cowell, John. The Interpreter: Or Booke containing the Signification of Words... mentioned in the Lawe Writers, or Statutes of this... Kingdome [Possibly: Cambridge, printed by Iohn Legate, 1607. 4°. STC 5900. Fore-edge: "Smith/& Cowels/Interp:". Present copy bound with 7.1.25, perhaps later than 1637.   **327.5.76²**]

Classis 7^{ae} Sectio 2^a

7.2.1 Turrecremata in Causas   1626–32
Two books bound together:
(1) Turrecremata, Johannes de [also Torquemada, Juan de]. Super primo volu. Causarum. Lugduni. Ioannes de Ionuelle dictus Piston imprim., 1519. F°, ff. 226. Adams T1167.
(2) Turrecremata, Johannes de. super secundo volu. Causarum. Lugduni, Ioannes de Ionuelle dictus Piston imprim., 1519. F°, ff. 219 + index. Adams T1168.
Donor (?): John Smith. Inscription on first title page: "Sum Johannis Smithi Liber ex dono Margarete Southewell virtue sororis sue". Fore-edge: "Turre/Cremata/In/Decret:/Causas/Doo[?] net".   **315.1.48**

7.2.2   Idem in decret   1625
Turrecremata, Johannes de [also Torquemada, Juan de]. Summa de
Ecclesia... Una Cum Eiusdem Apparatu... super decreto Papae Eugenii
IIII in Concilio Florentino de Unione Graecorum emanato. Venetiis, apud
M. Tramerzinum, 1561, 1562. 4°, ff. 412, 43+tabula. Adams T1178. Donor:
Dr John Richardson. Fore-edge: "Turrecr".   **333.2.14**

7.2.3   Corpus juris civilis 6 vol   1584–97
Five of the six vols. are as follows:
Justinian I, *Emperor of the East*. [Corpus Juris Civilis cum glossis.] in alma
Pariseorum achademia... imp. opera et impens U. Gering et B. Rembolt
soc. Vols. 3–5 per B. Rembolt, 1505–16. [Vol. I:] Codicis Iustiniani
amplissimum Argumentum. 1505. Adams J500. Fore-edge: "6".   **315.1.59**

[Vol. II:] Digesti... copiosum argumentum. 1515. Adams J546. Fore-edge:
"5".   **315.1.60**

[Vol. III] Infortiati Amplissimum argumentum. 1515. Adams J547. Fore-
edge: "7".   **315.1.61**

[Vol. IV:] Digestum Novum. 1516. Adams J548. Fore-edge: "Corpus
Iuris/1/N".   **315.1.62**

[Vol. V:] Cum Volumen, Ad Lectorem. 1516. Fore-edge: "4".   **315.1.63**

Donor: Edward Leeds. The vols. originally numbered 2 and 3, now
missing, may have been bound as one. The first four vols. listed are signed
by "Edouardus Leedis," a Master in Chancery, friend of Mildmay, and
an early college benefactor who died Feb. 17, 1589.

7.2.4   Covaruvij opera   1625
Covarruvias a Leyva, Diego, *Bp of Segovia*. Opera Omnia. [2 vols. in 1.]
Francofurti a. M., apud I. Saurium, impens. Rulandiorum, & F. N. Rothii,
1608. F°, pp. 610, 506+indices. Donor: Dr John Richardson. Inscription
on title page: "Ex dono D. Joh. Richardson &c". Fore-edge:
"Covaruv:/Opera".   **315.4.49**

7.2.5   Imperatorum Imagines   1597–1621
[Possibly: Strada, Jacobus de. Imperatorum Romanorum Omnium
Orientalium et Occidentalium Verissimae Imagines ex Antiquis
Numismatis Quam Fidelissime Delineatae.] Missing? A copy of the Tiguri,
1559 edition of this work with the engravings of Andreas Gesner
illustrating the heads of Roman emperors is in Emmanuel's library now
(315.1.33) bearing a title page inscription stating its ownership by William
Skinner. Skinner is probably the Emmanuel graduate (B.A. 1639–40) who

108

died in college in 1641, leaving books to the library. His copy may have replaced the original library copy.

7.2.6 Ptolomaei Geographia lat   1586
Ptolemaeus, Claudius. [Geographia] Ptolomaeus auctus, restitutus Emaculatus. Cum Tabulis. Argentorati, Ioannes Scotus literis excaepit, 1520. Fº, ff. 54 + 45 double-leaf and one single-leaf maps. Adams P2220. Proctor 10289. Donor: William Fleetwood. Inscription on title page: "Ex dono W. Fletewoode Record: London/1586".   **311.3.31**

7.2.7 Helvici chronol: et Remelini Anatom: 1622–6
Two books bound together:
  (1) Helvicus, Christophorus. Theatrum Historicum sive Chronologiae Systema Novum aequalibus Centuriarum & Decadum intervallis; cum assignatione Imperiorum, Regnorum. Giessae Hessorum, typis & sumpt. Nicolai Hampelii, 1618. Fº, pp. 39.
  (2) Remmelinus, Johannes. Catoptorum Microcosmicum, suis aere incisis visionibus splendens, cum historia, & Pinace. Augustae Vindelicorum, typis Davidis Francki, 1619. Fº, pp. 28. Fore-edge (vertically): "Helv/[?]/[?]".   **311.3.39**

7.2.8 Adricomij Theatrum terrae sctae   1625
Adrichomius, Christiaan. Theatrum terrae sanctae et Biblicarum Historiarum cum tabulis geographicis aere expressis. Coloniae Agrippinae, in off. Birckmannica, sumpt. Arnoldi Mylii, 1590. Fº, pp. 286 + 12 maps and index. Adams A185. Donor: Dr John Richardson. Inscription on title page: "Ex dono D. Joh. Richardson & c". Fore-edge: "Terra/Sanct".
                                                                                          309.1.18

7.2.9 Strabo gr 1   1621–2
Strabo. Rerum Geographicarum Libri XVII. Isaacus Casaubonus...emendavit, ac commentariis illustravit. [Gk & Lat.] *Tr.* G. Xylander. Lutetiae Parisiorum, typis Regiis, 1620. Fº, pp. 843, 282 + indices. Donor: Elias Travers. Inscription on front flyleaf: "Ex Dono} {λαθε βιωσ[ας] E. Travers; *pr*et: 23ˢ–6ᵈ/κύριοι πραξεων ἀλλ' οὐχ ἐξεων". Fore-edge: "Strabo".   **306.3.36**

7.2.10 Ortelij Thesaurus Geograph   1625
Ortelius, Abraham. Thesaurus Geographicus. Antuerpiae, ex off. Plantiniana, 1596. Fº. Adams 0348. Donor: Dr John Richardson. Inscription on title page: "Ex dono D. Joh. Richardson, etc." Fore-edge: "Orte-lius".   **318.2.10**

7.2.11 Medicorum Icones   May 12, 1613
Sambucus, Johannes. Veterum aliquot ac recentium Medicorum

Philosophorum*que* Icones.... cum eiusdem ad singulas Elogiis [Antwerp,] ex off. Plantiniana Raphelengii, 1603. F°. Donor: Laurence Wright. Inscription on fly-leaf: "Ex dono Laurentij Wrighti huius Collegij alumni/Anno Dom: 1613. Maij 12°." **307.3.62**

7.2.12   Stephanus de urbibus   1625
Stephanus, *Byzantinus*. De urbibus. *Ed.* Guilielmus Xylander. Basileae, ex off. Oporiniana, 1568. [Gk] Donor: Dr John Richardson. Missing. Register of Books Removed, p. 43, 1. 16: "Stephanus de Urbibus Gr:... Bas: 1558 Dr Rich". Emmanuel's present copy was a Sancroft gift: S11.1.28.

7.2.13   Novus Orbis   1597–1621
[1621 inventory (8.I.17): "Tipi Cosmographici declaratio et usus per Munsteru*m*"]
Grynaeus, Simon, *ed.* Novus Orbis Regionum ac Insularum Veteribus Incognitarum. [Includes a 12-page section at the beginning entitled:] "Typi Cosmographici et Declaratio et Usus, per Sebastianum Munsterum." [Possibly: Basile*ae*, apud Io. Hervagium, 1555. F°, pp. 667. Adams G1338. Donor (?): John Bingham. Signature on title page: "Johannes Bingham. 1598". **309.4.63**]

7.2.14   Munsteri Cosmogr^a: 1584–97
Two books bound together:
(1) Munster, Sebastian. Cosmographie universalis lib VI. Basileae, apud Henrichum Petri, 1552. F°, pp. 1163. Adams M1909.
(2) Gerbelius, Nicolaus. In descriptionem Graeciae Sophiani, praefatio. Basileae, ex off. Ioannis Oporini, 1545. F°, pp. 80, [13]. Adams G479. Fore-edge: "Munster*us*/20". **306.4.14**

7.2.15   Ptolomaei Almagest, Cornelij Celsi medic^a Alpharabius in Arist: Rhet
                                                                                  1597–1621
3 works bound together:
(1) Ptolemaeus, Claudius. Almagestu*m*. Venetii, ductu Petri Liechtenstein, 1515. F°, ff. 152. Adams P2213.
(2) Celsus, Aurelius Cornelius. [De Medicina Libri VIII.] [Title page missing.] Venetiis, Impressor Ioannes rubeus Vercellensis, 1493. F°, ff. 62. Hain 4837.
(3) Aristotle. [Rhetorica ex Arabico Latine reddita, interprete Hermanno Alemanno, praemissa Alpharabii Declaratione super eadem Rhetorica. Excerptum ex Aristotelis Poetica, per eundem Hermannum de Averrois textu Arabico. Venetiis, per magistrum Philippum Venetum, 1481.] [Title page missing.] F°. Hain 1681.
Donor: John Glanville. Inscription on Ptolemaeus title page: "Emmanuelis Collegij ex/dono Johannis Glanuille" and, in another hand, "Thys book belongeth to John [?] Felmingtem [?] A° 1575." Fore-edge (vertically): "Ptolom. Alm. C Celsus" and (horizontally): "36". **MSS 5.2.13**

7.2.16 Pomponius Mela cum Coment Vadiani   1622–6
Mela, Pomponius. [Three works: I:] De orbis situ Libri Tres. [*Ed.* I.
Vadianus.] [II:] Loca Aliquot ex Vadiani commentariis summatum re-
petita. [III:] Epistola Vadiani.... ad Rudolphum Agricolam iuniorem.
Basileae, apud Andream Cratandrum, 1522. F°, pp. 221, [54], [20]. Adams
M1056. Fore-edge: "P. Mela". Donor (?): Richard Baitmann. Inscription
on title page: "Richardi Baitmann".   **303.1.12**

7.2.17 Strabo Lat   1584–97
Three books bound together:
(1) Strabo. De situ orbis. Venetiis, a Philippo pincio, 1510. F°, ff.
    150 + index. Adams S1900.
(2) Avicenna. De animalibus per magistrum michaelem scotum de arabico
    in Latinum translatus. [Venice, c. 1500.] F°, ff. 54. Hain 2220.
(3) Solinus, C. Julius. De situ orbis terrarum.... Vibius Sequester de
    fluminibus. *Ed.* A. Gaboardus Pisauri ab Hieronymo Soncino, 1512. F°,
    ff. 42. Adams S1390.
Fore-edge: "Strabo/18".   **306.3.33**

7.2.18 Appiani et Gemmae Frisij Cosmogr[a]:   1625
Apianus, Petrus. Cosmographia, sive Descriptio universi Orbis, Petri
Apiani & Gemmae Frisii. Antuerpiae, ex off. Ioannis Withagii, 1584. 4°, pp.
479. Adams A1285. Donor: Dr John Richardson. Fore-edge: "Appi/ anij".
                                                                       333.1.75

7.2.19 Ptolomaei Geogr[a] graec   1622–6
Ptolemaeus, Claudius. De geographia libri octo. [Gk.] Basileae, παρ'
Ἱερωνύμῳ τῷ φρωβενίῳ καὶ Νικολαίῳ τῷ Ἐπισκοπίῳ, 1533. 4°, pp. 542.
Adams P2222. Fore-edge: "Ptolom/gr".   **331.2.55**

Classis 7*ae* Sectio: 3*a*

7.3.1. Herodotus gr lat   1625
Herodotus. Historiarum lib. IX.... Eiusdem Narratio de vita Homeri.
Editio secunda. *Trans.* L. Valla, *ed.* H. Stephanus. [Gk & Lat.] [Genevae,]
excud. Henricus Stephanus, 1592. F°, pp. 731 + index. Adams H398.
Donor: Dr John Richardson. Fore-edge: "Herodot:" Arms of William
Cecil, Lord Burghley, stamped on cover.   **306.3.19**

7.3.2 Thucidides gr lat   1625
Thucydides. De bello Peloponnesiaco libri octo. *Tr.*: Laurentius Valla, *ed.*
Henricus Stephanus. [Gk & Lat.] [Geneva,] excud. Henricus Stephanus,
Huldrichi Fuggeri typog. 1564. F°, pp. 297, 216 + index. Adams T666.
Donor: Dr John Richardson. Inscription on flyleaf: "Ex dono D. Joh.

Richardson, S.T.D. Collegij S.S.^{ae} Trinitatis Magistri, & hujus Collegij quondam Socij A.D. 1625". This copy replaced the library's first copy.

306.3.20

7.3.3   Xenophon gr lat   1584–97

Xenophon. [Possibly: Ἅπαντα τὰ σωζόμενα βιβλία... omnia quae extant opera.... annotationes Henrici Stephani. (Gk & Lat.) (Geneva,) excud. Henricus Stephanus, Huldrici Fuggeri typog., 1561. (Lacking the Latin version.) Fº, pp. 587, 43. Adams X10.   **306.3.17**]

7.3.4   Diodorus Siculus gr   1597–1621

Diodorus, *Siculus*. [Possibly: Bibliothecae historicae libri quindecim de quadraginta. *Ed*. Henricus Stephanus. (Gk) (Geneva,) excud. Henricus Stephanus, Huldrici Fuggeri typog., 1559. Fº, pp. 847. Adams D472.

310.1.12]

7.3.5   Polybius gr lat   1622–6

Polybius. Historiarum Libri priores quinque, Nicolao Perotto... interprete. Item Epitome sequentium librorum usque ad Decimumseptimum Wolfgango Musculo interprete. [2 pts, Gk & Lat.] Basileae, per Ioannem Hervagium, 1549. Fº, pp. 282, 323. Adams P1803. Fore-edge: "Polybius". Arms of William Cecil, Lord Burghley, stamped on cover.   **306.3.32**

7.3.6   Pausanius gr lat   1584–97

[1621 inventory (8.S.1): Παυσανιον της Ελλαδος περιηγησις]

Pausanias, *the Traveller*. Παυσανιου της Ἑλλαδος περιηγσις. Accurata Graeciae Descriptio. [Possibly: a Guilielmo Xylandro... recognita... Accesserunt Annotationes... a G. Xylandro inchoatae, nunc... a Frid. Sylb(urgii) continuatae... Addita etiam... Romuli Amasaei versio,... notatiunculis illustrata (2 pts, Gk & Lat.). Francofurti, apud Haer*ed*. Andreae Wecheli, 1583. Fº. Adams P522.   **313.4.34**]

7.3.7   Herodotus gr.   1584–97

Herodotus. Herodoti Libri Novem... Georgii Gemisti... de iis quae post pugnam ad Mantineam gesta sunt, Libri II. Una cum Ioachimi Camerarii Praefatione, Annotationibus, Herodoti vita. [Gk] Basileae, in off. Hervagiana, 1541. Fº, pp. 310. Missing. Register of Books Removed, p. 43, l. 18: "Herodotus cum Gemisto Grae: edit Cam.... Bas: 1541." Emmanuel's present copy (Adams H395) was a Sancroft gift: S11.1.37.

7.3.8   Dion gr   1584–97

Dion Cassius. Dionis Romanarum historiarum libri XXIII, a XXXVI ad LVIII usque. [Gk] Lutetiae, ex off. Rob. Stephani, 1548. Fº, pp. 498. Adams D503. Fore-edge: "Dion/gca".   **306.3.18**

7.3.9   Appian gr   c. 1584
Appianus, *of Alexandria*. Romanarum historiarum Celtica. Lutetiae, typis
Regiis, cura Caroli Stephani, 1551 [Gk] F°. pp. 395. Adams A1340. Donor:
Sir Walter Mildmay [not signed].   **FB.6**

7.3.10 Arriani Hist^a Alex: gr lat   1625
Arrianus, Flavius. De Expedit. Alex. Magni, Historiarum Libri VIII.
Alexandri Vita Ex Plut[archo]. Eiusdem Libri II, De Fortuna vel virtute
Alexandri. [Gk & Lat.] [Geneva,] Excud. Henr. Stephanus, 1575. F°. pp.
198, 68+index. Adams A2010. Donor: Dr John Richardson. Fore-edge:
"Arri/an*us*/gr.1." Arms of William Cecil, Lord Burghley, stamped on cover.
                                                                306.3.16

7.3.11 Arriani Periplus   1622–6
Arrianus, Flavius. Ponti Euxini & maris Erythraei Periplus.... *Ed*. I.
Guilielmus Stuckius. [2 pts, Gk & Lat.] Genevae, apud Eustathium
Vignon, 1577. F°, pp. 193, 109+indices. Adams A2015. Fore-edge:
"Arria/nus".   **306.4.51**

7.3.12 Agathia Hist^a gr lat   1622–6
Agathias, *Myrinaeus*. [Possibly: De imperio Iustiniani Imperatoris libri
quinque. *Tr*. B. Vulcanius. (Gk & Lat.)] Missing.

7.3.13 Aeliani Hist^{ae} variae gr lat   1622–6
Aelianus, Claudius. Variae historiae libri XIIII. *Tr*. Justus V. Wetter. [Gk
& Lat.] [Possibly: Editio postrema. (Lyon or Geneva?) apud Ioan.
Tornaesium, 1600. 16°, pp. 461, (18). Adams A223.   **322.7.54**]

7.3.14 Livius   c. 1584
Livius, Titus. Decades tres cum dimidia.... Beati Rhenani & Sigismundi
Gelenii adiunctae Annotationes. Addita est Chronologia Henrici Glareani.
Basileae, in off. Frobeniana, 1534–5, F°, pp. 69, 244, 243, 211, 91. Adams
L1330. Donor: Sir Walter Mildmay. Inscription on title page: "Sum
Gualteri Mildmaij quem libens/non mutabo/Gualteri Mildmaij/1558".
Fore-edge: "Livi*us*".   **FB.2**

7.3.15 Augustae Hist^{ae} Scriptores lat Minores   1611–21
Historiae Augustae scriptores Latini minores, a Ulio Fere Caesare ad
Carolum Magnum.... Opera Iani Gruteri; Cuius etiam additae notae. [3
pts.] Hanoviae impens. Claudii Marnii her., Iohannis & Andreae Marnii &
consort. 1611. F°, pp. 1202, 127, 177+indices. Fore-edge: "Hist: Aug:/i.ii".
                                                                306.3.28

7.3.16 Cornelius Tacitus   1622–6
Tacitus, Gaius Cornelius. Opera quae Exstant. *Ed*. Iustus Lipsius. Lugduni

Batavorum, ex off. Plantiniana, apud Franciscum Raphelengium, 1589. F°, pp. 335, 194, 64 + indices. Adams T36. Fore-edge: "C. Tacit". **306.3.34**

7.3.17 Lazius de republ: Rom: 1622–6
Two works: [I:] Lazius, Wolfgang. Reipublicae Romanae in Exteris Provinciis, Bello Acquisitis, Constitutae, Commentariorum Libri duodecim.... [II:] Zamosius, Stephanus. Analecta, Lapidum Vetustorum Et Nonnullarum In Dacia Antiquitatum. Francofurti ad Moenum, apud haered. Andreae Wecheli, Claudium Marnium & Ioannem Aubrium, 1598. F°, pp. 1108, 47 + indices. Adams L351. Fore-edge: "Lasius". **312.1.57**

7.3.18 Lipsij opera 2 vols   1626–32
Lipsius, Justus. Opera. [Possibly: Novae Formae Editio. (2 vols.) Lugduni, apud Horatium Cardon, 1613. F°. pp. 882, 899.   **305.2.14,15**]

7.3.19 Gruteri Inscriptiones 2 vol   1626–32
Gruterus, Janus. Inscriptionum Romanarum corpus absolutissimum. [Heidelberg,] in bibliopolio Commeliniano, 1616. F°. Missing. Register of Books Removed, p. 13, 1. 2: "Ja. Gruteri inscriptiones Romanae ... 2 V ... 1616".

7.3.20 Cuspinian de Caesar[b]   1622–6
Cuspinianus, Johannes. De Caesaribus atque Imperatoribus Romanis.... Vita Ioannis Cuspiniani, et de utilitate huius Historiae per D. Nicolaum Gerbelium. [Strasbourg, C. Mylius,] 1540. F°, pp. 762 + index. Adams C3134. Fore-edge: "Cuspin".   **306.4.12**
At some point after 1637 and before 1693 the Emmanuel library acquired a later edition of this work. The Register of Books Removed, p. 47, 1.25, shows: "Jo: Cuspinianus de caesaribus &, Impp Romanis.... Franc: 1601." This was replaced by a duplicate in Sancroft's bequest: S12.2.35[1]. We think the 1540 edition was acquired first because the fore-edge identification is in the manner of the library's fore-edge marking of books acquired in the mid-1620s.

7.3.21 Sigonius de Antiquo jure Rom: 1622–6
Sigonius, Carolus. [Possibly: De antiquo iure Populi Romani libri unde-cim. De republica Atheniensium libri IIII. De Atheniensium, Lacedae-moniorumque temporibus liber I. Lutetiae, apud Iacobum Du Puys (*Colophon:* Lugduni, excud. Ioannes Tornaesius) 1576. F°, pp. 667 + index. Adams S1100. Fore-edge: "Sigonius".   **311.4.10**]

7.3.22 Idem de fastis consular   1625
Sigonius, Carolus. Fasti Consulares, ac Triumphi acti a Romulo Rege usque ad Ti. Caesarem. Basileae, apud Nicolaum Episcopium Iuniorem,

114

1559. F°, pp. 388. Adams S1116. Donor: Dr John Richardson. Fore-edge: "Sigoni/Fasti [?]". **318.2.33**

7.3.23 Idem de Regno Italiae 1622–6
Sigonius, Carolus. Historiarum de Regno Italiae Libri. Missing. Emmanuel's present copy (Hanoviae, 1613–18) was a gift of Joseph Romney in the mid-seventeenth century. **304.3.22**

7.3.24 Ejusdem Hist Imper occidental 1622–6
Sigonius, Carolus. Historiarum de Occidentali Imperio Libri XX. Missing. Emmanuel's present copy (Francofurti, 1593; Adams S1119) was a gift of Joseph Romney in the mid-seventeenth century. **304.3.21**

7.3.25 Guicciardini Historia Italic 1622–6
[1626 and 1628 inventories (8.3.15): "Porchaccij hist: Ital:"]
Guicciardini, Francesco. La historia d'Italia. Ed. Thomaso Porcacchi. Vinegia, presso Giorgio Angelieri, 1583. 4°, ff. 9, 488, 112 + indices. Adams G1514. Foreedge: "Guicciard/Italice". **333.1.88**

7.3.26 Ejusdem Historia lat 2 vol 1584–97
Guicciardini, Francesco. Historiarum sui temporis libri viginti, ex Italico in Latinum. *Tr.* Cael. S. C[urio]. Basileae, excud. Petrus Perna suis & Henrici Petri impens., 1567. [2 vols.] 8°, pp. 1046, 971 + indices. Adams G1523. Fore-edges: "Guicciard/i/30"; "ii/31". Donor (?): John Leeds. Inscription on title page of vol. I: "Joha*nn*es Leeds me possidet. 1575". **324.5.29,30**

Classis 7^{ae} Sect: 4^{ae}

Sectio 4 is divided into four subsections. Our shelf location numbers, therefore, employ a hyphen to separate the subsection number from the book's position on the shelf within that subsection, e.g., 7.4.3–5 is the fifth book in the third subsection on the fourth shelf in Classis 7.

7.4.1–1 Historia de rebus memorab: Italicè 1597–1621
[1621 inventory (1.I.22): "Historia Marci Guazzi Ital."]
Guazzo, Marco. Historie di tutte le cose degne di memoria quai del anno 1524. [Possibly: Venetia, per Comin da Trino di Monferrato, 1544. 8°, ff. 408 + index. Adams G1453. Fore-edge (vertically): "Hist. Ital". **322.6.95**]

7.4.1–2 Carionis Chronicon Gallicè 1597–1621
Carion, Johannes. Croniques.... Avec les faits et gestes du seu Roy Francois, iusques au regne du Roy Henry deuxieme. *Tr.* Iean le Blond. Lyon, par Iean de Tournes, & Guillaume Gazeau. 1549. 16°, pp. 750 + index. Adams C720. Fore-edge: "Carion/gallice/32". **322.6.132**

7.4.2–1 Clavij Op*er*a 4 vol 1626–32
Clavius, Christophorus. Opera Mathematica [5 vols. in 4.] Moguntiae,

sumpt. A. Hierat, excud. I. Volmari, R. Eltz, & J. Albinus, [1611–]1612. F°.
Missing. Register of Books Removed, p. 17, 1.8: "Clavij opera
Mathematica ... 4 V ... Mogunt: 1612." Emmanuel's present copy was a
Sancroft gift: S6.1.31–34.

7.4.2–2   Alberti dureri Geomet^a pract^{ca} c.1584
Durer, Albrecht. Quatuor his suaru*m* Institutionum Geometricarum li-
bris, lineas, superfices & solida corpora Tractavit. Parisiis, ex off. Christiani
Wecheli, 1535. F°, pp. 581 [185]. Adams D1048. Donor: Sir Walter
Mildmay. Signature on title page: "Virtute non vi. Wa: Mildmaius:". **FB7**

7.4.2–3   Orontius in Euclidem   c. 1584
Two books bound together:
(1) Finé, Oronce. In sex priores libros Geometricorum elmentorum
    Euclidis ... demonstrationes ... cum ... textu graeco & interpretatione
    latina Bartholomaei Zamberti Veneti. Lutetiae Parisiorum, apud
    Simonem Colinaeum, 1544. F°, pp. 152 + index. Adams E997. Signature
    on title page: "Wa: Mildmay".
(2) Finé, Oronce. De Mundi Sphaera, sive Cosmographia, primare
    Astronomiae parte, Lib. V. Parisiis, ex off. Simonis Colinaei, 1542. F°,
    ff. 112. Adams F468.
Donor: Sir Walter Mildmay. Fore-edge: "Oron/tius/[faintly, in another
hand:] Orontius/22".   **FB5**

7.4.2–4   Ejusdem Geometria practica   1584–97
Finé, Oronce. De re & praxi geometrica, libri tres. [Possibly: Lutetiae apud
Aegidium Gourbinum, 1556. 4°, ff. 56 (59). Adams F466. Sometime after
1637 this was bound with Charles de Bouelles, Geometrie Practiques.
Paris, 1551.   **334.2.83**]

7.4.2–5   Stadij Ephemerides   1584–97
Stadius, Johannes. Ephemerides Novae et Exactae ... Ab Anno 1554. ad
Annum 1570. Coloniae Agrippinae, apud Haeredes Arnoldi Birckmanni.
1556. 4°. Adams S1623. Fore-edge: "Ephimerede/25".   **329.1.75**

7.4.2–6   Munsteri Horologiograph: 1597–1621
Munster, Sebastian. Horologiographia, Post Priorem Aeditionem ... re-
cognita. Basileae, excud. Henricus Petrus, 1533. 4°, pp. 334. Adams M1919.
Fore-edge (vertically): "munster" above (horizontally) "26".   **325.4.108**

7.4.2–7   Calendarium Palest Christman*n*   1622–6
Uri ben Simeon, Rabbi [sometimes Ori ben Simeon]. Calendarium
Palestinorum Et Universorum Iudaeorum ... scholiis ... illustratum ... *Tr.*
& *Ed.* Jac. Christmann. Francofurti, apud Ioan. Wecheli relictam Viduam,
impens. Petri Kopffi, 1594. 4°, pp. 159. Adams (U67) omits Emmanuel's

copy. Now bound with Morton Eudes, Catholike Traditions (London, 1610); this binding post-dates 1637.   **332.5.60**

7.4.2–8   Tonstalli Arithmetica   c. 1584
Tunstall, Cuthbert, *Bp of Durham*. De Arte Supputandi Libri Quatuor.
Parisiis, ex off. Roberti Stephani; 1529. 4°, pp. 271, [7]. Adams T1122.
Donor: Sir Walter Mildmay. Signature on fly-leaf and title page:
"Gualterus Mildmaius 1555." Fore-edge: (vertically) "Tonstall*us*" above
(horizontally) "27".   **FB12**

7.4.3–1   Godelmannus de Magis   1622–6
Godelmann, Johann Georg. Tractatus De Magis, Veneficis, et Lamiis,
deque his recte cognoscendis et puniendis ... in tres libros. [Possibly:
Francofurti, 1591. 4°.] Missing. This edition is listed in the catalogue of c.
1680 at I5.41. Emmanuel's present copy (Francofurti, 1601) was a Sancroft
gift: S14.2.28.

7.4.3–2   Valerij de val Epit: Lullij   1622–6
Valeriis, Valerius de. [Possibly: Aureum Sane Opus, In Quo Ea Omnia
Breviter Explicantur, Quae ... Raymundus Lullus, tam in scientarum ar-
bore, q*uam* in arte generali tradit. Augustae Vindelicorum, imprim.
Michael Manger, 1589. 4°, pp. 179 + index. Adams V57. Rebound with
other books after 1637.   **331.4.81³]**

7.4.3–3   Angelusij Ars Medica.   1622–6
Angelucci, Teodoro. Ars medica. [Possibly: Venetiis, apud Paulum
Meiettum, 1588. 4°, ff. 111. Adams A1111.   **331.4.104]**

7.4.3–4   Bodini daemonomania   1625
Bodin, Jean. De magorum daemonomania Libri IV. Basileae, per Thomam
Guarinum, 1581. 4°, pp. 488 + Preface. Donor: Dr John Richardson.
Missing. Register of Books Removed, p. 55, 1. 12: "Bodinus de Magorum
Daemonomania.... Bas: 1681 [i.e. 1581] Dr Rich." Emmanuel's present
copy (Adams B2220) was a Sancroft gift: S14.2.22.

7.4.3–5   Fernelius   1622–6
Fernelius, Johannes. Universa Medicina (*Ed.* G. Plantius.) Editio pos-
trema. (Therapeutices libri VII; De abditis rerum causis libri duo.)
Francofurti ad Moenum, apud Andream Wechelum, 1577. F°, pp. 248, 173,
101 + indices. Adams F258. Fore-edge: "Fernel:".   **311.4.62**

7.4.4–1   Drusij Comment ad voces Heb: No: Test   1625
Drusius, Johannes. Ad Voces Hebraicas Novi Testamenti commentarius.
Antuerpiae, ex off. Christophori Plantini, 1582. 4°, pp. 51. Missing. Donor:

Dr John Richardson. Register of Books Removed, p. 1, 1. 23: "Jo: Drusij comment: in voces hebreas N. Testm:ti .... Antw: 1582 ... Dr Richardson". Emmanuel's present copy (Adams D921) was a Sancroft gift: S1.3.44[3].

7.4.4-2   Ejusdem Parallela Sacra   1622–6
Drusius, Johannes. Parallela Sacra. [Heb., Gk, Lat.] [Possibly: Franekerae, excud. Aegidius Radaeus, 1588. 4°, pp. 124. Adams D933. Rebound with five other books of Drusius sometime after 1637.
328.2.102[1]]

7.4.4-3   Ejusdem Praeterita   1622–6
Drusius, Johannes. Annotationum in totum Iesu Christi Testamentum sive Praeteritorum libri decem. Missing.

7.4.4-4   Ejusdem Proverb: class 2ae   1622–6
Drusius, Johannes. Proverbiorum classes duae, in quibus explicantur Proverbia sacra & ex sacris litteris orta. Franekerae, excud. Aegidius Radaeus, 1590. 4°, pp. 392 + index. Adams D934. Fore-edge: "Drusius".
326.2.17

7.4.4-5   Grotij ordi [ink blot] Hollandiae Pietas   1622–6
Grotius, Hugo. Ordinum Hollandiae ac Westfrisiae Pietas ab Improbissimis Multorum Calumniis ... vindicata. [Possibly: Lugduni Batavorum, Iohannes Patius, 1613. 4°, pp. 100 [82]. Bound with several other books in the late seventeenth century.   **330.4.56[4]**]

7.4.4-6   Erastus de Excommunicatione   1622–6
Erastus, Thomas. Explicatio Gravissimae Quaestionis utrum Excommunicatio a sacramentorum usu arcet. Pesclavii, apud Baocium Sultaceterum, 1589. [London, J. Wolfe. STC 10511.] Missing. Register of Books Removed, p. 55, 1. 13: "Erastus de Excommunicatione ... Pesclav. 1589". Emmanuel's present copy (Adams E912) was a Sancroft gift: S14.2.23.

7.4.4-7   Pascalius de Coronis   1622–6
Paschal, Charles [also Carlo Pasquali]. Coronae, opus ... distinctum X. libris, quibus res omnis coronaria e priscorum eruta et collecta monumentis continetur. Parisiis, e typ. Petri Chevalerii, 1610. 4°, pp. 730 + Preface. Fore-edge: "Paschal. Coron".   **331.1.6**

7.4.4-8   Helvici Synopsis Histae   1622–6
Helvicus, Christophorus. Synopsis historiae universalis, ab origine mundi per quatuor summa imperia ... ad praesans tempus deducta. Missing.

7.4.4-9   Casaub Epistola ad Cardinal Peron   1622–6

118

Casaubon, Isaac. [Probably: Ad Epistolam...Cardinalis Peronii, Responsio. Londini, excud. I. Norton, 1612. 4°, pp. 72. STC 4740. Note: Emmanuel's copy was bound with other books after 1637. An apparent donor's signature was trimmed off the title page by the binder.

333.4.56⁵]

7.4.4–10   ad Frontone*m* Ducaeum.   1625
Casaubon, Isaac. ad Frontonem Ducaeum S.I. epistola. Londini, I. Norton, 1611. 4°, STC 4742. Donor: Dr John Richardson. Missing. Register of Books Removed, p. 27, 1. 7: "Is: Casauboni Epistola ad Frontonem Ducaeum. Lond: 1611 Dr Rich."

7.4.4–11   Acta Synodi Dordrac^{ae} 1622–6
Dort, Synod of. Acta Synodi Nationalis...Dordrechti habitae anno CI ƆIƆ CXVIII et CI ƆIƆ CXIX. [Possibly: Dordrechti, 1620. 4°. Fore-edge: "Syn Dord:/Acta".   **302.3.22**]

7.4.4–12   Puteani Stricturae in Casaub   1622–6
Puteanus, Erycius (also Eric Van de Putte). In Is. Casauboni ad Front. Ducaeum...epistolam stricturae. [Possibly: Lovanii, apud Iacobum Hulzium, 1612. 4°, pp. 39. Rebound with several other tracts, probably in the late seventeenth century.   **333.3.49⁴**]
A "memorandum" at the end of the 1637 catalogue includes "Puteani strictura, in Casaubon*um*" among the eighteen items "missing at the accounts of Easter 1637". In the left margin is written "this book shewed/at y̆ acc: octo: 18/1637", though it is unclear whether the latter statement pertains to the Puteanus volume or "Gratian one vol", listed just above it.

Classis 8^{ae} Sect: Super^r:

8.S.1   Marloratus in Gen   1625
Marlorat, Augustin. Genesis cum Catholica Expositione Ecclesiastica. Morgiis, sumpt. Ioannis le Preux & Eustathii Vignon, 1584. F°, pp. 353. Adams B1312. Donor: Dr John Richardson. Fore-edge: "Marlor./in gen:"
Arms of William Cecil, Lord Burghley, stamped on covers.   **306.2.16**

8.S.2   Idem in Novu*m* Testament   1626–32
Marlorat, Augustin. Novi Testamenti Catholica Expositione Ecclesiastica, [Possibly: Editio Septima. (Hanover?) sumpt. vid. Iohannis Commelini, 1620. F°, pp. 1194 + index.   **306.2.31**]

8.S.3   Polani Syntagma Theolog.   1625
Polanus, Amandus. Syntagma Theologiae Christianae,...Iuxta leges or-

dinis Methodici conformatum. Genevae, ex typog. Iacobi Stoër, 1617. F°, pp. 699 + indices. Donor: Thomas Hanscombe. Missing. Register of Books Removed, p. 30, 1. 2: "Amandi Polani Syntagma Theologia fol...Gen. 1617 Mr Hancom [i.e. Hanscombe]."

8.S.4   Danaei Opuscula   1626–32
Danaeus, Lambertus. Opuscula Omnia Theologica. Genevae, apud Eustathium Vignon, 1583. F°, pp. 1625 [2625]. Missing. Register of Books Removed, p. 29, 1.12: "Lamberti Danaei Opuscula Theologica (Duplicat) Mr Rich....Gen. 1583." Emmanuel's present copy (Adams D52) was a Sancroft gift: S9.1.31.

8.S.5   Iunij opera 2 vol   1625
Junius, Franciscus, *the elder*. Opera Theologica....Edito postrema....Praefixa est Vita Auctoris. Tomus Primus. Genevae, apud Petrum & Iacobum Chonet, 1613. F°, pp. [1086] + indices. Donor: Thomas Hanscombe. Inscription on front flyleaf: "Magister Thomas Hanscombe, hujus collegij socius moriens D.D." Fore-edge: "IVNIVS I." Vol. 2 is missing.   **309.3.25**

8.S.6   King Iames his workes   1616–21
James I, King. The Workes of...James,...Kinge of Great Brittaine, France & Ireland. London, Robert Barker & Iohn Bill, 1616. F°, pp. 569. Fore-edge: "King/James/Workes." STC 14344.   **310.1.24**

8.S.7   Bp Coupers workes   1625
Cowper, William, *Bp*. The Workes. [London] Thomas Snodham, Felix Kyngston for Iohn Budge, 1623. F°, pp. 1122 + index. STC 5909. Donor: Thomas Hanscombe. Flyleaf inscription: "1625/Magister Thomas Hanscombe huius/Collegij Socius, Moriens D.D." Fore-edge: "COWPERS/Workes."   **305.3.23**

8.S.8   Perkins his workes 3 vol   1597–1621
Perkins, William. The Workes. [3 vols.] Vols. 1 & 2: London, I. Legatt, 1612, 13; vol. 3: Cambridge, C. Legge, 1613. F°. STC 19650. Missing. Register of Books Removed, p. 29, 1. 18: "Will. Perkins Works 3 vol:....Lond: 1612."

8.S.9   Iuellus adversus Harding lat   1585–1621
Jewel, John, *Bp of Salisbury*. Adversus Thomam Hardingum volumen...Ex Anglico Conversum in Latinum, a Guilielmo Whitakero...*Tr.* Guilielmo Whitakero...Eiusdem...Apologia Ecclesiae Anglicanae. Genevae, apud Petrum Sanctandreanum, 1585. F°, pp. 108, [6], 204, 188, 40 + indices. Adams J180 (omits Emmanuel's copy). Fore-edge: "Juel: Lat/16."   **305.3.4**

8.S.10   Iewell agt Harding Engl   1584–1621
Jewel, John, *Bp of Salisbury*. A defence of the Apologie of the Churche of Englande, conteininge an answeare to a certaine booke... by M. Hardinge. Missing.

8.S.11   Whitakerus Cont Stapletonu*m*   1597–1621
Whitaker, William. Adversus Thomae Stapletoni... Defensionem ecclesiastiae authoritatis, duplicatio, pro authoritate S. Scripturae. Cantabrigiae, I. Legatus, 1594. F°. STC 25363. Missing. Register of Books Removed, p. 29, l. 34: "Gul. Whitakerus adversus Stapletonum.... Cant: 1594." Emmanuel's present copy was a Sancroft gift: S10.4.39.

8.S.12   Workes of Tindall Frith and Barnes   1584–97
Tyndale, William, John Frith, and Robert Barnes. The Whole workes of W. Tyndall, Iohn Frith, and Doct. [Robert] Barnes. *Ed.* J. Foxe. London, Iohn Daye, 1572–73. F°, pp. 478, 376 + indices. STC 24436. Donor: George Bishop. Inscription on title page: "ex dono, Geor: Bysshop." Fore-edge: "TINDAL/FRITH/BARNES/20."   **306.5.55**

8.S.13   Fox in Apocal.   1587–97
Foxe, John. Eicasmi, Seu Meditationes in Sacram Apocalypsin. [Possibly: Londini, impens. Geor. Byshop, 1587. F°, pp. 396 + index. STC 11237. Fore-edge: "FOX: APOC:/19."   **310.5.8**]

8.S.14   Lavater in Paralipo   1625
Lavater, Ludwig. In Libros Paralipomenon sive Chronicorum... Commentarius [with the Latin text]. Tiguri, excud. Christophorus Froschoverus, 1573. F°, ff. 244 + index. Adams L309. Donor: Dr John Richardson. Fore-edge: "LAVATER*us*/in Paralipom." Arms of William Cecil, Lord Burghley, stamped on covers.   **308.4.69**

8.S.15   Idem in Ezram   1622–6
Two books bound together:
(1) Lavater, Ludwig. Ezras. Liber Primus Ezrae, Homiliis XXXVIII... expositus. Tiguri, in off. Froschoviana, 1586. 4°, ff. 81 + index. Adams L311.
(2) Hospinianus, Rodolphus. Oratio De Origine Et Progressu Rituum Et Ceremoniarum Ecclesiasticarum. [Tiguri, Froschoverus?] 1585. 4°, ff. 15. Adams H1043. Fore-edge: "Lavater*us*/Esram." After 1637, this was bound with another volume.   **333.4.67¹**]

8.S.16   Felinus in Psalm: 1622–6
Bucer, Martin (*pseud:* Aretius Felinus), *ed.* Sacrorum Psalmorum libri quinque. [Possibly: Basileae, per Ioan. Hervagium, 1547. F°, pp. 612 + index. Adams B1426. Fore-edge: "3/(vertically) Felinus".   **301.3.3**]

8.S.17   Bucerus in 4^{or} Evang   1584–97
Bucer, Martin. Enarrationes perpetuae, in sacra quatuor Evangelia [with
the Latin text]. Argentorati, apud Georgium Ulricherum Andlanum, 1530.
F°, ff. 236, 104. Adams B3038. Fore-edge: "3/Bucerus in/Evaglia."**307.4.74**

8.S.18   Idem in Ep*istol* ad Rom et Ephes   1622–6
Two books bound together:
(1) Bucer, Martin. Metaphrasis et enarratio in epist...ad Romanos.
Basileae, apud Petrum Pernam, 1562. F°, pp. 39, 595+index. Adams
B3044.
(2) Bucer, Martin. Praelectiones...in Epistolam ad Ephesios. Basileae,
apud Petrum Pernam, 1562. F°, pp. 190+index. Adams B3047.
                                                                    308.4.68

8.S.19   Ejusdem Scripta Anglica   1584–97
Bucer, Martin. Scripta Anglicana Fere Omnia...a Conrado
Huberto...collecta...Adiuncta est Historia de Obitu Buceri, quaeq*ue* illi
& Paulo Fagio post mortem...contigere. Basileae, ex. Petri Pernae
Officina, 1577. F°, pp. 959. Missing. Register of Books Removed, p. 29, l.
24: "Mart: Buceri Scripta anglicana...Basil: 1577." Emmanuel's present
copy (Adams B3049) was a Sancroft gift: S9.2.20.

8.S.20   Ejusdem Gratul° ad Eccles Angl, et Respon: ad Esp*istol*as Stephani
Episcop Winton de coelibatu Sacerdotum.   1584–97
Bucer, Martin. Gratulatio...ad ecclesiam Anglicanam, de religionis
Christi restitutione: et, Responsio...ad duas Stephani [Gardiner]
Episcopi Vintoniensis...Epistolas, De coelibatu sacerdotum & coenob-
itaru*m*. [*Includes the* Disputata Ratisbonae, in altero colloquio, anno
XLVI] [Strassburg? officina Knoblochiana?] 1548. 4°, pp. 84, 692. Missing.
Register of Books Removed, p. 5, 11. 25–26 "[M. Bucerus,] Acta disputat:
Ratisbonens*is:* cum resp. ad Episc: Winton:/Gratulat: ad Eccles: Angl: de
relig: restitutâ...} 1548." Emmanuel's present copy (Adams B3037) was a
Sancroft gift: S3.4.29^{2}.

8.S.21   Idem de reconcili*atio*ne Eccles: 1584–97
[1621 inventory (7.I.11): "Idem de peccato Orig: & de Justif."]
Bucer, Martin. De vera Ecclesiarum in Doctrina, Ceremoniis, et Disciplina
reconciliatione & compositione....Responsio ad Calumnias Alberti
Pighii Campensis. [Strassburg, W. Rihelius?, 1540?] 4°, ff. 216. Adams
B3029. Fore-edge: "35/[?]/[?]/[?]/[?]/."   **329.1.23**

8.S.22   Idem de adminioe Eucharistiae   1584–97
Bucer, Martin. De vera et Falsa Caenae Dominicae Administratione.
Neuburgi Danubii, apud Iohannem Kilianum, 1546. 4°, pp. 312. Missing.
Register of Books Removed, p. 5, 1. 24: "M. Bucerus de administratione
Eucharistiae...Neuberg: 1546." Emmanuel's present copy (Adams B3031)
was a Sancroft gift: S3.4.29^{1}.

8.S.23 Ejusdem defensio adversus Episcop. Abricni Confe*ssionem*: et Lutheri Concio*nes* in 6*tum* Cap. Ephes et Coment in Ionam Lat: 1597–1621
Three books bound together:

(1) Bucer, Martin. Defensio adversus axioma Catholicum, id est crimi-nationem R. P. Roberti Episcopi Abrince*nsis*. Argentorati, per mathiam Apiarium, 1534. 8°. Adams B 3027.
(2) Luther, Martin. Caput sextum Divi Pauli ad Ephesios. [*Tr.* Vincentius Obsopoeus.] Haganoae, ex off. Petri Brubaccii, 1535. 8°. Adams L1795.
(3) Luther, Martin. Sermo super principe articulo nostro. Credo in Iesum Christum.—Enarrationes in Ionam prophetam. [Haganoae, ex off. P. Brubacchii,] 1530. [Lacks a comprehensive title page.] 8°. Mentioned but not described in Adams L1795. Fore-edge: "37."   **321.6.21**

8.S.24 Idem in Zephania*m*   1584–97
Bucer, Martin. Tzephaniah, Quem Sophoniam, vulgo voca*nt*, prophetarum epitomographus, ad ebraicam veritatem versus, & commentario ex-planatus. Missing. Edition unknown. "Memorandum" at end of 1637 inventory states that "Bucer in Zephan" was one of seventeen books "missing at the accounts at Easter 1637."

8.S.25 Bullinger in Ep*isto*las ad Cor   1584–97
Two books bound together:
(1) Bullinger, Heinrich. In priorem D. Pauli ad Corinthios epistolam ... commentarius. Tiguri, apud Christoph. Froscho., 1534. 8°, ff. 244. Adams B3242.
(2) Bullinger, Heinrich. In posteriorem D. Pauli ad Corinthios epistolam commentarius. Tiguri, apud Christophorum Froscho., 1535. 8°, ff. 128. Adams B3243. Fore-edge: "Bullingerus/Cor/28".   **321.6.9**

8.S.26 Idem in Ep*isto*las ad Gal, Ephes, Phil, Coloss: 1584–97
Bullinger, Heinrich. In D. Apostoli Pauli ad Galatas, Ephesios, Philippen. et Colossen*ses* epistolas ... commentarii. Tiguri, apud Christophorum Froschoverum, 1535. 8°, ff. 270. Fore-edge: "29/Bulling*us*/Gal[?]es." Adams B3244.   **321.6.10**

8.S.27 Idem in Catabapt et libellus de decimis   1584–97
Bullinger, Heinrich. Adversus omnia catabaptistarum prava dogmata ... lib. IIII per Leonem Iudae aucti [pp. 191–7, running head: "Libellus de Decimus"]. Tiguri, apud Christophorum Froschoverum, 1535. 8°, ff. 197. Adams B3191. Fore-edge: "30/[upside down] Bulli*ng*/5 Catab".   **326.4.101**

8.S.28 Idem de Scrp^ae authoritate et Episcop*orum* functio*ne*   1584–7
Bullinger, Heinrich. De Scripturae sanctae authoritate ... de*que* episcoporum ... institutione & functione. Tiguri, in officina Froschoviana, 1538. 4°, ff. 180. Adams B3206. Fore-edge: "24/Bul*us* de/[?]/[?]".   **329.1.6**

8.S.29   Ejusdem decades 4^{or} Sermonum 3 vol.   1584–97
Three volumes:
(1) Bullinger, Heinrich. Sermonum decades duae. Tomus primus. Tiguri, apud Froschoverum, 1549. 4°, ff. 121 + Preface. Adams B3255. Fore-edge: "25".   **330.2.45**
(2) Bullinger, Heinrich. Sermonum Decas tertia.... Tomus secundus. Tiguri, apud Froschoverum, 1550. 4°, ff. 164. Adams B2256. Fore-edge: "26".   **330.2.46**
(3) Bullinger, Heinrich. Sermonum decas quarta. Ad tomum secundum. Tiguri, apud Froschoverum, 1550. 4°, ff. 91. Adams B3257. Fore-edge: "27".   **330.2.47**

8.S.30   Idem in Apocal   1584–97
Bullinger, Heinrich. In Apocalypsim. Basileae, per Samuelem Regium, 1570. F°, pp. 313. Adams B3250. Fore-edge: "23".   **310.5.2**

Classis 8^{ae} Sect Inferior

8.I.1   Fulke on the Rhemists Test   1589–97
The Text of the New Testament... Translated out of the vulgar Latine by the Papists of the traiterous Seminarie at Rhemes... With A Confutation.... By William Fulke. London, Deputies of Christopher Barker, 1589. F°, ff. 496 + Preface. STC 2888.   [Possibly **305.4.57**]

8.I.2   Cartwright on the Rhem Test   1622–6
Cartwright, Thomas. A Confutation of the Rhemists Translation, Glosses, and Annotations on the New Testament. [Leyden, W. Brewster,] 1618. F °, pp. 761[763]. STC 4709. Fore-edge: "Cartwrig/in Rhem:/Test:".   **310.5.7**

8.I.3   Mortons Appeale   1625
Morton, Thomas, *Bp.* A Catholike Appeale for Protestants, Out of the Confessions of the Romane Doctors; particularly answering the mis-named Catholike Apologie for the Romane faith, out of the Protestants. Londini, Impens. Georg. Bishop & Ioh. Norton, 1610. F°, pp. 680. STC 18177. Donor: Dr John Richardson. Fore-edge: "Mortons/Appeale."   **303.4.75**

8.I.4   Bilsons survey of X^{ts} Sufferings   1622–6
Bilson, Thomas, *Bp.* The Survey of Christs Sufferings For Mans redemption: And of his Descent To... Hel. London, Printed by Melchisedech Bradwood for Iohn Bill, 1604. F°, pp. 678, [12] + index. STC 3070.
[Possibly: **312.4.49**]

8.I.5   Hookers Eccl Politie   1622–6
Hooker, Richard. Of the Lawes of Ecclesiasticall Politie. [Either: 6 pts. London, W. Stansby, sold by M. Lownes (pt 2, F. H. Fetherstone), 1617–

18. Fº. STC 13716; Or: London, W. Stansby, sold by M. Lownes, 1617–22. Fº. STC 13716ª.] Missing. Register of Books Removed, p. 29, 1. 40: "Hookers Ecclesiastical Policy 5 books.... Lond. 1617." Emmanuel's present holdings include a Sancroft gift (London, 1648): S9.3.52.

8.I.6   Raynoldus in Apocri 2 vol   1611–21
Rainolds, John. Censura Librorum Apocryphorum Veteris Testamenti... adversum Pontificos, imprimis Robertum Bellarminum. [2 vols.]. In Nobili Oppenheimio, sumpt. Vᵃᵉ L. Hulsii et H. Laurentii, 1611. 4º. Donor: Anthony Sawbridge. Missing. Register of Books Removed, p. 37, 1. 10: "Jo: Raynoldi censura librorum Apocriphorum 2 vol.... Oppenh: 1611. Ant Sabridge."

8.I.7   Ejusdem Collatio cum Hart   1625
Rainolds, John. The Summe of the Conference Between Iohn Rainoldes and Iohn Hart. London, Printed by Iohn Wolfe, for George Bishop, 1584. 4º. STC 20626. Donor: Dr John Richardson. Missing. Register of Books Removed, p. 31, 1. 42: "[Raynoldus] His conference with J. Hart (Dupl.) ... Lond: 1584 Dʳ Rich."

8.I.8   Strigelius in No: Test   1625
Strigelius, Victorinus. ὑπομνήματα In Omnes Libros Novi Testamenti. Lipsiae [in off. Voegelini, c. 1565]. 4º, pp. 304, 355. Donor: Dr John Richardson. Missing. Register of Books Removed, p. 21, 1. 29: "Vict: Strigelius in N. Testmᵗᵘᵐ... Lipsiae [n.d.] Id. [i.e. Dr Rich]." Emmanuel's present copy (Adams S1934) was a Sancroft gift: S7.3.16.

8.I.9   Ejusdem loci Communes pars 2ᵈᵃ   1622–6
Strigelius, Victorinus. Secunda Pars Locorum theologicorum... Philippi Melanthonis illustrantur. Ed. Christophorus Pezelius. Neapoli Nemetum, excud. Matthaeus Harnisch, 1582. 4º, pp. 486, [14]. Missing. Register of Books Removed, p. 31, 1. 40: "Vict Strigelii locorum com: pars 2ᵈᵃ.... Neap: 1582." Emmanuel's present copy (Adams S1940) was a Sancroft gift: S9.3.25.

8.I.10   Lubbertus Contra Socinum   1622–6
Lubbertus, Sibrandus. De Iesu Christo Servatore... contra Faustum Socinum. In Academia Franekerana, excudebat Æ. Radaeus, 1611. 4º, pp. 632 + index. Missing. Register of Books Removed, p. 37, 1. 11: "Sibr: Lubbertus de Xsto Servatore contra Socinum... Fran: 1611." Emmanuel's present copy was a Sancroft gift: S10.2.4.

8.I.11   Bertij Hymenaeus desertor   1622–6
Bertius, Petrus. Hymenaeus desertor, sive de sanctorum apostasia problemata duo. Missing. Emmanuel's present copy (Lugduni Batavorum, 1615) was a Sancroft gift: S9.3.4.

8.I.12 Faij Enchiridion 1625

Fayus, Antonius. Enchiridion Theologicum aphoristica methodo compositum ex disputationibus A. Fayi. Centuria I. Genevae, 1605. 4°. Donor: Dr John Richardson. Missing. Register of Books Removed, p. 31, l. 37: "Fayi Enchiridion Theologicum ... Gen: 1605, Dr Rich." Emmanuel's present copy was a Sancroft gift: S9.3.7.

8.I.13 Roffensis in Bellarminum 1614–21

[1621 inventory (5.S.4): "De potestate Papae in rebus temporalib*us*"] Buckeridge, John, *Bp of Ely* (& *of Rochester*). De Potestate Papae In Rebus Temporalibus, Sive In Regibus Deponendis Usurpata; Adversus Robertum Cardinalem Bellarminum, Libri Duo.... Authore Ioanne Roffensi [Possibly: Londini, ex officina Nortoniana apud Ioannem Billium, 1614. 4°, pp. 113, (5). STC 4002.] Missing. Emmanuel's present copy was a Sancroft gift: S9.3.11.

8.I.14 Feild of the Church 1622–6

Field, Richard. Of the Church, Five Books. Missing. Emmanuel's present copy (Oxford, 1628: STC 10858), was a gift of Dr John Breton in 1676: 312.5.9.

8.I.15 Sands Sermons 1622–6

Sandys, Edwin, *Abp of York*. Sermons. [Possibly: London, Iohn Beale for Thomas Chard, 1616. 4°, ff. 194. STC 21714. **332.5.71**] "Memorandum" at the end of the 1637 inventory states that "Sands Sermons" was one of seventeen works "missing at the accounts at Easter 1637."

8.I.16 Apologia pro juramento fidelitatis September 2, 1609

Two books bound together:

(1) James I, *King of England*. Apologia pro juramento fidelitatis primum quiden ἀγώνυμος: nunc vero ab ipso auctore edita. London, excud. Joannes Norton, 1609. 4°, pp. 116. STC 14405.

(2) James I, *King of England*. An Apologie for the Oath of Allegiance. London, Robert Barker, April 8, 1609. 4°, pp. 112. STC 14402. Donor: Samuel Ward. Inscription on flyleaf: "Septemb. 2. 1609./Liber Collegij Emmanuelis, ex dono Samvelis Warde nuper ejusdem collegij socij—." Fore-edge: "APOL:/pro juram/fidelis." **329.1.8**

8.I.17 Andresij responsio ad Apol: Bellarm: 1622–6

Andrewes, Lancelot. Responsio ad apologiam Cardinalis Bellarmini, contra praefationem Monitoriam Jacobi R. Londini, excud. Robertus Barkerus, 1610. 4°. STC 604. Missing. Register of Books Removed, p. 31, l. 38: "B. Andrews responsio ad Bellarmini Apologiam ... Lon: 1610." Emmanuel's present copy was a Sancroft gift: S4.3.10².

8.I.18 Bilsons church government 1625
Bilson, Thomas. The Perpetual Governement of Christes Church. London, Deputies of C. Barker, 1593. 4°. STC 3065. Donor: Dr John Richardson. Missing. Register of Books Removed, p. 37, 1. 24: "Bilsons perpetual government of the Church... Lond 1593 Dʳ Rich."

8.I.19 Abbotti Antilogia adversus Eudaemon 1625
Abbot, Robert. Antilogia Adversus Apologiam Andreae Eudaemon-Ioannis Iesuitae Pro Henrico Garneto Iesuita Proditore. Londini, ex off. Thomae Adams, 1613. 4°, ff. 201. STC 45. Donor: Dr John Richardson. Fore-edge: "ABBOTT/in Evde[?]." **334.2.40**

8.I.20 Pseudo Martyr 1625
[Donne, John.] Pseudo-martyr. Wherein this Conclusion is evicted. That Those Which are of the Romane Religion in this Kingdome... ought to take the Oath of Allegeance. London, W. Stansby for Walter Burre, 1610. 4°, pp. 392. STC 7048. Donor: Dr John Richardson. **334.3.38**

8.I.21 Tortura Torti 1622–6
Andrewes, Lancelot, *Bp*. Tortura Torti sive ad Matthaei Torti [*pseud.*, Card. Bellarmine] librum responsio. London, R. Barkerus, 1609. 4°, pp. 402. STC 626. Missing. The Register of Books Removed (p. 31, 1. 57 and p. 55, 1. 22) mentions two copies, both gifts of Mr John Richardson in the 1670s. Emmanuel's present copy was a Sancroft gift: S9.3.10.

8.I.22 Mornaenus ad Ebroicensem Episcop 1625
Mornay, Philippe de. Responsio ad librum Ebroicensis episcopi de colloquio Fontis bellaquei anno 1600 4 maii habito, in qua praecipuae hujus temporis controversiae... pertractanur ab... Philippo Mornaio. *Tr.* David Licquaeus. Hanoviae, apud C. Marnium et heredes I. Aubrii, 1607. 4°, pp. 442. Donor: Dr John Richardson. Fore-edge: "MORN/ad Ebro/ic." **333.4.42**

8.I.23 Paraeus de Eucharistia 1622–6
Pareus, David. Controversiarum Eucharisticarum una de litera et sententia verborum Domini in S. Eucharistia. Haidelbergae, 1603. 4°, pp. 281, [10]. Fore-edge: "Pareus/de Eucharistia." **334.3.40**

8.I.24 Whitakerus de Scriptura 1597–1621
Whitaker, William. Disputatio De Sacra Scriptura, contra... Robertum Bellarminum... & Thomam Stapletonum. Missing. Emmanuel's present copy (Cantabrigiae, 1588: STC 25366) was a Sancroft gift: S10.3.6.

8.I.25 Idem Contra Campianum 1622–6
Whitaker, William. Responsionis ad Decem illas Rationes, Quibus Fretus

Edmundus Campianus. Missing. Emmanuel's present copy (London, 1583: STC 25362) was a Sancroft gift: S9.4.33.

8.I.26   Downams defense   1625
Downame, George, *Bp.* A Defence of The Sermon Preached at the Consecration of the Bishop of Bath and Welles. [4 pts.] London, Thomas Creed, William Hall and Thomas Snodham, 1611. 4°, pp. 238, 148, 154, 168. STC 7115. Donor: Dr John Richardson. Fore-edge: "DOWNAM."
335.3.90

8.I.27   Parker de descensu X^{ti} 1625
Sanford, Hugh. De descensu Domini Nostri Iesu Christi ad Inferos libri quatuor. Ab Hugone Sanfordo...inchoati, opera...Roberti Parkeri, ad umbilicum perducti. [4 pts.] Amstelrodami in aedibus Aegidii Thorpii 1611. 4°. Donor: Dr John Richardson. Missing. Register of Books Removed, p. 21, 1. 35: "Rob: Parker de Xti descensu ad inferos...Amsterd: 1611. Dr Rich."

8.I.28   Cosins Apology   1622–6
Cosin, Richard. An Apologie for Sundrie Proceedings by Iurisdiction Ecclesiasticall. Missing. Emmanuel's present copy (London, 1593: STC 5821) was a Sancroft gift: S2.4.55. "Memorandum" at the end of the 1637 inventory lists "Cosins Apologie" as one of seventeen books "missing at the accounts at Easter 1637."

8.I.29   Dr Collins Ephata   1622–6
Collins, Samuel. Epphata to F. T. [i.e. T. Fitzherbert]; Or, The Defence of the...Bishop of Elie [Lancelot Andrews] Concerning his Answer to Cardinall Bellarmines Apologie. Cambridge, Cantrell Legge, 1617. 4°, pp. 554, [19]. STC 5561. Fore-edge: "Dr Collins".   **331.5.3**

8.I.30   Jacobi Regis in Bellarm: Responsio   1622–6
[Possibly: 2 books bound together:
(1) James I, *King of England*. Triplici nodo, triplex cuneus. Or an Apologie for the Oath of Allegiance, Against the two Breves of Pope Paulus Quintus and the late letter of Cardinal Bellarmine to G. Blackwel the Arch-priest (publ. in English and Latin versions).
(2) Matthaeus Tortus (*pseud.*, Card. Bellarmine). Responsio ad Librum Inscriptum Triplici nodo.] Missing.
The "Memorandum"at the end of the 1637 inventory states that "Jacobi Regis in Bellarm" was one of seventeen books "missing at the accounts at Easter 1637."

8.I.31   Barlowes Answer to a Catholique   1622–6
Barlow, William, *Bp of Lincoln.* An Answer to A Catholike English-Man.

[R. Parsons]... who passed his Censure Upon the Apology, made by
... Iames... King of Great Brittaine... for the Oath of Allegeance.
London, Thomas Haveland for Mathew Law, 1609. 4°, pp. 370. STC 1446.
[Possibly: 332.5.72. After 1637, this volume was bound with others of later
acquisition. The edges were trimmed and all flyleaves removed.]
The "Memorandum" at the end of the 1637 inventory states that
"Barlowes Answere to a Catholique" was among the seventeen books
"missing at the accounts at Easter 1637".

8.I.32   Blackwells Examinationes   1622–6
Blackwell, George. [Possibly: Mr. George Blackwel, (made by Pope
Clement 8, archpriest of England) his answers upon sundry his exam-
inations. London, R. Barker, 1607. 4°, pp. 41. STC 3105.] Missing. The
"Memorandum" at the end of the 1637 inventory states that "Blackwells
Examinations" was among the seventeen books "missing at the accounts at
Easter 1637." Emmanuel's present holdings include three copies of another
book – A large examination taken at Lambeth... of M. George Blakwell,
Londini, R. Barker, 1607. 4°, pp. 170. STC 3104 – including two Sancroft
gifts (S13.4.5; S10.3.27) and one bearing an illegible early signature on the
title page (William Skinner?): 331.5.67.

8.I.33   Brerewoods diversytie of Languages et de religionib nummisque antiq
                                                                    1622–6
Two books bound together:
(1) Brerewood, Edward. Enquiries Touching the Diversity of Languages
and Religions. [Possibly: London, (W. Stansby) for I. Bill, 1614. 4°.
STC 3618.]
(2) Brerewood, Edward. De Ponderibus et Pretiis Veterum Nummorum.
[Possibly: London, (W. Stansby) apud I. Billium, 1614. 4°. STC 3612.]
Missing.
The "Memorandum" at the end of the 1637 inventory states that
"Brerewoods Diversitie of Lang" was among the seventeen books "missing
at the accounts at Easter 1637." Emmanuel's present copy was a gift of Dr
John Breton in 1676: 330.5.63.

8.I.34   Dr James of the Corruptions of the Fathers   1622–6
James, Thomas, *Sub-Dean of Wells.* A Treatise of the Corruption of
Scripture, Councels, and Fathers, by the Prelats, Pastors, and Pillars of the
Church of Rome, for maintenance of Popery and irreligion. [5 pts.]
London, H. L[ownes]. For Mathew Lownes, 1612. 4°. Inscription on title
page: "ẽe musaeo/M Tompson/14 Julij/1620." STC 14463.   **323.4.13**
This is now bound with 8.I.36, below.

8.I.35   Ejusdem Catalogus MS   1625
James, Thomas, *Sub-Dean of Wells.* Ecloga Oxonio-Cantabrigiensis, tri-

buta in libros duos. [2 pts.] Londini, Arnoldus Hatfield, impens. G. Bishop, & I. Norton, 1600. 4°, STC 14453. Donor: Dr John Richardson. Missing. Register of Books Removed, p. 55, 1. 14: "Catal: M^{ss} Oxon Cant:... Lond 1600 Dr Rich." The present Emmanuel copy was a Sancroft gift: S14.2.44.

8.I.36   Coci Censura   1625
Cooke, Robert. Censura quorundam scriptorum, quae sub nominibus sanctorum et veterum auctorum... citari solent. Londini [R. Field] imp. Guil. Barret, 1614, 4°. STC 5469. Donor: Dr John Richardson. Contains a torn portion of what appears to be Richardson's gift plate on an end paper.
                                                                      323.4.13
This is now bound with 8.I.34, above.

8.I.37   Usserius de X^{nae} Eccl^{ae} successi*one* et statu   1625
Ussher, James. Gravissimae quaestionis De Christianarum Ecclesiarum continua successione & statu Historica Explicatio. Londini, excud. B. Norton, 1613. 4°, pp. 372. STC 24551. Donor: Dr John Richardson. Missing. Register of Books Removed, p. 11, 1. 3: "Ussherius de successione Ecclesiae Xtianae... (Dupl: Dr Rich) Lond: 1613 Mr Rich". Emmanuel's present copy was a Sancroft gift: S4.3.54.

8.I.38   Hookers Sermons   1622–6
Hooker, Richard. [Possibly two or more of the following, bound together:
(1) A Learned and Comfortable sermon of the Certaintie of Faith. Oxford, Joseph Barnes, 1612. 4°. STC 13707.
(2) A Learned Sermon of the Nature of Pride. Oxford, Joseph Barnes, 1612. 4°. STC 13711.
(3) A remedie against sorrow and feare. Oxford, Joseph Barnes, 1612. 4°. STC 13722.
(4) A Learned discourse of iustification. Oxford, Joseph Barnes, 1612. 4°. STC 13708.
(5) The answere of Mr R. Hooker to a supplication to the Privie Counsell. Oxford, Jos. Barnes, 1612. 4°. STC 13706.]
Missing. Register of Books Removed, p. 31, 1. 34: "Hooker's sermons — Oxf. 1612". Emmanuel's present copy, including the above works and six other treatises of various dates was a Sancroft gift: S9.3.52.

8.I.39   Moulins Defence of the Catholique faith   1622–6
Du Moulin, Pierre. A Defence of the Catholicke Faith: Contained in the Booke of... King Iames the first.... Against the Answere of N. Coeffeteau... Translated into English [by John Sanford or J. Digby, Earl of Bristol?]. London, W. Stansby for Nathaniel Butter and Martin Clerke, 1610. 4°, pp. 493. STC 7322   [Possibly: **331.5.11**]
Another copy was a Sancroft gift: S9.3.42.

8.I.40   Whites Way to the Church   1622–6

White, John, *of Eccles*. A Defence of the Way to the True Church against A.D. [J. Fisher, S.J.] his Reply. London, R. Field for W. Barret, 1614. 4°, pp. 557. STC 25390. Fore-edge: "WHITES/WAY/&c:".   **332.5.110**

8.I.41   Sparkes Answere to John de Albine   1625

Sparke, Thomas. An answere to master Iohn de Albines discourse against heresies. Oxforde, I. Barnes, 1591. 4°. STC 23019. Donor: Dr John Richardson. Missing. Register of Books Removed, p. 37, 1. 16: "Th: Sparks answer to Jo: d Albines discourse of Haeresies... Oxf: 1591 Dr Rich."

8.I.42   Carletons Jurisdict   1625

Carleton, George, *Bp.* Iurisdiction Regall, Episcopall, Papall. Londini, impens. Iohannis Norton, 1610. 4°, pp. 302. STC 4637. Donor: Dr John Richardson. Fore-edge: "iVRiS/Carlto*n*".   **332.5.98**

8.I.43   Taylors Sermons   1622–6

Taylor, Thomas. Iaphets First Publique Perswasion into Sems tents or Peters Sermon, which was the first Generall calling of the Gentiles, preached before Cornelius. Cambridge, Pr. by Cantrell Legge, 1612. 4°, pp. 366 + index. Fore-edge: "Taylor/Sermons." STC 23830.   **332.5.86**

8.I.44   Anti = Sanders   1622–6

[Possibly: Cowell, John. Anti-Sanderus, duos continens dialogos. Cantabrigiae. 1593, STC 5898.] Missing.

8.I.45   Catholique Traditions   1622–6

Eudes, Morton. Catholique traditions. [Possibly: *Tr.* from French by L. Owen. London, W. Stansby for Henry Fetherstone, 1610. 4°, pp. 238. STC 10562. This is now bound with 7.4.2–7, above.   **332.5.60**]

8.I.46   Fulke agt Heskins Sanders and Rastall   1584–97

Fulke, William. D. Heskins, D. Sanders, and M. Rastel, accounted... three pillars ... of the Popish Synagogue ... overthrowne. London, Printed by Henrie Middleton for George Bishop, 1579. 8°, pp. 803. STC 11433. Donor: George Bishop. Inscription on title page, almost obliterated: "[George] Bysshop." Fore-edge: "Fulk against/Heskins Sanders/et Rastel/31".

                                                                            328.5.68

8.I.47   [Fulke] agt Gregory Martyn   1584–97

Fulke, William. A Defense of the sincere and true Translations of the Holie Scriptures into the English tong, against the manifolde cavils... of Gregorie Martin. London, Henrie Bynneman for George Bishop, 1583. 8°, pp. 532, 71. STC 11430. Donor: George Bishop. Inscription on title page: "Ex dono Geor. Bysshop." Fore-edge: "Franc Greg:/Martin/2/35."

                                                                            328.5.69

8.I.48 [Fulke] agt Sanders   1584–97

Fulke, William. A Retentive, To Stay Good Christians, In True faith and religion, against the Motives of Richard Bristow. Also A discoverie Of The Daungerous Rocke of The Popish Church, commended by Nicholas Sander. London, Thomas Vautroullier for George Bishop, 1580. 8°, pp. 792. STC 11449. Donor: George Bishop. Inscription on title page: "Ex dono Geor. [Bysshop]." Fore-edge: "Fulke against/A rejender[?]/4/32".

328.5.67

8.I.49 Reioinder agt Bristow   1584–97

Two books bound together:
(1) Fulke, William. A Reioynder to Bristows Replie in defence of Allens scroll of Articles and Booke of Purgatorie. Also the cavils of Nicholas Sander... about the Supper of Our Lord... Confuted. London, H. Middleton for George Bishop, 1581. 8°, pp. 316. STC 11448. Inscription on title page: "ex do: Geor. Bysshop."
(2) Fulke, William. T. Stapleton and Martiall... confuted. London, Henrie Middleton for George Bishop, 1580. 8°, pp. 217. STC 11456. Donor: George Bishop. Fore-edge: "F. retentive/agt Bristow./3/33". **328.5.70**

8.I.50 Goodman of the fall of Mann   1622–6

Goodman, Godfrey. The Fall of Man. Missing. Emmanuel's present copy (London, 1616: STC 12024) was a Sancroft gift: S10.2.67.

8.I.51 Cartwrights 2 reply   1622–6

Cartwright, Thomas. Two volumes:
(1) The Second Replie Agaynst Maister Whitgiftes Second Answer. [Zurich, C. Froschauer,] 1575. 4°. STC 4714.
(2) The Rest of the Second Replie... Agaynst Master Whitgifts Second Answer. n.p., 1577. 4°. STC 4715.
Missing. Register of Books Removed, p. 37, 1. 17: "Cartwright's 2^d reply to Whitgift 2 parts & 2 vol: ... 1575, 77." Emmanuel's present copies were Sancroft gifts: S10.3.29^2 and S10.3.29^3.

Classis 9^{ue} Sectio super^r:

9.S.1 Rabanus de universo   1599

Rabanus Maurus, *Abp of Mainz.* [Opus De Universo.] [fol. 1, recto:] Epistola Rabani ad Ludovicum regem invictissimum &c. incipit foeliciter. [Strassburg, Adolf Rusch, the R-printer, c. 1465.] F°. Hain 13669. Donor: Richard Lister. Inscription on the top of f.1.: "RICHRDVS LISTERVS. EMAN:/COLLEGIO DEDIT. AN: DO: 1599." Fore-edge: "Rabanus/de vniverso" and, upside down, "38" or "58" (?). **MSS.2.1.7**

9.S.2 Aristot: op*era* gr lat 2 vol.   1625
Aristotle. Operum ... nova editio, Graece & Latine adscriptis ... emen-
dationibus: in quibus plurimae ... ex bibliotheca Isaaci Casauboni....
Accesserunt ... Kyriaci Strozae libri duo Politicorum Graeco-Latini. [2
vols.] Aureliae Allobrogum, apud Samuelem Crispinum, 1605. F°, pp. 946,
845 + index. Donor: Dr John Richardson. Fore-edge, vol. I:
"ARISTOT./OP./II"; vol. II: "II."   **310.1.57,58**

9.S.3 Plinius   1584–97
[1621 inventory (8.I.10): "Plinij histor."]
Pliny the Elder. Historia Naturalis. Missing? Emmanuel now owns several
copies, two of which could have been acquired before 1597 (Lutetiae
Parisiorum, 1532: Adams P1562, 308.3.9; and Lugduni, 1582: Adams
P1583, 310.1.4). A copy of Pliny's Liber Secundus ... de mundi historia
(Halae Suevorum. 1538: Adams P1565) was a Sancroft gift: S6.3.51.

9.S.4. Gesner de animalibus 3 vol.   1604–21
Gesner, Conrad. Historiae Animalium.... Editio Secunda. [4 vols. in 3.]
Francofurti, in Bibliop. Cambieriano, 1602–4. [Part of vol. 2: Ex off.
Typog. I Wecheli, impens. R. Cambieri, 1586.] F°, pp. 967; 806, 119; ff. 11,
85; pp. 1052, 38. Donor: Thomas Southaicke. Vols. 1 & 2 have bookplate:
"Ex dono T.S." with the London Grocers' Company arms. Fore-edges: "I,"
"II," and "III."   **311.4.20–2**

9.S.5 Franc Georgij Harmonia Mundi   1625
Georgius, Franciscus, *Venetus*. L'Harmonie du monde. *Tr.* Guy le Fevre de
la Boderie. Paris, chez Berthelemy Macé, 1588. F°, pp. 878 + table. Adams
G469. Donor: Dr John Richardson. Fore-edge: "Franciscus Georgius
veni."   **318.2.9**

9.S.6 Mocenicus   1622–6
Tractationum Philosophicarum Tomus Unus, In quo continentur I.
Philippi Mocenici ... Universalium Institutionum.... Contemplationes V.
II. Andreae Caesalpini, Aretini, Quaestionum Peripateticarum Libri V. III.
Bernardini Telesii Consentini, de rerum natura ... Libri IX. [Geneva]
Excud. E. Vignon, 1588. F°, coll. 963 + Preface & index. Adams T865.
Fore-edge: Mocēnic."   **305.3.51**

9.S.7 Volaterranus   1622–6
Maffeius, Raphael, *Volaterranus*. [Unknown work.] Missing. Emmanuel
owns a copy of his Opera (Lugduni, 1599: Adams M98), a Sancroft gift:
S12.2.40.

9.S.8 Plato Lat   1584–97
Plato. Opera. Latin. [Possibly: *Tr.* Ianus Cornarius.... Additis Marsilii

Ficini Argumentis & Commentariis. Basileae, in off. Frobeniana, per Hier. Frobenium et Nic. Episcopium, 1561. F°, pp. 1048 + index. Adams P1448.
306.3.37]

9.S.9   Plato gr: 1622–6
Plato. Omnia opera cum commentariis Procli in Timaeum & Politica. [Gk.] Basileae, apud Ioan. Valderum, 1534. F°, pp. 690. Adams P1437.
Fore-edge: "PLATO".   **305.3.62**

9.S.10.   Cardanus de Subtilitate   1584–97
Cardanus, Hieronymus (Cardano, Girolamo). De Subtilitate. Missing. The present Emmanuel copy (Lugduni, 1559: Adams C672) was a Sancroft gift: S2.4.36.

9.S.11   Aegidius in Aristot: poster   1584–97
Colonna, Egidio. [Colophon:] [Commentum] in librum posteriorum ana-lecticorum Aristotelis. Patavi, impresa ingenio Petri Mauter, 1478. F°. Hain 135. Title page and f. 1 missing. Fore-edge: (vertically, top to bottom) "Posteriora Ægidii", (horizontally) "4".   **MSS5.1.10**

9.S.12   Schegkius in Arist prior*um* et posterior*um*   1622–6
Schegk, Jacob, *the elder.* [Commentaries on the Prior and Posterior Analytics of Aristotle.] Missing.

9.S.13   Aristot Problem: Lat   1622–6
Aristotle. Problemata. [Latin.] Missing or [Possibly: Bernardino Baldi. In Mechanica Aristotelis Problemata exercitationes. Moguntiae, Vid. Ioannis Albini, 1621. 4°, pp. 194.   **329.1.54**]

9.S.14   Aristot Organon Lat   1584–97
Aristotle. Logica. [Lat.] Edidit Jacobus Faber. Stapulensis. F°. Missing.

9.S.15   Lambinus in Arist Eth   1584–97
[1621 inventory (8.I.6): "Ethica Aristot: GraecoLat. w. annot. Lamb. & Zuingeri."]
Aristotle. [Ethica.] De moribus ad Nicomachum Libri Decem. *Tr.* Dionysius Lambinus, *ed. and annotated by* Theodor Zwinger. [Gk & Lat.] Basileae, per Ioannem Oporinum, et Eusebium Episcopium, 1566. 4°, pp. 487. Adams A1811. Fore-edge: "Lamb:/in ETH/Arist:/6". Cover stamped in gold: "1567/GM/29 MAY."   **333.1.44**

9.S.16   Rodolphi Agricolae Log[a]   c. 1584
Agricola, Rodolphus. De inventione dialectica libri tres. cum scholi*is* Ioannis Mattaei Phrissemii. Coloniae, apud Heronem Alopecium, 1527. 4°, pp. 422 + index. Adams A357. Donor: Sir Walter Mildmay. Inscription and

signature on title page: "Virtute non vi, 1555", "Wa. Mildmay". Fore-edge: "Agricola".   **FB13**

9.S.17   Aristot Poetica Lat   1622–6
          Aristotle. Poetica. [Lat.] Missing. Emmanuel's present copy (London, 1623: STC 759) was a Sancroft gift: S6.2.57[2].

9.S.18   Aristot Physica cum coment Averois   March 19, 1629
          Aristotle. Physica Aristo. cum com. Averro. Aristote. Stagyrite Libri Physicorum octo. [*Tr.* & *ed.* Averroes & A. Zimara.] Lugduni, venund. apud Scipionem de Gabiano. [Colophon:] Papie*que* per Jacob. Paucidrapi*um* de Burgofranco, 1520. 8°, ff. 344. Adams A1895. Donor: Thomas Ball. Inscription on flyleaf: "Ex Dono Thom: Ball: Mar 19/1629." Fore-edge: (vertically) "Physica."   **329.1.52**

9.S.19   Melancthonis Ethica   1597–1621
          Two books bound together:
          (1) Melanchthon, Philipp. Ethicae Doctrinae Elementa et Enarratio Libri Quinti Ethicorum [Aristotelis]. Vitebergae, ex off. Iohannis Cratonis, 1550. 8°, pp. 254. Adams M1146.
          (2) Melanchthon, Philipp. Initia Doctrinae Physicae. Witebergae, Excud. Iohannes Lufft, 1572. 8°, pp. 393 + index. Adams M1163. Fore-edge: "Melanch:/Ethica/19."   **338.7.46**

Classis 9[ae] Sect: Inferior

The Inferior sectio is divided into two subsections. The numbering system is the same as that for Classis 7.4 See note, p. 115.

9.I.1–1   Demosthenes et Æschines gr lat   1597–1621
          [1621 inventory (8.S.27): "Demost & Aeschinis Opera cu*m* Ulpiani com*ment* novis*que* Scholis Graeco:lat"]
          Demosthenes. Demosthenis et Aeschinis opera Graecolatina. Missing. Emmanuel's present copy (Francofurti, 1604) was a Sancroft gift: S11.1.12.

9.I.1–2   Ciceronis op*era* 2 vol   1622–6
          Cicero. Opera. [2 vols.] Missing.

9.I.1–3   Plutarchi Moralia gr   1622–6
          Plutarch. [Possibly: Varia scripta, quae Moralia vulgo dicuntur. *Ed.* G. Xylander. [Gk] Basileae, per Eusebium Episcopium & Nicolai Fr. haeredes, 1574. F°, pp. 679. Adams P1636.   **313.4.35**]

9.I.1–4   Athenaeus gr: 1622–6
          Athenaeus, *Naucratita.* Dipnosophistarum... Lib. XV. [Gk.] Basileae, apud Ioannem Valderum, 1535. F°, pp. 333 [337] + indices. Adams A2097. Fore-edge: "ATHEN/Athenaīs".   **306.4.40**

9.I.1–5 Casaubon in Athenaeum   1622–6
Casaubon, Isaac. Animadversionum in Athenaei Dipnosophistas Libri
XV.... Secunda Editio Postrema. Lugduni, apud Antonium de Harsy &
Petrum Ranad. Excud. Guichardus Iullieron, 1600. F°, pp. 648. Adams
C821. Fore-edge: "Cas in/Athan".   **306.3.21**

9.I.1–6 Isocratis orationes Lat   c. 1584
Isocrates. Orationes omnes... Una Cum Novem... Epistolis. *Tr.*
Hieronymus Wolfius (*And* Castigationes In Isocratem, Per Hieronymum
Wolfium.) [2 pts in 1 vol.] Basileae, per Ioannem Oporinum, 1548. F°, pp.
251, 285 + indices. Adams 1221. Donor: Sir Walter Mildmay. Fore-edge:
"Isocrat/20".   **FB3**

9.I.1–7 Seneca   1584–97
Seneca, Lucius Annaeus. Opera. Missing. Emmanuel's present holdings
include two Sancroft gifts: (Basileae, 1557: Adams S886, S11.2.29; Lugduni,
1604: S11.3.60).

9.I.1–8 Plutarchi Moralia Lat   1584–97
[c. 1597 inventory (186): "Plutarchi opuscula."]
Plutarch. [Possibly: Opuscula Omnia. Basileae, In Off. And. Cratandri,
1530. F°, ff. 249 + index. Adams P1657. Fore-edge: "Plutarch/Opera/II"
and in another hand: "Plutar-/chi Op*us*/cula."   **306.4.46**]

9.I.1–9 Haddoni Orationes   c. 1584
[1621 inventory (8.5.20): "Haddoni Lucubrationes"]
Haddon, Walter. Lucubrationes passim collectae & editae. [2 pts.]
London, apud G. Seresium, 1567. 4°. STC 12596. Donor: Sir Walter
Mildmay. Missing.

9.I.1–10 Scaligeri vita etc: 1622–6
[Possibly: Scaliger, Joseph Justus. Epistola de vetustate et splendore gentis
Scaligerae, et Iul. Caes. Scaligeri Vita. Iul. Caes. Scaligeri oratio in luctu
filioli Audecti. Lugduni Batavorum, ex off. Plantiniana, apud Franciscum
Raphelengium, 1594. 4°, pp. 123. Adams S562.   **330.4.6**]

9.I.1–11 Dunaeus in demosthen   1622–6
Downes, Andrew. Praelectiones in Philippicam de pace Demosthenis.
[With Gk and Lat. text.] Londini, apud I. Billium, 1621. STC 7154. 8°.
Missing. Emmanuel now owns three copies, each apparently the gift of a
later seventeenth-century master of the college: William Dillingham
(338.8.43[2]), John Breton (329.7.55), and William Sancroft (S11.5.30).

9.I.2–1 Poetae Heroici gr 2 vol   1584–97
Poetae Graeci Heroici. Poetae graeci principes heroici carminis....

Homerus, Hesiodus, Orpheus, Callim., Aratus, Nicand., Theocrit., Moschus, Bion, Dionysius, Coluthus, Tryphiodorus, Musaeus, Theognis, Phocylides, Pythagorae aurea carmina. Fragmenta aliorum. *Ed.* Henricus Stephanus. 2 vols. Geneva, excud. Henricus Stephanus (II, H. Fuggeri typog.), 1566. F°, pp. 20, LXXII, 781; LVII, 489. Missing. Register of Books Removed, p. 43, 1. 4: "Poetae Graece Heroici edit H. Stephani... 1566." The present Emmanuel copy (Adams P1699) was a Sancroft gift: S11.2.5.

9.I.2–2   Homeri opera gr lat   1584–97
Homer. [Opera] [Gk & Lat.] [Possibly: Homeri quae extant omnia. Basileae, per Eusebii Episcopii opera ac impensa, 1583. Adams H767.

312.1.59]

9.I.2–3   Epitome Eustathij in Homerum Junij   1597–1621
Eustathius, *Bp of Thessalonica.* Copiae cornu sive Oceanus Enarrationum Homericum, ex Eustathii... commentariis... Hadriano Iunio autore. [Gk] Basileae, παρ' Ἱερωνύμω φροβενίω καὶ Νικολάω Ἐπισκοπίω, 1558. F°, pp. 571, 360 + Preface. Adams E1106.   **[Possibly: 313.4.36**]

9.I.2–4   Euripides   1584–97
[1621 inventory (8.S.13): "Euripides Graec. Lat."]
Euripides. [Works.] [Gk & Lat.] Missing. Emmanuel's present holdings include Tragoediae XIX [2 vols.] (Heidelbergae, 1597: Adams E1037), which was a Sancroft gift: S11.3.57,58.

9.I.2–5   Chaucer   1626–32
Chaucer, Geoffrey. The Workes. Missing.

9.I.2–6   Scaligeri poet   1622–6
Scaliger, Julius Caesar. Poetices. Libri septem. Missing. Emmanuel's present copies are a Sancroft gift ([Lyons,] 1561: Adams S596), and a 1673 gift of Mr John Richardson ([Lyons,] 1594: Adams S599): S5.1.35, 321.4.33.

9.I.2–7   Dydimus in Homerum   1584–97
[1621 inventory (8.S.14): "Homeri Ileas & Ulissia cum Scholijs Graec".]
Homer. Ilieas et Ulyssea cum interpretatione [Didymus]. [Gk.] [2 vols. in 1.] F°, pp. 594 [410], 284. Basileae, apud Io. Hervagium, 1535. Adams H748.   **FB.8**

9.I.2–8   Dionysius de situ orbis cum comet Eustathij et Mela Aethicus et Solinus
                                                                        1622–6
Dionysius, *Periegetes.* Dionysii Alex. et Pomp. Melae situs orbis descriptio Aethici cosmographia. C.I. Solini Polyhistor. In Dionysii poematium commentarii Eustathii. [Gk & Lat.] 3 vols. [Geneva,] excud. Henricus Stephanus, 1577. 4°, pp. 158, 47, 152. Missing. Register of Books Removed,

p. 43, 1. 31: "Dionysius Mela cum Solino &c... (Dupl: Mr Rich).... H.S. 1577." Emmanuel's present copy (Adams D648) was a Sancroft gift: S11.2.43.

9.I.2–9   Oppianus   1625
          Oppianus. Ἁλιευτικων βιβλια Ε. κυνηγετικων βιβλια Δ. [Copy contains Ἁλιευτικα only.] Parisiis, apud Adr. Turnebum, 1555. 4°, pp. 207. Adams 0204. Donor: Dr John Richardson. This volume was later bound with three other books.   **333.4.56**[1]

9.I.2–10   Nonni Dionysiaca   1622–6
          Nonnus, *Panopolitanus*. Dionysiaca. Missing? Emmanuel's present copies include a Gk edition (Antuerpiae, 1569: Adams N331) which was a Sancroft gift: S11.3.16.

9.I.2–11   Nicander gr lat cu*m* Scholijs   1622–6
          Two books bound together:
          (1) Nicander, *Colophonius*. Nicandri Theriaca, Eiusdem Alexipharmaca. Interpretatio innominati autoris in Theriaca. [Gk.] Coloniae, opera Ioan Soteris, 1530. 4°, pp. 103. Adams N209.
          (2) Nicander, *Colophonius*. Theriaca et Alexipharmaca cum scholiis. *Tr.* I. Lonicero. [Lat.] Coloniae, opera Iohan. Soteris, 1531. 4°, pp. 109. Adams N210.
          Donor (?): Robert Huicci. Inscription on title page: "Roberti Huicci liber." Fore-edge: "NIKA/NDER" and, vertically in another hand: "Nicander".
                                                       335.1.86

9.I.2–12   Lycophron gr Lat   1622–6
          Lycophron. Alexandra, sive Cassandra. [Gk & Lat.] Missing. Emmanuel's present copies include two (Basileae, 1546: Adams L2102, and [Heidelberg?] 1596: Adams L2108) which were Sancroft gifts: S11.1.39[1]; S11.6.104[1].

9.I.2–13   Boetius de consola*tione* philos: cum com*m*ent   1625
          Boethius, Anicius, Manlius Torquatus Severinus. De consolatione philosophie duplici cum commentario videlicet Sancti Thome et Iodoci Badii Ascensii. Parisii, venund. a Iohanne Petit, necnon Cadomi, a Roberto Mace, 1506. 4°. Adams B2286. Donor: Dr John Richardson.   **331.4.96**

9.I.2–14   Petrarchae Poemata Italicè   1584–97
          Petrarca, Francesco. [Possibly: Sonetti et Canzoni – Triomphi. Fiorenza, per li heredi di Filippo di Giunta, 1522. 8°, ff. 180. Adams P795.
                                                     329.7.110]

9.I.2–15 Guevara 2 vol 1584–97

(1) Guevara, Antonio de, *Bp.* Libro Primo Delle Lettere. *Tr.* Dominico di Catzelu. Vinegia, Appresso Gabriel Giolito de Ferrari, 1547. 8°, ff. 227. Fore-edge: "Gueuara/i/4". Not in Adams. **329.7.69**

(2) Guevara, Antonio de, *Bp.* Libro Secondo Delle Lettere. Vinegia, Appresso G. Giolito de Ferrari, 1546. 8°, ff. 260. Fore-edge: "ii/5". Not in Adams. **329.7.73**

9.I.2–16 Venceslaj Clementis a Lybeomonte, Viola De se 1637–?

Clemens, Venceslaus *à Lybeo–Monte.* Viola... nuncia ad seriam Meditationem Passionis & Resurrectionis ... Jesu Christi, n.p., 1637, 4°, pp. 56. **331.4.4**

Bound with 9.I.2–18 and two other books. This book and the next two items were apparently added to the collection and the inventory shortly after the catalogue had been compiled. The handwriting of these entries is different from that of the rest of the catalogue.

9.I.2–17 Ejusdem Garteriados seu aureae Periscelidos Lib. 1637–?

Clemens, Venceslaus, *à Lybeo-Monte.* Garteriados sive Aureae periscelidis Libri duo. Lugduni Batavorum, ex. off. W. Christiani, 1634. F°, pp. 52.
See note to 9.I.2–16. **308.5.77**

9.I.2–18 Ejusdem Trinobantiados Lib 1637–?

Clemens, Venceslaus *à Lybeo-Monte.* Trinobantiados Augustae sive Londoni Libri VI. n.p., 1636 (chronogrammatic date). 4°, pp. 204. **331.4.4**
Bound with 9.I.2–16 and two other books. See note to 9.I.2–16.

Pars Occidentalis

Classis I^{ae} Super^{r}: sect

²1.S.1 Bibliotheca Patrum gr 1 9 vol: 1627

La Bigne, Margarinus de, *ed.* Bibliothecae Veterum Patrum et Auctorum Ecclesiasticorum, Tomi Novem.... Editione Quarta,... duobus tomis graeco-latinis aucta. [12 pts in 9 vols.] Parisiis, [Grand Navire,] 1624. F°, coll. 1622; 788, 928; 1328, 1146; 1012, 518, 646; pp. 942; coll. 1365; 1251, 52; 1200, 14; coll. 1452. Donor: John Stoughton. Each volume has the inscription: "1627/Ex dono Johannis Stoughton. S. Theolog: D^{ris}/a hujus Collegij Socij."
Fore-edges:

(1) "Biblioth: /Patrum/I. Lat"	**304.1.4**
(2) "2.3."	**304.1.1**
(3) "4"	**304.1.2**
(4) "5.6.7"	**304.1.3**
(5) "viii"	**305.1.60**
(6) ".9."	**305.1.61**
(7) "Graecolat./.i."	**305.1.58**
(8) ".2."	**305.1.59**
(9) "Appendix"	**304.1.5**

²**1.S.2** Biblioth Patrum 2 vol. Margarini   1625
La Bigne, Margarinus de, *ed.* [Two volumes of the work described in ²1.S.1] Donor: Dr John Richardson. Missing. Register of Books Removed, p. 5, 1. 9: "Margarini de la Bigne Bibliotheca Patrum... 2V... Paris: 1654... Dʳ Rich." The date of the latter entry is clearly incorrect; Dr Richardson died in 1625. The edition in his donation was probably the Paris, 1624. Emmanuel's present holdings include two Sancroft gifts: Paris, 1576 in 4 vols. (Adams L4; S3.3.5–8) and Paris, 1644–54 in 15 vols. (S3.2.20–34).

²**1.S.3** Biblioth Patrum 2 vol. Grinaei   1620
Grynaeus, Johannes Jacobus, *ed:* Monumenta S. Patrum Orthodoxographia. [2 vols.] Basileae, ex off. Henricpetrina, 1569. F°, pp. 398, 2064. Adams M1736. Donor: William Branthwaite. Inscription on front end paper of each vol.: "Ex dono Domini Doctoris Branthwaite." Fore-edges: "Oxthodoxia/Patrum/I"; "II".   **303.4.29,30**
   The list of books willed to Emmanuel by William Branthwaite (Emmanuel College Archives LIB.2.4) cites this work as items 11 and 12: "Thalassij Sententiae, 2/Monumenta Patrum Orthodoxographa I}2 vol." The second volume begins with "Thalasii Sententiae Sacra."

²**1.S.4** Philo Judaeus gr lat   1620
Philo, *Judaeus.* Opera Exegetica in Libros Mosis, De Mundi Opificio, Historicos, & Legales. [Gk & Lat.] Coloniae Allobrogum, Petrus de la Rouiere, 1613. F°, pp. 904 + index. Donor: William Branthwaite. This book

140

does not bear the Branthwaite inscription, but its binding is similar to those of the Branthwaite donation. Fore-edge: "Philo. Iud." **301.3.54**

The list of books donated to Emmanuel by William Branthwaite (Emmanuel College Archives LIB.2.4) cites this entry as item 9: "Philo Judaeus in Libros Mosis."

²**1.S.5**   Justin Martyr gr Lat   1620
Justin, *Martyr, St.* Opera. [Gk & Lat.] Missing. Donor: William Branthwaite.

This is the first item in the list of books willed to Emmanuel by Branthwaite (Emmanuel College Archives LIB.2.4): "Justini Martyris Opera." The Register of Books Removed (p. 9, l. 24) mentions only a Paris 1636 edition, the gift of Mr John Richardson, probably in the 1670s.

²**1.S.6.**   Irenaeus et Acta Synodi Ephes gr   1584–97
Two books bound together:

(1) *Ephesus, Council of.* Acta Oecumenicae Tertiae Synodi Ephesi Habitae.... adversus Nestorium haereticum. [Gk] [Heidelberg,] e typog. Hieronymi Commelini, 1591. F°, pp. 319, [20]. Adams E210.

(2) Irenaeus, *St, Bp of Lyons.* Libri quinque Adversus portentosas haereses Valentini & aliorum... Opera. *Ed. & Comm.* Nicolaus Gallasius. [Paris] apud Ioannem le Preux, & Ioannem Parvum, 1570. F°, pp. 408, [22]. Adams I157.

Fore-edge: "Irenaeus/Acta synod/Ephesius".   **302.3.60**

²**1.S.7**   Origenis opera Lat 2 vol: 1584–97
Origenes. Opera. [Lat.] [2 vols.] Missing. Emmanuel's present holdings include two editions: Lugduni, 1536 (Adams O282) and Basileae, 1571 [2 vols.] (Adams O285); both were Sancroft gifts: S4.3.5, S4.3.3, 4.

²**1.S.8**   Dionysius Areopag et Maximus et pachimerus.   1622–6
Dionysius, *the Pseudo-Areopagite.* Opera Omnia quae Extant.... Accesserunt S. Maximi Scholia,... & Georgii Pachymerae paraphrasis in Epistolas. [Gk & Lat.] Lutetiae Parisiorum, ex off. Nirelliana sumpt. Sebastiani Cramoisy, 1615. F°, pp. [66], 390, 300, 187, 97 + indices. Fore-edge: "Dionys/Are°pag:".   **302.3.37**

²**1.S.9**   Clemens Alexandrinus gr lat   1620
Clement, *of Alexandria.* Opera... Quae Extant. *Ed.* Daniel Heinsius (with critical notes by Fridericus Sylburgius). [Gk & Lat.] Lugduni Batavorum, excudebat Ioannes Patius, pro Bibliopolio Commeliniano, 1616. F°, pp. 580, 50, 67. Donor: William Branthwaite. Inscription on flyleaf: "Ex dono Domini Doctoris Branthwaite." Fore-edge: "Clem".   **304.1.37**

The list of books donated to Emmanuel by William Branthwaite (Emmanuel College Archives LIB.2.4) cites this entry as item 6: "Clemens Alexandrinus". A copy of another edition of the Opera (Parisiis, apud M. Sonnium, 1590; Adams C2110) also contains the Branthwaite donation inscription, but it is a Sancroft book: S4.1.18. Moreover, it is in Latin only; it lacks fore-edge marking; and its inscription is in a hand different from that of the 1616 edition inscription. The inscription was probably added after the actual Branthwaite copy was lost. See also [2]1.S.23.

[2]**1.S.10**   Athanasij op*era* gr 1   1620
Athanasius, *St, Abp of Alexandria*. Opera. *Tr*. Petrus Nannius. [Gk & Lat.] [Heidelberg,] Ex officina Commeliniana, 1600–1. F°, pp. 858, 369 [365], coll. 266 [366]–644. Not in Adams (collation differs from Adams A2087, 2088, and 2089). Donor: William Branthwaite. Inscription on flyleaf: "Ex dono Domini Doctoris Branthwaite." Fore-edge: "Athanasius." **302.3.50**

The list of books donated to Emmanuel by William Branthwaite (Emmanuel College Archives LIB.2.4) cites this work as item 2: "Athanasij opera."

[2]**1.S.11**   Gregorius Thaumaturgus et Macarius et Basilius Seleucius gr lat 1622–6
Gregory, *St, Thaumaturgus, Bp of Neocaesarea, et alii*. Opera omnia. *Ed.* Gerardus Vossius, *et al.* [Gk & Lat.] Parisiis, sumpt. M. Sonii [&c], 1622. F°. Fore-edge: G. Thau*maturgi*:/Macarius/Basil./Seleu:". **301.3.53**

[2]**1.S.12**   Eusebij Hist[a] Eccles Idem de praeparat Evang et de demonst Evang et Socratis Hist[a] Theodor Sozom: gr   1584–97
Two vols. as follows:
(1) Eusebius, *Pamphili, Bp of Caesarea*. Ecclesiasticae Historiae... Lib.X. Eiusdem de vita Constantini Lib V. Socratis Lib. VII. Theodoriti episcopi Lyrensis Lib. V. Collectaneorum ex historia eccles. Theodori Lectoris Lib. II. Hermii Sozomeni Lib. IX. Evagrii Lib. VI. [Gk.] Lutetiae Parisiorum, ex off. Roberti Stephani, 1544. F°, ff. 350, 122. Adams E1093. **309.1.47**

(2) Three works:
(a) Evagrius, *Scholasticus*. [continued from above]. F°, ff. 123–181 [5].
(b) Eusebius, *Pamphili, Bp of Caesarea*. Evangelicae praeparationis Lib XV. [Gk.] Lutetiae, Ex officina Rob. Stephani, 1544. F°, pp. 498. Adams E1087.
(c) Eusebius, *Pamphili, Bp of Caesarea*. Evangeliae demonstrationis Lib. X. [Gk.] Lutetiae. In officina Rob. Stephani, 1545 [*colophon*: 1546]. F°, pp. 138 [318]. Adams E1082. **309.1.46**
The original single volume was separated and rebound as two, probably in the late seventeenth century. The title page has the signatures "Arundel" and "Lumley." Lumley Library 1097.

²**1.S.13**   Eusebij chron: cum animadversionibus Scaligeri Isag chron   1620
Eusebius, *Pamphili, Bp of Caesarea.* Thesaurus temporum. Eusebii
Chronicorum Canonum ... libri duo, interprete Hieronymo. Item auctores
omnes derelicta ... continuantes ... Eusebii ... Chronicorum ... reliquiae
graecae, *ed.* J. J. Scaliger. Eiusdem ... notae .... Ejusdem Isagogicorum
Chronologiae canonum libri tres. Missing. Donor: William Branthwaite.
The list of books donated to Emmanuel by William Branthwaite
(Emmanuel College Archives LIB.2.4) cites this work as item 13: "Eusebij
thesaurus temporum".

²**1.S.14**   Ephraem: Syrus gr 1   1626–32
Ephraem, *St, Syrus.* Opera? [Gk & Lat.] Missing.

²**1.S.15**   Basilij magni opera 2 vol. gr 1   1620
Basil, *the Great, St, Abp of Caesarea.* Opera Omnia, Quae Reperiri
Potuerunt. [Gk & Lat.] [2 vols.] Parisiis, apud Michaelem Sonnium, 1618.
F°. Donor: William Branthwaite. Inscription on the flyleaves of both
volumes: "Ex dono Domini Doctoris Branthwaite." Fore-edge of vol. II:
"Basil."   **302.3.44–5**
The list of books donated to Emmanuel by William Branthwaite
(Emmanuel College Archives LIB.2.4) cites this work as item 7: "Basilij
opera 2 vol."

²**1.S.16**   Nazianzeni opera gr lat 2 vol   1620
Gregory, *of Nazianzus, St, Patriarch of Constantinople.* Opera. *Ed.* Jac.
Billius Prunaeus. [Gk & Lat.] [2 vols.] Lutetiae Parisiorum, apud Clau-
dium Morellum, 1609–1611. F°. Donor: William Branthwaite. Inscription
on the flyleaves of both volumes: "Ex dono Domini Doctoris Branthwaite."
                                                            301.2.24, 25
The list of books donated to Emmanuel by William Branthwaite
(Emmanuel College Archives LIB.2.4) cites this work as items 3 & 4:
"Gregorii Nazianzeni 2 vol 1 vol/2 vol".

²**1.S.17**   Nysseni opera gr lat 2 vol   1620
Gregory, *St, Bp of Nyssa.* Opera Omnia Quae Reperiri Potuerunt. [Gk &
Lat.] [2 vols.] Parisiis, apud Michaelem Sonnium [Vol. II: apud Claudium
Morellum], 1615. F°. Donor: William Branthwaite. Inscription on the
flyleaf of each volume: "Ex Dono Doctoris Branthwaite". Fore-edges:
"Nyssen/i"; "Nyssen/ii".   **302.3.42, 43**
The list of books donated to Emmanuel by William Branthwaite
(Emmanuel College Archives LIB.2.4) cites this work as item 5: "Gregorij
Nisseni 2 vol."

²1.S.18   Epiphanius, gr Lat 2 vol   1622–6
Epiphanius, *St*. Opera Omnia... Dionysius Petavius... recensuit, Latine
vertit & animadversionibus illustravit. [Gk & Lat.] [2 vols.] Parisiis,
sumpt. M. Sonnii, 1622. F°. Missing. Register of Books Removed:
"Epiphanij opera Gr: Lat: Petavij... 2. V...Paris: 1622...." Emmanuel's
present copy was a Sancroft gift: S4.2.31, 32.

²1.S.19   Chrysostomi op*era* gr Savilij 8 vol   1597–1621
John, *Chrysostom, St*. Opera. [Gk.] *Ed*. H. Savile. Etonae, excudebat
Iohannes Norton, 1610–12. [8 vols.] F°. There are four issues with
various title pages: STC 14629–14629^c. Missing. Register of Books
Removed, p. 5, 1.10: "D. Chrysostomi opera Graece... ed: Savil:... 8 V...
Etonae." Emmanuel's present copy was a Sancroft gift: S3.3.10–17.

²1.S.20   Synesius gr Lat   1620
Synesius, *Bp of Ptolemais*. Opera Quae Extant Omnia. *Tr*. Dionysius
Petavius. [Gk & Lat.] Lutetiae, apud Hieronymum Drovart, 1612. F°.
Donor: William Branthwaite. Inscription on flyleaf: "Ex dono Domini
Doctoris Branthwaite".   **301.3.59**
   The list of books donated to Emmanuel by William Branthwaite
(Emmanuel College Archives LIB.2.4) cites this volume as item 8: "Synesij
opera".

²1.S.21   Cyrilli op*era* Lat   1597–1621
[1621 inventory (2.I.20): "Cyrillus Alexandrinus Lat"]
Cyril, *St, Abp of Alexandria*. Opera. [Lat.] Missing.

²1.S.22   Ejusdem Glaphyr gr lat   1626–32
Cyril, *St, Patriarch of Alexandria*. Γλαφυρὰ εἰς Πεντά τευχον. Scita &
elegentia commentaria in quinque priores Moysis libros. *Ed*. Andreas
Schottius [Gk & Lat.] Antuerpiae, apud hered. M. Nutii et I. Meursium,
1618. F°, pp. 360, [14]. Fore-edge: "Cyrilli/Glaphyr".   **301.3.60**

²1.S.23   Isidori Pelusiotae Ep*isto*lae gr lat 2 vol   1620
Isidore, *St, of Pelusium*. Epistolarum amplius mille ducentarum libri tres.
[Gk & Lat.] [2 vols.]. Donor: William Branthwaite. Missing. The list of
books donated to Emmanuel by Branthwaite (Emmanuel College Archives
LIB.2.4) cites this work as item 10: "Isidori Epistolae".
   As with ²1.S.9, a copy of this work ([Heidelberg,] 1605) has the
inscription on the flyleaf: "Ex dono Domini Doctoris Branthwaite." This
copy, however, was a part of the Sancroft donation: S4.3.2. The book lacks
any other evidence of early seventeenth-century Emmanuel ownership and
is much more likely to have been the gift of Sancroft than of Branthwaite.
The inscription, like that in ²1.S.9, was probably added after the actual
Branthwaite copy was lost.

²1.S.24 Theodoreti op*era* 2 vol   1620

Theodoretus, *Bp of Cyrus*. Opera. [2 vols.] Coloniae Agrippinae, apud Ioannem Birckmannum, 1573. F°, pp. 791, 634. Adams T480. Donor: William Branthwaite. Inscription on the flyleaf of each volume: "Ex dono Domini Doctoris Branthwaite." Fore-edges: "Theodoret:/Lat 1/25"; "Theodoret/Lat ii/26". The covers of both volumes are stamped with the Cambridge University arms and on vol. I the name R. Culverwel and on vol. II the initials R.C.   **302.3.51–2**

The list of books donated to Emmanuel by William Branthwaite (Emmanuel College Archives LIB.2.4) cites this work as item 14: "Theodoreti Opera."

²1.S.25 Theodoret Therapeut gr lat   1616

Theodoretus, *Bp of Cyrus*. Ἑλληνικῶν καθημάτων θεραπευτική. Graecarum Affectionum Curatio. *Ed.* Fridericus Sylburgius [Gk & Lat] [Heidelberg,] ex typog. Hieronymi Commelini, 1592. F°, pp. 218. Adams T484. Donor: Robert Booth. Inscription on title page: "Hic liber donatus Bibliothecae a Domino Roberto Booth quondam hujus collegii Socio. Anno Domini. i6i6."   **302.3.58**

²1.S.26 Damasceni op*era* gr lat et Cassianus   1584–97

John, *St, Damascene*. Opera omnia.... Ioannis Cassiani... Libri Aliquot. [Gk & Lat.] Basileae, ex off. Henricpetrina, 1575. F°, pp. 1275 [1295]. Missing. Register of Books Removed, p. 9, 1.34: "Damasceni opera ... Gr: lat:... Basil: 1575." Emmanuel's present copy (Adams J267) was a Sancroft gift: S4.3.9.

²1.S.27 Theophilact in Evang gr   1584–97

Theophylactus, *Abp of Ochrida*. Ἑρμηνεία εἰς τὰ τέσσαρα Εὐαγγέλια. Romae, [Antonio Blado] 1542. F°, pp. 581. Missing. Register of Books Removed, p. 9, 1. 36: "Theophylactus in 4 Evangelia... Gr: (*Dupl.*) Rome 1542". Emmanuel's present copy (Adams T594) was a Sancroft gift: S4.3.14.

²1.S.28 Oecumenius in Acta et Ep*isto*las gr et Aretha in Apocal: gr: 1597–1621

Oecumenius, *Bp of Tricca*. Expositiones Antiquae... ex diversis sanctorum patrum commentariis ab Oecumenio & Aretha collectae in hosce novi testamenti tractatus. Oecumenii quidem in Acta Apostolorum. In septem epistolas quae Catholicae dicuntur. In Pauli omnes. Arethae vero in Johannis Apocalypsim. [Gk.] [Possibly: Veronae, apud Stephanum & Fratres Sabios, 1532. F°, pp. 1014. Adams O111.   **301.3.64**]

²1.S.29 Photij Bibliotheca gr   1616

Photius, *Patriarch of Constantinople*. βιβλιοθήκη *Ed.* David Hoeschelius. [Gk] Augustae Vindelicorum, ex off. typog. I. Praetorii, 1601. F°, pp. 985.

Donor: Robert Booth. Inscription on flyleaf: "Hic liber donatus Bibliothecae/huic, a Domino Roberto Booth/quondam huius collegii socio./Anno domini. i6i6". Fore-edge: "BIBΛΙ/φΩΤ:". **303.4.31**

²**1.S.30**   Origenes Contra Celsum   1622–6
Origenes. Origenis contra Celsum libri VIII et Gregorii Neocaesar. Thaumaturgi Panegyricus in Origenem. *Ed.* David Hoeschelius. [Gk & Lat.] Augustae Vindelicorum, imprimebat D. Franck, 1605. 4°, pp. 511+index. Missing. Register of Books Removed, p. 11, 1.7: "Origines contra Celsum. Gr:lat: Hoeschelij... Aug: Vind: 1605". Emmanuel's present copy was a Sancroft gift: S4.3.29.

²**1.S.31**   Ejusdem Philocalia   1626–32
Origenes. Philocalia de obscuris S. Scripturae locis a SS. PP. Basilio Magno et Gregorio Theologo, ex variis Origenis commentariis excerpta. *Ed.* J. Tarinus. [Gk & Lat.] Parisiis, sumptibus P. de Forge, 1618. 4°, pp. 736+index. Missing. Register of Books Removed, p. 11, 1. 6: "Origines philocalia... Gr: lat:... Tarini... Paris 1618". Emmanuel's present copy was a Sancroft gift: S4.4.10.

²**1.S.32**   Theodoreti 3 dial gr   1622–6
Theodoretus, *Bp of Cyrus.* Dialogi tres contra quasdam Haereses. [Gk.] [Possibly: Romae, per Stephanum Nicolinum Sabiensem, 1547. 4°, ff. 142, [2]. Adams T493.   **329.2.6]**

Classis 1ᵃᵉ Inferioᵣ sectio

²**1.I.1**   Concilia Binij 1: 5 vol   1597–1621
Binius, Severinus. Concilia generalia et provincialia quotquot reperiri potuerunt. [5 vols.] Missing.

²**1.I.2**   Concilia 5 vol: Venetijs. 1585   1585–97
Councils of the Christian Church. Conciliorum Omnium, Tam Generalium, quam Provincialium... Volumina Quinque. [5 vols.] Venetiis, apud Dominicum Nicolinum, 1585. F°, pp. 1226, 870, 986, 927, 791. Adams C2773. Donor: Thomas White. Signature on the final page of each volume, sometimes on recto, sometimes verso: "Tho: White". Fore-edges: "Concilia/i/3"; "ii/4"; "iii/5"; "iiii/6"; "5/7".   **302.3.15–19**

²**1.I.3**   Concili*orum* Tomi duo priores crab   1625
Councils of the Christian Church. Conciliorum omnium tam generalium quam particularium tomus I-(II). *Ed.* Petrus Crabbe. [First 2 of 3 vols.] Coloniae Agrippinae, ex off. Ioannis Quentel, 1551. F°, pp. 1075, 1182. Donor: Dr John Richardson. Missing. Register of Books Removed: "P.

146

Crabbe concilia... 1um & 2um V... Col: Agrip: 1551. Dr Rich." Emmanuel's present copy (a full three-volume set, Adams C2770) was a Sancroft gift: S3.3.18–20.

²**1.I.4**   Canones Apostolo*rum* et vet concilio*rum* constitutiones et decreta pontificum   1584–97
Two books bound together:

(1) *Apostolic Canons.* Canones Apostolorum. Veterum Conciliorum Constitutiones Decreta Pontificum Antiquiora. De Primatu Romanae Ecclesiae. Moguntiae, in aed. Ioan. Schoeffer, 1525. Adams C542.

(2) Pius II, Pope (Aeneas Silvius, *Piccolomini*). Commentariorum... de Consilio Basileae Celebrato libri duo. [n.p., n.d., Basle, J. Parvus, c. 1542–per Adams] F°, pp. 349. Adams P1343. Fore-edge: "2", and (vertically, bottom to top): "Canon aposto et commentarii Aeneii Sylvii."   **304.4.18**

²**1.I.5**   Balsamon in Can: Apost   1626–32
Apostolic Canons. Canones SS. Apostolorum, Conciliorum Generalium & Provincialium: Sanctorum Patrum Epistolae Canonicae. *Comm.* Theodorus Balsamon, *Patriarch of Antioch. Tr.* Gentianus Hernes. [Gk & Lat.] Lutetiae Parisiorum, Typis Regiis, 1620. Missing. Register of Books Removed, p. 5, 1.7: "Balsamonis Canones apostolici; concilia &c.... (Dupl: Rich) Paris: 1620." Emmanuel's present copy was a Sancroft gift: S3.2.39.

²**1.I.6**   Zonaras in Can Apost   1626–32
Apostolic Canons. In canones ss. Apostolorum et Sacrorum Conciliorum. *Comm.* Johannes Zonaras. *Pref.* J. Quentin. [Gk & Lat.] Lutetiae Parisiorum, typ. Regiis, 1618. F°, pp. 1044, [16] + indices. Missing. Register of Books Removed, p. 5, 1.8: "Zonarae commentar: in canon: Apostolic: & concilia.... Paris 1618." Emmanuel's present copy was a Sancroft gift: S3.2.40.

²**1.I.7**   Gallicae Eccl^{ae} decreta Bochelij   1622–6
Gallican Church. Decretorum Ecclesiae Gallicanae ex conciliis eiusdem oecumenicis statutis Synodalibus... collectorum libri VIII. *Ed.* Laurentius Bochellus. Parisiis, apud B. Maceum, 1609. F°, pp. 1384, [31] + index. Fore-edge: "ECCL: GAL:/Dec: Boch:"   **302.3.21**

²**1.I.8**   Synodus Dordrac^a: 1619–21
Dort, Synod of. One of the several editions of the proceedings and results of the Synod held in 1619, presumably different from that listed at 7.4.4–11. [Possibly: Acta et Scripta Synodalia Dordraceni Ministrorum Remonstratium in Foederato Belgio. Hederwiici Ex off. Typographi Synodalis (1620).] Missing. Emmanuel's present copy was a Sancroft gift: S3.4.15.

Μικροπρεσβυτικὸν   1584–97
Μικροπρεσβυτικὸν. Veterum Quorundam brevium Theologorum... qui
aut tempore Apostolorum aut non multo post vixerunt, elenchus. Basileac,
apud Henrichum Petri, 1550. F°, pp. 662. Adams M1436. Fore-edge:
"MIKPO/ΠPEΣB/UTIKON/29", and below, faded: "Micro [?]/[?]".
                                                            301.2.51

²**1.I.10**   Philo Judaeus gr   1584–97
Philo, *Judaeus.* In Libros Mosis De Mundi Opificio, Historicos, De
legibus. Eiusdem libri singulares. [Gk.] Parisiis, ex off. Adriani Turnebei,
1552. F°, pp. 736. Adams P1033. Fore-edge: "Philo/ [?]/12".   **301.3.55**

²**1.I.11**   Iustinus Martyr gr   1584–97
Justin, *Martyr, St.* [Opera.] [Gk.] Lutetiae, ex off. Roberti Stephani, 1551.
F°, pp. 311. Missing. Register of Books Removed, p. 9, 1. 27: Justini
Martyris opera. Gr: R. Steph... Paris: 1551."

²**1.I.12**   Clemens Alexandrinus gr   1584–97
Clement, *St, of Alexandria. Τὰ εὑρισκόμενα ἁπανΓα.* Florentiae, ex
bibliotheca medicea, cudebat Laurentius Torentinus, 1550. F°, pp. 42, 347
[357]. Adams C2104. Fore-edge: "Clem/graece/18."   **301.2.22**

²**1.I.13**   Athanasius lat   1584–97
Athanasius, *St, Patriarch of Alexandria.* Opera [Lat.] Basileae, ex off.
Episcopiana, per Nicolaum et Eusebium Episcopios, 1564. F°, pp. 730, 142.
Adams A2084. Fore-edge: "Athanas/Lat/22". Donor: Richard Culverwell.
The Cambridge University arms and the initials of Richard Culverwell are
stamped on the binding.   **302.3.46**

²**1.I.14**   Basilus Mag: gr   1584–97
Basil, *St, the Great.* En amice lector, thesaurum damus D. Basilium. [Gk.]
Basileae, ex off. Frobeniana, [15]32. F°, pp. 674. Lumley 135. Adams B344.
Signatures on title page: "Thomas Cantuaren*sis*" and "Lumley". Fore-edge:
"Basilii/Magni oper/graec./11."   **304.4.29**

²**1.I.15**   Idem Lat   1584–97
Basil, *St, the Great.* Opera. [Probably: (*Ed.* Wolfgang Musculus) (2 vols. in
1.) Basileae, ex off. Hervagiana, 1540. F°, pp. 581 + index, 238 (438). Adams
B335. Donor: Edward Leeds. Signature on title page: "E Leeds."] This item
first appears on the catalogue of c. 1597 but is not mentioned on the 1621
catalogue. It reappears on the 1622 list, where it was apparently added
after the completion of the inventory.   **302.3.55**

²**1.I.16**   Nazianzenus gr   1584–97
Gregory, *St, of Nazianzus. ‟Απαντα, Γὰ μέχρι νῦν μὲν ευρισκόμενα. ’Εν*

βασιλεία, ἀναλώμασι Ἰωάννου Γοῦ ἐρβαγίου [1550]. Fº, pp. 140 [340], 95. Adams G1133. Fore-edge: "Naz./graec./ 15." Donor: Richard Culverwell. The arms of Cambridge University and the initials of Richard Culverwell are stamped on the cover. **301.3.65**

²**1.I.17** Idem lat   1584–97

        [1621 inventory (2.I.12): "Nazianzeni Orat. 30 Lat: & Gregory Nisseni pars."]

        Two books bound together:

        (1) Gregory, *St, of Nazianzus*. Orationes XXX. *Tr.* Bilibaldus Pirckheimer. Basileae, in off. Frobeniana per Hieronymum Frobenium & Nicolaum Episcopium, 1531. Fº, pp. 304, 126 (lacks end of second part from p. 67). Adams G1158.

        (2) Gregory, *St, Bp of Nyssa*. De Creatione hominis liber, supplementum Hexamerῶn Basilii Magni fratris. *Tr.* Dionysius Romanus Exiguus. Coloniae, ex off. Melchioris Novesiani, 1537. Fº, ff. 93 + index. Adams G1116. Fore-edge: "Nazian/Lat" and in another hand: "Greg*us*/Nazin" and "14."   **304.4.30**

²**1.I.18** Epiphanius gr   1584–97

        [1621 inventory (2.I.11): "Epiphanius contra 80 Haereses Graec"] Epiphanius, *St*. Contra Octoginta haereses opus eximium. [Gk.] [Possibly: Basileae, ἀναλωμασι Ἰωάννου του ‘Ερουαγίου 1544. Fº, pp. 543. Adams E250.   **303.4.49**]

²**1.I.19** Oecumenius in Acta et Ep*istolas* et Aretha in Apocal: Lat   1584–97

        Oecumenius, *Bp of Tricca*. Enarrationes Vetustissimorum Theologorum, in Acta quidem Apostolorum et in omnes D. Pauli ac Catholicas Epistolas ab Oecomenio: in Apocalypsim vero, ab Aretha... collectae. *Tr.* Ioannes Hentenius. Selecta quaedam fragmenta ex D. Epiphanio Cyprensi, Theodoreto Cyrensi Episcopis, aliisq*ue*... theologis.... Praeterea Remigii Altisiodorensis Episcopi... in undecim posteriores Prophetas, enarratio. Antuerpiae, in aed. Ioannis Steelsii, 1545. Fº, ff. 331. Missing. Register of Books Removed, p. 9, 11.28, 29: "Oecumenius in acta & epistolas... Lat: p*er* Hentenium/Remigius in minores prophetas...} Antw: 1545".

²**1.I.20** Zieglerus in Exod: et Levit: Borrhaius in 5 Libros Mosis, et Isychius in Levit et Gallasius in Exod, et Thom Aquinas in Cantic   1584–97

        [1621 inventory (2.S.24): Zieglerus in Gen. & Exod. Victor Afer de Generat*ione* verbi Dei; Borrhaus in Mosen, Isichius in Levit: Gallasius in Exodum & Thom: super Cantica Canticoru*m*]

        Five books bound together:

        (1) Ziegler, Jacob. Conceptionu*m* in Genesim mundi, & Exodum, Commentarii.... Marii Victorini Afri... De generatione divini Verbi. Basileae, apud Ioannem Oporinum, 1548. Fº, pp. 234 [246] + index. Adams Z151.

(2) Borrhaus, Martinus. In Mosem...Commentarii. In Librum... quem Genesim vocant... Exodum. Leviticum. Numeros. Deuteronomium. Basileae, ex off. Ioannis Oporini, 1555. F°, coll. 1116+index. Adams B2507.

(3) Hesychius, *of Jerusalem*. In Leviticum Libri Septem. Basileae, apud A. Cratandrum, 1527. F°, ff. 180. Adams H510.

(4) Gallasius, Nicolaus. In Exodum... Commentarii. Genevae, apud Ioannem Crispinum, 1560. F°, pp. 251, [11]. Adams G148.

(5) Aquinas, Thomas, *St*. Expositio devotissima super Cantica Canticorum. Venetiis, impens. Hered... O. Scoti & soc., 1516. F°, ff. 15, [1]. Adams B1567.

Donor: John Meredith. Inscription on first title page and on the vellum cover: "E dono Joannis Meredith Ministri Evangelii." Fore-edge: "28".

308.4.66

²**1.I.21** Antidotum adversus Haereses   1584–97

Sichardus, Johannes, *ed*. Antidotum contra diversas omnium fere seculorum haereses. [Possibly: Basileae, excud. Henricus Petrus, 1528. Adams S1065.   **303.4.54**]

Emmanuel also has a copy which was a Sancroft gift: S9.2.39.

²**1.I.22** Chron: Eusebij etc: 1622–6

Three works bound together:

(1) Sichardus, Johannes, *ed*. Chronica:... opus... ad annum... CIƆIƆ.LXXIX. per... viros claros continuatum.... Eusebius Pamphilius.... Hieronymus Presbyter. Prosper Aquitanicus. Matthaeus Palmerius Florentinus. Matthias Palmerius Pisanus: & alii adjectis quoque M. Aurelii Cassiodori... necnon Hermanni Contracti comitis Veringensis chronicis [&c.]. Basileae, ex off. Henricpetrina, 1579. F°, ff. 242+index. Adams F1078.

(2) Budaeus, Gulielmus: De Philologia Libri II. Parisiis, excud. Michael Vascosanus, in aed. Ascensianis, 1536. F°, ff. 46. Adams B3123.

(3) Budaeus, Gulielmus. De Studio Literarum recte et commode instituendo. Parisiis, excud. Michael Vascosanus, in aed. Ascensianis, 1536. F°, ff. 22. Adams B3126. Fore-edge: "Cronicon/Eusebij/H. Contr".   **308.4.16**

²**1.I.23** Chrisostomi opera lat. 4 vol   1597–1621

John, *Chrysostom, St*. Opera... recognita, suppleta, correcta,... Ex editione Graeco-Latina Frontonis Ducaei. [Lat.] [5 vols. in 4.] Parisiis, 1614. F°, coll. 1301+index; 1194, 1830; 1608; 1740, 120, 298. Fore-edges: "Chrysost: lat/i"; "ii/iii"; "iiii"; "iiii/v".   **305.1.28–31**

²**1.I.24** Hugo de S^{cto} Victore   1622–6

Hugo, *of St Victor*. Opera Omnia. Ed. & Comm. Thomas Garzonius. [3 vols. in 1.] Moguntiae, sumpt. Antonii Hierat, excud. Ioannes Volmari,

1617. F°, pp. 414, 427, 521 + indices. Fore-edges: "H: de Sanct: Vict:".

310.2.2

²**1.I.25**   Ricardus de Sᶜᵗᵒ Vict   1622–6
Richard, *of St Victor.* Omnia Opera. Parisiis, venundatur in ed. Ioannis
Petit, cura Andree boucard, 1518. F°, ff. 1–152, 1, 120–8, 11–112. Adams
R502. Fore-edge: "Ric:S/Victo/E,–da/Prow/Can."   **307.3.2**

²**1.I.26**   Sixti Senensis Bibliotheca   1625
Sixtus, *Senensis.* Bibliotheca sancta... ex praecipuis Catholicae Ecclesiae
Auctoribus collecta. *Ed.* J. Hay. Lugduni, sumpt. Sib. a Porta excud.
Stephanus Servin, 1591. F°, pp. 668 [664] + index. Adams S1271. Donor:
Dr John Richardson. Fore-edge: "Sixtus."   **305.2.40**

²**1.I.27**   Vellosilli advertae in 4ᵒʳ patres   1622–6
Vellosillus, Ferdinandus, *Bp of Lugo.* Advertentiae Theologiae Scholasticae
in B. Chrysost. et quatuor Doct. Ecclesiae [Saints Jerome, Ambrose,
Augustine, and Gregory]. Venetiis, 1601. F°, pp. 558. Fore-edge:
"Vellocil:/in. 4:ᵒʳ/patres".   **307.4.11**

²**1.I.28**   Nyssenus lat et Hilarius   1584–97
Two works bound together:
(1) Gregory, *St, Bp of Nyssa.* Opera... Omnia. [Lat.] *Tr.* Laurentius
Sifanus. Basileae, per Nic. Episcopium Iuniorem, 1562. F°, pp. 600.
Adams G1111.
(2) Hilary, *St, Bp of Poitiers.* Lucubrationes Quotquot Extant, Olim per
Des. Erasmum... emendatae... nunc denuo per D. Martinum
Lypsium collectae & recognitae. Basileae, apud Hier. Froben. et Nic.
Episcopium, 1550. F°, pp. 785 + index. Adams H555. Lumley 362.
Signatures on title page: "Cantuariensis" (Cranmer) and "Lumley". When
this volume was rebound, probably in the eighteenth century, the edges
were trimmed but the following remains on the upper right side of the fore-
edge: "seni".   **304.4.32**

²**1.I.29**   Rupertus 3 Vol   1625
Rupertus,· *Abbot of Deutz.* Three volumes:
(1) Libri XLII. De operibus sanctae Trinitatis. Lovanii, excud. S. Sassenus,
expens. vid. A. Birckmanni, 1551. F°, ff. 403 + index. Adams R922.
Donor: Dr John Richardson. Fore-edge: "Rupertus/i".   **304.4.68**
(2) Four works bound together:
(a) In XII Prophetas minores Commentariorum Libri XXXII. *Ed.* I.
Cochlaeus. Lovanii, excud. S. Sassenus, expens. Vid. A. Birckmanni,
1567. F°, ff. 213 + index. Adams R938.
(b) In Cantica Canticorum, de incarnatione Domini, Commentariorum
Libri VII. Coloniae, apud haer. A. Birckmanni, 1566. F°, pp.
72 + index. Adams R934.

(c) Commentariorum in Evangelium Iohannis, Libri XIIII. Coloniae, impens. Arnoldi Birckman, 1541. F°, pp. 311 + index. Adams R940.
(d) Commentariorum in Apocalypsim Iohannis, Libri XII. Coloniae, impens. Arnoldi Birckman, 1541. F°, ff. 195 + index. Adams R943. Donor: Dr John Richardson. Fore-edge: "Rupert:/ii." **304.4.69**

(3) Two works bound together:
(a) Opera Duo.... In Matthaeum De gloria & honore filii hominis, Lib. XIII. De Glorificatione Trinitatis & processione spiritus sancti. Lib. IX. Coloniae, impens. Arnoldi Birckman, 1540. F°, pp. 167, 103 + index. Adams R930.
(b) De Divinis Officiis Libri Duodecim. Coloniae Agrippinae, apud haer. Arnoldi Birckmanni, 1581. F°, pp. 181. Adams R920. Donor: Dr John Richardson (?). (The flyleaf, which probably bore the Richardson gift label, has been cut out.) Fore-edge: "Rupert./iii."
304.4.70

²**1.I.30**   Innocentij op*era*   1626–32
Innocent III, *Pope.* Opera. [2 vols. in 1.] Coloniae, apud Maternum Cholinum, 1575. F°, pp. 491, 814 + index. Adams I122. Fore-edge: "Innocen/tij 3^{tij} Opera." **303.4.32**

²**1.I.31**   Biblioth Studij Theolog   1584–97
Bibliotheca Studii Theologici, ex plerisque Doctorum prisci seculi monumentis collecta: Ex... Augustini liberis in epitomen ac locorum communium ordinem distributis: II.... Hieronymi Operibus... in Compendium redactis: III. Sententiis... Orthodoxorum Aliorum Patrum per locos communes digestis. [3 pts in 1 vol.] [Geneva,] apud Io. Crispinum, 1565. F°, pp. 469, 190, 235 + indices. Adams B1987. Fore-edge: "Bibliotheca/Aurlij theolog." **306.4.62**

²**1.I.32**   Prosperi op*era*   1584–97
Prosper, *St, of Aquitaine.* Opera. Lovanii, ex off. typog. Ioannis Bogardi, 1565. 4°, ff. 326 + index. Adams P2171. Fore-edge: "Prosper/28". **329.2.4**

²**1.I.33**   Pseudo Isidorus   1626–32
Isidorus, Mercator [Pseudo-Isidorus]. [Possibly: Pseudo-Isidorus et Turrianus vapulantes... Recensuit, notis illustravit... David Blondellus. (2 pts.).] Emmanuel's present copy (Genevae, 1628) was a Sancroft gift: S3.4.9.

²**1.I.34**   Apostol: Constitutiones gr   1625
Apostolic Constitutions. ΔιαΓαγαί. Constitutiones sanctorum Apostolorum A Clemente Romano. *Ed.* F. Turrianus. [Gk] Venetiis, ex off. Iordani Zileti, 1563. 4°, ff. 18, 195. Adams A1334. Donor: Dr John Richardson. Fore-edge: "Clemens". **325.4.61**

²**1.I.35**   Apostol: et Sct*arum* synod*orum* Canones   1622–6
Apostolic Constitutions. [Possibly: Κανόνες τῶν ᾿Αποστόλων καὶ τῶν ἁγίων
συνόδων. Apostolorum et Sanctorum Conciliorum Decreta. (Gk.) Parisiis,
per Conradum Neobarium, 1540. Adams C543. Bottom edge: "Decreta
apostolorum."   **325.4.62**]

²**1.I.36**   Medulla Patrum 4 vol.   1625
Scultetus, Abraham. Medulla theologiae patrum. [4 vols.] I. Ambergae, ex
typog. Forsteriano, 1613; II. Ambergae, 1606; III. [Leipzig] typis Got-
thardi Voegelini, 1609; IV. Heidelbergae, impens. Ionae Rosae, typis
Johannis Lancelloti, 1613. 4°, pp. 528, 400 + index, 482, 445 + index. Donor:
Dr John Richardson. Vols. 1 & 3 have the Richardson gift label on the
front end paper. Fore-edges: "Medulla/Patrum/Scultet;/I": "II"; "III"; "IV".
                                                                     327.3.79–82

²**1.I.37**   Theophyl in Ep*isto*las lat   1584–97
Theophylactus, *Bp of Ochrida.* In omnes D. Pauli Epistolas enarrationes.
[Possibly: *Tr.* Christophorus Porsena. Coloniae, Eucharius Cervicornus
excud. impens. Godefridi Hyttorpii, 1528. 8°, pp. 937. Adams T600.
                                                                      327.3.110]

²**1.I.38**   Euthymius in Evang lat   1584–97
Euthymius, *Zigabenus.* Commentaria in Sacrosancta quatuor Christi
Evangelia ex Chrysostomi aliorum*que*; veterum scriptis... collecta. Parisiis, apud Ioanne*m* Roigny, excud. Carola Guillard, 1544. 8°, ff.
430 + index. Adams E1117. Fore-edge: "31/Euthimi*us*/*in* eva*n*gelia."
                                                                      327.3.105

²**1.I.39**   Idem in Ep*isto*las lat   1584–97
Euthalius, *Bp of Sulca.* Narratio de divo Apostolo. Eutalii Diaconi Pro-
logus. [Includes commentaries on Paul's Epistles, Romans through
Hebrews.] [Paris, c. 1600.] 8°, ff. 285–748. Not in Adams. Fore-edge:
"32/Euthi*us* in/Paulum."   **326.4.80**

²**1.I.40**   Rupertus de vict verbi   1622–6
Rupertus, *Abbot of Deutz.* De Victoria Verbi Dei Libri Tredecim.
[Possibly: *Pref.* I. Petreius. Norembergae, apud Io. Petreium, 1524. 8°, ff.
227 + index. Adams R923.   **326.4.95**]
The catalogue of c. 1597 lists (no. 279) "Rupertus" but the item does not
reappear on the 1621 or 1622 inventories.

²**1.I.41**   Marci Erem^ae^ opuscula quaedam Theolog lat et Nicolai rescript ad
marcum excitatore*m* et Hesychii sermo ad Theodullu*m* lat: 1625
Marcus, *St, Eremita.* Opuscula qu*a*edam Theologica. *Tr.* I. Picus, *et al.*
[Also contains: Nicolai Cuiusdam, Rescriptum ad Marcum Exercitorem;

153

Marci Exercitoris, Disputatio cum Scholastico *and* Consultatio intellectus cum sua ipsius anima; Hesychii Presbyteri, Centuriae duae (ad Theodulum).] Lutetiae apud Audoënum Parvum, excud F. Morellus, 1563. 8°, pp. 542. Adams M555. Emmanuel's original copy was the first of twelve books listed as "wantinge" on April 12, 1626, which "Mr Johnso*n* is to be answerable for". Donor of the replacement copy: Dr John Richardson. Fore-edge: "Marcus/Eremita/Hesychij/Centura/34". **321.6.62**

²**1.I.42**   Lactantij op*era*   1584–97
[c. 1597 inventory (no. 85): "Lactantantius in oct."]
Lactantius Firmianus, Lucius Coelius. [Possibly: Divinarum institutionum Libri VII. Basileae, apud Andream Cratandrum, et Io. Bebelium, 1532. F°, ff. 149 + index. Adams L20. Fore-edge: "Lacta*n*/tius". Donor (?): Thomas Ughtred. Signature on title page: "Thomas Ughtred". **303.4.55**]

²**1.I.43**   Fulgentij op*era*   1584–97
Fulgentius, *Bp of Ruspa.* Opera. Item opera Maxentii Iohannis. Apud Coloniam Agrippinam, in aed. Hieronis Alopecii, impensa Godefridi Hittorpii, 1526. 8°, pp. 414, 138. Adams F1137. Fore-edge: "36" and (vertically) "Opera Fulge*n*tii". **321.6.90**

²**1.I.44**   Cassianus de incarnatio*ne* dni et Cyrilli sermo de eo qd verbum factum est homo et Maximus incarnatio*ne* verbi   1584–97
Two works bound together:
(1) John, *St, Cassianus.* De incarnatione Domini libri VII. (Contra Nestorium haereticum). Item Beati Cyrilli sermo, de eo quod verbum dei factum sit homo. Missing.
(2) Maximus, *Abbot and Confessor.* De incarnatione Verbi. Missing. This volume was possibly replaced by a Sancroft gift of a collection of works on the nature of Christ's incarnation: S9.2.41.

ᵛ²**1.I.45**   Philastrius˙ de Haeresibus   1584–97
Philaster, *Bp of Brescia.* De... haeresibus. Basileae, apud Henricum Petrum, 1539. 8°, pp. 407. Adams P995. Fore-edge: "Philastr./34". **322.5.8**

²**1.I.46**   Bodij unio dissidentium ex patribus   1584–97
Bodius, Hermannus, *pseud. (probably for J. Oecolampadius).* Unio Dissidentium. Libellus Omnibus unitatis et pacis amatoribus utilissimus ex praecipuis Ecclesiae Christianae doctoribus, per... Hermannum Bodium... selectus, ac per eunde*m* secundo recognitus. Antuerpiae, per Martinum Caesarem impens. Godefridi Dumaei, 1531. 8°, ff. 417. Adams B2251. Fore-edge: "Unio dissidentiu*m*/per her bodiu*m*/27". **321.6.39**

²**1.I.47**   Leonis op*era*   1584–97
[1621 inventory (3.S.10): "Opera Leonis Papae"]
Leo I, *Pope, called "The Great".* Opera. Missing.

²2.S(1).1   Tertulianus et Arnobius   1584–97

Tertullianus, Quintus Septimus Florens; Arnobius; and Arnobius Afer. Opera Tertulliani et Arnobii. *Ed. & comm.* Renatus Laurentius de La Barre [includes "Arnobius Afer in omnes psalmos," a work generally attributed to Arnobius Junior]. [2 pts.] Parisiis, apud M. Iulianum, 1580. F°, pp. 728, 240, [15]+index. Missing. Register of Books Removed, p. 9, 1. 20: "Tertulliani opera cum Arnobio in psalmos &c... dit: de la Bar... Paris: 1580." Emmanuel's present copy (Adams T413 omits Emmanuel's copy) was a Sancroft gift: S4.2.28.

²2.S(1).2   Cyprianus   1584

Cyprian, *St, Bp of Carthage.* Opera.... Adnotationes Iacobi Pamelij ... Editio altera. Parisiis, Apud S. Nivellium, 1574. F°, pp. 607, [2]. Adams C3165. Donor: Richard Culverwell. Inscription on title page: "Richardus Culverwell Colleg: Eman. D.D. L.M.Q. 1584. Res tuas age. 1584." Cambridge University arms and initials "R.C." stamped on the covers. Foreedge: "Cyprian*us*/15".   **302.3.41**

²2.S(1).3   Ambrosius 3 vol   1584–97

Ambrose, *Bp of Milan.* Omnia Quotquot Extant... Opera. *Ed.* Desiderius Erasmus, Sigismundus Gelenius and others, and Ioannes Costerius. [5 pts in 3 vols.] Basileae, per Eusebium Episcopium et haered. Nicolai Episcopii, 1567. F°. Missing. Register of Books Removed, p. 9, 1. 33: "P. Ambrosij opera... 3v.... Costerij... (Dupl: Rich)... Basil:1567." The present Emmanuel copy (Adams A942) was a Sancroft gift: S4.3.7, 8.

²2.S(1).4   Hieronymus 4 vol: 1584–97

Jerome, *St.*

    Although editions of Jerome's collected works were available long before 1584, it seems likely that this entry describes four separately published works. One of the volumes may have been Jerome's *Epistolae Selectae.* If so, it was later replaced by a copy donated by Mr John Richardson in the 1670s which was in turn replaced (Register of Books Removed, p. 11, 1. 28) by a Sancroft gift: S4.5.78. Three other items by Jerome, totalling five volumes, were also in Sancroft's gift and may have replaced the earlier copies, though the exchange is not recorded in the Register of Books Removed.

²2.S(1).5   Augustinus 8 vol: 1584–97

    (1)   Augustine, *St, Bp of Hippo.*

          Two works bound together:

          (a) De Civitate dei. *Comm.* Thomas Valois & Nicolaus Triveth. In Friburga, [Kilian Fischer,] 1494. F°. Hain 2068; Proctor 3214.

(b) De Trinitate. [Freiburg im Breisgau, Kilian Fischer,] 1494. F°. Hain 2040; Proctor 3215.

Fore-edge: "Augustin:/de civit: Dei."   MSS 6.1.7

(2) Augustine, *St, Bp of Hippo*. Prima (-Tertia) Quinquagena. In Explanatione*m* libri Psalmorum [with annotations at end]. Basileae pe*r* magistru*m* ioannem de Amerbach, 1497. F°. Hain 1975. Missing. Register of Books Removed, p. 9, 1.37: "D. Augustinus in psalmos ... Basil 1497". Emmanuel's present copy was a Sancroft gift: S4.3.16.

(3) Augustine, *St, Bp of Hippo*. Milleloquium Veritatis a F. Bartholomaeo de Urbino Digestum. Lugduni, Ad. Salamandrae, apud Senetonios Fratres, 1555. F°, coll. 2480 [2482]. Adams A2183.

Fore-edge: "Augustine/milleloquiu*m*".   **301.3.56**

(4-8) [Possibly: Augustine, *St, Bp of Hippo*. (Opera.) (10 vols. in 6.) Basileae, per A. et A. Frobenios, Fratres, 1569. F°. Adams A2166.

Fore-edges: I: "Aug./1111/I/II"

II: "August/III/1111"

III: "Augustin*us*/De civitate/Dei/V/VI"

IV: "Aug:/ aduers*us* her/eses/VII"

V: "Aug: Enara: In/Psal. Misticos/VIII/IX"

VI: "AVRE: AV/GVSTIN/X"

301.2.26–31]

If these six volumes were part of the eight-volume collection seen by the cataloguer, then one of the three works listed in nos. 1–3 is not. Uncertainty is compounded in this case because the major donations in the later seventeenth century by Breton, (Mr) John Richardson, and Sancroft all contained volumes of Augustine; these copies may have displaced some of the library's original volumes, though only one entry in the Register of Books Removed (see no. 2 above) lists such removals.

²**2.S(1).6**   Sedulius in Pauli Epi*sto*las   1584–97

Sedulius, *Scotus*. In Omnes Epistolas Pauli Collectaneum. Basileae, per Henricum Petrum, 1528. F°, ff. 110. Adams S855. Fore-edge: "5/Sedu/lius".

310.5.1

²**2.S(1).7**   Eucherij op*era*, et Salviani: Αντικείμενα de locis Script^ae in specie pugnantib*us* et Nazian: de Theolog: Lact   1597–1621

Three books bound together:

(1) Eucherius, *Bp of Lyon*. Lucubrationes.... piae. *Ed.* Ioannes Alexander Brassicanus. [2 pts in 1 vol.] Basileae, per Hieronymum Frobenium & Nicolaum Episcopium, 1531. F°, pp. 194, 310. Adams E970.

(2) Salvianus, *Massiliensis, Presbyter*. De Vero Iudicio et Providentia dei ... Libri VIII. *Ed.* Ioannes Alexander Brassicanus. Anticimenon Lib. III, incerto Autore. [2 pts.] Basileae, per Ioannem Hervagium,

Hieronymum Frobenium, et Nicolaum Episcopium, 1530. F°, ff. 58, 44. Adams S198.

(3) Gregory, *of Nazianzus, St, Patriarch of Constantinople.* De Theologia libri quinq*ue*. *Tr.* Petrus Mosellanus. Basileae, apud Io. Frobenium, 1523. F°. Adams G1147.

Fore-edge: "Eucheri*us*/Saluian*us*" [and in another, fainter hand:] "Eucherius/Saluianus/Gre*g*orius naza*n*zeus/27." **303.4.45**

²**2.S(1).8** Gregorius Magnus 1584–97
Gregory I, *St, Pope, called "the Great".* [Possibly: Confessio Gregoriana. *Ed.* F. Theodorus Petrus. Coloniae, apud Arnoldum Quentelium, 1597. 8°, pp. 341+index. Missing. Register of Books Removed, p. 11, 1.14: "Confessio Gregariana ... id: Petrei ... Colon: 1597". Emmanuel's present copy (Adams G1189) was a Sancroft gift: S4.4.64.]

²**2.S(1).9** Bedae op*er*a 4 vol: 1625
Bede, *St, The Venerable.* Opera. [8 vols. in 4.] Basileae, per Ioannem Hervagium, 1563. F°, coll. 220, pp. 221–374, coll. 375–542, pp. 353; coll. 673, 26, 1280; 122, 1138, 42, 1178; 663, 1138+index (vol. I). Adams B447. Donor: Dr John Richardson. Fore-edges: " Bedae, tom*us*/i*us* et ii*us*"; "iii*us* et iiii*us*"; "v*us* et vi*us*"; "vii*us* et viii*us*." **304.1.39, 40; 301.2.15, 16**

²**2.S(1).10** Cassiodorus in Psalm: 1622–6
Cassiodorus, Magnus Aurelius. Psalterii davidici expositio. Parisius, per Andream boucard, impens. Ioha*n*nis petit, venu*n*dat*ur* ab Ioa*n*ne parvo, 1519. F°, ff. 227. Adams C877. **310.5.15**

²**2.S(1).11** Alchuinus 1625
Alcuin, *ed.* Homiliae seu mavis sermones ... Hieronymi, Augustini, Ambrosii, Gregorii, Origenis, Chrysostomi, Bedae, Herici, Haymonis, aliorumque. Coloniae, ex off. Eucharii Cervicorni, 1530. F°, ff. 248. Adams A642. Donor: Dr John Richardson. Fore-edge: "Alcuin*us*" and vertically: "Homeliae seu sermo Doctoris/per Alcuinu*m* leuitam." **310.5.9**

²**2.S(1).12** Anselmus 1584–97
[1621 inventory (4.S.11): "Anselmus in o*m*nes Pauli Ep*isto*las"]
Anselm, *Abp of Canterbury.* In Omnes Pauli Apostoli epistolas enarrationes. Missing.

²**2.S(1).13** Bernardus 1584–97
[1621 inventory (3.S.3): "Bernardi Opera"]
Bernard, *Abbot of Clairvaux.* Opera Omnia. [2 vols. in 1.] Parisiis, 1586.

F°, coll. 1790, 1052 + indices. Adams B714. Fore-edge: "BERNARD".

304.1.13

Classis 2^{dae} Inferior Sect. 1ma

²**2.I(1).1**   Gnotosolitos   1597–1621
Geilhouen, Arnold. Gnotosolitos sive Speculum conscientiae. Bruxelle, 1476. F°. Proctor + 9327. Hain 7514.   **MSS.5.1.16**

²**2.I(1).2**   Campigni Summa Cathol: fidei   1625
Crespetius, Petrus. Summa Catholicae fidei, Apostolicae doctrinae, et Ecclesiasticae disciplinae, nec non totius Iuris Canonici. Lugduni, apud Ioannem Pillehotte, 1598. F°, pp. 895 + index. Adams C2934. Donor: Dr John Richardson. Fore-edge: "Campigny."   **310.2.10**

²**2.I(1).3**   Sanches de Matrimonio   1622–6
Sanchez, Tomas. Disputationum de Sancto Matrimonii Sacramento... tomi tres. [3 pts in 1 vol.] Antuerpiae, apud Haeredes Martini Nuti & Ioannem Meursium, 1614. F°, pp. 516, 411, 418 + indices. Fore-edge: "Sanches".   **308.3.46**

²**2.I(1).4**   Idem in decalogum   1625
Sanchez, Tomas. Opus Morale in Praecepta Decalogi. [2 vols. in 1.] Antuerpiae, apud heredes M. Nuti et Ioannem Meursium, 1614. F°, pp. 348, 396 + indices. Donor: Dr John Richardson. Fore-edge: "SANCHES".

308.3.47

²**2.I(1).5**   Sayri Clavis Regia   1626–32
Sayer, Robert (or, in religion, Gregory). Clavis Regia Sacerdotum, Casuum Conscientiae sive Theologiae Moralis thesauri locos omnes aperiens. Antuerpiae, apud I. Keerbergium, 1619. (*colophon*: Duaci, typ. M. Wyon, 1618). F°, pp. 1034 + index. Donor: Elias Pettit. Inscription on front flyleaf: "Ex dono Eliae Pettit, in Artibus/Magistri, & hujus Collegij quondam scholaris/Discipuli". Fore-edge: "Sayr".   **308.3.40**

²**2.I(1).6**   Laymanni Theologia Moralis   1627–32
Laymannus, Paulus. Theologia Moralis in V Lib. partita. [5 pts in 1 vol.] Lutetiae Parisiorum, sumpt. Petri Billaine, 1627. Donor: Elias Pettit. Inscription on flyleaf: "Ex dono Eliae Petit in Artibus Magistrj, & hujus/Collegij quondam scholaris discipuli." Fore-edge: "Laymannus."

308.3.39

²**2.I(1).7**   Filucius 2 vol: 1626–32
Filliucius, Vincentius. Moralium quaestionum de christianis officiis et

casibus conscientiae... tomus [primus]-secundus. [2 vols., title of vol. 1 defective.] Ursellis, sumpt. A. Hierati, 1625–6. F°, pp. 756+index. [Vol. 2 contains:] Ad duos priores tomos Quaestionum moralium appendix posthuma de statu clericorum.... Editio altera. Coloniae Agrippinae, sumpt. A. Hierat, 1626. F°, pp. 255+Schematismus+index. Donor: Elias Pettit. Inscription on the front flyleaf of each volume: "Ex dono Eliae Pettit in Artibus Magistrj, & hujus/Collegij quondam Scholaris discipulj." Fore-edges: "Filiucius/Tom. 1."; "Tom. II".   **308.3.20, 21**

[2].**I(1).8**   Henriquez Summa Theologiae Moralis   1625
Henriquez, Enrique. Summae theologiae moralis, libri quindecim. [2 pts in 1 vol.] Moguntiae, ex off. typog. I. Albini, 1613. F°, pp. 884, 116+index. Donor: Thomas Hanscombe. Inscription on first flyleaf: "Ex dono Magistri Hanscombe". Inscription on second flyleaf: "Magister Thomas Hanscombe, huius/Collegij Socius, Moriens. D.D." Fore-edge: "HENRIQUES".   **308.3.22**

[2].**I(1).9**   Soto de Just[a] et jure   1622–6
Soto, Domingo de. De Iustitia et Iure. Missing.

[2].**I(1).10**   Raymundi Summa   1622–6
Raymundus, St, de Penaforte. Summa de Casibus Poenitentiae. Missing.

[2].**I(1).11**   Azorij Institùt Moral: 3 vol   1622–6
Azor, Juan. Institutiones Morales... nunc primum in Germania editae. [3 vols.] Coloniae Agrippinae, apud Antonium Hierat, 1613–17. F°, pp. 926+index; coll. 1426+index; coll. 1222+index. Fore-edges: "Azorius/I"; "II"; "III".   **308.3.53–5**

[2].**I(1).12**   Paulus de Blanchis   1626–32
Blanchis, Paulus de. Tractatus Primus Disputationum de Difficilioribus Materiis Casuum, & dubiorum occurrentium in conscientia. Venetiis, apud Evangelistam Deuchinum, 1622. F°, pp. 615+index. Donor: Elias Pettit. Inscription on flyleaf: "Ex dono Eliae Pettit in Artibus Magistri, et/hujus Collegij quondam scholaris discipuli." Fore-edge: "Paulus/Blanchis."
                                                                               308.3.57

[2].**I(1).13**   Cordubensis Silva Casuum   1626–32
.Cordova, Antonio de. Quaestionarium Theologicum sive Sylva... variarum resolutionum casuum conscientiae. Venetiis, ex typographia Evangelistae Deuchini, sumptibus Baretii Baretii, 1604. Donor: Elias Pettit. Inscription on flyleaf: "Ex dono Eliae Pettit in Artibus Magistri &/huius Collegij quondam scholaris discipuli." Fore-edge: "[?] Cordubensis."
                                                                               307.4.12

²2.I(1).14   Summa Silvestri   1625
Silvester. Mazolinus, Summae Sylvestrinae Pars Prima [–Secunda]. [2
vols. in 1.] Lugduni, sumpt. Petri Landry, excud. Ioannem Tholozanum,
1594. 4°, pp. 515, 542 + indices. Adams S2154. Donor: Dr John Richardson.
Fore-edge: "SUM: SYLVES:".   **301.5.67**

²2.I(1).15   Raynerij Pantheolog: 2 vol: 1625
Rainerius, de Pisis. Pantheologiae tomus primus [–secundus]. [2 vols.]
Venetiis, apud Ioan. Baptistam a Porta, 1585. 4°, pp. 1207, 1232. Donor:
Dr John Richardson. Missing. Register of Books Removed, p. 51, 1. 34:
"Rayneri (de Pisa) Pantheologia – 2 vol: [Quarto]. . . . Ven 1585, Dr Rich".

²2.I(1).16   Antonini Summa Theolog: 4 vol: 1625
Antoninus, Abp of Florence. Summae Sacrae Theologiae, Iuris Pontificij
& Caesarei, Prima (–Quarta) Pars. [4 vols.] Venetiis, apud Iuntas, 1581–2.
4°, ff. 160, 304; 379; 536; 399 (vol. IV includes pp. 369–705 of an
unidentified collection of Latin sermons). Adams A1220. Donor: Dr John
Richardson. Fore-edges: "I/Antoninus"; "2"; "3"; "4".   **327.2.51–4**

²2.I(1).17   Opuscula de Authoritate Summi Pontificis et de residentia   1622–6
Nannini, Remigio, Florentino, ed. De Summi Pontificis Auctoritate, De
Episcoporum Residentia, et Beneficiorum Pluralitate, Gravissimo-
rum Auctorum Complurium Opuscula ad Apostolicae Sedis dignita-
tem maiestatemque. [2 vols. in 1.] Venetiis, ex off. Iordani Zileti, 1562. 4°,
ff. 255, 152. Adams N13. Fore-edge: "Opusc: de pon/ntif: authoriti/et de
resident."   **301.5.90**

²2.I(1).18   Nicolaus de Rebbe de utilitate Lecturae Theologiae et de residentia
                                                                       1622–6
Three works bound together:
(1) Rebbe, Nicolaus de. Tractatus de utilitate lecturae theologicae. . . . Et de
     prebendae theologalis origine, et primaeva fundatione. Duaci, ex off. B.
     Belleri, 1611. 4°, pp. 32.
(2) Rebbe, Nicolaus de. Tractatus Theologicus de residentia
     beneficiatorum quorum libet. Duaci, ex off. B. Belleri, 1612. 4°, pp. 32.
(3) Rebbe, Nicolaus de. Opus de dignitatibus et officiis ecclesiasticis. [2
     pts.] Duaci, ex off. B. Belleri, 1612. 4°, pp. 72, 83. Bound with these,
     probably after 1637, is: Thomas Godwin. Moses and Aaron. London,
     1626.   **333.4.35**

Classis 2ᵈᵃ Superior: Sect: 2ᵈᵃ

²2.S(2).1   Aquinatis opera 12 vol   1622–6
Aquinas, Thomas, St. Opera Omnia. Ed. Cosmas Morelles. [19 vols. in 12.]
Antuerpiae, apud Ioannem Keerbergium, 1612. F°. Fore-edges: I (pts 1–3):

"i/xi/Log & Philos:/Thom:"; II (pts 4–5): "II/12/Ethic: Polit:"; III (pts 6&7): "III/6/Sent 1234"; IV (pt 8): "IIII/4/Quae: Disput: Quod"; V (pt 9): "V/5/Contra gent:"; VI (pt 10): "VI/I/Prima Pars & 1^{2ae}"; VII (pt [11]): "VII/II/22^{ae}"; VIII (pt 12): "VIII/3/3^a pars & de papa/& concilio"; IX (pts 13, 14): "IX/7/Joh: Psal: Cant: Esa:/Jer: Lam: Mat:/Joan:"; X (pts 15, 16): "X/8/Cat Aurea & in Epist:/Pauli"; XI (pt 17): "XI/9/Opusc: distinct:"; XII (pts 18, [19]): "XII/10/Gen: Dan: Mach: Jac:/Pet: Joan: Jud:/& Index."

315.4.2–13

²**2.S(2).2**   Suarez de deo   1620–6*

Suarez, Franciscus. Commentaria ac disputationes in primam partem Divi Thomae, De Deo Uno et Trino. Moguntiae, sumpt. Hermanni Mylii Birckmanni, excud. Balthasar Lippius, 1620. F°, pp. 537, 352 + indices. Fore-edge: "Suarez/de/Deo/Op*uscu*la".   **315.4.31**[1]

*Suarez's works first appear on the 1621 inventory: (5.I.13) "Suarez: in 6 vols.". Between 1622 and 1626 the number of volumes grew to 11. We know (from the publication date of vol. 2) that the volumes in ²2.S(2).4 were acquired no earlier than 1625. However, we cannot know which of the other Suarez volumes were acquired before 1621 and which in the period 1622–6.

²**2.S(2).3**   Ejusdem 5 Tomi in Tertiam Thomae 3 vol   1617–26*

Suarez, Franciscus. Commentariorum ac Disputationum in Tertiam Partem Divi Thomae Tomi Quinque [in 3 vols.]. Moguntiae, ex off. typog. B. Lippii, sumpt. H. Mylii, [1610–] 1617. F°, pp. 835, 700 + index; 1090 + index; 746, 784 + indices. Fore-edges: "[?]/3$^{a[?]}$/"i & ii"; "iii"; "4.5."

315.4.22–4

*See note at ²2.S(2).2.

²**2.S(2).4**   Idem de virtute et relig 2 vol   1625–6*

(1) Suarez, Franciscus. Opus de Virtute et Statu religionis. [2 vols. in 1.] Lugduni, sumptibus Horatii Cardon, 1609–10. F°, pp. 662 + index, 734 + index. Fore-edge: "Relig:".   **315.4.26**

(2) Suarez, Franciscus. Operis de Religione Tomus Quartus, et Ultimus. Lugduni, sumpt. Iacobi Cardon & Petri Cavellat, 1625. F°, pp. 794 + index. Fore-edge: "2".   **315.4.27**

*See note at ²2.S(2).2.

²**2.S(2).5**   Idem de Legib   1597–1626*

Suarez, Franciscus. Tractatus de Legibus ac Deo legislatore. Missing. Emmanuel's present copy (Londini, 1679) was a Sancroft gift: S.2.1.

*See note at ²2.S(2).2.

²**2.S(2).6**   Idem adv*ersu*s sect: Anglic: 1614–26*

Suarez, Franciscus. Defensio Fidei Catholicae et Apostolicae adversus Anglicanae sectae errores, cum responsione ad Apologiam pro iuramento fidelitatis & praefationem monitoriam serenissimi Iacobi Magnae

Britanniae Regis. Coloniae Agrippinae, in off. Birckmannica, sumpt. Hermanni Mylii, 1614. F°, coll. 888 + index. Fore-edge: "Def". **315.4.28**
*See note at ²2.S(2).2.

²**2.S(2).7**   Idem de gra: 1621–6*
Suarez, Franciscus. De Divina Gratia. [2 vols. in 1.] Moguntiae, sumpt. Hermanni Mylii Birckmanni, excud. Balthasar Lippius, 1620[–1]. F°, pp. 446, 576 + indices. Fore-edge: "De Gratia".   **315.4.29**
*See note at ²2.S(2).2.

²**2.S(2).8**   Idem de Angelis et in 2^{dam} 1^{ae} Aquinatis   1621–6*
Suarez, Franciscus. Commentariorum ac disputationum in primam partem divi Thomae pars II, de Deo effectore creaturarum omnium, in tres praecipuos tractatus distributa, quorum primus de Angelis. Moguntiae, sumpt. H. Mylii Birckmanni, excud. B. Lippius, 1621. F°, pp. 699, 291, 223 + indices. Fore-edge: "De Angelis".   **315.4.32**

*See note at ²2.S(2).2.

²**2.S(2).9**   Ejusdem Metaphisica   1605–26*
Suarez, Franciscus. Metaphysicarum Disputationum,... Tomi Duo. [2 vols. in 1.] Moguntiae, excud. Balthasarus Lippius, sumpt. Arnoldi Mylii, 1605. Fore-edge: "SUAREZ/Metaphysica*rum*".   **315.4.25**
*See note at ²2.S(2).2.

²**2.S(2).10** Vasquez 8 Vol.   1622–6
Vazquez, Gabriel. Commentatiorum ac disputationum in Primam (–tertiam) partem Sancti Thomae. [8 vols.] Antuerpiae, apud P. et I. Belleros, 1621. F°, pp. 708; 739; 894; 882; 890; 567; 794; 441, 605 + indices. Fore-edges: "Vasquez/i".; "ii"; "iii"; "iiii"; "v"; "vi"; "vii"; "viii".
                                                                315.4.14–21

²**2.S(2).11** Gregor: de Valentia 4 Vol   1625
Valentia, Gregorius de. Commentariorum Theologicorum tomi quatuor. In quibus omnes quaestiones, quae continentur in summa Theologica D. Thomae Aquinatis, ordine explicantur. [4 vols.] Lutetiae Parisiorum, ex typog. R. Theoderici, & P. Chevalerii, 1609. F°, coll. 1436; 1292; 2106; 2228 + indices. Donor: Dr John Richardson. Fore-edges: "I/G: Valenti:"; "2"; "3"; "4".   **310.3.54–7**

²**2.S(2).12** Turrianus in 2^{dam} 2^{dae} Thom: 1625
Torres, Luis à. Disputationum in secundam secundae D. Thomae, de fide, spe, charitate et prudentia. Lugduni, sumpt. Horatii Cardon, 1617. F°, coll. 1295 + indices. Donor: Thomas Hanscombe. Inscription on first flyleaf: "Ex dono Hanscombe". Inscription on second flyleaf: "Magister Thomas

Hanscombe huius/Collegij Socius, moriens D.D." Fore-edge:
"TVRIAN*us*/In 2^{dam} 2^{dae}".   **310.3.41**

^{2}**2.S(2).13**   Cumel in 1^{am} et 2^{dam} Thom   1625
Zumel, Francisco. Variarum disputationum... tomi tres. Primus in
primam partem S Thomae,... secundus in ejusdem Primam Secundae...
Tertius in utramque partem. [3 pts in 1 vol.] Lugduni, sumptibus Ioannis
Pillehotte, 1609. F°. Donor: Dr John Richardson. Fore-edge: "CVMEL".
                                                                        310.3.42

^{2}**2.S(2).14**   Arragon in 2^{dam} 2^{dae} Thomae   1625
Aragon, Petrus de. In secundam secundae Divi Thomae... Commentaria.
De Iustitia Et Iure. Lugduni, expensis Petri Landry, 1596. F°, pp.
810 + index. Adams A1499. Donor: Thomas Hanscombe. Inscription on
second flyleaf: "Magister Hanscombe huius/Collegij/Socius, moriens D.D."
Arms [of the Hanscombe family?] on the covers. Fore-edge: "ARAGON
in/Thomam."   **310.3.40**

^{2}**2.S(2).15**   Salas in 1^{am} 2^{dae} Thom   1625
Salas, Juan de. Tractatus de Legibus, in Primam Secundae S. Thomae.
Lugduni, sumptibus Laurentii Durand, excud. A. Polerius, 1611. F°, pp.
632 + index. Donor: Dr John Richardson. Fore-edge: "Salas".   **310.3.46**

^{2}**2.S(2).16**   Koelinus in 1^{am} 2^{dae} Tho   1625
Koellin, Conrad. Expositio commentaria prima... in primam secundae...
S. Thomae Aquinatis. Venetiis, apud Franciscum Franciscium [*Colophon*:
apud Dominicum Nicolinum], 1589. F°, pp. 982. Adams K86. Donor:
Thomas Hanscombe. Inscription on flyleaf: "ex dono Magistri
Hanscombe." Inscription on title page: "Magister Thomas Hanscombe,
huius Collegij Socius moriens D.D." and "Res Tuas Age".   **310.3.43**

^{2}**2.S(2).17**   Bannes   1625
Two works bound together:
(1) Bañes, Domingo. Scholastica commentaria in primam partem... D.
    Thomae. Lugduni, apud Stephanum Michaelem, et socios, 1588.
    Adams B156. F°, coll. 880 + index.
(2) Bañes, Domingo. De Fide, Spe, et Charitate... Scholastica com-
    mentaria in Secundum Secundae Angelici Doctoris partem. Lugduni,
    apud Stephanum Michaelem, et socios, 1588. F°, coll. 1070
    [Emmanuel's copy lacks 911–1070]. Adams B157. Donor: Dr John
    Richardson. Fore-edge: "BAÑES".   **310.3.58**

^{2}**2.S(2).18**   Medina 2 vol   1626–32
Medina, Bartolomeo. Scholastica Commentaria in Thomae Aquinatis,...
Primam Secundae [et in Tertiae Partis quinquaginta novem priores

Quaestiones tertium librum Sententiarum complectentes]. [2 vols.] Coloniae Agrippinae, sumptibus P. Hennigii, 1618. F°. Fore-edges: "MEDINA/in Thom:/1"; "2".   310.3.35–6

²2.S(2).19   Cajetanus in Tho Sum 2 vol   1622–6
Cajetanus, Thomas de Vio, *Card*. [Commentary on the Summa Theologiae. of St Thomas Aquinas.] [2 vols.] Missing. Emmanuel's present copy (Lugduni, 1581; Adams A1438) was a Sancroft gift: S14.1.7,8.

²2.S(2).20   Pesantius in Tho   1625
Pesantius, Alexander. Commentaria brevia ac disputationes in universam Theologiam D. Thomae. Venetiis, apud Minimam Societatem, 1606. F°, pp. 1043 + index. Donor: Dr John Richardson. Fore-edge: "PESANTI".
                                                                     310.3.45

²2.S(2).21   Ripa in Tho   1625
Ripa, Raphael. Ad S. Thomae Aquinatis totam primam partem notationes, et dubitationes scholasticae. Venetiis, apud M. A. Somaschum, 1609. F°, ff. 461 + index. Donor: Thomas Hanscombe. Inscription: "1625, Magister Thomas Hanscombe huius Collegij Socius moriens D.D. Ex dono Magister Hanscombe." Fore-edge: "RIPA in Tho".   310.3.44

²2.S(2).22   Carbonis Epit Sum*mae* Thomae   1622–6
Carbone, Lodovico. [Possibly: Compendium absolutissimum totius Summae Theologiae D. Thomae Aquinatis... in quo universa eius doctrina partim conclusionibus quaestionum, partim vero argumentorum solutionibus, contenta proponitur. Coloniae, sumptibus Petri Cholini et Conradi Butgenii, 1609. 4°, pp. 1090 + index.   333.3.1]

Classis 2^{dae} Infer: sect: 2da

²2.I(2).1   Bonaventurae op*er*a 4 vol   1625
Bonaventura, *St, Card*. Opera, Sixti V. Pont. Max. Iussu Diligentissime emendata. [7 vols. in 4.] Moguntiae, sumptibus Antonii Hierati Coloniensis, 1609. F°. Donor: Dr John Richardson. Emmanuel's original copy of vol. I is missing and has been replaced by one with a gift inscription of Christopher Plunket dated 1638. Fore-edges: II: "4/Bonavent/ure"; III: "5"; IV. "6.7."   304.1.23; 310.3.22–4

²2.I(2).2   Soto in 4^m Sentent   1622–6
Soto, Domingo de. In quartum Sententiarum commentarii, nunc postremo.... recogniti. [Editio sexta] [2 vols. in 1.] Duaci, ex typog. Petri Borremans, 1612–13. F°, pp. 964 + indices. Fore-edge: "SOTO". 310.3.20

²2.I(2).3   Durandus   October 15, 1623
Durandus, Gulielmus, *of Saint-Pourçain, Bp of Meaux.* In Sententias
Theologicas Petri Lombardi Commentariorum, Libri Quatuor. Lugduni,
apud haered. Gulielmi Rovillii, 1595. F°, pp. 950 + index. Adams D1187.
Donor: Laurence Howlett. Inscription on title page: "Ex dono Laurentij
Howlet:/huius collegij socij 1623. Octob. 15." Fore-edge: "DURAND*US*".
                                                               310.3.21

²2.I(2).4   Estius in Sent 2 vol: 1625
Est, William Hessels van. In quatuor libros Sententiarum commentaria,
quibus pariter S. Thomae Summae Theologicae partes omnes mirifice
illustrantur. [4 vols. in 2.] Duaci, ex typographia P. Borremans, 1615–
1616. F°, pp. 311, 339; 235, 444 + indices. Donor: Thomas Hanscombe.
Inscription on flyleaf of vol. 1: "Magister Thomas Hanscombe,
huius/Collegij Socius, moriens D.D." Inscription on flyleaf of vol. II: "Ex
dono Magistri Hanscombe". Fore-edge "ESTIVS. I"; "II".   **310.3.26, 27**

²2.I(2).5   Faber in Sent.   1625
Faber, Philippus, *Faventinus.* Disputationes theologicae librum primum
(–quartum) Sententiarum complectentes.... Quibus Doctrina Scoti... di-
lucidatur. [4 pts in 1 vol.] Parisiis, [apud] Michaelem Sonnium, 1620. F°,
pp. 340, 199, 244, 235 + indices. Donor: Thomas Hanscombe. Inscription
on first flyleaf: "Ex dono Magistri Hanscombe". Inscription on second
flyleaf: "Magister Thomas Hanscombe, huius/Collegij Socius, moriens
D.D." Fore-edge: "FABER in Sent".   **310.3.25**

²2.I(2).6   Aureolus 2 vol   1622–6
Aureolus, Petrus, *Card., Abp of Aix.* Commentariorum in primum librum
sententiarum. Pars prima. [2 vols.] Romae, ex typog. Vaticana, 1596.
Adams A2266. (Vol. II: in Secundum–Quartum Sententiarum; in
Quodlibetas, 1605.) F°, pp. 1126 + index; 542, 326, 155, + indices. Donor:
Nicholas Morton. Inscription on front flyleaf of vol. 1: "Ex dono D*omini*
Nicolai   Morton/huius   Collegij   quondam   Socij."   Fore-edges:
"AVREOLVS/I"; "II".   **310.3.28,29**

²2.I(2).7   Capreolus 2 vol   Feb. 22, 1618
Capreolus, Johannes. In libros Sententiarum Amplissimae Quaestiones,
Pro Tutela Doctrinae S. Thomae Ad Scholasticum certamen egregie
disputatae. *Ed.* Matthias Aquarius. [4 vols. in 2.] Venetiis, apud haeredem
Hieronymi Scoti, 1589. F°, pp. 591, 588, 255; 462, ff. 84, pp. 86, 86, 75,
106, 155 + indices. Adams C614 (omits Emmanuel's copy). Donor: William
Sandcroft. Inscription on flyleaf verso in each vol.: "Hunc libru*m* Collegio
Emmanuelis D.D./Guilielmus Sandcroft ejusdem Collegij Socius} Feb. 22.
1618." Fore-edges: "CAPREOLVS"; "II".   **310.3.30,31**

²**2.I(2).8**   Bachon in Sent 2 vol   1626–32
Baco, Johannes (also John Baconthorpe). Quaestiones in quatuor libros
Sententiarum. [2 vols.] Cremonae, apud M.A. Belpierum, 1618. F°.
Missing. Register of Books Removed, p. 55, 1.1: "Jo: Bachonis Questiones
in 4 libr: sententiarum 2 vol:... Crem: 1618". Emmanuel's present copy
was a Sancroft gift: S14.1.13, 14.

²**2.I(2).9**   Alex: Alensis pars 1ª et 2ª 2 vol   1622–6
Alexander, *of Hales.* [Possibly: Universae Theologiae summa in Quatuor
Partes. Venice, 1575. (Vols. 1 & 2 only.) F°.] Missing. Register of Books
Removed, p. 55, 1.2: "Alexandri de Ales Summa Theologiae 4 vol:... Ven:
1575." Emmanuel's present copies include a Sancroft gift (Adams A697,
S14.1.18, 19), and a Breton gift (Coloniae Agrippinae, 1622: 310.2.8, 9).

²**2.I(2).10**   Carthusian in Sent 2 vol   1584–97
Dionysius, *Carthusianus.* De his quae secundum sacras scripturas & ortho-
doxor*um* patrum sententias, de sanctissima & individua trinitate semper
adoranda, catholice credantur, liber primus (–quartus). [The text of the
Sentences of Peter Lombard with the commentary of Dionysius
Carthusianus.] [5 pts in 2 vols.] Coloniae, expensis Peter Quentel, 1535. F°,
pp. 670, 611; 351, 608, 181+index. Adams D537. Lumley 261, 262.
Signatures on title page of vol. 1: "Thomas Cantuarien*sis*" (Thomas
Cranmer) and "Lumley" (John, first Baron Lumley). Fore-edges: "D.
Carth/in/Lomb./i.ii/7"; "in Lomb./3.4./8".   **309.3.2,3**

²**2.I(2).11**   Trigosus   1622–6
[1626 and 1628 inventories (5.S.13): "Trigosus: Epitom: Bonaventur"]
Bonaventura, *St, Card.* Summa Theologica Quam ex eius in Magistrum
sententiarum scriptis... collegit... commentariis illustravit... Petrus
Trigosus. Romae, ex typog. Vaticana, 1613 [–defaced, i.e. 1593]. F°, pp.
758+indices. Adams B2398. Fore-edge: "Trigos*us*".   **309.3.23**

²**2.I(2).12**   Scoti in sent pars 1ª et 2ª   1622–6
Duns, Johannes, *Scotus.* Commentary on the Sentences of Peter Lombard.
Missing. Emmanuel presently has several copies, including two Sancroft
gifts (Venetiis, 1506: Adams D1112, and Venetiis, 1627): S14.1.15, 16;
S14.1.17.

²**2.I(2).13**   Vincentij Specul: 4 vol   1622–6
Vincent, *of Beauvais.* Speculi Maioris... Tomi Quatuor. [4 vols.] Venetiis,
apud Dominicum Nicolinum, 1591. F°, ff. 424; 298; 280; 491. Adams
V811.   [Possibly: **310.2.57–60**]

²**2.I(2).14**   Altenstaig: Lexicon Theolog   1584–97
Altenstaig, Johann. Lexicon theologicum complectens vocabulorum de-

scriptiones, diffinitiones & interpretationes. Missing. Emmanuel's present copy (Coloniae Agrippinae, 1619) was a Sancroft gift: S13.3.8.

²2.I(2).15   Biel in Sent 2 vol   1625
Biel, Gabriel. Inventarium generale breve et succinctum contentorum in quattuor collectoriis Gabrielis. [1 vol. only: Vol. 2 is missing.] [Basel, J. de Pfortzen, 1508.] F°. Adams B2000. Donor: Dr John Richardson. Fore-edge: "Biel in/ium et/2 dum Sent".   **309.4.17**

²2.I(2).16   Petrus de palude   1622–6
Palude, Petrus de. [Possibly: Quartus sententiarum liber.] Missing. Emmanuel's present copy (Paris, 1514: Adams P124) was a Sancroft gift: S14.1.38.

²2.I(2).17   Gregorius Ariminensis   1625
Gregorius, Ariminensis. In Primum (–Secundum) Sententiarum nuperrime impressus... restitutus. Ed. Petrus Garamanta. [2 vols. in 1.] Parrhisiis, Ven. C. Chevallon [c. 1525]. F°, ff. (187, 133). Adams G1086. Donor: Thomas Hanscombe. Inscription on first flyleaf: "Ex dono Magistri Hanscombe." Inscription on second flyleaf: "1625./Magister Hanscombe/huius Collegii Socius moriens D.D." Fore-edge: "Greg./Arim."
318.4.13

²2.I(2).18   Holcot in Sent   1626–32
Holcot, Robert. Super quattuor libros sententiarum questiones. Lugduni, a Iohanne Trechsel, 1497. F°. Hain 8763. Fore-edge: "holcot super senten-tias".   **MSS.5.2.2**

²2.I(2).19   Occam in Sent   1626–32
William, of Ockham. Scriptum in primum [–quartum] librum senten-ciarum. Lugduni per Johannem Trechsel, 1495. F°. Hain 11942. Title page and first two ff. missing. Fore-edge: "Occamus/in sent."   **MSS.5.3.7**

²2.I(2).20   Soncinas in Sent   1622–6
Soncinas, Paulus. Epitomes quaestionum Ioannis Capreoli, super libros sententiarum. Pars prior (altera). Ed. Isidorus de Isolanis. Lugduni, ex-pensis Petri Landry, 1580. 4°, pp. 446, 226, ff. 15+index. Adams S1424. Fore-edge: "SONCNAS".   **334.2.73**

²2.I(2).21   Pelbarti Rosarium   1625
Pelbartus, Oswaldus, de Themeswar. Aureum Sacrae Theologiae Rosarium, Iuxta Quatuor Sententiarum Libros quadripartitum... Tomus Tertius [–Quartus]. [Emmanuel is missing pts I & II.] Venetiis, ex officina Daniani Zenarii, 1586. 4°, ff. 248, 260. Adams P554. Donor: Dr John Richardson. Fore-edge: "Pelbartus".   **330.2.30**

²**2.S(3).1**   Bradwardinus de causa dei   1618–21
Bradwardine, Thomas. De Causa Dei contra Pelagium. Londini, ex off-
icina Nortoniana, apud Ioannem Billium, 1618. F°, pp. 876. STC 3534.
Missing. Register of Books Removed, p. 29, 1.30: "Bradwardinus de causâ
de causa Dei... Lond: 1618".

²**2.S(3).2**   Cassandri opera   1622–6
Cassander, George. Opera quae reperiri potuerunt omnia. Parisiis, apud
H. Drouart, 1616. F°, pp. 1352. Missing. Register of Books Removed, p. 29,
1.9: "G. Cassandri opera... Par: 1616". Emmanuel's present copy was a
Sancroft gift: S9.1.23

²**2.S(3).3**   Guil: Parisiensis   1626–32
William, *of Auvergne, Bp of Paris*. Opera omnia. Venetiis, ex off. Damiani
Zenari [*colophon*: apud Ioannem Baptistam Natolinum], 1591. F°, pp.
1012 + index. Adams G1595. Fore-edge: "G. Paris/iensis."   **302.2.62**

²**2.S(3).4**   Contarenus   1626–32
Contarini, Gasparo, *Card*. Opera. Parisiis, apud Sebastianum Nivellium,
1571. F°, pp. 627. Adams C2560. Inscription on flyleaf: "N.P. empt.
Bononiae. 1589." Inscription on scrap of vellum reinforcing back binding:
"pretio viiˢ/27th Aug: 1618,/Mʳ B[e?]11". Fore-edge: "Contare*nus*".
                                                                      308.3.17

²**2.S(3).5**   Joh et Franc: Picus Mirandul   1625
Pico della Mirandola, Giovanni Francesco. Ioanni Pici Mirandulae...
Item, tomo secundo, Ioannis Francisci Pici... opera quae extant omnia...
Editio Ultima. [2 vols.: vol. I, works of Giovanni Pico della Mirandola;
vol. II, works of Giovanni Francesco Pico della Mirandola.] Basileae, per
S. Henricpetri, 1601. F°, pp. 519, 890 + indices. Donor: Thomas
Hanscombe. Inscriptions on title pages of both volumes: "Mʳ Thomas
Hanscomb hujus Collegij socius moriens. D.D." Fore-edges: "Mirand/1";
"Mirandul/2".   **306.4.56, 57**

²**2.S(3).6**   Lau*r* Iustiniani op*era*   1622–6
Lorenzo Giustiniani, *St*. Opera omnia. Venetiis, apud B. de Albertis, 1606.
F°, ff. 499 + index. Fore-edge: "iuSTINIA/NUS".   **308.3.48**

²**2.S(3).7**   Marsilius Patavinus   1584–97
[1621 inventory (4.S.8): "Marsilij Patavini defensor pacis siue de authoritate Papae"]
Marsiglio, *of Padua*. Defensor Pacis. Missing.

²**2.S(3).8** Gersonis op*era* 3 vol   1621–?
Gerson, Johannes. Prima (–Quarta) pars (Operum) [4 pts and index
in 3 vols.] Basileae, in off. Adami Petri, sumpt. Ludovici Hornken, &
Godofredi Hitorpii, 1517–18. F°. Adams G502. Vertically on fore-edges:
"Pri*ma* et 2ᵃ p*ars* gerso*nis*"; II: "3ᵃ p*ars* gersonis"; III: "4ᵃ p*ars* gersonis".
                                                                307.4.7–9

²**2.S(3).9** Andreae Frisij Tractatus   1584–97
[1621 inventory (4.I.4): "Fricius de Repub instituenda"]
Fricius, Andreas, *Modrevius*. De republica emendanda libri quinque...
quibus... accesserunt... de ecclesia liber secundus... Orationes item &
epistolae. Basileae, per Ioannem Oporinum, 1559. F°. Missing. Register
of Books Removed, p. 29, 1.14: "Andreas Fricius de Republicâ ordi-
nandâ & Ecclesiâ... Basil: 1559". Emmanuel's present copy (Basileae,
1554: Adams M1539) was a Sancroft gift: S9.1.34.

²**2.S(3).10** Vives de Veritate Xⁿᵃᵉ relig   1584–97
Vives, Johannes Ludovicus. De Veritate Fidei Christianae. Basileae, ex off.
Ioannis Oporini, 1543. Missing. Register of Books Removed, p. 38, 1.3:
"Lud: Vivis de veritate Fidei Xstianae... Bas: 1543". One of Emmanuel's
present copies (Basileae, 1544: Adams V959) was a Sancroft gift: S10.4.68.

²**2.S(3).11** Alvarez de planctu Eccl^{se}   1622–6
Pelagius, Alvarus, *Bp of Silves*. De Planctu Ecclesiae, Libri Duo. Venetiis,
ex off, Francisci Sansovini et soc., 1560. F°, ff. 100, 229. Adams P538.
Donor(?): Walter Rawly. Inscription on title page: "Ex dono clarissimi
Walteri Rawly, equitis armati". Fore-edge: "ALVAR*US*/pellagius/de/
planctu/Ec*cl*esiae".   **307.4.15**

²**2.S(3).12** Cardinalis Cusanus 2 vol   1622–6
Cusa, Nicolaus de, *Card*. Opera. [2 vols.] Missing. Register of Books
Removed, p. 51, 1.24: "Nic: de Cusa Opera... Bas. 1565". Emmanuel's
present copies (Parisiis, 1514: Adams C3130, and Basileae, 1565:
Adams C3131) were Sancroft gifts: S13.3.1,2 and S13.2.32.
    It does not seem likely that the one-volume 1565 edition listed in the
Register of Books Removed was the one present in the period 1622–37,
because the catalogues cite two volumes.

²**2.S(3).13** Alvarez de Auxilijs gr^{ae}   1625
Alvarez, Diego, *Abp of Trani*. De Auxilliis Divinae Gratiae et Humani
Arbitrii Viribus et Libertate, ac legitima eius cum efficacia eorundem
auxiliorum concordia. Coloniae Agrippinae, apud Antonium Boetzerum,
1622. 4°. Donor: Thomas Hanscombe. Inscription on flyleaf: "Magister
Thomas Hanscombe huius Colegij/Socius moriens D.D." Fore-edge:
"Aluarez de/auxiliis".   **334.2.71**

²**2.S(3).14**   Idem de Incarnat   1622–6

Alvarez, Diego, *Apb of Trani*. De incarnatione divini verbi disputationes LXXX. In quibus explicantur, et defenduntur, quae in tertia parte Summae Theologicae docet sanctus Thomas a Quaest. 1. Usque ad 24. Coloniae Agrippinae, apud Antonium Boetzerum, 1621. 4°, pp. 452 + index. Fore-edge: "Alvarez/de incar–/natione".   **334.2.72**

²**2.S(3).15**   Nicolai de Clemangis op*era*   1616

Clamenges, Nicolaus de. Opera omnia. [3 pts in 1 vol.] Lugduni Batavorum, apud I. Balduinum, impens. Lud. Elzevirii & Henr. Laurencii, 1613. 4°, pp. 191, 359, 86 + index. Donor: Robert Booth. Inscription on front flyleaf: "Hic Liber donatus Bibliothecae huic/a Domino Roberto Booth quondam/hujus Collegij socio./Anno Do*mini* i6i6." Fore-edge: "Cleman:".   **330.2.40**

²**2.S(3).16**   Espencaeus de Continentia   1622–6

Espence, Claude d'. Collectaneorum de continentia libri sex. Parisiis, ex off. Iacobi du Puys, 1565. 4°, pp. 824. Adams E946 (omits Emmanuel's copy). Fore-edge: "Espenceus/de contin."   **301.5.66**

²**2.S(3).17**   Onuphrius de primatu Petri   1625

Panvinius, Onuphrius. De primatu Petri, et, Apostolicae sedis Potestate. Venetiis, apud Franciscum Franciscium senensem, 1591. 4°, pp. 330 + index. Adams P193. Donor: Dr John Richardson. Fore-edge: "onu/phri/Onuph:/Panu:/de primat:/Petri". The binding is stamped with the arms of William Cecil, Lord Burghley.   **301.5.72**

²**2.S(3).18**   Barclaij Pietas   1625

Barclay, John. Pietas, Sive Publicae pro Regibus, ac principibus, et privatae pro Guilielmo Barclaio parente vindiciae, adversus... Cardinalis Bellarmini Tractatum, De Potestate Summi Pontificis in rebus Temporalibus. Parisiis, ex typis P. Mettayer, 1612. 4°, pp. 798. Donor: Dr John Richardson. Fore-edge: "Barclai*us*".   **329.1.1**

²**2.S(3).19**   Bennius   1622–6

[Possibly *either*: Beni, Paolo. De ecclesiasticus Baronii Cardinalis annalibus disputatio. Missing. Emmanuel's present copy was a gift of John Breton in 1676: 330.1.105; *or*: Benius, Jacobus. De privilegis i. consultorum. Missing.]

A copy of Paolo Beni's commentaries on Aristotle's Rhetoric (Venetiis, 1524[1624]) showing early Emmanuel ownership is still present: 304.1.57. But the subject matter would have been very much out of place in this classis (it ought instead to have been in classis 9), making it an unlikely referent for this entry.

²**2.S(4).1**   Tostatus 13 vol   1622–6
Tostado, Alfonso, *de Madrigal, Bp of Avila.* Opera omnia. [27 vols. in 13.]
Coloniae Agrippinae, sumpt. I Gymnici et A. Hierati, 1613. F°.
[Possibly: **307.2.41–53**]

²**2.S(4).2**   Salmeron 7 vol   1625
Salmeron, Alfonso. [Opera in two parts]
(1) Commentarii in Evangelicam historiam et in Acta Apostolorum: nunc
primum in lucem editi. [12 vols. in 5.] Coloniae Agrippinae, apud
Antonium Hierat et Ioan. Gymni, 1602–1604. F°.
(2) Commentarii in omnes Epistolas B. Pauli et Canonicas; in quatuor
tomos distributi ... Hic est primus (–quartus), in ordine autem XIII^{us}
(–XVI^{us}). [4 pts in 2 vols.] Coloniae Agrippinae, apud Antonium
Hierat et Ioannem Gymnicum, 1604. F°.
Donor: Dr John Richardson. Fore-edges: "Tom: 1.2:/SALMERON"; "To:
3.4"; "To: 5.6.7"; "To: 8.9"; "Tom. 10.11.12"; "13.14"; "Tom: 15.16".
                                                                          304.4.61–7

²**2.S(4).3**   Doway Bible 3 vol   1622–6
Bible [English]. Three volumes, as follows:
(1) Old Testament: The Holie Bible Faithfully Translated into English....
By the English College at Doway. [2 vols.] Doway, Lawrence Kellam,
1609–10. 4°. Darlow and Moule 231. Fore-edges: "Bible/Rhem./i";
"Bible/Rhem./ii".   **328.2.61, 62**
(2) New Testament: The New Testament of Iesus Christ faithfully trans-
lated into English... By the English College then Resident in Rhemes.
Set forth the second time, by the same College now returned to Doway.
Antwerp, Daniel Vervliet, 1600. 4°, ff. 404. Darlow and Moule 198.
Fore-edge: "Bible/Rhem/iii".   **328.2.63**

²**2.I(3).1**   Stapletoni opera 4 vol.   1626–32
Stapleton, Thomas. Opera quae extant omnia. [4 vols.] Lutetiae
Parisiorum, 1620. Missing. Emmanuel's present copy (310.2.3–7) is bound in
five volumes.

²**2.I.(3).2**   Ejusdem principia doctr^{lia}   1597–1621
Stapleton, Thomas. Principiorum Fidei Doctrinalium Demonstratio
Methodica. Parisiis, apud Michaelem Sonnium, 1581. F°, pp. 700 + index.
Adams S1652. Donor: Richard Culverwell. Cambridge University arms and
initials of Richard Culverwell stamped on the covers. Fore-edge:
"Stapleton/princ. doctr./11".   **305.1.7**

²**2.I(3).3**   Canisij Catechismus   1584–97
Canisius, Petrus. Opus Catechisticum, Sive De Summa Doctrinae
Christianae... Editio Ultima. Parisiis, apud Thomam Brumennium, 1579.
F°, coll. 1836. Adams C528. Fore-edge: "Canisii/catechism/12".   **308.3.36**

²**2.I(3).4**   Hosius   1584–97
[1621 inventory (4.I.7): "Hosij Opera omnia"]
Hosius, Stanislaus, Card., Bp of Ermland. Opera omnia. Missing. One of
Emmanuel's present copies (Antwerp, 1571: Adams H1023) was a Sancroft
gift: S13.2.24.

²**2.I(3).5**   Coccij Thesaurus Cathol: 2 vol   1625
Coccius, Jodocus. Thesaurus Catholicus, in quo controversia fidei... a
temporibus Apostolorum ad nostram usque aetatem... explicantur. [2
vols.] Coloniae, ex off. typog. Arnoldi Quentelii, 1600(–1601). F°, pp.
1138 + index; 1174 + index. Adams C2246. Donor: Dr John Richardson.
Fore-edges: "Coccius/To: I"; "To: 2".   **308.3.14, 15**

²**2.I(3).6**   Alphonsus de Castro Contra haereses   1626–32
Castro, Alfonsus de. Adversus omnes haereses. Missing. Emmanuel's present copy (Lugduni, 1546: Adams C967) was a Sancroft gift: S4.4.56.

²**2.I(3).7**   Sanderus de visibili monarchia   1622–6
Sanders, Nicholas. De Visibili Monarchia Ecclesiae, Libri VIII....
Accesserunt De Clave David seu de Regno Christi Libri Sex, contra
Calumnias Acleri pro visibili Ecclesiae Monarchia. [2 vols. in 1.]
Wirceburgi, apud vid. Henrici Aquensis, 1592. Adams S290. F°, pp. 808,
153 + indices. Donor: Dr John Richardson. Fore-edge: "SanDerus".
                                                      308.3.58

²**2.I(3).8**   Waldensis contr: Wicklif et 4ᵃ pars Homil Nausea   1622–6
Two books bound together:
   (1) Netter, Thomas, of Walden. Sacramentalia. Sextum videlicet volumen
       doctrinalis antiquitatum Fidei Ecclesiae Catholicae. [Paris,] impressum
       opera Iodoci Badii Ascensii, impens. Francisci Reginaldi, 1523. [Title
       page and first 6 pp. missing.] F°, ff. 344. Adams N195.
   (2) Nausea, Fridericus. Evangelicae veritatis Homiliarum centuriae tres....
       Addita est... quarta in ordine centuria. [Pt 4 only.] Coloniae, Petrus
       Quentell excud., 1532. F°, ff. 357–445. Adams N85.
Donor: Dr John Richardson. Fore-edge: "T. Waldens:/contra Wicl:".
                                                          307.3.6

²**2.I(3).9**   Pighius de Hierarch Ecclᵃᵉ   1584–97
Pighius, Albertus. Hierarchiae Ecclesiasticae Assertio. Coloniae, Melchior
Novesianus excud., 1538. F°, ff. [6], 267 + index. Adams P1192. Fore-edge:
"9/pighius campensis".   **307.3.4**

²2.I(3).10   Lindani Panoplia   1584–97
Lindanus, Wilhelmus (William van der Lindt), *Bp of Roermond*. Panoplia Evangelica sive de Verbo Dei Evangelico Libri Quinque Coloniae Agrippinae, excud. Maternus Cholinus, 1575. F°, pp. [22], 512, 71 + index. Adams L722. Fore-edge: "Lindan:/panoplia/13".   **307.3.8**

²2.I(3).11   Vadianus de Eucharistia   1584–97
Vadianus, Joachim. Aphorismorum Libri Sex de Consideratione Eucharistiae. [Zurich, C. Froschouer, c. 1536.] F°, pp. 256. Adams V6. Fore-edge: "Vadi/anus/de eu/chari/10" and, lower and faded: "[?]/Vadia*n*".
   307.3.10

²2.I(3).12   Klingij Loci Com: 1622–6
Clingius, Conrad. Loci Communes Theologici. Coloniae, apud haered. Arnoldi Birckmanni, 1562. Missing. Register of Books Removed, p. 29. 1.33: "Klingii loci communes chang'd *ye* Arch B's... Colon: 1562". Emmanuel's present copy (Adams C2222) was a Sancroft gift: S9.4.63.

²2.I(3).13   Coquaeus in Regem Jacobu*m*   1622–6
Coquaeus, Leonardus. Examen Praefationis Monitoriae Iacobi... Regis, praemissae Apologiae suae pro iuramento fidelitatis... In quo examine refellitur & Apologia ipsa Regis, & summi Pontificis brevia ad catholicos Anglos defenduntur. Friburgi Brisgoiae, apud Ioannem Strasserum, 1610. F°, pp. 509.   **307.3.7**

²2.I(3).14   Driedo 2 vol   1625
Driedo, Joannes, *à Turnhout*. Operum.... Tomus Primus (–Quartus). [4 vols. in 2.] Lovanii, ex off. Bartholomaei Gravii, 1566–72. F°, ff. 269, 155 + index; 172, 113 + index. Adams omits Emmanuel's copies. Donor: Dr John Richardson. Fore-edges: "Driedo/i"; "ii".   **307.4.1,2**

²2.I(3).15   Biel De Can Missae   1626–32
Biel, Gabriel. Sacri canonis misse tam mystica q*uam* litteralis expositio. Basilee, a Iacobo Pforczense, 1510. F°, ff. 269. Adams B2013. Inscription on folio iiii: "Liber collegij Trinitatis Cantabrig ex dono [?]". Fore-edge: "Biel/in Canon/Missa".   **307.4.23**

²2.I(3).16   Constantius de Eucharist   1584–97
Gardiner, Stephen (*pseud.* Marcus Antonius Constantius), *Bp of Winchester*. Confutatio Cavillationum, quibus sacrosanctum Eucharistiae Sacramentum, ab impiis Capernaitis impeti solet. Parisiis, apud Ioannem de Roigny, 1552. 4°, ff. 224. Adams G233. Fore-edge: "M. Anton:/Constan:/de Euchis/t./17".   **301.5.69**

²**2.I(3).17**   Lindani Apologia   1584–97
Lindanus, Wilhelmus (William van der Lindt), *Bp of Roermond*.
Apologeticum ad Germanos, pro Religionis Catholicae Pace. Antuerpiae,
ex off. Christophori Plantini, 1568. 4°, pp. 83, 176, 417. Adams L710.
Donor: Richard Culverwell. Fore-edge: "Lindani./Apolog:/14". Gilt initials
"R. C." (Richard Culverwell) stamped on cover.   **301.5.68**

²**2.I(3).18**   Watsons Quodlibets   1622–6
Watson, William. A Decacordon of Ten Quodlibeticall Questions
Concerning Religion and State. [Douay?] 1602. 4°, STC 25123. Missing.
Emmanuel's present copy was a Sancroft gift: S14.2.8.

²**2.I(3).19**   Alanus de Sacram   1622–6
Allen, William, *Card*. Libri tres. Id est, De Sacramentis in genere.
Antuerpiae, apud Iohannem Foulerum Anglum, 1576. 4°, pp. 653 + indices.
Missing. Register of Books Removed, p. 51, 1.29: "Gul: Alanus de
Sacramentis. ... Ant 1576". Emmanuel's present copy (Adams A754) was a
Sancroft gift: S13.3.10.

²**2.I(3).20**   Granatensis Introductio in Symbolum Fidei   1622–6
Granada, Luis de. Introductionis ad Symbolum Fidei, Libri Quatuor.
Coloniae, apud Gervinum Calenium & haeredes Ioannis Quentelii, 1588.
4°, pp. 826 + index. Adams G977. Fore-edge: "GRANATEN:".   **333.2.13**

²**2.I(3).21**   Turrecremata 2 vol   1622–6
Turrecremata, Johannes de [also Torquemada, Juan de], *Card*.
    Emmanuel's collection contains several volumes of Torquemada's works
of appropriate date and having fore-edge markings. [Possibly the following two volumes:

    (1) Super toto Decreto. Lugduni, I. de ionuelle dictus piston, 1519. F°, ff.
        299. Adams T1166.   **315.1.49**
    (2) Super tracta de penitentia. Super tracta de consecratione. Lugduni, I.
        de ionuelle dictus piston, 1519–1520. F°, ff. 94, 168. Adams T1169, 1170.
                                                      315.1.50

Fore-edges (vertically): "Io. De turrecremä sup destinctionibus"; "Io. De
turrecremä De penitï. et De con."]

²**2.I(3).22**   Roffensis de veritate Corp X^{ti} in Euchar: 1597–1621
Fisher, John, *St, Bp of Rochester*. De Veritate Corporis et Sanguinis Christi
in Eucharistia... Aeditio prima. Coloniae, per Petrum Quentell, 1527.
Adams F535. 4°, ff. 297 + index. Fore-edge: "Roffensis/de ueritat/corp:
Chri/19".   **334.3.68**

²**2.I(3).23**   Billicus Contra Melancthon   1584–97
Billick, Everhard. Iudicii Universitatis et Cleri Coloniensis adversus calum-

nias Philippi Melanthonis, Martini Buceri, Oldendorpii & eorum asseclarum, defensio. Coloniae, excud. Iaspar Gennepaeus, 1545. 4°, pp. 344. Adams B2043. Fore-edge: "18/Billicus".   **301.5.92**

²**2.I(3).24**   Weston de Tripl: officio hominis   1622–6
Weston, Edward. De triplici hominis officio. [3 pts.] Antuerpiae, apud I. Keebergium, 1602. 4°, Missing. Register of Books Removed, p. 17, 1.31: "Ed: Westonus de triplici hominis Officio. ... Amsterd: 1602". Emmanuel's present copy was a Sancroft gift: S6.3.31.

²**2.I(3).25**   Bussaei Apologet: adversus ubiquitarios   1625
Busaeus, Joannes, *Noviomagensis*. Apologeticus Disputationis theologicae de persona Christi, adversus Ubiquitarios. Moguntiae, in offic. typog. Ioannis Albini, 1609. 4°, pp. 590. Donor: Dr John Richardson. Fore-edge: "BVSE*US*".   **321.4.96**

²**2.I(3).26**   Pamelij Missale 2 vol   1622–6
Pamelius, Jacobus, *Bp of Saint-Omer*. Missale SS. Patrum Latinorum, sive Liturgicon Latinum, iuxta veterem Ecclesiae Catholicae ritum. [2 vols.] Coloniae, apud Arnoldum Quentelium, 1609. 4°. Fore-edges: "Missale/Pamelij/i"; "ii".   **325.4.59,60**

²**2.I(3).27**   Scioppij Eccles   1622–6
Schopp, Gaspar. Ecclesiasticus Auctoritati... Iacobi Magnae Britanniae Regis oppositus. Hartbergae, 1611. 4°, pp. 565 [550]+errata. Fore-edge: "SCiOPPi*US*".   **321.4.97**

²**2.I(3).28**   Bellarm: Contr venet et Gers   1622–6
Bellarmine, Robert, *Card*. Responsio... ad duos libros. Unum, cuius inscriptio est Responsio cuiusdam ... ad epistolam sui amici de Brevi & censuris a... Paulo V. Papa, adversus... Venetos publicatis. Et alterum... Tractatus... Ioannis Gersonis de excommunicationis Valore. Moguntiae, apud Balthasarum Lippium, & Nicolaum Steinium, 1606. 4°, pp. 80. Bound with four other books, apparently after 1637.   **333.4.46**[1]

²**2.I(3).29**   Gretseri Basilicon Doron   1625
Gretser, Jacob. βασιλικον Δωρον sive Commentarius Exegeticus in regis Iacobi Praefationem Monitoriam; et in Apologiam pro Iuramento fidelitatis. Ingolstadii, ex typ. Adami Sartorii, 1610. 4°. Donor: Dr John Richardson.   **333.4.85**

²**2.I(3).30**   Ejusdem Virgidemia   1622–6
Gretser, Jacob. I. Virgidemia Volciana. II. Antistrena Polycarpica. III. Notae in Notas Petri Molinei Calvinistae, super Epistolam Nysseno ad scriptam, de euntibus Hierosolymam. IV. Examen Tractatus de

Peregrinationibus, ab eodem Molineo editi. V. Correctiones Notarum in Epistolam Nysseni ad Eustathiam ... VI. Lithi Myseni Satyra Palinodica Commentario illustrata. Ingolstadii, ex typ. Adami Sartorii, 1608. 4°, pp. 428 + index. **333.4.59**

²**2.I(3).31** Agonisticum Spiri*tuale*   1622–6
Gretser, Jacob. Agonisticum Spirituale. Ingolstadii, ex typ. Adami Sartorii, 1609. 8°, pp. 280 + index. **333.4.58**

²**2.I(3).32** Magirus contr Parae*um*   1622–6
Magirus, Johann. De Sacrarum Scripturarum authoritate divina et canonica adversus Iesuitarum ... imposturas. Disputatio prima ... Notis ... illustrata. Cum vindicatione Censurae Moguntinae & discussione Exegeseos eiusdem D. Parei. Moguntiae, apud T. Albinum, 1604 **332.5.111**

²**2.I(3).33** Scioppius de Anti = X^{to} et in ipsu*m* Baldwinus et alius de Anti – X^{to} 1622–6
Three books bound together:
(1) Schopp, Gaspar. De Antichristo Epistola ad illustrissimum quemdam Germaniae principem protestantem scripta. Ingolstadii, ex typogr. A. Sartorii, 1605. 4°, pp. 275.
(2) Balduin, Friedrich. De Antichristo Disputatio ... Epistolae de 'Antichristo cuiusdam Gasperis Scioppii ... Opposita. Witebergae, typ. Cratonianis per I. Gorman, 1606. 4°.
(3) Wolf, Heinrich. Antichristus. [with Addendum: Disputatione de Antichristo ...] Tiguri, apud Iohannem Wolphium, 1592. 4°, ff. 39, [7]. Adams W229. **331.5.5**

²**2.I(3).34** Antididagma Coloniense   1584–97
Cologne, *Cathedral*. Antididagma seu Christianae et Catholicae Religionis per ... Dominos Canonicos Metropolitanae Ecclesiae Coloniensis propugnatio. Lovanii, excud. Servatius Zassenus, 1544. 8°, ff. 166. Adams C2374. Fore-edge: "28/Antidi/dagma". **338.5.30**

²**2.I(3).35** Peresius de Traditionib   1597–1621
Perez de Ayala, Martin, *Abp of Valentia*. De Divinis Apostolicis, atque Ecclesiasticis Traditionibus. Parisiis, apud Poncetam le Preux, 1549–50. 8°, ff. 312. Fore-edge: "Peresius/Aiala de/tradition:/24". Adams P679.
321.4.107

²**2.I(3).36** Erasmus de libero arbitrio, et Luth de serv arbit   1584–97
[1621 inventory (4.I.27): "Billicanus Lutherus Erasmus de Libero arbitrio"]
Four books bound together:
(1) Gerlacher, Theobaldus, *Bellicanus*. De libero arbitrio. [Basel,] Thomas Volffius, 1525. 8°, ff. 16 [title page through f.8 missing]. Adams B523.
(2) Erasmus, Desiderius. De Libero Arbitrio Διατριβή. Antuerpiae apud Michaelem Hillenium Hoochstratanu*m*, 1524. 8°. Adams E597.

176

(3) Luther, Martin. De Servo Arbitrio, ad D. Erasmum. [Place of printing erased from title] 1526. 8°. Adams L1899.

(4) Erasmus, Desiderius. Hyperaspistes Diatribae Adversus Servum Arbitrium Martini Lutheri. Basileae, apud Io. Frob., 1526. 8°. Adams E673. **321.6.37**

Classis 2^{dae} Infer: Sect 4^a

²2.I(4).1   Lyra 6 vol   1584–97

Bible [Latin]. Biblie iampridem renovate pars prima (–sexta) [titles vary] ... una cum glosa ordinaria: et litterali moralique expositione Nicolai de Lyra: necnon additionibus Burgensis: ac replicis Thorinai. [6 vols.] [Basel, J. & P. Froben, 1508.] Adams B985. Signatures on each title page: "Thomas Cantuariensis" (Thomas Cranmer) and "Lumley" (John, first Baron Lumley). Adams B985. Fore-edges: "Lyra/i/19"; "ii/20"; "iii/21"; "iiii/22"/; [vol. V was trimmed when rebound]; "6/24".

303.2.61,62; 302.2.1– 4

²2.I(4).2   Hugo Cardinalis 6 vol   1584–97

Bible [Latin]. Prima [–sexta] pars huius operis: continens textum biblie, cum postilla domini Hugonis Cardinalis. [Vols. 1–6 contain the Old Testament, Apocrypha & Gospels only; vol. 7 is missing.] [Basel, Johann de Amerbach, 1498–1502.] F°. Adams B982 (omits Emmanuel's copy). Hain 3175. Signatures on each title page: "Thomas Cantuariensis" (Thomas Cranmer) and "Lumley" (John, first Baron Lumley). Fore-edges (vertically): "HVGO I"; "HVGO II"; "HVGO III"; "HVGO IIII"; "HVGO V"; "HVGO VI". Top edges: "hug j."; "hug 2."; "hug. 3."; "hugo 4."; "hugo 5."; "hug. 6." **MSS 6.1.13–18**

²2.I(4).3   Carthusiani opusc: 2 vol   1597–1621

Dionysius, *Carthusianus*. Operum Minorum Tomus Primus (–secundus). [2 vols.] Apud Sanctam Ubiorum Coloniam Iohannes Soter excudebat, 1532. F°, ff. 560 + index; 544 + index. Adams D534. **302.2.57,59**

²2.I(4).4   Idem in Pentateuch   1584–97

Dionysius, *Carthusianus*. Enarrationes ... in quinque Mosaicae legis libros. Coloniae suis impensis Petrus Quentel excudebat, 1534. F°, ff. 412 + index. Missing. Register of Books Removed, p. 21, 1.13: "Dion: Carthusianus in Pentateuch: ... Colon: 1534." The present Emmanuel copy (Adams D551) was a Sancroft gift: S7.2.22.

²2.I(4).5   Idem in Libros Historic   1622–6

Dionysius, *Carthusianus*. Enarrationes ... in libros Iosue. Iudicum. Ruth. Regum. I. II. III. IIII. Paralipomenon. I. II. Coloniae, suis impensis Petrus

177

Quentell excudebat, 1535. F°, ff. 305. Adams D554. Fore-edge: "Histor".

302.2.44

²**2.I(4).6**   Idem in Psalmos   1584–97

Dionysius, *Carthusianus*. Insigne commentariorum opus, in Psalmos omnes Davidicos. Parisiis, apud Iohannem Lodoicum Tiletanum ex adverso Collegii Remensis, 1542. F°, ff. 327. Adams D559. Signatures on title page: "Thomas Cantuarien*sis*" (Thomas Cranmer) and "Lumley" (John, first Baron Lumley). Fore-edge: "Psal/12".   **302.2.43**

²**2.I(4).7**   Idem in Prover*b*   1584–97

Dionysius, *Carthusianus*. Enarrationes piae ac eruditae in quinque libros Sapientiales, hoc est, Proverbia, Ecclesiasten, Canticu*m* Canticorum, Sapientiam, Ecclesiasticum. Coloniae, per Iasperum Genepium, 1539. F°, ff. 302. Adams D573. Signatures on title page: "Thomas Cantuarien*sis*" (Thomas Cranmer) and "Lumley" (John, first Baron Lumley). Fore-edge: "Prou/11".   **302.2.45**

²**2.I(4).8**   Idem in Proph   1584–97

Two books bound together:

(1) Dionysius, *Carthusianus*. Enarrationes ... in quatuor prophetas maiores. Coloniae, expensis Petri Quentel, 1543. F°, ff. 435. Adams D564. Signatures on title page: "Thomas Cantuarien*sis*" (Thomas Cranmer) and "Lumley" (John, first Baron Lumley).

(2) Dionysius, *Carthusianus*. Enarrationes ... in XII. prophetas minores. Coloniae [Petrus Quentel], 1539. F°, ff. 155. Adams D569.

Fore-edge: "Proph/13".   **302.2.46**

²**2.I(4).9**   Idem in Evang   1584–97

Dionysius, *Carthusianus*. In Quatuor Evangelistas Enarrationes. Coloniae, per Iasparem Gennep*ae*um, 1538. F°, ff. 383. Adams D581. Signatures on title page: "Thomas Cantuarien*sis*" (Thomas Cranmer) and "Lumley" (John, first Baron Lumley). Fore-edge: "Euang/14".   **302.2.47**

²**2.I(4).10**   Idem in Ep*isto*las   1584–97

[1621 inventory (3.I.10): "Dionis: in Acta A*post*oloru*m*. Epist. & Apocalyps."]

Two books bound together:

(1) Dionysius, *Carthusianus*. In omnes beati Pauli epistolas commentaria, iam tertio. ... recognita. Coloniae, apud Petrum Quentell, 1538. F°, ff. 190.

(2) Dionysius, *Carthusianus*. In Epistolas Omnes Canonicas, in Acta apostolorum, & Apocalypsim. Coloniae, expensis Petri Quentell, 1536. F°, ff. 183 Adams D595. Signatures on first title page: "Thomas

Cantuarien*sis*" (Thomas Cranmer) and "Lumley" (John, first Baron Lumley). Fore-edge: "Epist./15".   **302.2.47A**

²2.I(4).11   Idem in Job, Act, Jacob, et Apocal   1625
               Two books bound together:
               (1) Dionysius, *Carthusianus*. Enarrationes in Lib. Iob. Tobiae. Iudith.
                   Hester. Esdrae. Nehemiae. I. Machabaeorum. II. Machabaeorum.
                   Coloniae, impensis Petri Quentell, 1534. Fº, ff. 208 [218]. Adams D576.
               (2) Dionysius, *Carthusianus*. In Epistolas omnes canonicas, in Acta aposto-
                   lorum, & in Apocalypsim enarrationes. [On the same title page,
                   stamped under the above:] Adiectae sunt expositiones Hymnor*um*
                   ecclesiasticorum eiusdem Dionysij, fol. 181. Coloniae, in aedibus
                   Quentelianis, 1533. Fº, ff. 212. Adams D601. Donor: Dr John
                   Richardson. Fore-edge: "Iob, Apoc./Acta. Iacob/etc."   **302.2.48**

²2.I(4).12   Ejusdem Postillae 2 vol   1597–1621
               [1621 inventory (3.I.12): "Dionis in Ep*isto*las & Evang: Dominic. pars 1ª";
               (3.I.13): "Dionis. Carthus. de Sanctis"]
               [Possibly the following two books:
               (1) Dionysius, *Carthusianus*. Epistolarum ac Evangelior*um* Dominicalium
                   totius anni Enarratio, adiunctis Homiliis & Sermonibus variis... Pars
                   prima de Tempore. Coloniae, P. Quentell suis impensis excudebat,
                   1533.   **302.2.61**
               (2) Dionysius, *Carthusianus*. Homiliarum in Epistolas & Evangelia ser-
                   monum*que* de sanctis, opus praeclarum.... Pars Altera de Sanctis.
                   Coloniae, P. Quentel suis impensis excudebat, 1533.   **302.2.60**
               Adams D604]

Note: One volume of the shorter works of Dionysius has been in the Emmanuel collection from the time of the
earliest list. For some reason, however, this book was not recorded in the catalogues of 1626, 1628, 1632 or 1637.
We describe the book here as belonging to this classis:

               [1621 inventory (3.I.3); "Dionis. Carth. in Lib. Boetij, Cassiani & Scala
               Paradisi"]
               Dionysius,   *Carthusianus*.   Operum   Minorum   Tomus   Tertius....
               Commentaria in libros... Boethij... Iohannes Cassianus ... in opera
               Iohannes Climaci explanatio. Coloniae, ex off. M. Novesiani 1540. Fº, ff.
               237, 199, [1], 131. Adams D535. Signatures on title page: "Thomas
               Cantuarien*sis*" (Thomas Cranmer) and "Lumley" (John, first Baron
               Lumley). Fore-edge: "Op*us*cula/l*us*/Carthusian*us*/&/Cassian*us*/3/9". **301.3.1**

Classis 3*ae* Super*r* Sect. 1*a*

²3.S(1).1   Villalpandus 3 vol   1626–32
               Villalpandus, Joannes Baptista and Pradus, Hieronymus. In Ezechielem
               explanationes et apparatus urbis, ac templi Hierosolymitani. [3 vols.]
               Romae, [I:] ex typog. Aloysii Zannetti, 1596; [II + III:] Typis Illefonsi

Ciacconii, excud. Carolus Vulliettus, 1604, 1602–1605. F°, pp. xv, 360; 104, 655; xvi, 573. Missing. Register of Books Removed, p. 51, l. 14: "J. Bapt: Villalpandus in Ezechielem 3 vol:... Rom$\begin{cases}1596.,\\1604\end{cases}$ Emmanuel's present copy (Adams P2050) was a Sancroft gift: S13.1.1–3.

²3.S(1).2   Maldonat in Evang   1625
Maldonatus, Joannes. Commentarii in quattuor Evangelistas. Lugduni, sumpt. Horatii Cardon, 1602. F°, Coll. 1965 + index. Donor: Dr John Richardson. Fore-edge "MALDON in Evang."   **303.2.56**

²3.S(1).3   Lorinus in Psal 3 vol   1625
Lorinus, Joannes. Commentariorum in Librum Psalmorum tomus I (–III). [3 vols.] Lugduni, sumptibus Horatii Cardon, 1612–1616. F°, pp. 1086 + index; 1079 + index; 1239 + index. Donor: Dr John Richardson. Fore-edge: "LORINUS in/Psalm. Tom. i."; "Tom ii"; "Tom iii".
                                                                      303.2.51–3

²3.S(1).4   Idem in Acta   1625
Lorinus, Joannes. In Actus Apostolorum commentaria. Lugduni, apud Horatium Cardon, 1609. F°, pp. 896 + index. Donor: Dr John Richardson. Fore-edge: "LORINUS in Acta".   **303.2.54**

²3.S(1).5   Idem in Epistolas Johannis et Petri   1625
Lorinus, Joannes. In catholicas tres B. Ioannis, et duas B. Petri Epistolas Commentarii. Lugduni, sumpt. H. Cardon, 1609. F°, 421 + index. Donor: Dr John Richardson. Fore-edge: "LORIN: in epistolas Iohannis Petri".
                                                                      303.2.55

²3.S(1).6   Idem in Ecclesiasten   1625
Lorinus, Joannes. Commentarius in Ecclesiasten. Accessit expositio eiusdem in Psalmum LXVII. Moguntiae, apud B. Lippium, 1607. 4°, pp. 538 [534] + index. Donor: Dr John Richardson, 1625. Missing. Register of Books Removed, p. 21, l. 30: "Jo: Lorinus in Ecclesiast: & Ps: 67um ... Mogunt: 1607. Id [i.e., Dr Rich.]". Emmanuel's present copy was a Sancroft gift: S7.3.20.

²3.S(1).7   Pineda de gestis Salomonis   1625
Pineda, Joannes de. Ad suos in Salomonem Commentarios Salomon praevius, id est, De Rebus Salomonis Regis libri octo. Lugduni, apud H. Cardon, 1609. F°, pp. 584 + indices. Donor: Dr John Richardson. Fore-edge: "PINEDA".   **301.2.7**

²3.S(1).8   Oleaster in Pentat   1625
Oleastro, Hieronymus ab. Commentaria in Pentateuchum. Lugduni, apud

Petrum⁻ Landry, 1588. F°, pp. 650. Adams O151. Donor: Dr John
Richardson. Fore-edge: "Oleastro/in Pentat:".   **301.3.2**

²3.S(1).9   Cornel a lapide in 4 Proph majores   1626–32
Lapide, Cornelius à (Van den Steen). Commentaria in quatuor Prophetas
Majores. [4 pts in 1 vol.] Parisiis, 1622–6. F°. Fore-edge: "C. a. Lapide/in 4
prophet./major:".   **307.2.56**

²3.S(1).10 Idem in 12 Proph: minores   1626–32
Cornelius a Lapide (Van den Steen). Commentaria in Duodecim
Prophetas Minores. Lugduni, sumptibus C. Landry, 1625. F°. Fore-edge:
"C. a Lapide/in 12 prophet./minor:".   **307.2.57**

²3.S(1).11 Idem in Acta, Epistolas, Canonicas: et Apocal: 1627–32
Cornelius a Lapide (Van den Steen). Commentaria in Acta Apostolorum,
Epistolas Canonicas, et Apocalypsin. [3 vols. in 1.] Antuerpiae, apud
Martinum Nutium, 1627. F°, pp. 392; 604; 374. Fore-edge: "C. a Lapide/in
Acta: Epistol: Can/+Apocalipse:".   **306.2.2**

²3.S(1).12 Idem in Epistolas Pauli   1622–6
Cornelius a Lapide (Van den Steen). Commentaria in omnes Divi Pauli
epistolas. Missing. Emmanuel's present copy (Antuerpiae, 1627) was a gift
of John Breton in 1676: 306.2.3.

²3.S(1).13 Christoph a Castro in Ier: Thren: et Baruch   1625
Castro, Christophorus a. Commentariorum in Ieremiae Prophetias,
Lamentationes et Baruch libri sex. Parisiis, apud M. Sonnium, 1609. F°, ff.
xxviii, coll. 1122. Donor: Dr John Richardson. Fore-edge: "C a Castro/in
Ierem./Lament Baruc:".   **302.2.8**

²3.S(1).14 Idem in proph minores   1622–6
Castro, Christophorus a. Commentariorum in Duodecim Prophetas libri
duodecim. Moguntiae, apud I. T. Schöwetterum, 1616. F°, pp.
582+indices. Missing. Register of Books Removed, p. 51, 1. 21:
"Christoph: Castrus in 12 Prophetas... Mogun: 1616". Emmanuel's present copy was a Sancroft gift: S13.2.17¹.

²3.S(1).15 Lucas Brugensis 2 vol   1626–32
Lucas, Franciscus, of Bruges. [Possibly: Notationes in Sacra Biblia.
Antuerpiae, ex off. Christophori Plantini, 1580. 4°, pp. 467. (Second vol.
missing.)   **334.2.58**]

²3.S(1).16 Stella in Lucam   1625
Stella, Didacus (Estella, Diego d'). In... Evangelium secundum Lucam
Ennarrationum Tomus Primus (–Secundus). Antuerpiae, apud Petrum &

Ioannem Belleros, 1622. F°, pp. 340, 384. Donor: Dr John Richardson. Fore-edge: "STELLA/IN/LVCAM".　　　　　**302.2.9**

²**3.S(1).17**　　Espencaeus in Tim　　　　　　　　　　　　　1625
Espence, Claude d'. In priorem D. Pauli ad Timotheum Epistolam, Commentarii et digressiones. Lutetiae Parisiorum, ex off. typog. Michaelis Vascosani, 1561(–64). F°, pp. 426. Donor: Dr John Richardson. Missing. Register of Books Removed, p. 21, 1. 7: "Espencaeus in Epistolas Pauli ad Timotheum... Paris: 1561 Dr Rich". Emmanuel's present copy (Adams B1930) was a Sancroft gift: S7.1.31[1].

²**3.S(1).18**　　Benzo in Magnific　　　　　　　　　　　　　1625
Benzoni, Rutilio, *Bp of Loretto.* Commentariorum ac Disputationum in Beatissimae Virginis Canticum Magnificat Libri Quinque. Venetiis, apud Iuntas, 1606. F°, pp. 192, 244, 260, 95, 57 + index. Donor: Dr John Richardson. Fore-edge: "Benzo in/Magnif:".　　　　　**304.4.53**

²**3.S(1).19**　　Toletus in Ioh　　　　　　　　　　　　　　1625
Toletus, Franciscus, *Card.* In... Ioannis Evangelium commentarii. Coloniae Agrippinae, in off. Birckmannica, sumpt. Arnoldi Mylii, 1599. F°, coll. 1056, 576 + index. Adams T782. Donor: Dr John Richardson. Fore-edge: "Toletus/in Johannem".　　　　　**304.4.58**

²**3.S(1).20**　　Idem in Epistolam ad Rom　　　　　　　　　　1625
Toletus, Franciscus, *Card.* In Epistolam Beati Pauli ad Romanos Commentarii et annotationes. Accesserunt ejusdem cardinalis xv sermones in Psalmum primum et tricesimum: ac duo in ejusdem Epistolae loca tractatus. Moguntiae, apud B. Lippium, sumpt. A. Mylii, 1603. 4°, pp. 782 + index. Donor: Dr John Richardson. Missing. Register of Books Removed, p. 21, 1. 24: "Toletus in Romanos & Psalmum 31^{mum}... Mogunt: 1603. Dr Rich:". Emmanuel's present copy was a Sancroft gift: S7.2.48.

²**3.S(1).21.**　　Idem in Lucam　　　　　　　　　　　　　1625
Toletus, Franciscus, *Card.* Commentaria in... Evangelium secundum Lucam. Venetiis, apud Georgium Variscum, & Socios, 1601. F°, pp. 795 + index. Donor: Dr John Richardson. Fore-edge: "TOLET/in/ LVCaM".　　　　　**304.4.57**

²**3.S(1).22**　　Gasp: Sanctius in Isaiam　　　　　　　　　　1625
Sanctius [Sanchez], Gasparus. In Isaiam prophetam Commentarii cum paraphrasi. Moguntiae, apud Iohannem Theobaldum Schönwetterum, 1616. F°, pp. 736 + index. Donor: Dr John Richardson. Fore-edge: "G:SANCT/in ISAIA:".　　　　　**302.2.6**

²3.S(1).23   Idem in Zachariam   1625
           Sanctius [Sanchez], Gasparus. In Zachariam Prophetam commentarii cum
paraphrasi. Lugduni, apud H. Cardon, 1616. 4°, pp. 333 + index. Donor: Dr
John Richardson. Missing. Register of Books Removed, p.21, 1. 25: "Gasp:
Sanctius in Zachariam... Lugd: 1616. Id [i.e., Dr Rich.]". Emmanuel's
present copy was a Sancroft gift: S7.3.7.

²3.S(1).24   Idem in Cant   1625
           Sanctius [Sanchez], Gasparus. In Canticum Canticorum commentarii.
Cum expositione Psalmi LXVII. Lugduni, apud H. Cardon, 1616. 4°, pp.
397 + index. Donor: Dr John Richardson. Missing. Register of Books
Removed, p. 21, 1. 27: "[Gasp: Sanctius] in Cantica... & Psalm: 67um...
Dr. Rich." Emmanuel's present copy was a Sancroft gift: S7.3.6.

Classis 3^{ae} Super^r Sect 2^a

²3.S(2).1   Destructorium Vitiorum   1597–1621
           Alexander, *Anglus*. Destructorium Vitiorum. Missing. Emmanuel's present
copy (Nuremberge, 1496: Hain 652, Proctor 2111) was a Sancroft gift:
S13.2.38.

²3.S(2).2   Postilla Wicelij   1584–97
           Wicelius, Georgius. Postilla, hoc est, enarratio... super Evangelia et
Epistolas de Tempore & de Sanctis per totum annum. Apud Coloniam
Agrippinam, excud. Petrus Quentel, 1545. F°, pp. 351, 391. Adams W123,
W126. Donor(?): John Wickliffe. Signature on flyleaf: "Jhan Wickliffe".
Fore-edge: "Postilla Wi/cellij/13".   **305.3.22**

²3.S(2).3   Bromyardi Summa Praedicant   1584–97
           Bromyard, John de. Summa praedicantium. [Nuremberg,] per Joannem
Stuchs, sumpt. Anthonii Kobergers, 1518. F°, ff. [406]. Adams B2895.
Donor(?): Robert Cronkar. Signature on title page: "Robtus Cronkar".
                                                            308.4.15

²3.S(2).4   Nauseae Homiliae   1584–97
           Nausea, Fridericus, *Bp of Vienna*. Evangelicae veritatis Homiliarum
Centuriae tres. [Coloniae, Petrus Quentell excud.,] impens. Arnoldi
Birckman, 1532. F°, ff. [445]. Adams N85. Donor(?): Robert Cronkar.
Fore-edge: "Nauseae Homl/2". Signature on paste-down: "Robert Cronkar
clericus".   **308.3.51**

²3.S(2).5   Clichtovei Elucidatorium Eccles   1584–97
           Clichtoveus, Judocus. Elucidatorium ecclesiasticum. Missing.

²**3.S(2).6**   Erasmi Eccles^{tes}   1584–97

Erasmus, Desiderius. Ecclesiastae, sive de ratione concionandi. Antuerpiae, apud Michaelem Hillenium in Rapo, 1535. 8°, ff. 231. Adams E626. Fore-edge: "Erasm/Ecclesiaste".   **323.5.112**

²**3.S(2).7**   Sermonum Pomerium 2 vol   1622–6

Pelbartus, Oswaldus, *de Themeswar*. Pomerium sermonum. Missing.

²**3.S(2).8**   Costeri conciones 2 vol   1625

Costerus, Franciscus. Conciones in Evangelia Dominicalia. *Tr. & Ed.* Theodorus Petreius. 2 vols. Coloniae Agrippinae, sumpt. Antonii Hierati, 1608. 4°, pp. 430, 397 + indices; 552, 178 + indices. Donor: Dr John Richardson. Fore-edges: "Costeri/Conciones/i"; "2".   **330.2.32**

²**3.S(2).9**   Iacobus de voragine   1622–6

Voragine, Jacobus de. Sermones aurei in Evangelia. Moguntiae, sumpt. Petri Cholini, 1616. 4°, pp. 375. Fore-edge: "Iacobus de/Vorag." **330.2.37**

²**3.S(2).10**   Diez Summa praedicant   1597–1621

Diez, Philippe. Summa praedicantium. Antuerpiae, ex off. Martini Nutii, 1600. 4°, pp. 559, 538 + indices. Adams D454. Fore-edge: "DIEZ". **333.2.20**

²**3.S(2).11**   Clicthovei opusc^a   1622–6

Two books bound together:

(1) Clichtoveus, Judocus. De puritate conceptionis beatae Mariae virginis, [etc.] [4 tracts]. Ex off. emissum in alma Pariseorum academia, Venale habetur in off. H. Stephani, 1513. 4°, ff. 105. Adams C2208.

(2) Eucherius, *St, Bp of Lyons*. Formularum Intelligentiae Spiritalis Liber. Basileae, per Andream Cratandrum, 1530. 4°, pp. 131. Adams E969.

Fore-edge: "Clichto/uei hom".   **334.3.70**

²**3.S(2).12**   Sasbouti Homiliae   1625

Sasbout, Adam. Homiliae accurate recognitae. [2 pts.] Coloniae Ubiorum, ex off. Bernardi Gualteri, 1613. 4°, pp. 54, 273. Donor: Dr John Richardson. Fore-edge: "Saus = /bout/Homil".   **334.3.66**

²**3.S(2).13**   Royardi Homiliae 4 vol   1584–97; 1625

(1) Royardus, Johannes. Homiliae in epistolas dominicales.... Pars Aestiva. Antuerpiae, in aed. Ioannis Steelsii, 1543. 8°, ff. 160 + index. Adams R832. Donor: Dr John Richardson. Fore-edge: "Royard/i/27", and, in another hand: "Royardi pars I^a/epistolarum estiua/lium de sanctis".   **321.7.61**

(2) Royardus, Johannes. Homiliae in omnes epistolas dominicales.... Pars Hyemalis. Antuerpiae, in aed. Ioannis Steelsii, 1543. 8°, ff. 152 + index. Adams R831. No gift label. Fore-edge: "ii/28", and, in another hand: "Royardus".   **321.7.59**

(3) Royardus, Johannes. Homiliae in Evangelia dominicalia.... Pars Aestiva. Parisiis, apud Vivantium Gaultherotum, 1542. 8°, ff. 294 + index. Adams R834. No gift label. Fore-edge: "iii/29", and, in another hand: "Royardi pars evang/esti/valium". **321.7.60.**

(4) Royardus, Johannes. Homiliae in Evangelia Dominicalia.... Pars Hyemalis. Parisiis, apud Vivantium Gaultherot sub signo D. Martini, 1542. 8°, ff. 294 + index. Not in Adams. No gift label. Fore-edge: "iiii/30", and, in another hand: "Royardi/pars/euangelius/hyemalis". **321.7.57**

²**3.S(2).14**   Pippinus in Gen 2 vol   1584–97

Pepin, Guillaume. Expositio in Genesim. [2 vols.] Parisiis, apud Joannem Parvum in ed. Claudii Chevallonii, 1528. 8°, ff. 430; 359. [Possibly: Adams P626. **321.7.67,68**]

²**3.S(2).15**   Bernardinus Ochinus 3 vol   1584–97

(1) Ochino, Bernardino. Prediche... (Prima parte). [Basle, 1562(?)] 8°. Adams O31. Fore-edge: "Bernard/Ochino/i". **338.5.35**

(2) Ochino, Bernardino. La terza parte della prediche. [Basle, a 1543.] 8°. Adams O34. Fore-edge: "II". **338.5.36**

A third volume is missing. This is perhaps the volume recorded on the "Memorandum" which lists books "wanting" on Oct. 4, 1610: "Barnardi Ochini. serm. p. 2." and again on Apr. 12, 1627 with the note that "Mr. Johnson [was] to be responsible for" it and other books: "Ochini pars".

²**3.S(2).16**   Culmanni Conciones 2 vol   1584–97

Culmann, Leonhard. Secundus (–Tertius) Tomus sacrarum contionum. [2 vols.] Norimbergae, in off. Iohannis Montani, & Ulrici Neuber, 1550. 8°, ff. 312; 322, Adams C3050. Fore-edges: "Culmanni/conc: pars 2us/30"; "Culmanni/conc. pˢ 3ᵗˢ/31". **326.4.98,99**

²**3.S(2).17**   Haymonis Homiliae 2 vol   1584–97

Haymo, *Bp of Halberstadt.* Homiliarum sive concionum popularium pars aestivalis (–hyemalis). [2 vols.] Coloniae, ex. off. Eucharii Cervicorni, 1534. 8°, pp. 615; 734. Adams H90. Fore-edges: "32/pars aestivaˡⁱˢ/haymoⁱˢ"; "33/haymoⁱˢ/pars hiemaliˢ". **321.7.62,63**

Classis 3ᵃᵉ Superʳ sect 3ᵃ

²**3.S(3).1**   Hen: Steph: Thesaurus Ling Grae 4 vol   1584–97

Stephanus, Henricus. Thesaurus Graecae linguae. [5 pts in 4 vols.] [Geneva,] excudebat H. Stephanus, 1572. F°. Missing. Register of Books Removed, p. 13, l. 35: "[H. Stephani] Lexicon.... 4v.... 1572". Emmanuel's present copy (Adams S1791) was the gift of H. Hubbard, who was a fellow from 1732 to 1778.

²3.S(3).2   Suidas gr   1584–97
Suidas. τὸ μὲν παρὸν βιβλίον, Σουίδα.... Venetiis, in aed. Aldi, et Andreae
soceri [1514.] F°. Adams S2062. Isaac 12834. Fore-edge: "SUiDAS/22".

318.3.3

²3.S(3).3   Budaei Lexicon   1622–6
Budaeus, Gulielmus. Lexicon sive dictionarium Graeco–latinum. Missing.
One of Emmanuel's present copies ([Geneva,] 1562: Adams B3142) was a
Sancroft gift: S11.1.21,22.

²3.S(3).4   Mottensis tab^ae ling gr   1622–6
Aleandro, Girolamo, *Card., Abp of Brindisi.* Tabulae... graecarum mu-
sarum. [Possibly: Lovanii, imprim. Theodoricus Martinus Alustensis, 1516.
4°. Adams A651.   **331.4.76**]

²3.S(3).5   Urbani Gram gr   1597–1621
Bolzanius, Urbanus. [Possibly: Grammaticae Institutiones. Basileae, apud
V. Curionem, 1524. 4°, ff. 249. Adams B2364.   **332.2.44**]

²3.S(3).6   Hesych Lexic gr   1628–32
Hesychius, *Alexandrinus.* Δεξικόν. Missing. One of Emmanuel's present
copies (Florentiae, 1520: Adams H507) was a Sancroft gift: S11.1.28¹.

²3.S(3).[7]   2 Chappell Folio (?) Bibles
This unnumbered entry was probably added between 1637 and 1645 since
two large folio Bibles appear in a chapel inventory dated 1645 but not in a
chapel inventory of 1637. The handwriting and ink are different from
those of the rest of this catalogue.

Classis 3^ae Inferio^r Sect. 1^a

²3.I(1).1   Ludolphus de vita X^ti   1584–97
Ludolphus, *de Saxonia.* Vita Iesu Christi. Missing. One of Emmanuel's
present copies (Antuerpiae, 1618) was a Sancroft gift: S8.2.38.

²3.I(1).2   Masius in Iosh.   1625
Masius, Andreas, *ed.* Iosuae Imperatoris historia [Heb., Gk, & Lat.]
Antuerpiae, ex off. Christophori Plantini, 1574. F°, pp. 154, 350. Donor: Dr
John Richardson. Missing. Register of Books Removed, p. 21, 1. 9: "Andr:
Masius in Iosuam... Antw: 1574: Dr Rich". Emmanuel's present copy
(Adams B1325) was a Sancroft gift: S7.1.34.

²3.I(1).3   Serranus in Levit et Ezech   1625
Two books bound together:
(1) Serranus, Petrus. In Levitici Lib. Commentaria. Antuerpiae, ex off.

Christophori Plantini, 1572. F°, pp. 264 [260] + index. Adams S994.

(2) Serranus, Petrus. Commentaria in Ezechielem Prophetam. Antuerpiae, ex off. Christophori Plantini, 1572. F°, pp. 289 + index. Adams S996.

Donor: Dr John Richardson. Fore-edge: "Seran:/in $\begin{cases} \text{Leuit}_{,,} \\ \text{Ezek} \end{cases}$". **304.3.18**

²**3.I(1).4**   Sadolet in Ep*istol* ad Rom: 1584–97
Sadoletus, Jacobus, *Card. Bp of Carpentras*. In Pauli Epistolam ad Romanos Commentariorum Libri Tres. Lugduni, Sebastianus Gryphius excud., 1536. F°, pp. 231. Adams S72. Fore-edge: "6/Sado/let*us*/[?]".
                                                                                    306.2.32

²**3.I(1).5**   Gorranus in Evang   1584–97
Gorran, Nicolaus de. Commentaria... in Quatuor Evangelia. Coloniae, Petrus Quentel excud., 1537. F°, ff. 587. [Possibly: Adams G880.
                                                                                    303.4.14]

²**3.I(1).6**   Idem in Ep*isto*las   1584–97
Gorran, Nicolaus de. Postilla... Super Epistolas Pauli [Hagenau,] impens. Johannis Rynman, 1502. F°. Proctor 11616, Adams G 881. Fore-edge: "Gorranus/in epistol./11".   **310.5.3**

²**3.I(1).7**   Ausbertus in Apocal   1622–6
Ambrosius Ansbertus. In... Apocalypsim libri decem. Coloniae, per Eucharium Cervicornum, opera & impensa Godefridi Hittorpii, 1536. F°, pp. 442 + index. Adams A956. Fore-edge: "AusBert [?]/Apocal/[?]" and two illegible lines in another hand.   **308.4.73**

²**3.I(1).8**   Cajetanus in Evang et Act   1622–6
Cajetanus, Thomas de Vio, *Card*. Evangelia cum commentariis.... in quatuor evangelia & Acta Apostolorum. Parisiis, veneunt in aed. Ioannis Parvi, 1540. F°, ff. 290 + index. Adams C142. Fore-edge: "Caieta:/in euang:/in act:".   **302.2.56**

²**3.I(1).9**   Zachar Chrysopol de concord Evang   1625
Zacharias, *Bp of Chrysopolis*. In unu*m* ex quatuor sive de concordia evangelistarum, libri quatuor. [Cologne,] Eucharius Cervicornus excud., 1535. F°, pp. 383. Adams Z20. Donor: Dr John Richardson. Fore-edge: "Zachar/concord/euang" and "Zacha^{ius}/31".   **310.5.6**

²**3.I(1).10**   Haymo in Psalmos   1625
Haymo, *Bp of Halberstadt*. Pia Brevis Ac Dilucida in Omnes Psalmos Explanatio. Friburgi Brisgoiae, excud. Ioannes Faber Emmeus, 1533. F°, pp. 345. Adams H100. Donor: Dr John Richardson. Signature of Thomas Blage (d. 1611) on the title page. Fore-edge: "Haym°/in psal:".   **303.4.13**

²3.I(1).11   Turrecremata in Psalmos   1626–32
Turrecremata, Johannes de [also Torquemada, Juan de], *Card*. [Expositio
super Psalterium (Basel, Johann Amerbach, not after 1482).] F°, pp. [124].
Title page missing. Hain 15689. Proctor 7618.   **MSS 6.2.1**

²3.I(1).12   Catena aurea in Psal   1584–97
[Possibly: Puteo, Franciscus de. Cathena Aurea super Psalmos.] Missing.
One of Emmanuel's present copies (Parisiis, 1520: Adams P2294) was a
Sancroft gift: S8.3.25.

²3.I(1).13   Arias Montanus in 12 proph minores   1622–6
Montanus, Benedictus Arias. Commentaria in Duodecim Prophetas.
Missing.

²3.I(1).14   Idem in Iosh   1625
Montanus, Benedictus Arias. De Optimo Imperio, sive in Lib. Iosuae
Commentarium. Antuerpiae, ex off. Christophori Plantini, 1583. 4°, pp.
713. Adams M1637. Donor: Dr John Richardson. Fore-edge:
"MONTAN/IN JOSH."   **330.2.34**

²3.I(1).15   Ejusdem Antiquitates Iudaicae in Vet Test   1625
Montanus, Benedictus Arias. Antiquitatum Iudaicarum Libri IX. Lugduni
Batavorum, ex off. Plantiniana, apud Franciscum Raphelengium, 1593. 4°,
pp. 200. Adams M1630. Donor: Dr John Richardson. Fore-edge: three
illegible lines of writing.   **334.1.83**

²3.I(1).16   Ribera in 12 proph minores   1625
Ribera, Francisco de. In Librum Duodecim Prophetarum commentarii.
Coloniae Agrippinae, in off. Birckmannica, sumpt. Arnoldi Mylii, 1593. F°,
pp. 807 + indices. Adams R473. Donor: Dr John Richardson. Fore-edge:
"RIBERA IN/12 PROPH".   **308.4.61**

²3.I(1).17   Idem in Apocal   1625
Ribera, Francisco de. In sacram Beati Ioannis Apostoli, & Evangelistae
Apocalypsim Commentarii.... His Adiuncti Sunt, Quinque libri de
Templo. Lugduni, ex off. Iuntarum, 1592. 4°, pp. 447, 320 + indices. Adams
R478. Donor: Dr John Richardson. Fore-edge: "RIBERA IN/APOCAL".
                                                                 330.2.27

²3.I(1).18   Pererius in Gen Tom 2^{dus} et 3 2 vol   1625
(1) Pererius, Benedictus, *Valentinus*. Commentariorum et Disputationum
in Genesim, Tomus Secundus. Lugduni, ex off. Iuntarum, 1593. 4°, pp.
577, 100 + indices. Adams P659. Donor: Dr John Richardson. Fore-
edge: "Pererius/To: 2 in/Genes:".   **332.1.30**
(2) Pererius, Benedictus, *Valentinus*. Tertius tomus Commentariorum in

Genesim. Lugduni, ex off. Iuntarum, 1596. 4°, pp. 782 [792]. Adams
P660. Donor: Dr John Richardson. Fore-edge: "To: 3".   **332.1.31**

²3.I(1).19   Idem in Exod   1625
Pererius, Benedictus, *Valentinus*. Primus tomus selectarum Disputationum
in Sacram Scripturam, continens super libro Exodi centum trigenta septem
Disputationes. Lugduni, sumptibus Horatii Cardon, 1602. 4°, pp.
501 + index. Donor: Dr John Richardson. Fore-edge: "Pererius/in Exod".
                                                                       332.1.32

²3.I(1).20   Idem in Ioh   1625
Pererius, Benedictus, *Valentinus*. Quartus Tomus... qui est prior tomus
disputationum in Evangelium B. Ioannis super novem primis eius
Evangelii capitibus. Lugduni, sumpt. H. Cardon, 1608. 4°, pp. 539 + index.
Donor: Dr John Richardson. Fore-edge: "Pererius/in Joha*n*nem". **332.1.33**

²3.I(1).21   Idem in Ep*isto*lam ad Rom   1625
Pererius, Benedictus,*Valentinus*. Secundus Tomus Selectarum Disputationum
in Sacram Scripturam, continens centum octoginta octo disputationes super
Epistola beati Pauli ad Romanos. Lugduni, sumpt. H. Cardon, 1604. 4°, pp.
675 + index. Donor: Dr John Richardson. Fore-edge: "Pererius/ad Rom:".
                                                                       332.1.29

²3.I(1).22   Magalianus in Ep*isto*l ad Tim et Tit   1625
Magalianus, Cosmas. Operis hierarchici, sive, de ecclesiastico principatu
libri III, in quibus̈ Epist. tres B. Pauli... commentariis illustrantur,...
Timotheo... duae, una Tito. Lugduni, sumptibus H. Cardon, 1609. 4°.
Donor: Dr John Richardson. Missing. Register of Books Removed, p. 21,
1. 28: "Cosm: Magalianus in Epist: ad Titum, & Timotheum... Lugd:
1609. Id. [*i.e.*, D' Rich]". Emmanuel's present copy was a Sancroft gift:
S7.3.9.

²3.I(1).23   Delrio Phar*us* S Scrpt^ae   1625
Delrio, Martin Anton. Pharus Sacrae Sapientiae. Lugduni, sumptibus
Horatii Cardon, 1608. 4°, pp. 583 + index. Donor: Dr John Richardson.
Fore-edge: "DeL-RiO/in Gen:".   **330.2.29**

²3.I(1).24   Idem in Threnos   1625
Delrio, Martin Anton. Commentarius Litteralis in Threnos, id est
Lamentationes Ieremiae. Lugduni, sumptibus Horatii Cardon, 1608. 4°, pp.
230 + index. Donor: Dr John Richardson. Fore-edge: "Delri°/in thr/en."
                                                                       330.2.28
A "memorandum" at the end of the 1637 catalogue includes "Delria in
Threnos" among the eighteen items "missing at the accounts at Easter
1637". The name "M' Johnson" is written in the left margin, indicating his

189

responsibility for the volume. The entire entry was later lined out and the comment added to the right: "in $\overset{e}{y}$ Library at the accounts octob. 26th 1645".

²**3.I(1).25** Ioh de Hay Ap*aratus* in Evang   1622–6
Sixtus, *Senensis* (John de Hay). Apparatus Evangelicus. Duaci, 1611. 4°. Missing.

²**3.I(1).26** Lindani Paraph in Psal   1584–97
Lindanus, Wilhelmus (Willem van der Lindt), *Bp*. Paraphrases in Psalmos Davidicos. Missing. Emmanuel's present copy (Coloniae, 1610) was a Sancroft gift: S17.6.30.

²**3.I(1).27** Tittlemannus in Ep*isto*las   1597–1621
Titelmann, Franz. Elucidatio in omnes Epistolas Apostolicas, quatuordecim Paulinas, & Canonicas septem. [Possibly: Antuerpiae, apud Michaelem Hillenium, 1532. 8°. Adams B1844. Fore-edge (vertically): "Titleman in Epist./Paulin:".   **321.7.58**]

²**3.I(1).28** Isido: Brixianus in Nov: Test   1584–97
Clarius, Isidorus, *Bp of Foligno, ed*. Novi Testamenti vulgata quidem editio. Missing.

²**3.I(1).29** Guilliandus in Ep*isto*las Canon   1584–97
Guilliandus, Claudius. In canonicas Apostolorum septem epistolas. Missing.

²**3.I(1).30** Haymo in Ep*isto*las pauli   1584–97
Haymo, *Bp of Halberstadt*. In divi Pauli epistolas omneis interpretatio. Missing. Emmanuel's present copy (n.p., 1531: Adams H113) was a Sancroft gift: S7.5.18.

Classis 3ᵃᵉ Infer: Sect 2ᵃ

²**3.I(2).1** Zuingeri Theat vitae hum: 10 vol   1622–6
Zwinger, Theodor. Theatri Humanae Vitae. [10 vols.] Basileae, per Eusebium Episcopium, 1586 [*colophon*: 1587]. F°, pp. 4373. Adams Z215. Donor: William Bownest. A MS note on the flyleaf verso of vols. I & X: "Liber Guilielmi Bownest in artibus Baccalaurei, et huius Collegij, scholaris discipuli". All the other volumes bear his signature. Fore-edges: "De a*n*i*m*i Bonis/&c/1"; "De corpo:/ris Bonis/&c/270/2"; "De Fortunae/Bonis &c/.581./3"; "De Habitib*us*/Organicis/Theoricis/Practicis (?)/.1083./4"; "De Prudentia/&[Fortitudine/.1634./5"; "De Temperantia/

190

:2203:/6"; "De Justitia/.2997./7"; "De Meccanicis/habitib*us*/ De Instru-
mentis/fine, loco, et/tempore actionu*m*/humanar*um*/.3623./8"; "De Vita/
Solitaria/Religiosa/Politica./Oeconomica/.4050./.9."; "Index/.10.".

310.2.45–54

²**3.I(2).2**   Ejusd Lat in Arist Eth   1584–97
Zwinger, Theodor. Aristotelis... De moribus ad Nicomachum Libri
Decem. Tabulis perpetuis quae Commentariorum loco esse queant,
explicati & illustrati. Basileae, per Ioan. Oporinum & Eusebium
Epsicopium, [c. 1566.] F°, pp. 40, 338 + index. Adams Z208. Fore-edge:
"ZVINGER/ARIST:/Ethic:/5".   **301.1.59**

²**3.I(2).3**   Pierij Hieroglyphica   1625
Valerianus, Joannes Pierius. Hieroglyphica. Sive De Sacris Aegyptiorum,
Aliarumque Gentium Literis Commentarii... A. Caelio Augustino Curione
duobus Libris aucti. Lugduni, apud Bartholomaeum Honoraty, 1597. F°, ff.
441. Adams V53. Donor: Dr John Richardson. Fore-edge: "Pierij Hierog."
Cover stamped with arms of William Cecil, Lord Burghley.   **305.2.12**

²**3.I(2).4**   Coelius Rhodiginus   1625
Rhodiginus, Ludovicus Coelius. Lectionum Antiquarum Libri Triginta.
Coloniae Allobrogum, excud. Philippus Albertus, 1620. F°, coll.
1720 + index. Donor: Thomas Hanscombe. Missing. Register of Books
Removed, p. 13, 1. 11: "C. Rhodigini lectiones antiquae... Genev: 1620: Mʳ
Hanscomb". One of Emmanuel's present copies ([Franfurt a.M.,] 1599;
Adams R454) was a Sancroft gift: S5.1.30.

²**3.I(2).5**   Wolfij Lectiones memorab: 2 vol   1622–6
Wolf, Johannes. Lectionum memorabilium et reconditarum centenarii
XVI. Lavingae, sumt. autoris impressit Leonhardus Rheinmichel, 1600. F°,
pp. 1012. Missing. Register of Books Removed, p. 47, 1. 24: "Jo: Wolfii
Lectiones memorabiles 2 vol:... Lavinge 1600". Emmanuel's present copy
(Adams W236) was a Sancroft gift: S12.2.38,39.

²**3.I(2).6**   Stuckij Antiquitates conviviales   1622–6
Stuckius, Johannes Gulielmus. Antiquitatum convivialium libri III. Tiguri,
excud. Christophorus Froschoverus, 1582. F°, ff. 397 + index. Missing.
Register of Books Removed, p. 13, 1. 22: "Stuckius de Convivijs... (*Dupl*:
Mʳ Rich)... Tiguri. 1582". Emmanuel's present copy (Adams S1960) was a
Sancroft gift: S5.2.21.

²**3.I(2).7**   Erasmi adagia   1622–6
Erasmus, Desiderius. Adagiorum... Chiliades Quatuor, cum ses-
quicenturia; magna... emendatae & expurgatae. Quibus Adiectae Sunt
Henrici Stephani Animadversiones... His Accesserunt, Appendix ad
Chiliades Erasmi. Coloniae Allobrogum, excud P[etrus] Aubertus, sumpt.

Caldorianae Soc., 1612. F°, coll. 1610 [1616]+index. Donor: Thomas Blosse. Signature on title page: "𝕭losse./ex dono fratris". Covers stamped with gold intials: "TB".   **305.2.34**

²**3.I(2).8**   Ejusdem Epi*sto*lae   1622–6
Erasmus, Desiderius. [Possibly two books bound together:
(1) Opus Epistolarum. Basileae, ex off. Frobeniana, apud H. Frobenium, 1529. F°, pp. 1010+index. Adams E855.
(2) Epistolarum Floridarum Liber unus, antehac nunquam excusus. Basileae, in off. I. Hervagii, 1531. F°, pp. 147. Adams E859.
Fore-edge (vertically): "EPLE. ERAS./EPISTOLE: ERASMI".   **305.3.5**]

²**3.I(2).9**   Polyanthea   1584–97
Nannus, Dominicus, *Mirabellius*, & Amantius, Bartholomaeus. Polyanthea.... Opus Suavissimis Floribus Celebriorum Sententiarum Tam Graecarum Quam Latinarum, Exornatum. [Possibly: Coloniae, apud M. Cholinum, 1567. F°, pp. 1019+index (Emmanuel's copy lacks p. 1019+index). Adams N24.   **306.4.60**]

²**3.I(2).10**   Gyraldi op*era*   1625
Giraldus, Lilius Gregorius. Operum quae extant omnium tomi duo. Basileae, per Thomam Guarinum, 1580. F°, pp. 666, 634. Donor: Thomas Hanscombe. Missing. Register of Books Removed, p. 13, l. 14 "Gr: Gyraldi Opera... Basil: 158... Mʳ Hanscomb." Emmanuel's present copy (Adams G716) was a Sancroft gift: S5.1.37.

Classis: 3ᵃᵉ Infer: Sect 3ᵃ

²**3.I(3).1**   Ioha*nne*s de Ianua Catholicon   1586
Balbus, Johannes, *de Janua*. Summa que vocant catholicon. [Strassburg, the "R" printer, n.d.] F°, 372 unnumbered leaves. Hain 2251; Proctor 246. Donor: William Fleetwood. Signature on first page: "Ex dono W. Fletewoode Recordatoris/London 1586". Fore-edge: "Cathol:". **MSS.2.1.2**

²**3.I(3).2**   Calepinus   1622–6
Calepinus, Ambrosius. Dictionarium undecim linguorum... respondent... latinis Vocabulis hebraica, graeca, gallica, italica, germanica, belgica, hispanica, polonica, ungarica, anglica. Onomasticum... adiunximus. Basileae, per S. Henricpetri, 1605. F°, pp. 1582, 302. Missing. Register of Books Removed, p. 13, l. 3: "Calepini Dictionarium... Basil: 1605". Emmanuel's present copy was a Sancroft gift: S5.1.7.

²**3.I(3).3**   Minsh diction 2 vol   1626–32
(1) Minsheu, John. Ἡγεμὼν εἰς τὰς γλῶσσας, id est, Ductor in Linguas,

The Guide Into Tongues. & Vocabularium Hispanicolatinum Et Anglicum.... A Most Copious Spanish Dictionarie, With Latine and English. Londini, [W. Stansby?] apud Ioannem Browne, 1617. F°. STC 17944. Fore-edge: "Minshaei Dict".   **313.1.70**

(2) Minsheu, John. Emendatio, ... seu Augmentatio sui Ductoris in Linguas, The Guide Into Tongues...in...novem Linguis. London, John Haviland, 1627. F°. STC 17947. Fore-edge: "Min/sheu". **313.1.71**

²**3.I(3).4**   Priscianus   1599

Priscianus, *Caesariensis.* Volume*n* maius cum expositione... Ioannis de Aingre.... eiusdem volume*n* minus: & de duodecim carminibus: ac etiam de acce*n*tibus cu*m* expositione... Danielis Caietani Venetiis, per Bonetum Locatellum, impens. Octaviani Scoti, 1496. F°, ff. 283. Hain 13364; Proctor 5071. Donor: Richard Lister. Inscription on title page: "RICHARDVS: LISTERVS/EMAN: COLLEGIO/DEDIT. ANN: DO: 1599."   **MSS 5.2.18**

²**3.I(3).5**   Dictionariu*m* Latino = Gallic   1584–97

Stephanus, Robertus, *the elder.* Dictionarium Latinogallicum. [Possibly: Lutetiae, ex off. Rob. Stephani, 1544. F°, pp. 731. Adams S1804. **318.4.18**]

²**3.I(3).6**   Noni*us* Marcell*us* et Sext*us* Fest*us* Pompeius et M: Terentius Valla 1622–6

Nonius Marcellus; Festus, Pompeius; and Terentius Varro, Marcus. The works of these three authors were published jointly in some eight different editions between 1480 and 1511. Missing.

²**3.I(3).7**   Dictionarium Latino-Germanicum   1584–97

Missing. Among Emmanuel's present copies of early Latin–German dictionaries are two Sancroft gifts (Petrus Dasypodius, *ed.*, Argentorati, 1540: Adams D139; [Antwerp?, c. 1580]: Adams D417): S5.4.19 and S5.5.29.

²**3.I(3).8**   Smith de pronunct: Ling Anglicae   1584–97

Two books bound together:

(1) Smith, Sir Thomas. De recta & emendata linguae Anglicae scriptione, dialogus. Lutetiae, ex off. Roberti Stephani, 1568. 4°, ff. 44.

(2) Smith, Sir Thomas. De recta & emendata linguae Graecae pro-nuntiatione. Lutetiae, ex off. Roberti Stephani, 1568. 4°, ff. 50 [48].

Missing. Register of Books Removed, p. 13, 1. 44: "Th: Smith de recta scription: Anglicae, & pronuntiat: Graece linguae... Paris: 1568." Emmanuel's present copy (Adams S1313 & S1314) belonged to Sir Walter Mildmay and is among the founder's books: FB.11. However, it was presented to Emmanuel in 1825.

²**3.I(3).9**   Melancthonis Gram lat: 1604–21
Melanchthon, Philipp. Grammatica Latina...Recognita et Locupletata.
Accessit tractatus de Orthographia. Vitebergae, 1569. 8°, pp. 517. Adams
M1153. Donor: Thomas Southaicke. Fore-edge: "melancthon/grammar./
18".   **329.7.94**

BOOKS LOST OR REPLACED, 1597–1637

The following list records all books which, after inclusion on at least one inventory, subsequently disappeared from the collection. Sometimes these books were replaced by new gifts or purchases, and sometimes they were simply lost. The listing follows chronological groupings, first showing books which appeared only on the earliest inventory. The first line in each entry is an exact transcription of the way the book was listed on the final inventory on which it appeared. The date of that inventory and the location on it are listed to the left of this transcription. At the right-hand side of the entry, as in all the items on the 1637 catalogue, is the date, or period, of acquisition. Where possible, we have suggested items on the 1637 catalogue which replaced the books removed, giving the full 1637 catalogue location. Because the evidence for identification of missing items is necessarily scanty, we have not made guesses about the particulars of dates and places of publication, but have named just authors and titles where possible. Where different inventories provide complementary information, we quote an earlier as well as the latest inventory to indicate more fully the basis for our identification.

Books lost or replaced between c. 1597 and 1621

Final catalogue location		Acquired
1597.4	Biblia Lat. in fol.	1584–97
1597.22	Observationes hebr in pentateuchen.	1584–97
1597.30	Gerardus de Iudaicis disciplinus Veltuyck, Gerard. Itinera deserti. De Iudaicis disciplinis.	1584–97
1597.31	Vatablus in psal. Vatablus, Franciscus, *annot.* Liber Psalmorum Davidis.	1584–97
1597.47	Collectaneum de Tropis Script. [also 1597.369] Westhemer, Bartholomaeus. Collectanea troporum, Sacrae Scripturae candidatis utilissima.	1584–97
1597.62	Theod. Lat in duobus Tomis. Theodoretus, *Bp of Cyrus.* Opera in duos tomos distincta.	1584–97

1597.76	Bedae opera in omnes canon: libros. Bede, *the Venerable*, *St.* [Possibly: In septem epistolas canonicas Commentaria.]	1584–97
1597.94	Bonaventura 2. Vol. super sent. Bonaventure, *St.* Commentary on the sentences of Peter Lombard.	1584–97
1597.105	Brentius in Levitt. Brenz, Johannes. In Leviticum.	1584–97
1597.106	Ecclastica hystoria Alberti Crantij Crantz, Albert. Ecclesiastica historia, sive Metropolis. [Replaced by 1637.6.2.7]	1584–97
1597.108	Eucherius in Genes: lib Regum &c. Eucherius, *Bp. of Lyon.* Commentarii in Genesim, & libros Regum.	1584–97
1597.114	Philippus presbyter in Iob. Philippus, *Presbyter.* In historiam Iob.	1584–97
1597.117	Sacrae Ceremoniae [Possibly: Piccolomini, Agostino Patrizio. Rituum ecclesiasticorum sive sacrarum cerimoniarum s.s. Romanae ecclesiae.] [Possibly replaced by 1637.6.2.4]	1584–97
1597.126	Dryedo de ecclasticis script & dogma Driedo, Johannes. De ecclesiasticis scripturis & dogmatibus.	1584–97
1597.138	Bucerus in Epist. Bucer, Martin. [Possibly: Metaphrases et enarrationes epistolarum D. Pauli tomus primus.] [Possibly replaced by 1637.8.S.18]	1584–97
1597.143	Petrus Martyr de Eucharist. Martyr, Peter, *Vermilius.* [Possibly: Defensio Doctrinae Veteris et Apostolicae De Sacrosancto Eucharistiae Sacramento.] [Replaced by 1637.5.I.12]	1584–97
1597.144	Musculus super Psalm: Musculus, Wolfgang. In Psalterium commentarij.	1584–97
1597.151	Zanchius de divinis attribut. Zanchius, Hieronymus. De natura dei, seu de divinis attributis, libri V. [Replaced by the Zanchius Opera: 1637.5.I.14]	1584–97
1597.154	[Musculus] Loci communes Musculus, Wolfgang. Loci communes Sacrae theologiae.	1584–97
1597.169	Herodotus Lat [Wanting 1610.5.S.5: "Herod. hist:"] Herodotus. Historia. [Lat.]	1584–97

1597.176	Selecte Orationes.	1584–97
1597.178	[Appianus] Latine. [Wanting 1610.5.S.9: "Appian. Lat."] Appianus, *of Alexandria.* [Possibly: De bellis civilibus Romanorum.]	1584–97
1597.182	Iulius Solinus [Wanting 1610.5.I.19: "Solinus de rebus mirab."] Solinus, Gaius Julius. Solinus de mirabilibus mundi.	1584–97
1597.193	Onufrius. Panvinius, Onuphrius. [Possibly replaced by either 1637.6.5.7 or ²1637.2.S(3)17]	1584–97
1597.194	Novus orbis per Columbum & Paulum Venetum. Two books bound together: (1) Grynaeus, Simon, *ed.* Novus Orbis. (2) Paulus, *Venetus.* [Unknown]. [Replaced by 1637.7.2.13]	1584–97
1597.200	Scapulae Lexicon Scapula, Johannes. Lexicon graecolatinum novum.	1584–97
1597.201	Ulpianus in Olynthiacas & Philipp: Demosthenis [Wanting 1610.5.S.21: "Vlpian. Com. in Olyn: & Philip Dem:"] Ulpian, *the Rhetorician.* Commentarioli in Olynthiacas, Philippicasq Demosthenis orationes. [Gk]	1584 97
1597.203	Iohannes de Sacrobosco manuscript [Wanting 1610.5.I.24: "Ioh. de sacro: de sphaera. M.S."] [See T. James, p. 137, Vol. 9: "*Io. de sacro Bosco de Sphaera.* Transcriptum exemplar quo nihil elegantius."] John, *de Sacrobosco* (Holywood). De sphaera mundi. Ms.	1584–97
1597.207	Polytica graeca. [Wanting 1610.5.I.8: "Arist. polit. graec."] Aristotle Politica. [Gk]	1584–97
1597.208	Sophocles gr. [Wanting 1610.5.S.18: "Soph. Trag: graec."] Sophocles. Tragediae. [Gk]	1584–97
1597.209	Turnebus. Turnebus, Adrianus.	1584–97
1597.210	Iovij 12 vicecomites. [1610.1.I.25: "Iovij Vitae 12 vic. com: Med. pr."] Giovio, Paolo, *Bp of Nocera.* Vitae duodecim Vicecomitum Mediolani Principum.	1584–97

1597.212	Ovidij Epist cum Com: Badij [1610.5.S.25: "Ovid. Epl. cum. Com:"] Ovid. Heroidum Epistolae [with a commentary by Jodocus Badius, *Ascensius*].	1584–97
1597.213	cosmographia Appiani. Apianus, Petrus. Cosmographia. [Possibly replaced by 1637.7.2.18]	1584–97
1597.216	Osorius de nobilitate. [Wanting 1610.5.S.29: "Ozorij Lib. de nobil: civil:"] Osorius, Hieronymus, *Bp of Silves*. De Nobilitate Civili et Christiana.	1584–97
1597.220	Clenardi gram gr. Clenardus, Nicolaus. Institutiones in linguam Graecam.	1584–97
1597.221	Platonis Phaedo graecolat. [Wanting 1610.5.I.9: "Platonis Phaed. graecol."] Plato. Phaedo. [Gk & Lat.] [*Tr.* Marsilio Ficino.]	1584–97
1597.222	Aesopi fabulae gr. Stephanus. [Wanting 5.I.10: "Aesopi vit. & fab. graec."] Aesop. Vita & fabulae. [Gk]	1584–97
1597.228	Sleidani Com: in oct. [Wanting 1610.1.I.29: "Io: Sleid. de statu reip: & relig"] Sleidan, Johann. De statu religionis et republicae.	1584–97
1597.232	Oecolampadius in Aesaiam. Oecolampadius, Johannes. In Iesaiam prophetam.	1584–97
1597.233	[Oecolampadius] In Ezechielem. Oecolampadius, Johannes. In prophetam Ezechielem commentarius.	1584–97
1597.234	[Oecolampadius] In Danielem. Oecolampadius, Johannes. In Danielem prophetam libri duo.	1584–97
1597.235	Bedrotes contra imagines Strasburg, *Preachers*. Non esse ferendas in templis Christianorum imagines et statuas. Autoribus Ecclesiasticis Argentoraten [i.e. Martin Bucer]. Iacobo Bedroto interprete.	1584–97
1597.236	Zuinglius ad Lutherum. Zwingli, Ulrich. Amica exegesis, id est, expositio eucharistiae negocii, ad Martinum Lutherum.	1584–97
1597.237	Lutherus de 10. praecept & potest. papae [Two books probably bound together:] (1) Luther, Martin. Decem Praecepta Wittenbergensi praedicata populo.	1584–97

(2) Luther, Martin. Resolutio Lutheriana Super Propositione Sua Decima Tertia, De Potestate Papae.
[Replaced by 1637.2.S.1]

1597.239	Erasmi Enchyridia.	1584–97
	Erasmus, Desiderius. Enchiridion Militis Christiani.	
1597.242	Oecolamp. de Euchar.	1584–97
	Oecolampadius, Johannes. [Possibly: De genuina verborum Domini, Hoc est corpus meum, iuxta vetustissimos authores, expositione liber.]	
1597.243	Luth: sup 5um 6.7. capita Math.	1584–97
	Luther, Martin. Enarrationes Doctissimae in Quintum, Sextum, & Septimum capita Matthaei. [Replaced by 1637.2.S.1]	
1597.245	Luther in psal. 21	1584–97
	Luther, Martin. Lucubrationes in Psalmum XXI. [Replaced by 1637.2.S.1]	
1597.246	Petrus Mart de Sacram:	1584–97
	Martyr, Peter, Vermilius. [Possibly: Tractatio de sacramento eucharistiae, habita in celeberrima universitate Oxoniensi.] [Replaced by 1637.5.I.12]	
1597.249	Luth. de abroganda Missa	1584–97
	Luther, Martin. De abroganda missa privata Martini Lutheri Sententia. [Replaced by 1637.2.S.1]	
1597.251	Luth. de ordine Episcoporum	1584–97
	Luther, Martin. Adversus falso nominatum ordinem episcoporum libellus. [Replaced by 1637.2.S.1]	
1597.267	Brentius de providentia	1584–97
	Brenz, Johannes. (?)	
1597.269	A. Com: backing the Turke cause.	1584–97
	[Possibly: Cambini, Andrea. Two very notable commentaries, of the original of the Turks....]	
1597.272	Maurus de clericorum Institut.	1584–97
	[Wanting 1610.3.S.26: "Rab. Mau. de cler. instit."] Rabanus Maurus, Abp of Mainz. De clericorum institutione & ceremonijs ecclesiae, ex Veteri & Novo Testamento.	
1597.273	Octavius.	1584–97
	Minucius Felix, Marcus. Octavius.	
1597.274	Rivius de erroribus pontificorum	1584–97
	[Wanting 1610.4.S.39: "Rivij lib. de erroribus pontif."]	

Rivius, Johannes. De erroribus pontificorum, seu de abusibus ecclesiasticis.

1597.276	Defensio doctrinae Christianae.	1584–97
1597.278	Pereius de tradit Ecclesiae Perez de Ayala, Martin, *Abp of Valentia*. De divinis apostolicis, atque ecclesiasticis traditionibus.	1584–97
1597.279	Rupertus. Rupertus, *Abbot of Deutz*.	1584–97
1597.281	Erasmus Chatech. Erasmus, Desiderius. Catechismus.	1584–97
1597.283	Apologia pro Luper.	1584–97
1597.284	Nicholaus Hannacus. [Possibly: Nicolas Hanapus, *Patriarch of Jerusalem*. Exempla sacrae scripturae ex utroque testamento.]	1584–97
1597.285	Historia de Turcis.	1584–97
1597.288	Erasmus de matrimoniae Christiano Erasmus, Desiderius. Christiani matrimonii institutio.	1584–97
1597.290	Luther in Hoseam. Luther, Martin. In Hoseam Prophetam... Enarratio. [Replaced by 1637.2.S.1]	1584–97
1597.291	Concivnculae Lutheri. Luther, Martin [either: Conciunculae Quaedam in deiparae virgini et aliquot Divis festos dies; or: Conciunculae quaedam amico cuidam praescriptae.] [Replaced by 1637.2.S.1]	1584–97
1597.294	Margarita Theologica Spangenberg, Johann. Margarita Theologica.	1584–97
1597.296	Loci Communes Melancthoni [Wanting 1610.4.S.41: "Melancth: Loc. com."] Melanchthon, Philipp. Loci Communes Theologici. [Replaced by 1637.2.S.2]	1584–97
1597.298	Chatechismus Lucae Lossij. Loss, Lucas. Catechismus, hoc est, Christianae Methodus.	1584–97
1597.300	Euthymius in psalm. [Wanting 1610.7.S.33: "Euthym: in Psal:"] Euthymius, *Zigabenus*. Commentationes in omnes Psalmos.	1584–97
1597.304	Lutheri praelectiones in 15. psal. graduum Luther, Martin. In Quindecim Psalmos Graduum Commentarij. [Replaced by 1637.2.S.1]	1584–97

1597.305	[Luther] summaria in psal. & annot. in Ecclesiasten Two works bound together: (1) Luther, Martin. Summaria in Psalmos Davidis. (2) Luther, Martin, annot. Ecclesiastes Solomonis. [Replaced by 1637.2.S.1]	1584–97
1597.307	Lutherus in Epistolas & Evang: Tom. 1. Luther, Martin. Primus Tomus Enarrationum in Epistolas & Evangelia. [Replaced by 1637.2.S.1]	1584–97
1597.308	Oecolamp: in psal. cum Bulling. αποδειξει verae religionis Two books bound together: (1) Oecolampadius, Johannes, comm. Liber Psalmorum Davidis cum catholica expositione Ecclesiastica. (2) Bullinger, Heinrich. Antiquissima fides et Vera Religio.... Heinrychi Bullingeri Apodixis, sive clara & evidens demonstratio.	1584–97
1597.315	Haepinus in psal. 19. Aepinus, Johannes. Commentarius in Psalmum XIX.	1584–97
1597.316	Franciscus Lambert in Lucam [Wanting 1610.4.I.47: "Lambert in Lucam"] Lambert, Francois, of Avignon. In Divi Lucae Evangelium commentarij.	1584–97
1597.317	Luther in psal. 51. Luther, Martin. Enarratio Psalmorum LI. Misere mei Deus, & CXXX. De profundis clamavi. [Replaced by 1637.2.S.1]	1584–97
1597.318	Melancthon in Evang: dominical Melanchthon, Philipp. Explicationum... in Evangelia Dominicalia. [Replaced by 1637.2.S.2]	1584–97
1597.322	Calvini Institut. [Wanting 1610.4.S.36: "Calv. Instit:"] Calvin, John. Institutio christianae religionis. [Replaced by 1637.5.S.1]	1584–97
1597.323	Opera Maroti Gall: [Wanting 1610.5.I.30: "Clem. Marot. Epistolae] Marot, Clement.	1584–97
1597.324	Pauli Beroti histor Iudaica Berotus, Paulus(?). Historia Iudaica.	1584–97
1597.325	Erasm: de sarcienda Ecclesiae Concordia Erasmus, Desiderius. Liber de sarcienda ecclesia concordia.	1584–97

1597.330	Alardi Selectae Epist. Alardus *of Amsterdam*. [Possibly: selectae aliquot similitudines.]	1584–97
1597.331	Melancthon in Romanos. Melanchthon, Philipp. Commentarii in Epistolam Pauli ad Romanos. [Replaced by 1637.2.S.2]	1584–97
1597.333	Lutheri annot in Deut. Luther, Martin, *annot*. Deuteronomion Mose. [Replaced by 1637.2.S.1]	1584–97
1597.336	Melancthon ad Colloss. Melanchthon, Philipp. Scholia in Epistolam Pauli ad Colossenses. [Replaced by 1637.2.S.2]	1584–97
1597.338	Lutherus ad Galat. Luther, Martin. In Epistolam Pauli ad Galatas... commentarius. [Replaced by 1637.2.S.1]	1584–97
1597.341	Bucerus ad Ephes: Bucer, Martin. Praelectiones in epistolam ad Ephesios. [Replaced by 1637.8.S.18]	1584–97
1597.350	Lutheri Homiliae In .1. ad Cor: 15. Luther, Martin. Homiliae Christianissimae et lectu dignissimae in decimum quintum caput prioris epistolae divi Pauli ad Corinthios de resurrectione mortuor(um). [Replaced by 1637.2.S.1]	1584–97
1597.352	Selectae Orationes Melancthonis Melanchthon, Philipp. Selectae Declamationes.	1584–97
1597.356	Sarcerij Rhetorica. Sarcerius, Erasmus. Rhetorica plena ac referta exemplis.	1584–97
1597.357	Lutherus de Sublimiori mundi potestate Luther, Martin. De Sublimiore Mundi Potestate... Liber. [Replaced by 1637.2.S.1]	1584–97
1597.360	Fulconis *R*esponsio ad Stapeltonu*m* [Wanting 1610.5.S.34: "Fulk against staplet. Lat."] Fulke, William. Ad Thomae Stapletoni... Controversiarum cavillationes & calumnias... G. Fulconis... responsio.	1584–97
1597.369	Tropi scripturae p*er* Westemeru*m* [also 1597.47] Westhemer, Bartholomaeus. Collectanea troporum, Sacrae Scripturae candidatis utilissima.	1584–97
1597.383	Hier biblia in 5 vol. in 16. Bible [Lat.] Vulgate. 16°. 5 vols.	1584–97

1597.384	Calvini cronica gallice.	1584–97
1597.392	Decreta Burchardi	1584–97
	[Wanting 1610.3.S.24: "Burchardi decreta"]	
	Burchardus, *Bp of Worms.* Decretorum libri XX.	

Books permanently lost or replaced between c. 1597 and 1610

Final catalogue location		Acquired
Wanting 1610.1.S.35	Liber psalm. cum Annot. Steph:	1597–1610
	Stephanus, Henricus, *annot.* Liber Psalmorum Davidis.	
Wanting 1610.4.I.27	Lutheri Apol: a Thed. impre dam:	1597–1610

Books permanently lost or replaced between 1621 and 1622

Final catalogue location		Acquired
1621.2.S.26	[crossed out:] Κυρον Θεοδόρου τοῦ προδρόμου.	1584–97
	[Wanting 1610.7.S.30: "Cyri Theod. Epigr. graec."]	
	Theodorus, Cyrus, Prodromus. Epigrammata. [Gk]	
1621.7.S.23	Bernardus Cantabrig: de vera tranquil.	1584–97
	Bernard, John. Oratio ... de vera animi tranquilitate.	

Books permanently lost or replaced between 1622 and 1626

Final catalogue location		Acquired
1622.1.S.19	Zachariae Chrisopolitanj de concordia Evang	1584–97
	Zacharias, *Bp of Chrysopolis.* In unum ex quatuor sive	
	de concordia evangelistarum, libri quatuor.	
	[Replaced by [2]1637.3.I(1)9]	
1622.1.I.3	Nicephorj histor Ecclesiast	1584–97
	Nicephorus Callistus. Historia Ecclesiastica. [Lat.]	

1622.1.I.9	Chronica Sebastianj Francj Mordens Belgice. Franck, Sebastian. Chronicazeitbüch vund Geschichtbibell.	1597–1621
1622.1.I.13	Bedae Ecclesiast. Histor. Anglic. Bede, *St, The Venerable. Historia Ecclesiastica Gentis Anglorum.* [Replaced by ²1637.2.S(1).9]	1584–97
1622.2.S.7	Proverb. Solom. cu*m* annotat. Munsterj: Bible, Proverbs. [Heb.] Proverbia Salomonis. [*Tr. & Annot. Sebastian Munster.*]	1584–97
1622.2.S.8	Tridecim articulj fidej Iudaeoru*m* [1597.39: "Iosephus de artic fidei Iudaeoru*m* in oct."] Maimonides, Moses. Tredecim articuli fidei Iudaeorum. [Includes the compendium historiarum of Joseph Ben Gorion.] [Heb. & Lat.] [*Ed.* Sebastian Munster.] 8°. Vuormaciae, apud P. Schoefer, 1529.	1584–97
1622.2.S.21	Diction. Chald: Eliae Levitae. [On the c. 1597 list, 1597.19 "Lexicon Chaldaicu*m*" is yoked with 1597.20 "Thargu*m* .1. Chaldaica Paraphrasis in Bibl."] Two books bound together: (1) Elias, *Levita.* Lexicon Chaldaicum. (2) Bible, Pentateuch. [Aramaic] Targum.	1584–97
1622.2.S.22	Luther*us* in Genesin. Luther, Martin. [Probably: In Genesin enarrationum ... tomus secundus (–quartus).]	1584–97
1622.2.S.27A	Marcus Heremita &c [1621.2.S.29: "Marcus Heremita & Hesichij presbyter centur. Lat."] Marcus, *St, Eremita.* Opuscula quaedam Theologica [also contains Hesychius Presbyter, centuriae duae (ad Theodulu*m*)]. [Replaced by ²1637.1.I.41]	1584–97
1622.2.I.4	Chrysostom. Tom. 1*us* in Vetus Testam: Lat. John, *Chrysostom, St.* Opera. [Lat.] vol. 1 of 5.	1584–97
1622.2.I.5	Chrysost: Tom. 2*us* in Mat: Marc: Luc: Lat. John, *Chrysostom, St.* Opera. [Lat.] vol. 2 of 5.	1584–97
1622.2.I.6	Chrysostom: Tom*us* 3*us* in Ioh: & acta Apost. John, *Chrysostom, St.* Opera [Lat.] Vol. 3 of 5.	1584–97
1622.2.I.7	Chrysost. Tom. 4*us* in Paulj Ep*isto*las John, *Chrysostom, St.* Opera [Lat.] Vol. 4 of 5.	1584–97
1622.2.I.8	Chrysost: Tom 5*us* Lat John, *Chrysostom, St.* Opera. [Lat.] Vol. 5 of 5.	1584–97
1622.2.I.10	Epiphani*us*: contra Haereses	1584–97

Epiphanius, St, *Bp of Salamis*. Contra octoaginta haereses opus. [Lat.]
[Replaced by ²1637.1.S.18]

1622.2.I.14	Theophilact. in 4ᵒʳ Evang: Lat. Theophylactus, *Abp of Ochrida*. In quatuor Evangelia enarrationes. [Lat.] [*Tr*. Iohannes Oecolampadius.]	1584–97
1622.3.S.8	Operae Bedae Bede, *St, The Venerable*. Opera. [Replaced by ²1637.2.S(1).9]	1597–1621
1622.3.S.9	Beda de Temporum ratione Bede, *St, The Venerable*. Opuscula complura de tem- porum ratione. [Replaced by ²1637.2.S(1).9]	1584–97
1622.3.S.11	Thomae Theolog: 2: Volˢ. [1597.92: "Thomae Summa summarum 2. vol] Aquinas, Thomas, *St*. Summa Theologica. 2 vols. [Replaced by ²1637.2.S(2).1]	1584–97
1622.3.S.12	Thomas in 4: Evang: [1597.89: "Thomas in Evang: & Epist."] Aquinas, Thomas, *St*. Catena aurea in quatuor evan- gelia & commentaria in Epistolas Pauli. [Replaced by ²1637.2.S(2).1]	1584–97
1622.3.S.13	Thomas super Sentent. Aquinas, Thomas, *St*. Super libris sententiarum Petri Lombardi. [Replaced by ²1637.2.S(2).1]	1584–97
1622.3.S.14	Thomas contra Gentiles. Aquinas, Thomas, *St*. Summa Contra Gentiles. [Replaced by ²1637.2.S(2).1]	1584–97
1622.3.S.19	Bonaventure in Luc. 2. vols Bonaventure, *St*. In secundum Lucam evangelium commentarij. [Replaced by ²1637.2.I(2).1]	1584–97
1622.3.I.4	Iohann. Clinaris.	1621–2
1622.4.S.5	Dionis: de caelestj Hierarchia. Dionysius, *The Pseudo-Areopagite*. De coelesti hierarchia.	1584–97
1622.4.S.12	Dreidonius de Libertate Christiana. Driedo, Johannes. De libertate Christiana. [Replaced by ²1637.2.I(3).14]	1584–97
1622.5.S.20	[crossed out:] Lactantius Graec. [inserted after the deletion: "Theophylact Graec"]	1622
1622.6.I.12	Chemnitij Locj Theolog: Chemnitz, Martin. Loci Theologici. [Replaced by 1637.2.S.5]	1584–97

1622.7.S.1	Musculus in Iohann Musculus, Wolfgang. Commentarii in evangelium Ioannis.	1584–97
1622.8.S.2	Thucidides de bello Pellop. Gr. Lat. Thucydides. De bello Peloponnesiaco. [Gk & Lat.]	1584–97
1622.8.S.15	πλανύδες Gr: M: S: Planudes, Maximus. A Greek manuscript.	1597–1621
1622.8.S.18	Budaej Comment. Linguae Graec. Budaeus, Gulielmus. Commentarii linguae Graecae.	1584–97
1622.8.I.2	Aristotelis opera Lat. Aristotle. Opera. [Lat.] [Replaced by 1637.9.S.2]	1584–97 1584–97
1622.8.I.7	Ethica Aristotelis Gr. Aristotle. Ethica. [Gk] [Replaced by 1637.9.S.2]	
1622.8.I.14	Strabo de Situ Orbis. Gr. Strabo. De situ orbis. [Gk]	1584–97
1622.8.I.20	[crossed out:] Finaej Geograph [Possibly: Finé, Oronce. De mundi sphaera.]	1622
1622.9.S.5	Magister Sententiarum Petrus, Lombardus. Sententiarum libri quatuor.	1584–97
1622.9.I.2	Decretales Greg: 9 Pontif: Vol: 1um Gregory IX, Pope. Epistolae Decretales.	1584–97
1622.9.I.3	Decretales Bonifac. 8. Vol: 2um Boniface VIII, Pope. Sextus decretalium liber. [This is volume 2 of a set with 1622.9.I.2.]	1584–97

Books lost or replaced between 1626 and 1628

Final catalogue location		Acquired
1626.1.I.15	[crossed out:] Reuchlin de arte Caballist: Reuchlin, Johann. De arte cabalistica.	1622–6
1626.2.I.37A	Mercatorij Tab. Gall. Mercator, Gerard. Galliae tabule, geographicae.	1597–1621

Books lost or replaced between 1628 and 1632

Final catalogue location		Acquired
1628.3.I.5	[crossed out:] Aretius in Psalm. [Possibly: Bucer, Martin (pseud. Aretius Felinus), ed.	1584–97

Sacrorum Psalmorum libri quinque.]
[Possibly replaced sometime before 1626 by 1637.8.S.16]
Note: The 1597.107 entry "Philinus super Psalm" is probably the same book.

1628.7.3.15	[crossed out:] Trithemius de Scriptoribus Eccles. Trithemius, Johannes. De scriptoribus ecclesiasticis.	1622–6
1628.7.3.16	[crossed out:] Ejusdem Epistolae Trithemius, Johannes. Epistolarum familiarum libri duo.	1622–6
1628.8.3.11	[crossed out:] Lipsius de milit: Rom. Lipsius, Justus. De militia Romana libri quinque: commentarius ad Polybium.	1622–6
1628.8.3.12	[crossed out:] Idem de cruce Lipsius, Justus. De cruce libri tres.	1622–6
1628.8.3.13	Ejusdem epistolae selectae Lipsius, Justus. Epistolarum selectarum centuria prima.	1622–6
1628.8.3.14	[crossed out:] Staplet de magn. Eccles. Rom. & Lip Vir. Hal Two books bound together: (1) Stapleton, Thomas. Vere admiranda, seu, de magnitudine Romanae ecclesiae Libri duo. (2) Lipsius, Justus. Diva Virgo Hallensis, beneficia ejus et miracula.	1622–6
1628.10.S.17A	[in right margin:] Averr: pars. Theodor. Peta. de Hoem [?]	1626–8

Books listed as "new bought" at the end of the 1626 list, lost or replaced sometime before 1632

Final catalogue location		Acquired
NEW 23	Mosche Misnacorum	1626–32
NEW 42	Cusani pars Nicholas, of Cusa. [Possibly one volume of ²1637.2.S(3).12 temporarily misplaced among the "new bought" books]	1626–32
NEW 49	Isidori Epistolarum lib 5us Isidore, St, of Pelusium. De interpretatione Divinae Scripturae epistolarum.	1622–6

There is no evidence of any book being lost, removed or replaced between 1632 and 1637.

APPENDIX: DONORS 1584–1637

* before a name indicates that the book(s) contain only a signature. Others contain more definite statements that the books were indeed donations.
** indicates that the book(s) donated are no longer present.

Date	Donor	Cash amount	Items donated	Vols.	Connection with Emmanuel
1584 (?)	*Sir Walter Mildmay		12	12	Founder.
1584 (?)	*Richard Culverwell		5	5	Probably the brother-in-law of Laurence Chaderton. Early benefactor.
1584–90 (?)	Richard Ashton	£13.6s 8d "ad Bibliothecam ornandam"			Early benefactor.
1584–97	George Bishop		5	5	London bookseller and printer; Warden and Master, Stationers' Company. No apparent connection.
	*Hugh Broughton		1	1	No apparent connection.
	*Robert Cronkar		2	2	No apparent connection.
	*Edward Leeds		3	6	Early benefactor. Died Feb. 17, 1589.
	*John Leeds		1	2	No apparent connection.
	John Meredith		1	1	No apparent connection.
	*Thomas Ughtred		1	1	No apparent connection.
	*Thomas White		1	5	Admitted 1596, B.A. 1600–1; M.A. 1604; Fellow 1603; died 1606.
	*John Wickliffe		1	1	No apparent connection.
1586	*William Fleetwood		3	3	Recorder of London. No apparent connection.
1597	George Barcroft		1	1	No apparent connection.
1597–1621	William Bedell		2	4	Matric. 1584–5; B.A. 1588–9; M.A. 1592; B.D. 1599; Fellow 1593.
	John Glanville		1	1	Matric. 1587; B.A. (?1591–2); M.A. 1595.

Date	Donor	Cash amount	Items donated	Vols.	Connection with Emmanuel
1598	Samuel Wright		1	1	Admitted 1587. B.A. 1590–1; M.A. 1594.
	Thomas Crocus		1	1	No apparent connection.
	*John Bingham		1	1	No apparent connection.
c. 1598	**Laurence Chaderton		1	2	First Master, 1584–1622.
	*John, first Baron Lumley		16	25	No apparent connection.
1599	Richard Lister		3	3	B.A. 1588–9; M.A. 1592; Fellow c. 1593.
1600	Ralph Cudworth		4	4	Matric. 1588–9; B.A. 1592–3; M.A. 1596; B.D. 1603; D.D. 1619; Fellow until 1609.
1600–21	Thomas Bywater		3	3	No apparent connection.
	Samuel Starlinge		1	1	Admitted 1589; B.A. 1593–4; M.A. 1597; B.D. 1603–4; Fellow c. 1596.
1601	John Newcourt		1	1	No apparent connection.
1604	Thomas Pickering		1	2	Admitted 1589; B.A. 1592–3; M.A. 1596; B.D. 1603; Fellow 1596. Died 1625.
1605–21	Thomas Southaicke		18	45	No apparent connection.
c. 1607	"Mr. Shipton" (John?)		?	?	Matric. 1604; B.A. 1607–8; M.A. 1611.
1609	Samuel Ward		1	1	B.D. 1603; Fellow 1595.
1611	Joseph Alliston		1	1	Matric. c. 1595; B.A. 1598–9; M.A. 1602; B.D. 1609; Fellow 1601–11.
1611–21	**Anthony Sawbridge		1	2	No apparent connection.
1612	John Cotton		1	1	M.A. 1606; B.D. 1613; Fellow 1606.
1613	Laurence Wright		1	1	Admitted 1606: B.A. 1609–10; M.A.1613.
	*John White		1	1	No apparent connection.
1614	Samuel Bisse		1	1	No apparent connection.
1616	Robert Booth		4	4	M.A. 1610; Fellow 1609.
1617–32	Thomas James		1	1	Matric. 1611; B.A. 1614–15; M.A. 1618.

210

1619	William Branthwaite	12	17		M.A. 1586; B.D. 1593; D.D. 1598; Fellow 1585–1607.
	William Sandcroft	1	2		Admitted 1596; B.A. 1600–1; M.A. 1604; B.D. 1611; D.D. 1629; Fellow 1604–16; Master 1628–37.
1619–21	John Foxcroft	1	1		Matric. 1611; B.A.1614–15.
1621–2	*Elias Travers				B.A. 1604–5; M.A. 1608; B.D. 1615; D.D. 1620; Fellow 1609–21. Nephew of Walter Travers who was a friend of Laurence Chaderton and an early benefactor.
1622–6	*Richard Baitmann	1	1		No apparent connection.
	*Thomas Blosse	1	1		Matric. 1612.
	William Bownest	1	10		Matric. 1617; B.A. 1620–1.
	*Robert Huicci	1	1		No apparent connection.
	Nicholas Morton	1	2		Admitted 1612; B.A. 1615/16; M.A. 1619; Dixie Fellow.
1623	Walter Rawly	1	1		No apparent connection.
	*M. Tompson	1	1		No apparent connection.
	Lawrence Howlett	1	1		Migrated from Sidney Sussex, 1607; B.A. 1608–9; M.A. 1612; B.D. 1619; Fellow 1613–21. Died 1626.
1625	Thomas Hanscombe	17	28		Migrated from Trinity to Emm., 1614; B.A. 1616–17; M.A. 1620; Fellow 1620. Died 1625.
	John Richardson	136	172	£120	M.A. 1585; B.D. 1592; D.D. 1597; Fellow 1585.
1626–32	Elias Pettit	5	6		Admitted 1619; B.A. 1622–3; M.A. 1626. Died 1634.
	*John Smith	1	1		Not definitely identified; four John Smiths

Date	Donor	Cash amount	Items donated	Vols.	Connection with Emmanuel
					matriculated at Emmanuel before 1632. One of these was admitted 1595; B.A. 1598–99. Died 1632.
1627	Richard Hunt		1	2	Admitted 1610; B.A. 1613–14; M.A. 1617; Fellow 1618; B.D. 1624; *or:* B.A. 1624.
	John Stoughton		1	9	Admitted 1607; B.A. 1610–11; M.A. 1614; B.D. 1621; D.D. 1626; Fellow 1616.
1628, 1629	Thomas Ball		3	4	M.A. 1625; Fellow 1625.
1628–32	Henry Featherstone		1	4	London bookseller. No apparent connection.
1630	Anthony Tuckney		2	2	Admitted 1613; B.A. 1616–17; M.A. 1620. Elected Fellow 1619, but became chaplain to Earl of Lincoln first. Returned, and for 10 years a tutor. B.D. 1627. Cousin of John Cotton.
1631–32	John Poole		1	1	Admitted 1624; B.A. 1627–8; M.A. 1631.
1632	John Crossly		1	1	Matric. 1624; B.A. 1627–8; M.A. 1631.
1633	Nicholas Preston		1	1	Admitted 1625; B.A. 1628–9; M.A. 1632; B.D. 1639; D.D. 1661.
1636–37	Edward Thornton		5	5	Admitted 1624–5; B.A. 1628–9; M.A. 1632. Died 1635.

INDEX

Barletius, Marinus 100
Barlow, William 26, 128
Barnes, Robert 121
Baronius, Caesar 84, 92, 96, 170
Baruch, Moses ben, *Almosnino* 60
Basil, *St, the Great* 17, 143, 148
Bayly, Thomas 75
Baynes, Ralph 58
Becanus, Martinus 76
Bede, *The Venerable* 78, 79, 157, 196, 204, 205
Bedell, William 3, 23, 24, 33 (n56), 66, 94, 209
Bedrotus, Jacobus 198
Bellarminus, Robertus, *Card.* 26, 73, 75, 84, 94, 125, 126, 127, 128, 170, 175
Beni, Paolo 170
Benius, Jacobus 170
Benzoni, Rutilio 182
Bernard, *Abbot of Clairvaux* 157
Bernard, John 203
Beroaldus, Matthaeus 98
Berotus, Paulus 201
Bertinoro, Obadiah 61
Bertius, Petrus 125
Bertramus, B. Cornelius 56
Beza, Theodore 10, 19, 54, 82, 83, 84
Bible, Arabic 55
Bible, Aramaic 59, 204
Bible, Chaldaic 53, 55
Bible, English 54, 171, 186
Bible, French 53
Bible, German 56
Bible, Greek 53, 54, 55, 56, 66, 77
Bible, Hebrew 53, 54, 55, 56, 57, 59, 60, 62, 204
Bible, Irish 55
Bible, Latin 53, 54, 55, 57, 62, 66, 76, 79, 80, 81, 85, 95, 177, 195, 202
Bible, Polyglot 53, 54, 55, 57
Bible, Syriac 53
Bibles, mentioned, 10, 13, 16, 18, 19, 21, 22, 24, 25, 31, 32 (n47), 48
Bibliander, Theodorus 64, 86
Biel, Gabriel 167, 173
Billick, Everhard 6, 174
Bilson, Thomas, *Bp* 124, 127
Bingham, John 110, 210
Binius, Severinus 146
Bion, *of Smyrna* 137
Bishop, George 22, 23, 209
Bisse, Samuel 84, 210
Bizzarus, Petrus 100
Blackwell, George 129

Blage, Thomas 187
Blanchis, Paulus de 26, 159
Blond, Jean le 115
Blosse, Thomas 192, 211
Bochellus, Laurentius 147
Bodin, Jean 117
Bodius, Hermannus 7, 154
Bodleian Library 14, 74
Boethius, Anicius 138, 179
Bolzanius, Urbanus 186
Bomberg, Daniel 22, 53–4
Bonaventure, *St* 164, 166, 196, 205
Boniface VIII, *Pope* 206
Booth, Robert 23, 101, 144, 146, 170, 210
Borrhaus, Martinus 150
Boussard, Gaufridas 95
Bownest, William 190, 211
Bradford, John 76
Bradshaw, William 3
Bradstreet, Simon 4
Bradwardine, Thomas 168
Branthwaite, William 3, 19, 22, 23, 24, 33 (n57), 49, 140, 141, 142, 143, 144, 145, 210
Brassicanus, Joannes Alexander 156, 157
Brenz, Johannes 19, 68, 87, 196, 199
Brerewood, Edward 129
Breton, John 27, 81
Breul, Jacobus de 99
Bristow, Richard 132
Bromyard, John de 183
Broughton, Hugh 80, 209
Brunus, Conrad 104
Bucer, Martin 5, 19, 63, 121, 122, 123, 175, 196, 198, 206
Bucholtzer, Abraham 97, 98
Buckeridge, John, *Bp of Ely* 126
Budaeus, Gulielmus 104, 105, 150, 186, 206
Budaeus, Joannes 82
Budé, Guillaume, *see* Budaeus, Gulielmus
Bugenhagen, Johannes 87
Bullinger, Heinrich 19, 123, 124, 201
Burchardus, *Bp of Worms* 203
Burroughs, Jeremiah 3
Busaeus, Johannes 175
Bywater, Thomas 78, 79, 210
Bzovius, Abraham 96

Caesalpinus, Andreas 133
Caietanus, Daniel 193
Cajetanus, Thomas de Vio 164, 187

Calepinus, Ambrosius 192
Callimachus 137
Calsio, Mario de 56
Calvin, John 19, 28, 32 (n47), 81, 82, 83, 201
Calvinus 203
Calvinus, Johannes, *J.D.* 103
Cambini, Andrea 199
Cambridge University
  colleges: Christ's 2, 11; Clare College 22; Clare Hall 2; Emmanuel *see* Emmanuel College; Gonville and Caius 3, 24, 26; King's 5, 18, 28; Peterhouse 3, 24; St John's 4; Sidney Sussex 3, 23, 24; Trinity 3, 4, 5, 10, 18, 21, 24, 26, 28, 173
  curriculum 11
  library 14
Camden, William 25, 101, 103
Campianus, Edmundus 128
Canisius, Petrus 6, 172
Canons, Apostolic 147
Capello, Marco Antonio 94
Capito, Wolfgang Fabricius 69
Capreolus, Johannes 23, 165, 167
Carafa, *Card.* 54
Carbone, Lodovico 164
Cardanus, Hieronymus 134
Careless, John 76
Carion, Johannes 100, 115
Carleton, George 131
Cartwright, Thomas 26, 124, 132
Casaubon, Isaac 24, 92, 109, 118, 119, 133, 136
Cassander, George 168
Cassianus, Joannes 145, 179
Cassiodorus, Magnus Aurelius 96, 157
Castellion, Sebastian 7, 70
Castrioti, Georgius, *see* Scanderbeg
Castro, Alfonsus de 172
Castro, Christophorus a 181
Catzelu, Dominico di 139
Cecil, William, Lord Burghley 98, 99, 111, 112, 113, 119, 121, 170, 191
Cedrenus, Georgius 96
Celsus, Aurelius Cornelius 110
Cevallarius, Antonius 56
Chaderton, Laurence 2, 18, 19, 21, 22, 53–4, 210
Chalcocondylas, Laonicus 99
Chamier, Adrien 85
Chamier, Daniel 85
Chandieu, Antoine de la Roche 83
Chaucer, Geoffrey 11, 137

Chemnitz, Martin 23, 43, 65, 66, 205
Choniates, Nicetas Acominatus 99
Christmann, Jakob 116
Chrysostom, *St see* John, *St, Chrysostom*
Chytraeus, David, *the elder* 72
Cicero, Marcus Tullius 11, 64, 79, 135
Clamenges, Nicolaus de 170
Clarius, Isidorus 190
Clark, John Willis 5, 8
Clauser, Conrad 99
Clavius, Christophorus 12, 115
Clemens, Venceslaus 139
Clement, *of Alexandria* 141, 142, 148
Clenardus, Nicolaus 64, 198
Clichtoveus, Judocus 183, 184
Clinaris, Johannes 205
Clingius, Conrad 173
Clugh, Alexander 28
Coccius, Jodocus 172
Cogelius, Charieus 71
Colet, John 80
Collins, Samuel 26, 128
Cologne, *Cathedral* 7, 176
Colonna, Egidio 134
Columna, Petrus, *Galatinus* 57
Coluthus 137
Cominaeus, Philippus 101
Consilium Basileense 79
Concordance, Biblical 54, 56
Conradus, *Abbot of Auersperg* 91
Constantine I, *Emperor of Rome, the Great* 95
Constantius, *see* Gardiner
Constitutions, Apostolic 152, 153
Contarini, Gasparo 168
Cooke, Robert 130
Coquaeus, Leonardus 173
Cordova, Antonio de 26, 159
Cornarius, Janus 133
Cornwall, Francis 3
Cosin, Richard 128
Costello, William T. 11, 12
Costerius, Joannes 155
Costerus, Franciscus 184
Cotton, John 3, 4, 23, 24, 43, 66, 210
Councils of the Christian Church 146
Covarruvius a Leyva, Diego 108
Cowell, John 26, 107, 131
Cowper, William, 120
Cranmer, Thomas 14, 15, 17, 32 (n44), 41, 76, 97, 151, 166, 177, 178, 179
Crantz, Albert 92, 196
Crespetius, Petrus 158
Crocus, Thomas 32 (n40), 90, 210

Cronkar, Robert 183, 209
Crooke, Thomas, *see* Crocus, Thomas
Crossley, John 74, 212
Cudworth, Ralph 13, 23, 26, 77, 78, 79, 210
Culmann, Leonhard 7, 185
Culverwell, Ezekiel 3
Culverwell, Richard 2, 22, 32 (n41), 49, 97, 145, 149, 155, 171, 174, 209
Curio, Caelius Augustinus 101, 115
Curterius, Johannes 74
Curtis, Mark H. 12
Cusa, Nicholas of, 26, 95, 169, 207
Cuspinianus, Johannes 114
Cyprian, *St* 22, 155
Cyril, *St* 144

Danaeus, Lambertus 120
Daniel, Samuel 25, 102
Dasypodius, Petrus 193
Delrio, Martin Anton 189
DeMonte, Robertus 101
Demosthenes 135
Didymus 137
Diez, Philippe 184
Digby, J. 130
Diodorus, *Siculus* 112
Dion Cassius 112
Dionysius *Alexandrinus* 137
Dionysius, *Carthusianus* 16, 17, 166, 177, 178, 179
Dionysius *of Halicarnasus* 137
Dionysius, *the Pseudo-Areopaqite* 141, 205
Dionysius Romanus Exiguus 149
Dister, Johannes 55
Dod, John 26
Donne, John 26, 127
Dort, Synod of 119, 147
Downame, George 128
Downes, Andrew 136
Dreschler, Wolfgang 101
Driedo, Johannes 173, 196, 205
Drusius, Johannes 117, 118
Dudley, Thomas 4
Du Moulin, Charles 10, 11, 106
Du Moulin, Pierre 130
Duns, Johannes, *Scotus* 166
Duran, Solomon ben 60
Durandus, Gulielmus 165
Durer, Albrecht 10, 12, 116

Eckius, Johannes 60
Edward VI, King 5

Elias, *Levita* 57, 59, 61, 62, 63, 204
Elizabeth, Queen 2, 4
Emili, Paolo, see Aemilius, Paulus
Emmanuel College
  early history 2–4,
  founding 2
  library, books removed 20, 21, 24, 40
  library, donations to: 22–26, 31 (n26), 34–35
  library furnishings 7–9
  library growth 22–29
  library holdings in, discussed:
    aesthetics 18, Arabic books 27, casuistry 25, Counter-Reformers 18, 25, 26, divinity 10, 18, 26, ethics 18, geography 28, grammar 18, Greek 18, 19, Hebrew books 15, 18, 21, 27, history 11, 18, 25, law 11, 18, 28, lexicography 18, literature 11, 18, logic 18, Lutherans 19, 20, 32, manuscripts 15, mathematics 11, 12, 18, 28, moral theology 25, 26, philology 18, polity 18, 19, preaching 18, Reformers 18, 19, 20, 25, 32, rhetoric 10, 11, 18, science 18, surgery 28
  library inventories 1, 9, 13–15, 18–21, 39, 46
  early Puritan character 2–4,
  statutes 2, 10, 33 (n67)
England, livings in 77
Ens, Caspar 93
Ephesus, Council of 141
Ephraem, *St, Syrus* 143
Epiphanius, *St* 144, 149, 205
Erasmus, Desiderius 7, 17, 21, 24, 48, 55, 60, 66, 151, 155, 176, 177, 183, 191, 192, 199, 200, 201
Erastus, Thomas 118
Espence, Claude d' 170, 182
Estella, *see* Stella
Estienne, *see* Stephanus
Estius, Gulielmus 76, 165
Eucherius, *St* 156, 184, 196
Euclid 12, 74
Eudes, Morton 131
Euripides 137
Eusebius, Pamphili 17, 95, 97, 142, 143
Eustathius, *Bp of Thessalonica* 137, 176
Euthalius, *Bp of Sulca* 153
Euthymius, *Zigabenus* 153, 200
Evagrius, *Scholasticus* 142
Eytzinger, Michael 94
Ezra, Abraham Aben 59, 64

Faber, Jacobus 134
Faber, Philippus 165
Fabricio, Theodosio 73
Fagius, Paul 5, 59
Fayus, Antonius 126
Fazellus, Thomas 100
Featherstone, Henry 74, 212
Felinus, Aretius, see Bucer
Felmington, John 110
Fernelius, Johannes 117
Ferronus, Arnoldus 100
Festus, Pompeius 193
Fevre, Guy le, de la Boderie 133
Ficino, Marsilio 198
Field, Richard 126
Filliucius, Vincentius 26, 158
Finch, Sir Henry 105
Fine, Oronce 10, 12, 116, 206
Fisher, John, 7, 126, 131, 174
Fitzherbert, Thomas 128
Flacius, Matthias, *Illyricus* 48, 66
Fleetwood, William 14, 22, 32 (n43), 45, 98, 109, 192, 209
Fore-edge markings 6–7, 9, 47
Foster, Samuel 12
Fowberius, Robertus 78
Foxcroft, John 79, 211
Foxe, John 91, 95, 121
Francis I, king of France 31
Franck, Sebastian 204
Freher, Marquard 103
Fricius, Andreas, *Modrevius* 6, 169
Frisius, Gemma 111
Frith, John 121
Fulgentius, *Bp of Ruspa* 154
Fuliambe, G. 62
Fulke, William 22, 124, 131, 132, 202
Fuller, Thomas 3
Funck, Johann 97

Gaguin, Robert 100
Galatinus, see Columna, Petrus
Gallasius, Nicolaus 82, 141, 150
Gallican Church 147
Garamanta, Petrus 167
Gardiner, Stephen, *Bp of Winchester* 6, 89, 122, 173
Garnet, Henry 127
Garzonius, Thomas 150
Gaskell, Philip 5, 10, 26
Gast, Johannes 68, 71
Geilhouen, Arnold 158
Gelenius, Sigismundus 113, 155
Gemblacensis, Sigebertus 101

Gemma, Reiner, *Frisius* 111
Genebrard, Gilbert 97
George, Castriota, see Scanderbeg
Georgius, Franciscus, *Venetus* 133
Gerbelius, Nicolaus 110, 114
Gerlacher, Theobaldus, *Bellicanus* 7, 176
Gerson, Johannes 169, 175
Gesner, Andreas 108
Gesner, Conrad 23, 98, 133
Giovio, Paolo 96, 197
Giraldus Cambrensis 78
Giraldus, Lilius Gregorius 192
Giustiani, Lorenzo, *St* 168
Glanville, John 110, 209
Glareanus, Henricus 113
Gobellinus, Joannes 92
Godefroy, Denys 103
Godelmann, Johann Georg 117
Godwin, Francis 94
Godwin, Thomas 160
Goldast, Melchior 104, 106
Goodman, Godfrey 132
Gorion, Joseph ben 64, 204
Gorran, Nicolaus de 15, 18, 77, 187
Gothofredo, *see* Godefroy
Granada, Luis de 174
Gratianus, *Bononiensis* 106
Gratius, Ortuinus 92
Grauer, Albert, see Grawer, Albert
Grawer, Albert 72, 73
Great Migration to New England 4
Gregoras, Nicephorus 99
Gregorius, Ariminensis 167
Gregory, *St, of Nazianzus* 143, 148, 149, 157
Gregory, *St, of Nyssa* 17, 143, 149, 151, 175, 176
Gregory, *St. Thaumaturgus* 142
Gregory I, *Pope, the Great* 77, 79, 157
Gregory IX, *Pope* 206
Gretser, Jacob 26, 175, 176
Grimstone, Edward 99
Grotius, Hugo 118
Gruterus, Janus 25, 94, 113, 114
Grynaeus, Simon 12, 74, 110, 197
Grynaeus, Johannes Jacobus 140
Gualtherus, *see* Walther
Guazzo, Marco 115
Guevara, Antonio de, *Bp* 139
Guicciardini, Francesco 25, 115
Guidacerius, Agathius 64
Guilliandus, Claudius 7, 190

Haddon, Walter 10, 11, 31 (n26), 136

Hall, Joseph 3, 26
Hanscombe, Thomas 24, 25, 65, 94, 95, 120, 159, 162, 163, 164, 165, 167, 168, 169, 191, 192, 211
Harding, Thomas 120, 121
Harmenopulus, Constantius 105
Hart, John 125
Harvard College 4
Harvard, John 4
Hay, John de, see Sixtus
Haymo, *Bp of Halberstadt* 157, 185, 187, 190
Hegesippus 92
Heinsius, Daniel 141
Heller, Yom Tov Lipmann 61
Helvicus, Christophorus 109, 118
Hemmingius, Nicolaus 23, 66
Henriquez, Enrique 26, 159
Henry VIII, King 11, 19
Hentenius, Joannes 149
Herbert, George 11
Hernes, Gentianus 146
Herodotus 111, 112, 196
Hesiod 137
Heskins, Thomas 131
Hesychius, *Alexandrinus* 186
Hesychius, *Presbyter of Jerusalem* 150, 154, 204
Hieronymus, *Pragensis* 74
Hieronymus, *St, see* Jerome, *St*
Hilary, *St* 17, 151
Hoeschelius, David 145, 146
Hoffman, Christoff 19, 68, 71
Holbein, Hans 54
Holcot, Robert 167
Holdsworth, Richard 21, 24, 27
Homer 31, 137
Hooker, Richard 124, 130
Hooker, Thomas 3, 4
Hooper, John 76
Horrocks, Jeremiah 12
Hosius, Stanislaus 6, 26, 172
Hospinianus, Rodolphus 91, 121
Hostiensis, Henricus de Segusio 103
Howlett, Laurence 165, 211
Hugh, *St, of Cher* 16, 18
Hugo, *of St Victor* 150, 177
Huicci, Robert 138, 211
Hunt, Richard 105, 212
Huss, Johann 74
Hutter, Elias 54, 56

Iarhi, R. Selomo 59
Innocent III, *Pope* 152

Irenaeus, *St* 141
Isaac, Samuel ben, *of Uceda* 60
Isidore, *St, Bp of Seville* 80
Isidore, *St, of Pelusium* 144, 207
Isidorus, Mercator 152
Isidorus de Isolanis 167
Isocrates 10, 11, 136

Jacob, Moses ben, *of Coucy* 64
James I, King 3, 23, 120, 126, 128, 129
James, Thomas 13, 15, 129
James, Thomas, *of Lincoln* 91, 210
Jansenius, Cornelius 75
Jardine, Lisa 10–11
Jayne, Sears 1, 14, 27
Jerome, *St* 18, 54, 76, 79, 80, 152, 155, 157
Jewel, John 120, 121
John, *of Aingre* 193
John, *of Ardern* 81
John, *St, Cassianus* 154
John, *St, Chrysostom* 13, 18, 43, 80, 144, 150, 157, 204
John, *St, Damascene* 145
John, *de Sacrobosco* 197
Johnson, Francis R. 14
Johnson, Mr 185, 190
Johnson, Robert 27
Jonathan, *ben Uzziel* 59
Jonvillaeus, Carolus 82
Joseph ben Gorion 58
Josephus, Flavius 17, 18, 97
Josephus Hebraicus, *see* Joseph ben Gorion
Junius, Franciscus 55, 120
Junius, Hadrianus 137
Justin, *Martyr, St* 141, 148
Justinian I, *Emperor of the East* 103, 108
Justinianus, Augustus 55

Kempis, Thomas à 77
Kimchi, David 58, 59, 61, 62
Kimchi, Moses 63
Kircher, Conrad 56
Kis, Stephanus, *Szeqedinus* 67
Koellin, Conrad 163

La Barre, Renatus Laurentius de 155
La Bigne, Margarinus de 139, 140
Lactantius Firmianus, Lucius Coelius 79, 154
Laetus, Julius Pomponius 106
Lambert, François, of *Avignon* 201
Lambertus, *Schaffnaburgensis* 101

Tryphiodorus 137
Tuckney, Anthony 4, 24, 74, 80, 212
Tunstall, Cuthbert 10, 12, 117
Turnebus, Adrianus 197
Turpinus, Johannes 101
Turrecremata, Johannes de 107, 108, 174, 188
Turrianus, Franciscus 152
Tusanus, Jacobus 105
Twyne, Brian 103
Tymms 76
Tyndale, William 121

Ughtred, Thomas 154, 209
Ulpian, *the Rhetorician* 197
Ursinus, Zacharias 75
Ussher, James 130

Vadianus, Joachim 6, 111, 173
Valentia, Gregorius de 162
Valerianus, Joannes Pierius 191
Valeriis, Valerius de 117
Valla, Laurentius 11, 111
Valois, Thomas 155
Van de Putte, *see* Puteanus
Van den Steen, *see* Lapide
Van der Lindt, *see* Lindanus
Van Est, *see* Estius
Vasquez, Gabriel 162
Vatablus, Franciscus 195
Vellosillus, Ferdinandus 151
Veltuyck, Gerard 195
Venice 24, 94, 175
Vergilius, Polydorus 101
Villalpandus, Joannes Baptista 179
Vincent, *of Beauvais* 166
Viret, Pierre 85
Vives, Johannes Ludovicus 6, 169
Voragine, Jacobus de 184
Vossius, Gerardus 142
Vulcanius, B. 113

Wales, livings in 77
Wallis, John 12
Walsingham, Thomas 101, 102
Walther, Rudolph 71, 86
Ward, Nathaniel 4

Ward, Samuel 3, 19, 23, 24, 126, 210
Watson, William 174
Weinrichius, George Silesius 72
Westhemer, Bartholomaeus 195, 202
Westminster Assembly 3, 4
Weston, Edward 175
Wetter, Justus V. 113
Whitaker, William 120, 121, 127
White, John 78, 210
White, John, *of Eccles* 131
White, Thomas 146, 209
Whitgift 132
Wicelius, Georgius 183
Wickliffe, John 183, 209
William, *of Auvergne* 168
William, *of Ockham* 104, 167
Willis, Robert 5, 8
Wilson, Edward 33 (n57)
Wolder, David 56
Wolf, Heinrich 176
Wolf, Johannes 89, 191
Wolfius, Hieronymus 99, 136
Wotton, Sir Henry 3, 24, 94
Wright, Laurence 110, 210
Wright, Samuel 13, 77, 210
Würtemberg 73
Wycliffe, John 54, 80, 81

Xenophon 112
Xylander, Guilielmus 109, 110, 112, 135

Yates, John 3
Yehiel, Asher ben 56

Zacharias, *Bp of Chrysopolis* 187, 203
Zambertus, Bartholomaeus 116
Zamosius, Stephanus 114
Zanchius, Hieronymus 19, 23, 90, 196
Zasius, Udalricus 60
Ziegler, Jacob 149
Zimara, Marco Antonio 135
Zonaras, Ioannes 99, 147
Zumel, Francisco 162
Zurich 71
Zwinger, Theodor 134, 190, 191
Zwingli, Ulrich 19, 86, 198